Student Retention Success Models in Higher Education

Edited by Clinita Arnsby Ford, Ph.D.

Published by
CNJ Associates, Inc.
P. O. Box 10042
Tallahassee, FL 32302-2042

Cover Design

The Quilt reflects the cultural diversity on the nation's college and university campuses; with differences, as in the quilt blocks, harmonizing for togetherness in the learning community. The Quilt represents all areas of an institution joined side-by-side in a unified retention program covering the entire institution. The Quilt represents the nurturing, caring and feelings of warmth and security provided to students through the model programs featured in this book.

Cover created by Charlie Designs

Acknowledgements

The editor is grateful to Dr. Marvel Lang who initiated the idea for this book and was co-editor of my previous two books, Black Student Retention in Higher Education (1988) and Strategies for Retaining Minority Students in Higher Education (1992); my husband, James R. Ford, Sr.; my secretary and assistant, Janice R. Nails-Love; Genevieve W. Thomas, who gave me my first faculty position in higher education; Dr. Courtney E. Walker, the first to appoint me to an administrative position in higher education; Dr. Charles A. Taylor, Lynn Alten, Denise Carty, Nancy Richardson and Vivian L. Hobbs for professional assistance and guidance; Elizabeth Johanna for the book design; and each author for the diligent effort in the preparation of manuscripts.

Clinita Arnsby Ford, Ph. D.
Editor

Publisher's Cataloging in Publication
    (Prepared by Quality Books Inc.)
Student retention success models in higher education/edited by Clinita Ford.
    p. cm.
    Includes index.
    ISBN 0-9649919-0-X

    1. Minorities—Education (Higher)—United States.
    2. Minority college students.
    3. College dropouts. I. Ford, Clinita A.
    LC3727.S88 1996   378. 1'9829'073
                                  QBI96-20043

ISBN: 0-9649919-0-X

Dedication

This book is dedicated to my parents, the late Anita Hunter Arnsby and the late Clinton N. Arnsby; my aunt, Alma Hunter Salter; my uncle, Dr. Norvell W. Hunter; my husband, James R. Ford, Sr.; my children, James Jr., Janita and JaKathryn; and my grandchildren, James III, Carlanita, Tanner and Ari.

About the Editor

Clinita A. Ford, Ph.D., is a nationally acclaimed lecturer and consultant on Black Student Retention in higher education. She has edited and co-edited three books on student retention, has written chapters in several books and has appeared on nationwide teleconferences. She is the founder and director of the annual National Higher Education Conference on Black Student Retention, which began in 1985.

Dr. Ford received her B.S. degree from Lincoln University (MO) at the young age of 19 years, her M.S. from Columbia University and her Ph.D. degree from Kansas State University; where she was one of the first recipients of the General Foods Fellowship. She has established a distinguished career that has earned her many awards and honors. She has been noted in American Men and Women of Science, Personalities of the South, Who's Who in American Education; International Who's Who of Professionals; Who's Who of American Women; Strathmore's Who's Who and Outstanding Educators of America. Other honors and awards include Distinguished Alumni Award from Kansas State University, Alumni Achievement Award and Honorary Doctorate from Lincoln University, Teacher of the Year Award from Florida A. and M. University and induction in the National Black College Alumni Hall of Fame.

Currently Dr. Ford is a retired professor at Florida A. and M. University. She spends much of her time developing retention conferences and providing consultant services.

Table of Contents

Table of Contents

Foreword

The eighteen years of consulting in two-year and four-year institutions and the experiences gained through the National Higher Education Conference on Black Student Retention, of which I am the founder and director, have provided the opportunity for me to become familiar with some of the nation's most effective student retention programs.

Student retention is a problem faced by all institutions. It is addressed in many ways. Recognizing the scope and complexity of the problem, the special interest in the downward spiral of retention of minority students and the resulting challenge to institutions, we decided to publish a book of model programs that would be useful in academia for developing new initiatives or improving the effectiveness of existing retention initiatives.

Over two dozen university administrators, faculty and staff of successful retention programs were selected to author chapters in Student Retention Success Models in Higher Education. These are models from state university systems, national projects, two-year, four-year, public, private, historically black, and predominantly white, institutions. The institutions are located in all sections of the country, coast-to-coast, giving a broad perspective of initiatives. The final product is one of the best collections of student-centered retention programs ever published.

As we approach a new millennium, the effectiveness of retention efforts assume a greater importance. Demographic projections are that the pool of minority high school graduates will expand, but will not be equivalently absorbed and retained in higher education. Our challenge is to increase retention and graduation rates. Universities understand that attrition is costly.

Student Retention Success Models in Higher Education is a resource for capturing ideas from some of the best programs. It is full of information which you can adapt to the characteristics of your learning community. Whether you are newly appointed or long-term tenured, you will find exciting information on retention programs. Each chapter contributes something different. You have many choices.

Clinita A. Ford, Ph. D.
Editor

Increasing Retention Rates Among Students of Color: The Office of AHANA Student Programs at Boston College

by Donald Brown

Overview:

Under representation and high rates of attrition among black and Hispanic/Latino students in higher education are matters of grave concern. So grave that, unless addressed in a substantive way, they may prove catastrophic for the nation.

At a time when there is both a national and global demand for a highly skilled and trained work force, high school dropout rates among black and Hispanic students hover around forty percent. In some of the larger cities, on occasion the dropout rate has exceeded seventy percent.

If these frighteningly high dropout rates are not enough of a problem, the nation is further imperiled by the inordinately high attrition rates among many black and Hispanic students who do succeed in going to college.

In this chapter the author discusses these issues by reviewing the literature related to factors that contribute to the underrepresentation of Black and Hispanic students in higher education. The latter portion of the chapter describes what Boston College is doing through its Office of AHANA Student Programs to retain and to graduate AHANA (African-American, Hispanic, Asian, and Native American) students.

INTRODUCTION

"A black male in California is three times more likely to be murdered than to be accepted to the University of California." — Alexander Astin

Twenty years ago, the attrition rate among students of color at Boston College was seventeen percent. Today, as a result of an array of support services, the retention rates for a target group of students of color, who come to the university having been cheated educationally, are ninety five percent after four years and ninety three percent after five years. The aforementioned retention rates are in sharp contrast to the national figures provided by the American Council on Education in its Twelfth Annual Status Report on Minorities in Higher Education (1993), which lists the percentage of all students graduating from 298 NCAA Division I colleges and universities, in the year covered by the report, as fifty four percent. The graduation rate for white students during the same period was fifty six percent; for Asian students, sixty three percent; for Hispanics, forty one percent; for blacks, thirty two percent, and for Native Americans, thirty percent.

With increasing regularity, citizens are expressing concern over the far-reaching effects that inordinately high drop-out rates at both the high school and college levels will have on the future well-being of this nation.

Causes of Underrepresentation and High Rates of Attrition among Black Students

Scores of researchers have attempted to pinpoint the exact cause of the decline in enrollment, as well as the high rate of attrition, among black students in higher education. Among these researchers is Pamela Christoffel who, in her research and development update for the College Board (1986), synthesizes research done in the area of retention. She makes the following observation which is especially true for black and, as shown later, Hispanic students in higher education: "… the decision to drop out of school is nearly always a combination of factors. Among these, as others have hitherto pointed out are: academic boredom, uncertainty about what to study and transitional/adjustment problems." With respect to specific barriers for black students, however, she lists the following: low levels of parental education; poor high school preparation; lack of advising at the high school level about academic and career choices; poor study habits; low degree-level goals; and lack of financial aid.

Walter Allen (1987), a prolific writer on the subject of black student retention in higher education, corroborates and expands on Christoffel's list by suggesting that declining enrollments and high rates of attrition among blacks (and Hispanics) are due in large measure to the following variables:

a) poverty and lack of role models;

b) uneven quality of secondary school preparation;

c) toughening of requirements for college enrollment;

d) increased admissions reliance on standardized tests; and

e) alterations in financial aid packaging.

A. Poverty and Lack of Role Models

Christoffel, Allen and virtually scores of other researchers are unanimous in their sentiment that the poor economic status of black families is a major reason that black students do not go to college.

University of Chicago sociologist William Julius Wilson, author of The Truly Disadvantaged (1987), for instance, is quite specific in linking declining enrollments to what he describes as a burgeoning "underclass." In his assessment of the status of blacks in higher education Wilson cites poverty and the absence of role models as two of the major reasons that blacks and other poor students struggle while in high school and choose not to go to college.

The vicious cycle of poverty among black families is perpetuated when black high school students are virtually forced to attend schools where learning does not take place; schools that are no more than breeding grounds for criminal activity. Scores of media have highlighted the fact that many inner city schools have, for all practical purposes, become armed camps where violence is the order of the day; where students, almost out of necessity, must be more concerned about personal safety than with receiving the knowledge imparted in the classroom.

B. Quality of Secondary Preparation

In addition, many black students who desire to learn are seriously disadvantaged by the lack of resources and the poor quality of teaching. Orfield (1987) points out that schools attended by black and other students of color are distinguished in yet another way: they are the most segregated schools in America. According to Orfield, 63.4 percent of all black students attend predominantly minority high schools. Troubled by the segregated nature and poor quality of instruction that black students receive, Orfield made this strong assertion: " ... the children being socialized and educated in these underclass schools are even more comprehensively isolated from mainstream middle class society than were black children of the South whose problems led to the long battle over segregated education."

Holman (1985) points to another unsettling reality of the black students' educational experience in America. He suggests that far too many black students are veering away from the college preparatory track as early as the elementary grades. " ... They become resigned to societal norms of human inequity at a very early stage in their educational experience. They do so by taking fewer of the basic courses necessary for developing the skills, study habits and content required to excel in science, math and technology in the intermediate, high school and college years " (Holman, 1985).

If black students are not discouraged from taking college preparatory programs before they arrive at high school, it often happens once there. In her report entitled, Equality and Excellence: The Educational Status of Black Americans, Hammond (1985) indicts a good number of inner city high schools by stating that teachers, guidance counselors and other school officials direct black students to programs where they will be trained for lower status occupations. As a consequence, black students are underrepresented in academic programs and overrepresented in vocational programs. Hammond also observed that in high school, "... for the most part, black students take fewer years of mathematics, physical and social science courses than white students and the focus of the courses, mathematics, for example, tend to be on general skills rather than algebra, geometry, trigonometry or calculus" (Sudarkasa, 1988).

C. Toughening of Requirements for College Enrollment

Despite all of the rhetoric about affirmative action and being desirous of going to any length to increase the numbers of black students on their campuses, many schools have resorted to a system which essentially tells prospective black students that irrespective of their differing backgrounds, educational and otherwise, the same measuring rod used to assess white student eligibility will be used to assess their qualifications; and if they do not measure up, they will not be admitted. Notwithstanding warnings by Astin (1975) and other researchers that an admissions system based on test scores alone would have a disparate effect on black students, more and more colleges continue to place a high premium on standardized tests when making admissions decisions.

D. Increased Reliance on Standardized Tests

An increased reliance on standardized tests does not augur well for a wider degree of participation among black and Hispanic students in higher education. As pointed out in One Third of a Nation (1988), black students have made noticeable progress on the Scholastic Aptitude Test. Evidence of this is a rise in their scores of twenty one points on the verbal and twenty points on the math section of the examination. Notwithstanding these gains, however, blacks still lag far behind whites in performance on the SAT. Of the 1.05 million high school seniors who took the SAT in 1985, just over 70,000 (three percent) were black. Seventy three percent of black students taking the exam scored below 400 on the verbal section and sixty four percent scored below 400 on the math portion. For whites, only 31 percent had verbal scores below 400 and only twenty two percent had math scores that low (ACE, 1988).

4

E. Alterations in Financial Aid Packaging

In addition to the "get tough" posture being assumed by many colleges and universities, a shift in financial aid packaging and a reduced commitment to affirmative action have had serious implications for black student attendance at colleges and universities. While some researchers believe availability of financial aid has little implication for a student's decision to enroll in college, there is increasing evidence that adequate financial aid, especially in light of the poor financial status of many black families, is vitally important. Sudarkasa (1988) remarks that the importance of financial aid for black students becomes apparent when one considers that in 1981 nearly half (48 percent) of all black college-bound seniors came from incomes under $12,000 as compared to only ten percent of their white counterparts.

Solomon Arbeiter (1987) points out that whereas grants had previously represented nearly two-thirds of the aid package, loans have emerged as the major portion, now constituting more than one-half of the financial aid package. Arbeiter makes the important observation, that when faced with the prospect of enormous loans at the close of four years, in some cases amounting to half of what the family earns in a year, many black students have chosen, despite their increased graduation rates from high school, not to attend a college or university.

Underrepresentation and Attrition of Hispanic Students

As in the cases of black students, several themes emerge as causes of under-representation and high rates of attrition among Hispanic students in higher education. They are as follows:

- poor preparation at the elementary and secondary school levels;

- lack of support and encouragement from teachers and guidance counselors;

- insufficient financial aid;

- transition/adjustment problems;

- family circumstances; and

- inadequacy of support services.

With respect to the current involvement of Hispanics in higher education, the American Council on Education – Office of Minority Concerns – points out that " ... while Hispanics have made considerable gains in the number of degrees earned since 1971, given their proportionate numbers in the overall population, they continue to be one of the most underrepresented groups in American Higher Education. In the academic year 1985, Hispanics represented

8.2 percent of the eighteen to twenty-four-year-old population, but only 4.3 percent of the enrollments in higher education, and received only 2.7 percent of the baccalaureate degrees" (American Council on Education, 1987).

Inadequate Preparation

Clearly, the lack of adequate preparation at the elementary and secondary school levels is one of the major contributors to the lack of Hispanic involvement in higher education. The National Council of La Raza states that in far too many instances Hispanic students begin their education at a serious disadvantage; in many instances, Hispanic youth come to the school experience from households where little or no English is spoken (Orum, 1986). Frequently, they are recent immigrants. Unable to speak the language and having little knowledge of American culture, problems for these youth are compounded by being enrolled in school systems that are sorely lacking in the resources and personnel necessary to respond to the academic, psychological, linguistic and cultural needs of students whose natural tongue is not English (p.10).

Fields (1988) points out that between grades one and four, twenty-eight percent of Hispanic students are enrolled below their normal grade level, as compared to twenty percent of white children. Between the fifth and eighth grades, the numbers increase so that nearly forty percent of Hispanic students are behind grade level, compared to twenty-five percent of whites. By the ninth and tenth grades, forty-three percent of Hispanic students are behind.

Even more alarming is the fact that at the high school level Hispanic students are not enrolled in the kinds of courses that allow for admission or, if admitted, for them to compete favorably in college. The National Commission on Secondary Education for Hispanics (1984) points out that over forty percent of Hispanic high school seniors are enrolled in general curriculums; thirty-five percent are enrolled in vocational curriculums; and only twenty-five percent are enrolled in college preparatory courses.

A major cause for alarm are the poor grades being earned by many Hispanic students who succeed in getting into college preparatory courses. Data taken from the U.S. Department of Education's High School and Beyond study (1980) indicated that Hispanic high school graduates were less likely than white high school graduates to have earned "A's" in school, and almost twice as likely to have earned grades of "D" or "F" in the core courses of English, math, and social science.

As was mentioned in the discussion of black students, one of the consequences of either not taking college preparatory courses or doing poorly while in them, is poor performance on standardized tests. La Raza (Orum, 1986) points out that nearly forty states now require students to pass competency examinations before graduating from high school. Moreover, colleges and universities are beginning to rely more and more on SAT and ACT examination scores in deciding who to admit. Hispanics are less likely than any other group to take these tests (p.11); evidenced by the results of the High School and Beyond Study (1980) which indicated that while fifty-two percent of Hispanic high school students had planned on attending college in the next year (1981), only twenty-eight percent had taken the SAT as compared to thirty-four percent of black and thirty-eight percent of white students. La Raza also points to the results of the Department of Education's National High School and Beyond Achievement Test (1980) on which seventy-six percent of the Hispanic high school students who took the test scored in the bottom half of all students nationwide (p.16).

Stereotyping and Lack of Support

Several other factors contribute to the poor quality of the secondary school experience for some Hispanic students. One of these factors is a perception by students of being labeled, stereotyped, or made to feel inadequate because of a lack of proficiency at speaking the English language. Ramirez's research (1981) cites evidence that both white and Hispanic teachers had a tendency to ascribe negative qualities towards students who spoke with an accent, used a non-standard version of English, or, who spoke a non-standard version of Spanish (Olivas, p. 307). In a similar vein, the research of Ryan and Caranza (1975) found that, for the most part, students who spoke English with an accent were judged by white teachers to be less intelligent than students who did not speak with an accent (Olivas, p. 318).

Lack of Support From Guidance Counselors

Low self-esteem and inadequate support from guidance counselors are other major factors that impede Hispanic students' success at the high school level, thus affecting their decision to pursue higher education. An analysis of an Educational Testing Service study on career education and counseling among Hispanic students, conducted by La Raza in 1982, revealed that Hispanic students were less likely than other groups of students to view their counselors as a resource. Moreover, it was determined that counselors in schools with large Hispanic enrollments were less likely to reach out to the Hispanic students or engage in discussions or counseling sessions regarding their aspirations.

Family Circumstances

Colon and Caus (1988) represent the sentiment of a host of Hispanic researchers in pointing out that family plays an exceedingly important role in the Hispanic students' decision to pursue education, whether it is at a high school or college level. Hispanic families are extremely close knit and each member feels a deep sense of obligation to contribute to the family's economic and social well-being.

La Raza (1984) points out that functional illiteracy among Hispanic adults is disproportionately high, with some studies reporting a range between 13.5 percent and fifty-six percent of Hispanic adults who are functionally illiterate (p. 18). With respect to this issue of adult illiteracy, in general, Astin (1975) advances the view that the educational status of the parent(s) has profound implications on whether a student remains in or drops out of school. The educational aspirations of students are thwarted when they do not have role models in the home with whom they identify.

One of the problems experienced by Hispanic high school students, and later those successful in getting into college, is having to choose between attending school or working to help sustain the family and themselves.

In light of the combined effects of being held back, performing poorly on standardized tests, receiving little or no encouragement and support from teachers and guidance counselors, and being concerned about the economic well-being of the family it is easy to understand why some Hispanic students have given up on the notion of acquiring an education.

Insufficient Financial Aid and Support Services

Paramount among the effects of inadequate elementary and secondary preparation, poverty, low expectations, and little support from teachers and guidance counselors is having limited career and educational options. Fortunately, one option available for Hispanic students, indeed all students, given their open-door admissions policy, has been two-year community colleges. According to statistics compiled by the Association of Community and Junior Colleges, fifty-six percent of all Hispanic students in higher education attend junior college. Sarah Melendez, former assistant director of the American Council on Education's Office of Minority Concerns, points out the problem with junior college attendance among Hispanics is that seventy percent of Hispanic students who enroll in junior college do not graduate; and of the thirty percent who persist to graduation, only one in seven who is desirous of transferring to a four-year college actually does so (Melendez, 1987).

With respect to an explanation as to why so few students make the transition from two- to four-year colleges and universities, Melendez, Santiago, Magallan and Lara (1987) make some interesting observations. Melendez points out that some Hispanic students, who lack English language skills, have to spend a considerable amount of time in non-credited remedial courses before being allowed to enroll in mainstream courses. Therefore, financial aid does not go as far for them as it would for someone going directly into regular courses. Due to this, many Hispanic students are forced to work up to as much as thirty or forty hours per week, to supplement financial aid allocations (p. 7).

In addition to the financial problems that many Hispanic students encounter, Magallan (1987) believes that the curriculum of many junior colleges, while exceptional at providing remedial assistance, do not take into consideration contributions made by persons of Hispanic descent. As a result of not seeing themselves in what they are studying, many of these students become bored with their studies and lose the motivation necessary to persist throughout the two or three years of junior college.

Francisco Lara of the Tomas Rivera Center, a Hispanic think tank in California, cites at least three other reasons why Hispanic students are not making the transition from two- to four-year institutions: "they are not receiving the quality of information and assistance that makes the transfer process less of an arduous task; they lack clearly thought-out career and educational goals; and there is a lack of clearly articulated agreements between two- and four-year institutions concerning transfers" (Lara, 1987).

Hispanic Attrition at the Four-Year Level

The problems of declining enrollments at the high school level and the poor transfer rates from junior college are surpassed by high rates of attrition among Hispanic students at the four-year level. In 1978, Brown, Rosen and Olivas provided a status report of Hispanic students at the four-year level by pointing out that while they made up 5.6 percent of the total U.S. population at that time, they comprised only 4.0 percent of undergraduate enrollments and earned just 2.8 of all bachelor's degrees (Olivas, 1982). Today, Hispanics continue to be grossly underrepresented among the ranks of those earning bachelor's degrees. As was mentioned at the outset of the chapter, the graduation rate of Hispanic students, after six years, was forty-one percent (ACE, 1993).

The Problem of Adjustment

Fields (1988) makes the observation that if the first few weeks and months of the collegiate experience are difficult for most students, they are especially difficult for Hispanic students, many of whom leave home reluctantly and then find themselves having to live with persons whose attitudes, values, backgrounds and experiences are vastly different from their own. Fiske (1988) refers to this experience as "juggling two cultures," and believes it is especially difficult for Hispanic students to subjugate their background, culture, and experiences for what is taught both in and out of the classrooms of predominantly white institutions.

Fields points out that feelings of being discriminated against, similar to those of black students, are prevalent among Hispanic students attending predominantly white colleges and universities. Many Hispanic students complain there is a commonly-held perception among white students that Hispanics are less than qualified to attend the institution. Despite the extent to which they may have been prepared academically, the perception seems to be that all Hispanic and black students enter the university through special admissions programs for high-risk students. This sort of thinking, coupled with an unwelcoming campus climate, has made, in Field's estimation, the transition from home to college an extremely difficult proposition—so difficult, in fact, that many Hispanic students simply resolve it makes little sense to remain in an unwelcoming environment when they could find a job to support themselves, as well as to help their families (p.22).

Boston College's Commitment to Retain and Graduate Students of Color

Driven by a commitment to social justice which dictated that more had to be done to fulfill its goal of retaining and graduating students of color, in 1978 Boston College gave its director of the Office of Minority Student Programs (this author) the charge of altering an embarrassingly high attrition rate of eighty-three percent for a target group of black and Hispanic students. Those students had been identified by the university's admissions office as having high levels of motivation and potential, but as requiring assistance if they were to succeed at the university. The strategies used to reduce the high rates of attrition and the establishment of a solid system of academic support services will constitute the remainder of this chapter.

The Evolution of the Office of AHANA Student Programs

Over the course of this director's tenure, a great deal has transpired at Boston College. One important change has been in the name of the office charged with serving students of color. Many students viewed the term "minority" as pejorative, and therefore used the services of the office sparingly. Through the efforts of two of these students, the name of the office was changed to AHANA Student Programs. The term, AHANA, is an acronym for African American, Hispanic, Asian, and Native American. This term is being used by more than thirty colleges and universities, school districts, clubs, and organizations.

There is no question that the most important achievement of the Office of AHANA Student Programs over the years has been the complete reversal of a seventeen percent retention rate in the late 1970s to a current retention rate of ninety-three for the target group served by the office. The target group served by the AHANA office consists of approximately sixty students who are required to participate in a six-week summer academic enrichment program called the Options Through Education Transitional Summer Program. This group includes students who enter the university with SAT scores nearly four hundred points below that of the typical Boston College student. They are the first in their family to attend college; they are students who attended high schools in districts where the dropout rate has, on occasion, exceeded 70 percent; and, they are students who, unless provided with substantial financial aid packages, could not otherwise afford to attend Boston College. While the Office of AHANA Student Programs gives virtually all of its attention to the target group during the summer, during the academic year the office's doors are open to all AHANA students who wish to use its services.

Another milestone for the Office of AHANA Student Programs and, indeed, for the university as a whole, was the election in 1994 of a black male and a Hispanic female to the positions of president and executive vice president of undergraduate government at Boston College. William Dorcena and Cecilia Gutierrez, both seniors who were encouraged by the AHANA office to pursue positions of leadership in the undergraduate government, campaigned on the promise to unify the campus and to promote diversity. The election of Dorcena and Gutierrez is a testament to the ability of AHANA and white students to work together to improve campus life.

Over the years, the Office of AHANA Student Programs has received a number of accolades, honors, and acknowledgments for its efforts at assisting AHANA students at Boston College. These have included recognition by the Faculty Senate at Boston College; identification by the Educational Testing Service as a model retention program in a report titled, Improving Minority Retention: A Search for Effective Institutional Practices (Clewell and Ficklen,1986); and, a Retention Excellence Award from the Noel Levitz National Center for Student Retention.

While such tributes are important, nothing has been more exhilarating than watching students categorized as "average" realize their dream of graduating from Boston College. Comments such as those from Cecilia Gutierrez, '95, executive vice president of undergraduate government, encourage the staff of AHANA Student Programs to continue its important work: "I use the AHANA house a lot. I would not have gotten anything done without it. The staff takes time for you, even if they are in the middle of something. It's nice to know we have this at B.C.—it's a great support for AHANA students." In a similar vein, Nancy Joseph, '95, a nursing student, encourages AHANA students to utilize the services of the AHANA office and to "get to know the people at the AHANA house. Take advantage of every service they offer; it's a great support network." Faculty members have also been encouraging, as manifested in the remarks of psychology professor, Ramsey Liem: "AHANA is a very important and effective organization. It fulfills its primary function of academic, personal and social counseling and it clearly contributes to the extremely high retention rate among students of color once they're on campus. AHANA students can come to Boston College with faith in that support."

There is nothing magical about Boston College's success at preparing AHANA students for the highly competitive world that awaits them. The institution's success is directly linked to having developed and implemented an effective support system that addresses the academic, psychological, and social needs of AHANA students. In "Improving Minority Retention: A Search for Effective Institutional Practices" Clewell and Ficklen, 1986) suggest that successful retention programs possess the following characteristics: presence of a stated policy; high levels of institutional commitment; substantial degree of institutionalization; comprehensiveness of services; dedicated staff; and non-stigmatization of students.

The Office of AHANA Student Programs has been successful because it possesses virtually all of these characteristics. Chief among them is an array of comprehensive support services administered by a gifted, dedicated, and talented staff. These staff members have high expectations of the students entrusted to their care and, consequently, fully expect each of them to graduate.

Several issues need to be clearly thought out as colleges and universities contemplate developing strategies aimed at recruiting, retaining, and graduating AHANA students: All of the components that shall be discussed are in place in Boston College's Office of AHANA Student Programs.

1. Clear Sense of Mission and Commitment at the Highest Levels of the Institution

If an institution is to be successful at retaining AHANA students, or for that matter, any student, it must have a clear sense of its mission. It must honestly ask itself if it has the capacity to meet the educational and other needs of the student(s) it is considering recruiting. If the answer is "no," the matter is quite simple: the institution should not attempt to recruit the student(s).

On the other hand, if the institution believes it can work with a student and agrees to accept him/her, there should be an attending commitment that it will do whatever is necessary to ensure the student is provided with the quality of instruction, the assistance, nurturance and support required to negotiate the university.

The preceding speaks to a commitment emanating from the highest levels of the university. Indeed, if a college or university is serious in its desire to recruit and retain black students, boards of trustees must tell presidents, and presidents must tell vice presidents, deans, and department heads, etc., that the institution is fully committed to creating a climate where all of its students regardless of race, color or creed can flourish academically. Furthermore, boards of trustees—via their chief executive officer, the president—must communicate to the campus community that the task of retaining black and Hispanic students shall not be the responsibility of any one office, but rather shall be everyone's responsibility; even if responsibility means nothing more than creating a hospitable environment where black, Hispanic and other AHANA students feel welcome. Commitment requires that boards of trustees, presidents, deans, department heads and faculty all share in conveying to the university community that racism has no place in the community; and that the kind of community being sought is one that respects diversity and where mutual respect and responsibility are the principles that govern how one conducts him or herself. Commitment at the highest levels of the university means the institution (after carefully examining the special needs, backgrounds, cultures, and experiences of black and Hispanic students) will set in place programs that respond not only to the academic but psychological, social and cultural needs of students of color. Anything short of establishing a strong support service system for AHANA students amounts to nothing more than rendering lip service.

Finally, commitment at the top means the university recognizes the important role that AHANA faculty, staff, and administrators play in the lives of AHANA students and will therefore seek to hire members of these groups, not only in faculty positions, but also in administrative positions at the highest levels of the institution.

2. Honesty in the Recruitment Process

Once an institution has realistically assessed its capacity to respond to the needs of its AHANA students, the next step in the process is that of recruitment. Edward Anderson (1978) stresses that a carefully thought-out recruitment plan is the first step in the retention process. He emphasizes that recruiters should be honest in pointing out to guidance counselors, teachers, parents and students the type of student(s) the institution is best suited to serve. Furthermore, to offset any misunderstanding that might come about later on in the admissions process, or after the student has been admitted, Anderson stresses the university has a moral obligation to be as candid as possible in telling students about the likelihood of being admitted; of obtaining financial aid; of finding housing; and, perhaps most important, of being victimized by racism. In addition to the preceding, the recruiter should feel obliged to point out the size of classes, who will be teaching them (professors or teaching assistants), and what students can expect to learn; and, further, the recruiter should be prepared to point out how a degree in a particular major will be perceived by graduate and professional schools and/or prospective employers.

3. Innovative Admissions Policies

In this era of concern over the dearth of black and Hispanic students entering higher education, colleges and universities are virtually in a war over enrolling the "best and brightest." Little, if any, thought is being given to affording marginal students an opportunity to attend such institutions. Nettles, et. al., (1985) and a host of other researchers believe that high schools grades, SAT and ACT scores and the kinds of curriculum in which a student is enrolled in high school are the best predictors of success in college. Sedlacek and Webster (1974), however, offer a differing perspective on measures that they believe are better determinants of black and Hispanic student success in college, including:

a. positive self-concept;

b. realistic self-appraisal;

c. understanding and ability to deal with racism;

d. preference for long-term goals;

e. availability of a strong support person;

f. leadership experience; and

g. demonstrated community service.

There are hundreds of Boston College AHANA students who, over recent years, have not only succeeded academically but have become very effective student leaders at the university. Had traditional methods been applied when the admissions office looked at these students' applications, rather than non-cognitive variables, they would not have been accepted to Boston College. It does not make sense to exclude, because of poor performance on a standardized test, students who would probably do well if afforded an opportunity and provided with necessary academic support services.

4. Mandatory Summer Orientation Program

An essential component of an effective retention plan is a summer orientation program for those students identified as needing academic assistance. At the heart of such programs is a statement to the student, that in the light of deficiencies that he or she possesses, participation in the program is mandatory. Secondly, if the program is to be successful, and if courses are offered on a credited basis, the program should be no less than six weeks in length.

Further, a contractual agreement between students and the program needs to be entered into at the outset of the program, clearly outlining what the program expects from the student and, conversely, what the student can expect from the program. Expectations should be delineated for the summer program, and for the academic year as well. A critical aspect of the contractual agreement should be a commitment by the student that he or she will exact as much from the summer program and academic year as possible.

More important than contractual agreements are the objectives of a summer program for high-risk AHANA students. Such a program should, at the very least, do the following:

• Diagnose students' academic levels of abilities and tailor academic offerings geared to meeting their needs.

• Provide programs of instruction in math and English.

• If on a diagnostic test a student demonstrates a capacity to handle a credited course in math, English, science, he/she should be allowed to do so.

14

- Provide students with a program of instruction in the use of computers.
- Introduce students to a variety of academic and administrative resources on campus, e.g. libraries, laboratories, computer centers and deans'offices.
- Provide academic advisement regarding course selection and requirements in majors.
- Offer classes, workshops and seminars regarding the realities involved in attending college.
- Structure workshops and classes aimed at assisting students with note-taking, test-taking, study habits, time management, decision-making, and budgeting skills.
- Utilize the campus' career center to get students to begin thinking about graduate education and career opportunities.
- Provide recreational outlets so that students can relax and establish relationships with each other.

5. Academic Support Services

Although a summer orientation program is important in preparing high-risk AHANA students for the rigors of the academic year, the academic year program is important to the survival of all AHANA students. At some point in their academic careers, AHANA students will need to turn to someone for help. Institutions that do not have an academic support program are strongly urged to establish one.

Again, all of the services suggested here are offered to students served by the Office of AHANA Student Programs at Boston College:

1. Tutorials: Because even the brightest students will at times experience difficulty with a course, a tutorial program needs to be set in place to respond to the need of any student who might come into the office at any time for help. At Boston College, tutoring is provided by both AHANA and non-AHANA undergraduate and graduate students.

2. Academic Advisement: This service must be provided because AHANA students will need help in selecting appropriate courses in their major, as well as courses compatible with interest and desires. At Boston College, this advisement is provided by four graduate students hired by the Office of AHANA Student Programs.

3. Personal Counseling: As has been mentioned, predominantly white colleges and universities can be lonely, alienating, and isolating places for AHANA students. It is essential that assistance is provided to better enable students to deal with the environment. The best personnel to provide help are trained counselors. At Boston College, graduate students are hired and trained to provide counseling to AHANA students. In addition, administrative aides or

peer counselors are hired to reach out to fellow students, helping them where possible to resolve difficulties, but more importantly, to counsel them to use the office's services.

4. Academic Performance Monitoring: This is essentially an early warning system that requires faculty to report those students who are experiencing academic and personal difficulties. By knowing the problems that a student is experiencing early on, the program can better assist him/her at passing courses that he/she might otherwise fail. The principal responsibility for monitoring AHANA student performance rests with the graduate assistants.

5. Career Counseling: It is vitally important that students see what's in store for them at the close of their four-year experience. Questions they may have about careers need to be answered. Job sites that interest them should be visited (alumni can be helpful here). Students should be provided with information regarding graduate and professional schools internships, fellowships, scholarships, work study and summer opportunities. etc.

6. Comprehensive Financial Aid: Dr. Frank Hale, vice provost for Minority Affairs Emeritus at the Ohio State University, makes the observation that " ... commitment without cash is counterfeit" (1988). Hale feels it is unrealistic to expect poor students (whose parents in many instances earn less than ten thousand dollars a year) will take out huge loans to subsidize their education, when they recognize these loans will place an undue burden on the family. Rather than subject the family to a large loan burden many AHANA students simply decide not to attend college. It is clear, then, that if colleges and universities want to increase the presence of AHANA students, they have to reach into their coffers to make resources more readily available. No support measure is more important that this.

7. Mentoring: Studies abound pertaining to the important role faculty play in shaping the academic lives of students. Premier among these researchers are Pascarella and Terenzini (1979) who believe the relationships established between faculty and students outside of the classroom are critically important in a student's academic and social growth and development. If faculty-student interactions are important to all students, these relationships are doubly important for AHANA students. This is doubly important given the pervasive inhospitable and cold climate that exists on far too many predominantly white campuses. White faculty members at predominantly white colleges and universities, in particular, need to enter into mentoring relationships with AHANA students. These relationships call on faculty to advise, assist and generally support assigned students at negotiating the undergraduate years; and, equally important, encourage the student to consider graduate school with an eye toward a career in teaching.

The 1992 academic year was very special for the Office of AHANA Student Programs as it marked the launching of the Benjamin Elijah Mays Mentoring

Program. Divided into two components (a three-day summer institute aimed at training mentors for their important work and the actual academic year program), the specific aim of the program is to provide AHANA students with an opportunity to have a personal connection with a faculty member who can help to guide them through the university environment. The Mays Program also attempts to ameliorate potential isolation by pairing AHANA students with faculty members who are willing to develop a relationship and follow their proteges through the four years of college. At present there are one hundred fifteen mentors and 150 proteges enrolled in the program.

Since mentors and students come from a variety of cultures and racial back-grounds, the institute offers sessions on cross-cultural communications; responsibilities of mentors; and techniques for building relationships, all presented by experts in the field. Students participate in the institute as well, telling their stories and describing how mentors have assisted them in making the transition and adjustment to college life.

8. Involvement in the Community: The isolation that most AHANA students experience on predominantly white campuses could be partially overcome if opportunities were found for students to become involved in off-campus activities. This is especially true in those cases where the campuses are far removed from the community. Given the academic problems experienced by large numbers of black and Hispanic students at the elementary and secondary school levels, two critically important services that could be provided by black and Hispanic college students are tutoring and mentoring of younger students.

Given the magnitude of the dropout problem among black and Hispanic students, the task of exciting youngsters about college should begin at the elementary and middle school grades. Preparation should begin early, and there are a host of models that colleges and universities may want to look at. At Boston College there is Project 2000, wherein AHANA students have adopted a fourth-grade class at one of Boston's elementary schools. Some forty fourth-graders are brought to campus for a Saturday program during which skills are imparted in math, English, science, and computer literacy. Moreover, it is hoped that positive values through group discussion will be instilled and that the youth will become excited about learning.

9. Religion as a Critical Element: Marvalene Styles Hughes (1987) highlighted the important role religion plays in the lives of black students attending predominantly black and predominantly white colleges and universities. On asking black students at both types of institutions an open-ended question aimed at determining what contributed to their success in college, an equal number of students cited their faith in God as being critically important.

Given the importance of religion in the lives of AHANA students at Boston College, the Office of AHANA Student Programs has recently added another service called the Gospel Caravan. The aim of the Gospel Caravan is that of affording AHANA students desirous of attending an off-campus worship service on Sunday morning an opportunity to attend a worship service of their choice. All that is required of a student is that he/she be present and board the bus at the appointed time.

10. The Importance of Evaluation: If an institution is to be effective in meeting the needs of its students, it must occasionally assess what works and what does not work. Quite simply, there is need for an institutional self-study. Similarly, if a retention effort is to succeed there is need for a program evaluation periodically to determine the programs' strengths and weaknesses. The wise program director, on pinpointing his/her weaknesses, will move swiftly to correct them.

Summary and Conclusion

The aim of this chapter has been to point out the challenges faced by AHANA students prior to and on enrolling in the nation's colleges and universities. Moreover, it offers a solution in the form of a well-thought-out retention plan. The attrition rates for AHANA students nationwide are totally unacceptable—unacceptable because as this country enters the next century, when literally one third of the nation's workforce will be people of color and women, there is an imperative to insure that AHANA students at every level of the educational pipeline receive the best education possible. Such is not the case at present, as far too many AHANA students are victimized by an inadequate education.

Several variables seem to predominate in the high dropout rates among far too many AHANA students who go on to college, including poor preparation at the high school level; feelings of alienation and isolation; inadequate financial aid; and a lack of support services. Dr. Frank Hale states:

> *"We have insisted on bombarding them with the methods, tactics and strategies we know best. We have said, 'we will do for you what we have done for others, but we will not vary our approach; your unique background, experience and culture notwithstanding.' We ask of them a greater degree of change than institutions are willing to make." (Hale, 1982).*

The message is clear. If this nation is seriously concerned about its very survival, it has to conduct its business in a different way. At the post-secondary level, colleges and universities have to go out of their way to ensure the environment is more welcoming and that AHANA students have the academic support services necessary to excel and to graduate.

—Dr. Donald Brown is the director of the Office of AHANA Student Programs at Boston College in Boston, Massachusetts.

Endnotes

Allen, W.R. (1982). National Study of Black College Students. University of Michigan, Department of Sociology, Ann Arbor, MI.

Anderson, E. (1978). A Retention Design Applied to an Equal Opportunity Program in: Noel (ed.) Reducing the Dropout Rate. Jossey Bass, San Francisco, CA.

Arbeiter, S. (1987). Black Enrollments: The Case of the Missing Students. Change Magazine. Vol. 19, (pp. 14-19).

Astin, A. (July 1989). Student Involvement/Retention: How Well Are You Doing? Remarks Delivered at the National Conference on Student Retention.

Blake, E. Jr. (May/June 1987). Equality for Blacks: Another Lost Decade or New Surge Forward? Change Magazine. Vol. 19.

Christoffel, P. (March 1986). Minority Student Access and Retention: A Research and Development Update. College Entrance Examination Board. New York, NY.

Clewell, B. and Ficklen. (1986). Improving Minority Retention in Higher Education: A Search for Effective Institutional Practices. Princeton, N.J. Educational Testing Service.

Davila, E.M. (October 1988). Cited in Black Issues in Higher Education.

Fields, C. (1988) The Hispanic Pipeline: Narrow, Leaking, and Needing Repair. Change Magazine. Vol. 20, (pp. 20-27).

Fiske, E.B. (1988). The Undergraduate Hispanic Experience: A Case of Juggling Two Cultures. Change Magazine. Vol. 20, (pp. 18-47).

Fleming, Jacqueline. (1984). Blacks in College. Jossey Bass, San Francisco, CA.

Hale, F.W., Jr. (1982) Serving Two Masters: Perspective of a Black Administrator With a Minority Focused Function at a Predominantly White Institution. Proceedings of the First National Conference on Issues Facing Black Administrators at Predominantly White Institutions.

Hale, F.W., Jr. (June 1988). Strategies for Overcoming Barriers to Access and Retention. Remarks delivered at the National Conference on Blacks in Higher Education.

Hammond, L.D. (1985). Equality & Excellence: Educational Status of Black Americans. College Entrance Examination Board. New York, NY.

Hughes, M.S. (1987). Black Students' Participation in Higher Education. Journal of College Student Personnel. Vol. 28, (pp. 532-537).

High School and Beyond. (1980). U.S. Department of Education: National Center for Education Statistics. Washington D.C.

Holman, C.M. (October 1985). "How to Stop the Miseducation of Black Children." Ebony.

Lara, F. (April 1987). Cited in Black Issues in Higher Education.

Levine, A. and Hirsch, D. (May/June 1988). "On Making Meaningful Impact: Hostos President Isaura Santiago." Change Magazine. (pp. 48-53).

Magallan, R. (April 1987). Cited in Black Issues in Higher Education.

"Make Something Happen" (1984). National Commission on Secondary Schooling for Hispanics: Hispanic Policy Development Project. Washington, D.C.

Melendez, S. (April 1987). Cited in Black Issues in Higher Education Vol. 4, no. 2.

Minorities in Higher Education: Twelfth Annual Status Report, 1993. American Council on Education. Washington, D.C.

Nettles, M., Gosman, E.J., Thoney, A.R., and Dandridge, B.A. (1985). Causes and Consequences of College Students' Performance: A Focus on Black and White Students' Attrition Rates, Progression Rates, and Grade Point Averages. Tennessee Higher Education Commission. Nashville, TN.

Olivas, M. (1982). Federal Higher Education Policy: The Case of Hispanic Education, Evaluation, and Policy Analysis.

"One Third of a Nation" (1988). Report of the Commission on Minority Participation in Education and American Life. American Council on Education, Washington D.C.

Orum, L. (1986) "The Education of Hispanics: Status and Implications." The National Council of LaRaza. Washington, D.C.

Pascarella, E.T., and Terenzini, P.T. (1979). "Student-Faculty Informal Contact and Persistence: A Further Investigation." Journal of Educational Research. Vo. 50, (pp. 545-595).

Sedlacek, W.E., and Webster, D.W. (1978). Admissions and Retention of Minority Students in Large Universities: Journal of College Student Personnel. 19:242-248.

Sudarkasa, N. (January 1988). Black Enrollment in Higher Education: The Unfulfilled Promise of Equality. State of Black America: National Urban League Report.

Watson, B. (January 1981). The Quality of Education for Black Americans. State of Black America: National Urban League Report.

Wilson, R. (November 1986). Black Education in the Workforce: A Demographic Analysis. Remarks delivered at the Annual Meeting of the National Alliance of Black School Educators. Washington, D.C.

Wilson, W.J. (1987). The Truly Disadvantaged: The Innercity, The Underclass, and Public Policy. The University of Chicago Press, Chicago, IL.

U.S. Bureau of the Census. (August 1987). Monthly Income and Poverty Status of Families and Persons in the U.S. 1986, Current Population Reports. Government Printing Office, Washington, D.C. No. 157 (p.60).

U.S.A. Today. (June 5, 1988).

Working Collaboratively: Strategies for Success

by Lillian B. Poats and Emma Amacker

Overview:

Cooperative programs which are designed to enhance the recruitment and retention of minority students have become an integral concern to institutions of higher education. Pipeline issues which suggest that the numbers of minority students graduating from high school may negatively impact the ability of colleges and universities to enroll these students have made it necessary for collaboration to become a vital strategy.

This chapter is designed to provide a discussion surrounding the issues which arise when colleges and institutions engage in meaningful collaborative efforts with public schools. Additionally, it seeks to outline five basic strategies which can serve as guiding principles in the development and implementation of collaborative programming.

As colleges and universities compete for well prepared students in the future, the recruitment and retention of minority students may very well be dependent upon their ability to reach these youngsters prior to their enrollment at the college level. Collaborative programs represent a way not only to encourage students to continue their education, but also a way to familiarize students with America's campuses.

Introduction

In an era of economic constraints and a declining applicant pool, cooperative efforts become a more viable option for America's colleges and universities. It is clear the recruitment of minority students to higher education is dependent, in many ways, upon the collaborative efforts which the institution is willing to engage in. This is often referred to as "a pipeline issue."

If fewer minority students are graduating from high school with acceptable academic performance, then there will be fewer students who meet the eligibility requirements for entrance into colleges and universities. This fact has led many colleges and universities to engage in collaborative programs with public education. Initially, most programs are focused at the high school level, where the attempt is to provide tutorial services and familiarization activities designed to enhance the probability that students will attend college.

The involvement of the university in this arena has not been without debate. While most regard this involvement as necessary to assure students are prepared for entrance into college, many in higher education scorn these activities. The reality of attrition and declining enrollment, however, suggests colleges and universities must become involved in assuring there are qualified students in the pipeline prepared to meet the challenges of higher education.

Undoubtedly, the involvement of college and university personnel with high school students is beneficial to all parties. It allows for the university personnel to gain a realistic understanding of America's schools; and secondly, it allows individuals within the secondary schools to gain a better understanding of the expectations held by colleges. One prevailing issue, however, for individuals who have spent time engaged in this process, is that intervention strategies should begin prior to the high school level. The need to extend these efforts to the middle school and often the elementary school level becomes painfully clear. You don't begin at the high school level to encourage students to study science. These efforts must begin in the primary stages of a student's educational career. The result of this dialogue has been the extension of academic services, as well as mentorship programs to the elementary and middle school level.

In networking to create positive learning environments, educators can become involved in collaborative efforts which include innovative inservice training and staff development designed to provide new and creative ways of thinking about teaching and learning. As this dialogue develops, educators will be able to discuss expectations and share information which will enhance the educational environment. Current networks designed to facilitate educational reform require that America's school systems focus on effective ways to develop quality students. Developing working relationships with post-secondary institutions can only enhance the probability that the quality of instruction will increase. Not only does this create more effective school systems, it positively impacts those individuals in the pipeline for college enrollment.

A key element in the networking process must be the ability to work collaboratively. This is difficult, in many instances, because it is somewhat natural for the university to want to assume a leadership role and dictate to the public school districts what needs to be done. However, the success of collaborative programs is totally dependent on the ability of individuals to work in a cooperative manner. There are many stories of failed efforts of colleges and universities working with school districts. A critical review of many such programs suggests there are some essential elements for working collaboratively. These essential elements address cooperative efforts involving various levels of the college and university experience, high schools, middle schools and elementary schools. The literature is complete with various models of institutional connections designed to enhance the probability that minority students will engage in higher education. The following suggestions provide generic strategies and guidelines which can be used in all configurations:

1. Philosophically agree upon a global perspective.

This suggests that institutions and/or individuals involved should maintain a focus on the overall goal of the venture, i.e. to recruit minority students to colleges. This posture eliminates the competition aspect of the venture or the stratification of institutions. The guiding premise then becomes to recruit students to higher education not a specific program or campus. Often when several colleges are involved in a project, there is the temptation to stratify institutions based on perceived status and/or prestige. This places institutions in competition with each other, sometimes to the detriment of the student. The lack of a clear focus on a global perspective may allow the project to dissipate into an individualistic focus which does not meet the needs of all parties involved. The focus may be on institutional desires rather than on student needs.

The need to agree upon a global perspective is equally important whether there are several institutions on the same level (i.e. two four-year institutions) or institutions of differing levels (i.e. a four-year, a two-year college and a high school). It forces institutions to look at the overall goal rather than to reduce the effort to specific institutional goals. This principle will need to be kept central during the developmental stages of the project.

2. Develop a formalized document which outlines the specific responsibilities and activities of all institutions involved.

It is imperative that all participating institutions feel comfortable with the terms of the agreement; especially those individuals directly responsible for the implementation. Individuals should be brought into the project based on their interest and willingness to be involved in the program. It is not a good idea to assign individuals to a project of this nature. A written document should outline the administrative reporting responsibilities in each institution involved, as well as for the total project. This document should be very specific with regards to fiscal accountability. It provides an organizational framework so it is clear who is responsible for making decisions related to the project. In instances where external funding is sought, this document has the essential components of the proposal. It is necessary, however, to be very clear in this document so that all parties understand and are comfortable with the organizational structure. Many projects have gone awry because of a lack of agreement or understanding of responsibilities. At the same time, partnerships built on a multi-level structure must allow for a sense of autonomy for institutions involved and the ability for them to have input regarding their activities. There is a clear need to be flexible and make allowances when the institutional culture dictates.

3. Top level support is critical.

Success can only be expected when the goals and vision of the collaboration are voiced from the top leadership of the institutions. Top leadership is defined as the superintendent, president and/or dean. Other individuals in the organizational hierarchy must understand the program; however, support of the top administrative official sets the tone for universal acceptance of the program. The program is more likely to gain support from individuals in the organization when it has been sanctioned by the top administrators. It is critical that top-level administrative support be the guiding force for any collaborative project. It is helpful when this support is demonstrated with a written affirmation as witnessed by signing the interinstitutional agreement. This support for the project should be evident through involvement of top administrative officials. Opportunities should be provided for top administrative officials to participate in activities. This might involve formal greetings and/or remarks on programs. Additionally, administrators should have an opportunity to interact with professionals from the various institutions involved in the project. Invitations to attend planning meetings should always be extended to administrators. Lastly, but most importantly, administrators should have the opportunity to visit and dialogue with program participants. Interaction with the students sends a positive message regarding the value of the program. Top administrative support, then, should be evidenced by participation in activities, as well as by financial support. Many brilliant program ideas have been lost due to the lack of top administrative support. It is the job of the project director to continuously market the project in a positive light.

4. Network in a cooperative manner.

Network in a cooperative manner with those who have the same global objectives (i.e. the recruitment and retention of minority students into higher education), who may not be formally linked to the program. In most cases, this is reflected in cooperation between individuals who coordinate similar programs. Participation in professional organizations allows for the formation of networks to share information and compare issues. In conjunction with this, the stories of success as well as failures must be told. Conference participation and presentation of papers which highlight the program serve to enhance insight into sought goals. The dissemination of information about the project provides a vehicle to dialogue with other individuals with similar goals. Networking in a positive manner can only serve to enhance the quality of the program.

5. Communicate! Communicate! Communicate!

Communication is perhaps the most challenging issue in a collaborative effort. Institutions and individuals come to the project with differing viewpoints, cultures and intentions. In addition to being mindful of this, it becomes necessary to pay very careful attention to the modes of communication. In addition to observing basic rules of courtesy, honesty and politeness, participants may need to develop skills enhancing positive communication in a collaborative effort. As with other forms of communication, a critical factor here will be genuineness. When individuals are genuine and truthful a certain degree of trust will develop. Without such trust, the effort may be doomed for failure from the beginning. All communication should be maintained with a high degree of professionalism. Once individuals have gained a mutual respect for each other, interactions will take on a positive note. One must be mindful of the nature of interaction among individuals from the beginning of the project. It may be necessary for the project director to work strategically to foster positive communication among all parties involved. Openness in communication is critical to project success. Institutions and individuals involved must feel freedom to discuss problems, concerns and other issues related to the project.

It is imperative that communication be fostered through periodic meetings designed to share ideas, answer questions, and allow for dialogue among representatives from the various institutions. Well-planned and well-implemented meetings which focus on program issues are well received. Individuals will use this as a forum to dialogue. If individuals come to the forum with personal agendas, this becomes a perfect opportunity to work on achieving that global perspective — the idea that everyone is in this for the same reason. Respect emanates from continuous dialogue and discussion. Individuals will come to understand the various institutional perspectives and will be able to move beyond that specific agenda to achieve the goals of the program.

The guiding principle in working collaboratively is to recognize that institutions and individuals often differ in their approach. However, it is imperative that participants continue to focus on the ultimate goal. This is extremely important for the success of collaborative programs. While it is necessary to acknowledge that each school will not function in the same manner. It is just as important to resist the monolithic thinking which suggests that "difference equals deficiency." Institutional methods and culture will differ, however, the goal may be achieved. In their own way, each institution may have a major impact on the recruitment and retention of increased numbers of minority students into higher education. The additional benefit to working collaboratively is found in the idea that dialogue among individuals and institutions can enhance the support which minority students receive. While some institutions may not exhibit a high degree of sensitivity initially, the dialogue may assist in developing a better understanding of the issues involved in minority student recruitment and retention.

Summary

Colleges and universities no longer have the luxury of sitting back and blaming high schools for underprepared students. The recruitment and retention of minority students is fundamentally tied to the ability to assure that these students are prepared for the academic challenges which colleges offer. Collaborative work with institutions who have large minority populations becomes a viable way of attracting these students into the ranks. One must recognize, however, that this is sometimes a difficult task for individuals in higher education. It is difficult, primarily because colleges and universities have enjoyed an "ivory-tower" atmosphere which did not always require that they reach out. The ability to work collaboratively, then, becomes an asset which institutions can use. For some institutions, the acknowledgement that colleges must reach out to public schools is the first step to creating effective networks. The dialogue designed to facilitate the building of specific programs is then more likely to occur. Much of this work is done by individual faculty and staff members on behalf of the institution.

When faculty and staff leave their comfortable offices in the academy, they often find themselves ill-equipped to interact and function effectively in the school environment. These strategies represent a challenge for well intentioned faculty and staff who engage in collaborative efforts designed to enhance the recruitment and retention of minority students.

—Dr. Lillian B. Poats is Associate Professor in the Department of Educational Leadership and Counseling at Texas Southern University in Houston, Texas.
—Dr. Emma Amacker is Assistant Professor in the Department of Curriculum and Instruction at Texas Southern University in Houston, Texas.

The Bridge: A Viable Retention Program for African-American Students

by Constance A. Chapman and Beatrice L. Logan

Overview:

Each year many African-American students enroll in colleges and universities. College enrollment for these students is an exciting period—a feeling of great accomplishment. The students begin their postsecondary education with anticipation that the next four years of their lives will be filled with stimulating academic experiences, culminating with a degree. What happens to this enthusiasm, then, since less than half of these students persist through graduation? Retention studies suggest that the attrition rates of African-American students are five to eight times higher than their white counterparts. What can colleges and universities do to salvage the postsecondary pursuits of African-American students?

A retention program called The Bridge was implemented over a decade ago at Georgia State University (GSU) in Atlanta. This summer enrichment program, established expressly for African-American students, helps them to assess their interests, values, and abilities while improving their skills in reading, writing, mathematics, and study skills. At the same time it emphasizes the importance of coping and persistence in college life.

The single, overriding theme in the Bridge is that education is not something that just happens, but something each individual must create for him/herself. In the past ten years The Bridge, which is in place on four other Georgia campuses, has helped shape African-American students at predominantly white colleges to graduate as positive, qualified, adept learners — ready as anyone to face future career challenges. This article describes this unique program and its components.

Introduction

Statistics show the attrition rates of African-American students enrolled in higher education institutions on predominately white campuses has grown as rapidly as their enrollment. Why does this problem exist? Georgia State University (GSU) has looked to research to gain understanding of this phenomenon. Data reveal that attrition rates of African Americans students are five to eight times higher than those of their white counterparts. Stewart (1991) reported that while the rate of white students graduating within a six-year time frame (the average number of years students have taken to graduate recently) is fifty percent, minority graduation is only twenty-five. In essence, African American students have not fared well.

Tinto (1975, 1987) and Astin (1977, 1984) identified some possible causes for student attrition. Tinto identified academic and social integration as determinants that influence students' decisions to persist in school or drop out. He found that students arrive on campus with various built-in characteristics which play significant roles in their persistence. These characteristics are influenced by their family backgrounds, pre-college educational achievements, academic abilities, and other personal attributes.

Astin (1977, 1984) emphasized the importance of student participation in campus life, such as involvement in sports, clubs, sororities, fraternities, etc. He submitted that this involvement helps students bond with the institution. The overriding theme of both Astin and Tinto appears to be that students who bond to the university and develop close relationships with peers, faculty and staff are more likely to remain matriculated until graduation.

Later, Nettles (1991) found another factor that influenced what Tinto called "academic integration." He wrote:

> *Academic integration is a factor which includes students' satisfaction with faculty relationships; their feelings that the faculty of the university is sensitive to the interest, needs, and aspirations of students; the ease with which students feel they can develop close personal relationships with faculty members on campus; the perception of students that their faculty are good teachers; and the students' satisfaction with the quality of instruction at their university.*

If the problem of African-American student retention on predominately white campuses is to be resolved, two relevant questions must be answered. What can be done to reverse the high attrition rates of African-American students? What intervention strategies are needed to give African-American students the same chance to succeed as other students?

Lang and Ford (1988), and Haniff (1991) submitted that students' perception and their willingness to persist to graduation are directly influenced by faculty members who are sensitive, caring, and supportive. As appropriately stated by Haniff, "this caring and these relationships cannot be legislated or programmed.

It is precisely because such relationships cannot be legislated, that programs to facilitate black students on white campuses must exist, limited though they are" (p. 248). Davis (1991) said such programs are especially important for the retention of African-American students.

Levin and Levin (1991) reviewed research literature on retention programs and proposed five characteristics essential for such programs. They are: " (a) proactive interventions; (b) small tutorial groups; (c) the teaching of study skills, learning strategies, and test-taking techniques in the context of courses in which students are enrolled; (d) the development of students' basic language skills (i.e. reading, writing, speaking, and listening abilities); and (e) quality instruction" (p. 325).

In setting up such programs, Pounds (1989) encourages predominately white institutions to include three major elements: (a) meaningful ways to involve students in campus life; (b) positive bonds with faculty and staff; and (c) protection from threatening situations. These pertinent factors described by Levin and Levin, Pounds, and others are integral elements of Georgia State University's retention program, The Bridge.

Development Of The Bridge

In 1984, the U.S. Department of Education, Office of Civil Rights, found that African-American enrollment in the University System of Georgia was not compliant with the 1978 Desegregation Plan. In order to alleviate this situation, the Board of Regents selected six institutions to conduct a pilot project— "The Bridge." GSU was one of them. The original mission of the program was to increase the retention of African-American students. Initially this was a four-week program with primary emphasis on classroom instruction in reading, mathematics and science. Although classroom instruction is important, other factors also impact retention. Consequently, since the inception of this program, The Bridge at GSU has expanded its mission to help participants develop more holistically. This includes appreciation of self-worth, multi-cultural awareness, collaborative learning, participation in campus organizations and activities, and development of leadership skills.

Program Operations & Activities

The Bridge is a four-week, nonresidential, summer enrichment program open to approximately forty students who meet the following criteria: a) they must be accepted for matriculation in the Division of Learning Support Programs (LSP), which means that they are deficient in one or more of the basic skill areas— mathematics, reading, composition; b) they must be African-American; and c) they must apply to the program.

Once students are accepted into The Bridge, they are placed in appropriate levels of noncredit courses in mathematics, reading and composition which have been determined by students' performance on the SAT/ACT, the Collegiate Placement Examination (CPE), and their high school mathematics and English averages. The mathematics component is divided into three levels (097, 098, 099); reading, two levels (070, 071); and composition, two levels (080, 081). The Bridge students also take a seminar entitled Personal and Academic Development, a course required of LSP students.

After students have been placed in appropriate levels, they are divided into two groups of twenty students. Because of the disparity in students' mathematical skills, a concerted effort is made to homogeneously group them according to their mathematics scores.

The courses offered during The Bridge are designed to familiarize students with the level of competence expected in college courses and to increase their performance in these skill areas. At the end of the program, students who demonstrate readiness are progressed to the next level. For example, a student who is placed in Composition 080 and demonstrates ability to write effective essays, free of grammatical and structural errors, by the end of the program is placed in Composition 081 for fall quarter.

Academic courses serve to achieve The Bridge program's goal of helping students to become acquainted with the ramifications of the university experience. Each of these courses requires diligent work in and out of class. While work begins at the students' level of competence, instructors expect the same level of effort and achievement that they expect of students during regular academic classes.

Each academic course also helps students to build self-esteem, become aware of other cultures, engage in collaborative learning, and participate in campus activities. Additionally, in order to instill racial pride and awareness, all of the courses offered during The Bridge focus on some aspect of the African-American experience.

Mathematics

The purpose of this course is to strengthen students' mathematical skills by providing practice in logical problem-solving. Students receive four hours of class-room instruction per week, plus two hours of computer instruction in mathematics theory and operations. In addition to learning techniques necessary for solving problems on the Whimbey Analytical Skills Inventory (WASI), concerted effort is made to help students understand and use mathematics in real-life situations. Examples are computing predicted grade point average (PGA) and determining the monetary worth of jobs, calculations which often confuse students of color. Students are also required to gather research on a person of African descent who has made significant contributions to this field.

Language Arts

Reading and composition are encompassed in the language arts course which meets eight hours per week. One purpose of the course is to develop efficient reading, writing and study skills through a main-idea approach. This instructional approach assumes reading and writing to be related communication skills, each supporting and enhancing the other.

The second purpose of this course is to develop writers as readers through collaborative learning. Peer conferences encourage collaborative learning which help students to develop confidence. Chapman (1991) wrote that "one of the ways to help students develop…confidence is to teach them how to be critical readers of their own writing. Peer conferences can teach this skill" (p. 20). Consequently, during The Bridge, peer conferences are held after each writing assignment.

The third purpose of the course is to enhance racial pride. This is accomplished through assigned readings and discussions which focus on the African American experience in the historical context of slavery and the movement for social equality. These discussions help students develop their critical thinking skills and examine their personal assumptions prior to engaging in formal and informal letter and essay writing. There is also a broader effort to examine other issues of discrimination such as the treatment of Native Americans and negative stereotyping of minorities by the media. Students read literature by black writers and leaders like Toni Morrison, Gloria Naylor, and Martin Luther King, Jr.

Personal and Academic Development Seminar

This course is designed to help students acquire academic and personal skills that will enable them to succeed at GSU. In addition to helping students build self-esteem and bond to the university, this seminar emphasizes study skills, time management, goal setting, memory and listening skills, note-taking and test-taking strategies, and library skills. Students are also guided through structured exercises designed to familiarize themselves with university support services, faculty members, college organizations and careers. They receive academic advisement, and are encouraged to express their frustration and to explore their fears about beginning their postsecondary education in a culturally diverse institution.

Academic and Personal Support

Besides regular classes, The Bridge offers other support for students. They are introduced to the learning lab where they can get one-on-one tutoring or work on computer-generated exercises to enhance their skills in reading, mathematics and composition.

Students are also instructed in the basics of word processing during the seminar class. They are then able to refine this skill during mathematics and language arts classes which are scheduled once per week in a computer classroom. Students are encouraged to make presentations during class meetings and plan special events like The Bridge closing ceremony. GSU student leaders are invited to speak about their organizations and the advantages of becoming active in those groups.

Special Activities

Probably the most important retention tool is building student's self-respect and self-worth. Without this feeling of self-worth, students cannot be expected to bond with the university. The Bridge activities which help to promote this feeling of self-worth are omnipresent. On Friday of each week, the groups combine for special activities. These include meetings with successful leaders, authors, and professionals like former U.N. Ambassador Andrew Young, and Georgia author Dori Sanders.

Special activities also include field trips to educational events and sites. These include the Black Arts Festival held in Atlanta bi-annually, visiting art galleries, and attending concerts where students can experience the work of talented black men and women.

A major field trip each year is an all-day visit to the Civil Rights Institute in Birmingham, Ala., which chronicles civil rights events that occurred before most of The Bridge students were born. There, they get an emotional taste of life before the movement began. They also begin to see the importance of Dr. Martin Luther King, Jr. and others who worked for the freedom of African Americans. For their language arts class, students are required to write letters describing their experience to a close relative or friend. For example, one student wrote:

> *"The visit opened my eyes and made me realize all of the things my people went through to get me where I am today. This in itself, along with my self-motivation, has motivated me to do my best in school. It has also motivated me to do whatever is necessary to help my people excel."*

Funding and Staff

At Georgia State, The Bridge program falls under the aegis of the Division of Learning Support Programs. The professional staff includes an administrative coordinator and three instructors (mathematics, seminar, language arts). Dr. Michael Hovland (1994), senior consultant at Noel•Levitz Centers in Iowa City says an important factor in successful programs is choosing the right people to staff them. He further elaborated that "the people running programs are more important than the programs they run" (p. 29). In agreement with this philosophy, GSU has chosen outstanding and dedicated LSP teachers who have expressed an interest in the recruitment and retention of African American students.

There are also two junior staff members, one male and one female, who act as peer advisors. Peer advisors are important members of The Bridge staff. They are former Bridge students who have demonstrated outstanding leadership and interpersonal skills and are familiar with campus logistics. These students are chosen and trained by The Bridge coordinator months before the program begins. Training centers around group dynamics, university resources and procedures, simulated problem resolution, job responsibilities, etc. Each peer advisor is assigned to one of the two groups. Their jobs entail attending all classes, and functioning as friends and confidants for the students. The peer advisors also assist the instructors in various ways such as distributing supplies, taking students to see counselors, etc. They also work closely with the program coordinator to plan and carry out program activities.

Staff Meetings

Once per week, The Bridge staff — teachers, peer advisors, and the coordinator — meets to evaluate goals for the previous week and synchronize classroom activities for the next week. The staff also shares information and insights about the program and discusses students who need additional tutoring, counseling, etc. During these meetings, special attention is also given to the peer advisors' input since they have a unique liaison with students, enabling them to hear things not privy to teachers.

Indicators of Program Success and Accomplishments

Although quantitatively unmeasured, one of the indicators of The Bridge's success is the change in attitude of students who participate in the program. As Robert & Thomson (1994) point out, minority students are ashamed to be associated with learning assistance programs, especially when they have earned above average high school grade-point averages. The Bridge offers a chance for these students to become aware of their weaknesses in a non-threatening setting with students who have similar backgrounds and experiences. The Bridge is designed to give students the opportunity to see learning assistance as an important tool for improving their skills, rather than as a burden which chokes their self-esteem. As one student put it:

> *"The Bridge program helped me understand the reason for the LSP and that it is going to help me in the long run. I feel at this point in my life that I have made the right decision to pursue my education."*

Another indicator of The Bridge's success is the one year retention rates of participants. As reported by the annual report of LSP, The Bridge students' rate of retention after one year is about twenty percent higher than that of students who do not participate in the program (see Tables 1 and 2 for retention statistical data).

Bridge students also work harder and are more enthusiastic about their studies. One mathematics instructor commented that one of her fall quarter classes was composed mostly of The Bridge students. She stated:

> *"It was the most hard-working, task-oriented class that I have ever had. They were*

eager to learn, listened carefully, asked excellent questions and even did extra work without being told to. It was a pleasure I had seldom experienced in a LSP class."

Retention data also suggest that students who actively participate in campus functions are more likely to persist. Because students gain self-confidence during The Bridge program and are made aware of the importance of extra-curricular activities, they become active in various campus affairs after their Bridge experience. For example, one ex-Bridge student served as director of the GSU television station; another organized what has become a locally popular singing group; and several others have been freshman orientation guides; others have participated in special leadership training programs; and some students have become active in the Student Government Association. All of these students have completed at least three years at GSU.

Table 1

The Bridge

RETENTION OF STUDENTS
FOR FOUR OR MORE QUARTERS
N=%*

1984	1985	1986	1987	1988	1989	1990	1991	1992	1993	1994
86	83	95	69	81	85	74	77	88	77	N/A

* Does not include students in The Bridge program who never enrolled at Georgia State University.

Sources: Gold, Deming, & Stone (1992)
Stone, (1994).

Table 2

Performance of 1992 Bridge Students in Three High-Risk Courses
N= 44

	Math 104	English 111	Political Science 101
Number Students Enrolled	39	34	29
Number Students Passed	27	26	25
Number Students Failed	12	8	4

Grades Earned

A = 28	(6.8%)	
B = 148	(36.1%)	
C = 112	(27.3%)	

Total Percentage of Students Earning A, B, or C = 70.2%

Impact on Increasing Minority Students at The Institution

Georgia State University's operation of The Bridge program for ten consecutive years underscores its commitment to the recruitment and retention of a diverse student population. Since retention data suggest the largest attrition rates occur during the freshmen year (Tinto, 1987), the university regularly tabulates the number of students returning for their second year. Retention data reveal the average persistence rate of The Bridge students from 1984-1994 is eighty-two percent. This high retention rate is attributed to the structure of the program, which "requires" cross-campus involvement with university departments, services and organizations. Moreover, since The Bridge is a major GSU program that focuses on the holistic development of African American students, its high retention rate has a major impact on the university as a whole.

Another way The Bridge has impacted the university is by involving white faculty and staff. They serve as program instructors, mentors, academic advisors, positive role models, etc. This promotes close faculty/staff/student relationships, making students feel accepted, respected and supported, therefore, enhancing their chances for retention and graduation.

Problems and Probable Solutions

As with most programs, there are problems which seem unsolvable. For The Bridge, the main problem is funding. Even though both salaries and operating costs have increased significantly, The Bridge has received the same amount of money since the program began. Further, since Board of Regents' guidelines prohibit spending any funds on food, all monies for such expenditures have to be raised from other sources. Fortunately, the program has been able to get funding once per year from the Georgia State Foundation to finance The Bridge and closing ceremonies. However, raising funds to launch other activities like the Three-Tiered Mentoring Program are complicated. It has been suggested that soliciting funds for the program outside of the university – from large local businesses, for example – would represent a conflict of interest since the university itself regularly solicits and receives funds from these sources.

Another problem is the inability to attract more male students. This problem is, in part, due to the fact that male high school students submit their applications for admission to GSU very late. For example by April 1, 1994, the program staff had received names and addresses of thirty females but only four males. Usually, the first forty students who apply for the program – twenty females and twenty males are accepted. In order to ensure a balance, spaces are held for males until the week before the program begins. Nevertheless, females usually outnumber males in the program two to one.

One solution to the problem of the scarcity of males in the program is to contact them during their senior year in high school, invite them to campus, introduce them to possible careers and to former Bridge students. These students could become acquainted with the college early in the year and become mentors throughout the application process. GSU does have a minority recruiter, but since students have more influence on other students, this contact might prove more fruitful.

A third problem is the inability to offer jobs to students who attend The Bridge. Although the program is essentially free, most students need to work in order to earn money for clothing, food and leisure time activities. Consequently, it is essential that they secure jobs for the summer. This is difficult since The Bridge hours require attendance from 9:00 a.m. until 1:30 p.m.

Visions and Perspectives

In their description of The Bridge at GSU, Gold, Deming & Stone (1992) reported that an important component of the program involved the mentoring of students by faculty members. They wrote:

"Each mentor contacted five or six students on a regular basis, met with them for social functions, and monitored their academic progress through the year" (p. 112).

By the end of the 1994 program, however, mentoring of Bridge students had dwindled, partly because faculty members were frustrated because students seldom returned their calls and partly because the component was not closely monitored.

Continuous contact had been deemed essential in order to increase the retention rates of the students in this program, and it had been decided that each student would profit from having a faculty mentor. Further, it was projected that students might persist longer if they, themselves, acted as mentors to other students. In fact, Levitz and Noel (1990) said "studies have shown that freshmen who can name a campus-affiliated person they can turn to with a problem are more than twice as likely to return for the sophomore year as those who cannot" (p. 10). With this in mind, a 3-Tiered Mentoring Program was launched.

During the winter quarter of 1995, letters were sent to all the 1994 Bridge students explaining the program and requesting those who were interested to attend a meeting. Of the forty students who were sent letters, fifteen attended the meeting. Subsequently, they were all assigned to faculty and staff members who had volunteered to act as mentors.

In early April, The Bridge students were given the names and addresses of black students who had been accepted to GSU. Each student wrote a letter and enclosed a photograph to students on their lists. Students who respond will become mentees of The Bridge students who originally contacted them.

One critical problem young college students have is choosing realistic careers. Unwise choices often make students lose confidence in themselves, causing failures and eventual dropout. The Bridge program could be instrumental in circumventing this unfortunate situation by offering an apprenticeship/academic program where students would be able to spend half their time working in their chosen career and the other half attending classes. Being exposed to the rigors of a career and learning about the skills needed to perform in it successfully would certainly be a giant step towards retention.

The success of any program can only be determined over time. However, even though one-year retention rates were collected for The Bridge, there was no comparative data after that first year. How does the performance of Bridge students compare with non-Bridge students? One-year retention rates average sixteen percent higher, but what about other factors? Were there more graduates among Bridge students? Which group had the highest GPA? Did one group take longer to complete undergraduate requirements? Which group had the most stopouts? Dropouts? This study is well on the way.

Insights and Advice

Replicate Other Successful Programs

Probably the best advice to those who wish to initiate bridge programs is to identify successful programs and move toward emulating them. One such program is in place at the University of California, Berkeley which has reported a minority graduation rate of sixty percent (Robert and Thomson, 1994). Administrators of this program attribute its success to several key elements: students live on campus; they receive academic help, financial aid, encourage- ment to participate in campus activities and organizations; and they are closely counseled all the way to graduation.

Conduct On-going Comparative Studies

Often the focus is on individual students who have been successful as a result of a retention program, rather than on the program as a whole. Consequently, factors are often overlooked that make retention a myth rather than a miracle. It is important, therefore, to conduct studies which will realistically compare the success of students in special retention programs to non-program students. These studies can accomplish two things: 1) they can help uncover weak components of the program; and 2) they can provide viable data for increased funding.

Cooperation of Administrators

This ingredient is essential for the successful execution of any program, especially ones which involve the retention of minority students. Hovland (1994) provides some insight:

> *I think that in the best programs you see a kind of concurrent "top-down" and "bottom-up" approach. Enacting a new mission doesn't work at all well if it's all top-down; if you have a strong president who declares "this is what we're going to do," it's doomed from the beginning. And if it's too much a bottom-up effort, it's going to fail as well...(developing such programs must) be seen as a legitimate part of the school's mission, if only for the pragmatic reason that otherwise resources won't be committed to that area (p. 30).*

Other essential components of a successful retention program must be:
- activities designed to build self-esteem, and racial pride;
- peer mentoring/networking;
- faculty and staff as volunteer mentors; support group meetings for program participants;
- small group study sessions outside of class;
- student involvement in campus activities and leadership training;
- intrusive counseling;
- recognition of students for academic achievements; and
- nomination of students for university recognitions and awards.

Sadly, the problem of African American student retention on predominately white campuses has remained a problem because many administrators focus only on the recruitment of these students. High attrition rates among African American students nicely feed the bell curve theory and so, many institutions encourage so–called retention programs which are largely "bottom-up", an approach Hovland (1994) said is "doomed from the beginning" (p. 30). However, the task of increasing the graduation rates of African American students is surmountable. Programs must meet the needs of the students and employ the entire university community, faculty, staff, and administrators.

—Dr. Constance A. Chapman is a 1995-96 Fullbright recipient and Assistant Professor of Composition at Georgia State University in Atlanta, Georgia.
—Dr. Beatrice L. Logan is Assistant Professor and Counselor in the Division of Learning Support Programs at Georgia State University in Atlanta, Georgia.

References

Astin, A. (1977). Four critical years. San Francisco: Jossey-Bass.

Astin, A. (1984). Student involvement: A developmental theory for higher education. Journal of College Student Personnel, 25, 297-308.

Chapman, C. (1991). The peer conference: A key to developing writers as readers. Georgia Journal of Reading, Fall\Winter, 20-25.

Davis, R. (1991). Social support networks and undergraduate student academic-success-related outcomes: A comparison of black students on black and white campuses. In W. R. Allen, E. G. Epps, and N. Z. Haniff (Eds.), Colleges in Black and White: African American Students in Predominately White and in Historically Black Public Universities (pp. 143-157) Albany, N. Y: State University of New York Press.

Ford, C. (1990). In W. E. Cox & F. L. Matthews. Dr. Clinita Ford on retaining America's Black collegians. Black Issues In Higher Education, 6 (22), 16-19.

Gold, M. Deming, M. P., & Stone, K. (1992). The Bridge: A summer enrichment program to retain African-American collegians. Journal of the Freshman Year Experience, 4 (2), 101-117.

Haniff, N. Z. (1991). The institution and racism. In W. R. Allen, E. G. Epps, and N. Z. Haniff (Eds), Colleges in Black and White: African American Students in Predominately White and in Historically Black Public Universities (pp. 247-256). Albany, N. Y: State University of New York Press.

Hovland, M. (1994). In G. A. Kluepfel, Developing successful retention programs: An interview with Michael Hovland. Journal of Developmental Education, 17(3), 28-33.

Lang, M. & Ford, C. (1988). Black student retention in higher education. Springfield, IL: Charles E. Thomas.

Levin, M., & Levin, J. (1991). A critical examination of academic retention programs for at-risk minority students. Journal of College Student Development, 32, 323-334.

Levitz, R., & Noel, L. (1990). Connecting students to institutions: Keys to retention and success. In Retention Resources: The 1990 National Conference on Student Retention in Washington, D. C. (pp. 8-14). Iowa City , IA: Noel•Levitz Centers.

Nettles, M. T. (1991). Racial similarities and differences in the predictors of college student achievement. In W. R. Allen, E. G. Epps, and N. Z. Haniff (Eds.), Colleges in Black and White: African American Students in Predominately White and in Historically Black Public Universities (pp. 75-91). Albany, N. Y: State University of New York Press.

Pounds, A. W. (1989). Black students. In M. L. Upcraft & J. N. Gardner (Eds.), The freshman year experience: Helping students survive and succeed in college (pp. 277-286). San Francisco: Jossey-Bass.

Robert, E. R., & Thomson, G. (1994). Learning assistance and the success of underrepresented students at Berkeley. Journal of Developmental Education, 17 (3), 4-14.

Stewart. D. M. (1991). Higher education. In D. W. Hornbeck & L. M. Salamon (Eds.), Human Capital and America's Future (pp. 193-219). Baltimore: John Hopkins University Press.

Stone, K. (1994). Annual Report (1993-1994). Atlanta, GA: Georgia State University, Division of Developmental Studies

Tinto, V. (1975). Dropout from higher education: A theoretical synthesis of recent research. Review of Education Research, 45, 89-125.

Levitz & D. Saluri (Eds.), Increasing Student Retention (pp. .28-43). San Francisco: Jossey-Bass.

Tinto, V. (1987). Leaving college: Rethinking the causes and cures of student attrition. Chicago: the University of Chicago Press.

Tinto, V. (1990). Principles of effective retention. Journal of The Freshman Year Experience, 2(1), 35-48).

Pre-Orientation: Gaining a Competitive Edge

by Roland L. Byrd

Overview:

The transition from high school to college is a major step in the lives of newly accepted college freshman students. Howard University's Pre-Orientation Program is a four-day weekend activity that is designed to assist the new college student in making the transition from high school to college as successful as possible. Students who have generally been admitted to the institution by April 1st are contacted and invited to attend. The program is strictly voluntary. For those students who choose to participate, their parents are also encouraged to attend.

Through seminars, workshops, panels, testing, student advisement, and recreational activities, the participants are introduced to the university's orientation and registration procedures; made aware of university programs, services, and resources available to assist them in their college development; tested for their academic potential; advised of their academic strengths and/or demonstrated weaknesses, including recommendations for improvement; presented with tips on preparing for entry-level courses and study techniques for success; and are given the opportunity to experience living on campus and creating friendships with fellow students in a small group setting. Through these involved interventions, the Pre-Orientation Program has become an initial step in the retention of students at the university. Students attain an advanced awareness of college life and gain a "competitive edge" in their preparation for college study.

Historical Origin and Program Development

The Center for Academic Reinforcement (CAR) at Howard University was the originator of the university-wide Pre-Orientation Program. An autonomous unit which reported directly to the Office of the Vice President for Academic Affairs, the CAR provided academic assistance, instructional programs and counseling services during the first semester or first year for students who had been identified as having demonstrated deficiencies but unrealized potential. Many students were entering college without the proper attitude and motivation for learning and without the academic preparedness required for gaining a college degree. Deficiencies were not limited to academic subject areas but related also to the attitudinal mindset of the student.

For years the director of the CAR, Dr. George Rhodes, Jr., had pondered over ways by which the CAR could provide better assistance for the students of the university in general, and this classified population in particular. Through preliminary studies and observations made by university counselors and advisors, several obstacles were discovered to be impeding students' success in obtaining their higher education. The obstacles which seem to most affect the performance and retention of students at Howard were:

- lack of college preparedness,
- financial problems,
- poor class attendance,
- misconceived expectations regarding their responsibility and role in achieving academic success.

The existing programs were attempting to address these problems; however, they did not confront or challenge the student early enough. Thus, in an attempt to provide a beginning cure for the ills of student anxieties, frustrations, and negative levels of motivation which impede academic success, Dr. Rhodes presented his notion of a new outreach component in March 1989. The primary focus of this component was the development of a strong auxiliary program designed to assist incoming freshmen to successfully bridge the gap from high school to college. Consequently, this pre-orientation program was conceived and initially began in May 1989.

The implementation of this program was centered around the belief that early motivation, stimulation, identification, and intervention were major factors for academic success. This pre-program would offer to ease the transition from high school to college. The situation would be less pressured, the circumstances would be less threatening, and the environment would be comforting.

The program objectives were, and continue to be:

- to identify academic strengths/weaknesses of each student,
- to propose recommendations and provide resources to assist students in

overcoming weaknesses and to further enhance strengths,

- to motivate students to have the proper attitude for academic success, and
- to acquaint students with the procedures and resources of the university in an attempt to eliminate possible anxieties encountered by freshmen.

Implementation Strategies

The original Pre-Orientation Program was designed to span four consecutive weekends (9:00 a.m. to 5:00 p.m., Saturdays only). Letters were sent out to newly-accepted freshmen who lived in surrounding locales. This structure, however, limited the possible pool of participants. Based on recommendations by parents of this first group, the structure was changed to a weekend format, Friday morning through Sunday afternoon, for the second year of the program. This new format immediately allowed for the participation of all new entrants to the university, regardless of locality. However, immediately after the first year of the program with the new weekend format, it was discovered that the timeframe was too short for all of the information and activities that were presented. In order to be more effective, the decision was made to extend the weekend from Thursday to Sunday. This remains the current structure of the program.

Once the program took the three-to-four-day format, several other activities were added. These activities included academic advisement by students' advisors in their respective schools and colleges and a pre-registration of their courses for the fall semester. The campus tour was extended and included a "drive-by" view of the other campuses of the university, as well as key highlights of Washington, D.C. Social activities included an evening of fun and games in the Student Center and an evening of group presentations (skits) on "adjusting to college life". A sample of the Pre-Orientation weekend agenda is highlighted below:

Pre-Orientation Weekend Agenda

Thursday
- Program registration
- Opening session
- Testing
- Workshop
- "Getting-to-Know-You"

Saturday
- Testing
- Workshops
- Tour
- Group Presentations
  (Students & Parents)

Friday
- Testing
- "About the University"
- Academic advisement
- Group sessions
- Recreation

Sunday
- Weekend highlights
- Individual feedback
- Program evaluation
- Program closing

Three CAR administrators served as co-coordinators of the program. They were this author, assistant director; Ms. Kimberly Gregg, counselor; and Ms. Carol Henley, computer specialist. Ms. Henley, however, was the key coordinator. The Offices of the President and the Vice President for Academic Affairs were involved from the beginning. Often the president himself and/or the vice president was available to meet the program participants. Other offices were asked to participate, and they all graciously consented. These units included the following:

- Academic advisors
- Academic computing
- Admissions & records
- Athletic department
- Counseling
- Financial aid
- Food service
- Health services
- Howard University Hotel
- Library
- Physical facilities
- Public relations
- Recruitment
- Registrar's Office
- Residence life
- Security
- Student center
- Student life

With these different levels of involvement, the implementation of the program became a university-wide effort.

To accomplish the program objectives of early identification and intervention, all participating students were tested to determine their academic proficiencies in mathematics, reading, English, and study skills. Based on test results, the students were counseled, individually, on their demonstrated strengths and weaknesses and advised what they could do over the summer months to assist in decreasing or eliminating the deficiencies.

In an attempt to motivate, stimulate, and inform the students, workshops on test-taking, time management, and study skills, preparation for freshman English and mathematics, computer literacy, etc., were conducted for both students and parents. The program also acquainted the students with the orientation, registration, financial aid, and housing acquisition processes within the university. To reduce initial anxieties and tensions, "getting-to-know-you" and recreational activities were presented.

With the four-weekend program, all costs associated with it were absorbed by the CAR program. Participants were only responsible for their transportation cost in getting to the university. However, when the program shifted to a one-weekend activity, students were then required to cover the cost for food and housing in a dormitory on campus. Students who traveled alone were picked up from the train depot, bus station, or airport by the university. Parents were encouraged to stay at the Howard University Hotel so that they would be near the program. With long days, this allowed parents to move about with more comfort. Those who had relatives or friends in the area occasionally opted to stay with them.

From the beginning of the program, an important component was the involvement of parents. Parents were invited to participate and a schedule of activities was prepared for them as well. They attended all informational sessions with the students, were encouraged to attend workshops and recreational activities, and had sessions designed specifically for them. This was an opportunity for them to be better informed about the educational options and challenges that their child would be facing, to network with other parents, to discuss common concerns, experiences, and possible solutions to related educational issues.

For both the students and parents, this trip to Howard University represented an opportunity to visit the university and the surrounding area. Additionally, along with the wealth of information received during this conference, the trip may be the convincing factor which allowed them to make a more informed decision to attend Howard.

Program Success and Accomplishments

Since its inception, the Pre-Orientation Program has had one major goal and that continues to be to greatly impact the success and retention of students admitted to Howard University. The program has been conducted for six years, with some 1,130 prospective entering freshmen students in attendance, encompassing fourteen different groups and averaging over eighty students per weekend group. Students came from all parts of the country, including U.S. territories. More than ninety-five percent of the students who participate enter the university the following fall semester. The chart below shows the program format and attendance by year:

Pre-Orientation Participation

Year	Program Format/# of Groups or Weekends	Participants
1989	consecutive Saturdays (one group)	66
1990	Friday-Sunday weekend (three groups)*	271
1991	Thursday-Sunday weekend (four groups)*	210
1992	Thursday-Sunday weekend (three groups)*	267
1993	Thursday-Sunday weekend (two groups)*	198
1994	Thursday-Sunday weekend (one group)*	118

* represents # of weekends, one group per weekend

Initially, the success of the program was best measured by how the program was perceived by the participants—both students and parents. Each student received a program evaluation form and the parents received a parental version. These were filled out at the end of the program. Students were asked to evaluate the overall merits of the program, as well as the individual activities. One hundred percent of the students evaluating the program felt that the objectives of the program were met and they would recommend it to other new students. The activity students felt was the most beneficial was the "Test Advising and Counseling" session. Additionally, ninety-three percent indicated that they would be interested in attending future activities associated with this program.

Likewise, one hundred percent of the parents evaluating the program felt that the program met all of the stated objectives and they would recommend it to other parents for their children. They specifically stated:

• the program was very well organized and informative;

• the program's staff was very congenial and made their children feel welcomed; and

• the program prepared their child for college life.

Follow-up activities were also a major component of the program. When the students returned to the university in the fall, they attended a special "Welcome Back Reception" for pre-orientation participants. The thrust of this activity was to encourage the students to chart a course for themselves beginning their first day on campus. They were given instruction concerning the completion of their pre-registration process and encouraged to sign-up for academic survival workshops, the second activity planned for them during the orientation week. Also, near the end of the semester, review sessions were scheduled to assist them in preparation for their final examinations.

During the course of the semester, counseling and advising were made available for all program participants. Individual or small group sessions were conducted as deemed necessary. Counseling sessions were structured to let students know that they had a place to go where they could confer with someone and feel comfortable about getting a response. An accepting atmosphere and warm environment was created.

Academically, students records were viewed to determine enrollment at the university, whether mid-term deficiencies had been received, and for final grades in courses and cumulative grade-point averages. Complete data on the first year of the program have been compiled and are presented here for review.

Of the sixty-six students who participated in the original group, approximately four percent of all new entering students for the fall of 1989, there were thirty-one males and thirty-five females. All of these students were registered for the fall 1989 semester, and approximately eighty-five percent of them were accepted into the engineering, liberal arts, business, or communications programs. Their average SAT scores were 427 (verbal) and 461 (math), with ranges of 280-600 and 350-620, respectively. Comparable SAT scores for all new entrants of the university were 426 (verbal) and 456 (math).

During their first semester, only ten (fifteen percent) received mid-term deficiencies. Of these ten, only two ended up on probation at the end of the semester. However, eleven other students had grade-point averages (GPAs) less than 1.60 and were on probation at the end of the semester as well, making a total of thirteen or twenty percent of the total group. One of these students has since graduated. Approximately thirty-four percent of all new students were on probation at the end of their first semester at the university.

The average semester GPA for the group was 2.40. Thirty percent of the students had GPAs of 3.00 or better, with eighteen percent making the dean's list (minimum 3.20). One student had a perfect 4.00.

Through 1994, thirty-one (forty-seven percent) of the participating students have graduated, ten with honors. Although not with honors, eight other students graduated with GPAs between 3.00 and 3.19. The lowest GPA of the graduates was 2.54. The average amount of time it took these students to graduate was four and a half years, with one or two summer sessions included. Another ten students (fifteen percent) are still enrolled at the university and should complete their requirements for graduation within the year.

The benefits of this program have been numerous. In meeting its objectives, the Pre-Orientation Program has achieved these measures for students and parents, as well as for the university.

The basic benefits are listed below:

Students	Parents	University
• early assessment and advisement	• first-hand information	• better-prepared students
• reduction in anxiety and tension	• networking with other parents	• positive retention strategy
• sense of being part of the university	• degree of comfort and satisfaction	• better image of the university
• early support mechanisms		

This program gives students the needed insight into college life before it becomes the real world and while it is non-threatening. For the parents, this early awareness allows them to participate with their child in this selection process and to ease their mind regarding how their child will survive at the university. The institution benefits by getting a more-informed incoming student and a better product with which to work. The atmosphere of comradery and the attitude that "we are all in this together" which is generated at the end of each weekend session is indescribable.

As a part of its success, the program has been presented twice at national conferences, once at the National Higher Education Conference on Black Student Retention (1990) and at the National Freshman Year Experience Conference (1993). Additionally, in 1992, Ms. Carol Henley, the principal administrator, was honored as an "Outstanding Freshman Advocate" by this conference. This honor recognized the educational experiences presented to first-year students, and specifically the methodology employed in carrying out this experience.

Shared Insights and Perspectives for the Future

As students approach their college careers, many of them have mixed emotions and unrealistic expectations of these very valuable years. The college experience is a mystery to some and presents a degree of difficulty in making the transition from high school. Students need to have clear and realistic academic goals, and their assessment of their abilities must be congruent with those of the institution. With these attributes in place, success becomes an easier task.

An "early alert" program, such as Pre-Orientation, is an ideal mechanism for providing students with information about what college life is all about and what to expect of college prior to enrolling. Pre-Orientation allows the students to know and understand their value, potential, abilities, and skills, and how the institution views these traits. It assists in reducing anxiety and in turning uncertainty into certainty.

Orientation to college is an ongoing process. It should never be restricted to the time period prior to enrollment in college. Constant assessment and follow-up procedures should occur throughout the student's first year in college. Counseling should be provided to assist in fostering assertiveness, decision-making, and persistence. This allows for the identification of student needs, deficiencies, and problems so that early intervention can occur.

The success of pre-orientation rests with a quality program. The program must include counseling/advising, assessment and follow-up, along with constant resources to facilitate learning and successful academic performances. These elements will assist the students in developing the discipline required for university-level academic work.

A committed staff is a necessity, because the implementation of the program requires long hours and dedicated service. Staff members must be competent, sensitive, patient, and personable. They must express a natural and genuine interest in the welfare of students.

The employment of previous participants as student workers (mentors) adds to the quality of the program. They can offer insight into the program from a different viewpoint, a dimension which allows for greater reinforcement on the part of the student participants. The sharing of their perspectives, experiences, and strategies used in successfully completing their freshman year would be invaluable. The student mentors also stimulate interest on the part of the participants to become involved in campus life and student organizations. This helps to solidify the students' alliance with the university.

A pre-orientation program should also be self-supporting. Although the program participants pay for the bulk of the cost for conducting the program, operating funds would assist in keeping the cost at a minimum for the participants. For incoming freshman students, this time of year is "peak time" in their lives; they are graduating from high school as well as preparing to go to college. The cost of participating in the program could be a burden for some students and their parents, thereby limiting the number of students able to participate.

The pre-orientation program should be conducted throughout the early summer months (May and June) and not limited to one or two weekends. This experience and exposure are too valuable not to be shared with all students. The ultimate goal of such a program is to have all new incoming freshman students participate, so that they all can gain that competitive edge.

—Roland L. Byrd (M.S. in ed), serves as the Assistant Director of the Center for Academic Reinforcement, in the School of Education, at Howard University, in Washington, D.C.

I'M READY Project
(Increasing Minority Representation
through Educating and Developing Youth)
by Katie M. McKnight

Overview:

The problem of minority access and retention in higher education will not go away. Not until we plug the leaks that lead to increasing attrition and drop out will we resolve the retention problems. Within this conceptual framework, the I'M READY Project was conceived and designed as a comprehensive program of recruitment and retention aimed at students from 7th grade through the senior year of the College of Nursing BSN Program. The program's strategies attract students to nursing, provide academic counseling, develop an attachment to health professions, and establish long term mentoring relationships.

The successful key to this retention model is the commitment to test, refine, and implement specific strategies at various levels of the students' educational pursuits while mentoring them in the process. Bonding in relationships served as a highly motivating factor in the academic achievement of each student.

The significant involvement of parents, teachers, and administrators play an important role in the development of the students' career choices. Therefore, the participation of this group enhances the students' ability to succeed in a supportive environment that fosters academic enhancement and skills in the educational arena.

Introduction

During the past decade, minority access and retention in higher education has become one of the most hotly debated, controversial, and yet one of the most salient issues in American higher education. Beginning with the publication of Jacqueline Fleming's "Blacks in Colleges" in 1984 and the inauguration of Dr. Clinita Ford's National Black Student Retention Conference in 1985, the issues of minority student access and retention in general, and black student retention in particular, have continuously gained prominence. Since that time the volume of literature and research on these problems has increased immensely; the number of people involved in programs and projects to address these problems has grown tremendously; and the number of programs at institutions to increase retention have become significantly high.

The proliferation of minority retention programs at institutions at least suggests there is a genuine recognition of the problem. Many institutions are seriously grappling with the issues and concerns that translate into high attrition rates for minority students. One fact is certain — there is now a good understanding and knowledge of the reasons for the high attrition rates and the needs for special retention programs for minority students, especially for black students at predominantly white institutions. There is also a good understanding of the problems too many black students face in the larger society and on white college campuses that affect their success in college.

Some of those problems have been summarized recently by Feagin (1992, p.546), paraphrasing Keller (1988-1989):

1. The campus subculture is hostile to blacks at many institutions, and the faculty and deans remain insensitive.

2. A growing number of blacks are enrolling in the military, in part because of the more hospitable environment there.

3. Financial aid has been declining.

4. The decline is mainly among black males; something is wrong with black men, probably drugs, prison, and unemployment.

5. Poor preparation for college work, as seen in SAT scores, is a major factor.

6. With more jobs available, many blacks go to work rather than college.

7. The deterioration of the black family means a lack of discipline and emphasis on education.

8. The high incidence of drug use inhibits study.

9. Attitudes of blacks, such as a lack of effort, are a problem.

10. There is a lack of adult leadership emphasizing education.

Although the purpose here is not to debate these facts, while they are undeniably true concerning the circumstances of many black students, specifically, and to a certain extent, these findings place too much blame on the victims of a long history of overt institutionalized social and economic discrimination. In his article, Feagin (1992) points out those factors at institutions that affect black student attrition and retention that are beyond their control.

In these times of dwindling resources, budget cuts, and distressful fiscal conditions, many institutions are pondering whether they can afford to continue to sustain programs aimed toward such a small portion of their student population. Indeed, at most white institutions especially, retention programs are viewed as being particularly for the benefit of black students. Yet, when examining enrollment and dropout statistics, it is found that attrition rates are at an all-time high for students across the spectrum of the college population. This means that institutions could do well by expanding the scope of their retention efforts while at the same time incurring some savings in recruitment efforts to replace those non-returning students.

The problem of minority access and retention in higher education will not go away. Not until the leaks that lead to increasing attrition and dropout are plugged will the retention problems be resolved. The leaks are many and getting larger. For example, too many blacks and other minority students are lost in the transition from secondary school to college; too many never make the transition to college enrollment. Then, too many of those who do enroll in college drop out before completing their degrees. Of those who do graduate from college, only a small percentage go to graduate and professional schools to earn advanced degrees. This is why access and retention programs are crucially important. In order to rectify these situations, special efforts must be formalized and they must become institutionalized.

At the University of Illinois at Chicago (UIC), a predominantly white institution, they have developed and successfully implemented the I'M READY (Increasing Minority Representation through Educating And Developing Youth) program as a recruitment and retention model for the College of Nursing.

In Table 1, racial/ethnic distribution of students at the University of Illinois at Chicago (UIC) indicates that African Americans make up less than ten percent of the population, in contrast to the white population that makes up fifty-five percent. A similar picture is true for the College of Nursing. African Americans are still less than ten percent and the white student population is nearly sixty-five percent. The Hispanic student population is about seven percent in the College of Nursing and eleven percent of the total campus enrollment.

Table 1

University of Illinois at Chicago Racial/Ethnic Distribution Comparison of Fall Terms 1989-1993 Total Undergraduates

Racial/Ethnic Category		Fall 1989	Fall 1990	Fall 1991	Fall 1992	Fall 1993
Native American	N	45	48	47	51	52
	%	0.3%	0.3%	0.3%	0.3%	0.3%
African American	N	1,681	1,827	1,703	1,739	1,722
	%	10.5%	11.1%	10.8%	10.7%	10.5%
Asian	N	2,491	2,668	2,695	2,839	3,001
	%	15.6%	16.3%	17.0%	17.6%	18.3%
Hispanic	N	1,726	1,904	2,066	2,325	2,547
	%	10.8%	11.6%	13.0%	14.3%	15.5%
Caucasian	N	9,316	9,073	8,481	8,422	8,241
	%	58.4%	55.1%	53.6%	51.8%	50.1%
Foreign	N	377	354	369	363	373
	%	2.4%	2.3%	2.3%	2.2%	2.2%
Unknown	N	309	541	476	524	498
	%	1.9%	3.3%	3.0%	3.2%	3.0%
Total	N	15,945	16,465	15,837	16,263	16,434
	%	100%	100%	100%	100%	100%

Background

With this factor in mind, the College of Nursing established the I'M READY Project, funded by the Robert Wood Johnson Foundation at $380,773 over a period of four years, and an additional $394,000 for a continuation grant for the program through 1998.

The goal of the project is to increase the number of African American and Hispanic students admitted to and graduated from the UIC College of Nursing. Recruitment and retention strategies to increase the percentage of minority registered nurses will improve nursing's ability to meet the demand for health care delivery within a multicultural society. The project aims to increase the supply of minority registered nurses by recruiting, retaining through academic and social support strategies, and graduating more minority students from the UIC College of Nursing.

The I'M READY project is designed as a comprehensive program of recruitment and retention aimed at students from seventh grade through their senior year at the College of Nursing BSN program. The program's strategies attract students to nursing, provide academic counseling, develop an attachment to health professions, and establish long-term mentoring relationships. These strategies are initiated in three phases over the first three project years. Five grade schools and five high schools in the Chicago Public School (CPS) system were chosen for the project in an effort to: a) build long-term relationships between the College of Nursing (CON) and the (CPS) staff in each school; b) facilitate frequent one-to-one contact between CON counselor and student by minimizing travel time; and c) ensure that the Chicago Public School where each student is enrolled offers the academic program needed by the student.

The first year involves organizing the project efforts and implementing strategies for seventh and eighth grade minority students in the five Chicago Public Schools as reflected in Chart 1.

Chart 1
University of Illinois at Chicago College of Nursing
I'm READY Program
Parent Advisory Council (7th and 8th Graders)
Student and Parent Information Chart

Activities	Where	When	Who
Health Career Awareness Session	Local School	Twice a Year	UIC-College of Nursing Academic Counseling
Career Orientation Interview	Local School	Once a Year	UIC-College of Nursing Academic Counseling
Parent Advisory Council	UIC	Twice a Year	UIC-Office of Chancellor
Academic Counseling	Local School	Bimonthly	UIC-Academic Counselor
One-Half Day Tour of UIC/Lunch	UIC	Twice a Year	Project Staff UIC Staff, Member
One-Half Day Workshop for 8th graders on highschool selection and curriculum pattern	UIC-College of Nursing	Once a Year	UIC-Support Staff Project Staff, Early Outreach
Summer Seminar for 8th grade students: • Adjustments to High School • Study Skills • Time Management • Note Taking • Test Taking Skills • Extracurricular Activities	UIC-College of Nursing	Summer (July)	UIC-Support Staff Project Staff Early Outreach

The program involves academic counseling, career awareness, understanding nursing and health service delivery; and developing long-term relationships between aspiring and actual nursing students. The academic counselor meets individually with each of the selected students, to establish a long-term relationship, monitor students' progress, and clarify the purpose of the I'M READY program. These individual meetings occur at least bimonthly throughout the program. The academic counselor periodically conducts focus group sessions with the students to discover their views of health care careers, and to learn how to interest them in nursing.

In the fall term students attend a one-day program at the UIC where they become acquainted with faculty, alumni and current nursing students by attending a lecture, observing nursing students' demonstrate clinical laboratory skills, and attending an informal meeting with nursing students where mentor/mentee dyads are determined based on mutual agreement. The alumnus or nursing student is a personal contact for the student throughout the program; a new mentor is assigned only if the alumnus or nursing student cannot continue the relationship after BSN graduation. Complementary tickets to UIC sporting events are offered to each CPS student. This visit thus creates for the CPS students a peer group of future nurses. In the spring term, students attend a half-day tour of the University of Illinois Hospital and Clinics (UIH), where they meet with nurses who work in various clinical roles and learn about the variety of career opportunities in nursing. Nursing student mentors are encouraged to attend this tour with their CPS student mentees. A focus group session is conducted by the counselor shortly after this tour.

During the summer term, students and their parents participate in a half-day workshop given by CPS counselors from selected high schools and the academic counselor. The primary purpose of the workshop is to assist students in focusing on a plan of studies that is appropriate for a health career. The eighth grade graduates attend a one-week high school preparatory summer seminar on adjusting to high school life, study skills, time management, note-taking skills, test-taking skills, and selection of extracurricular activities. Orientation and summary sessions of the seminar are also attended by the students' parents.

Upon completion of the high school preparatory seminar, the UIC College of Nursing offers a place in the BSN program when each student is ready to enter, contingent on successful completion of an appropriate college preparatory curriculum, graduation from high school, and completion of an appropriate pre-nursing curriculum at UIC Liberal Arts and Sciences (LAS). At entry into high school, students have: 1) gained exposure to both professional nursing in a hospital setting and UIC academic student life; 2) begun a potentially long-term mentoring relationship with a UIC CON student or other related health professional; 3) received academic counseling appropriate for their academic goals; 4) participated in high school orientation and skills training; and 5) been offered a future place in UIC CON BSN program.

Specific strategies for retention of the high school minority students in the I'M READY program includes the following activities; 1) academic counseling, 2) College of Nursing Days, 3) PSAT Review, 4) SAT-ACT Review, 5) summer academic program, 6) summer workshops, 7) CON-UIH Volunteer and Employment Experience, and 8) testing skill workshops.

Over the past four years, the strategies for the high school students were evaluated and refined. The strategies have proven to be most successful and cost effective in the recruitment and retention model.

From the high school population of students it has been learned that students change their career choices and goals. Therefore, the I'M READY staff must be able to assist the student in his/her transition.

Although student interviews and focus sessions can successfully be conducted at the high schools, other recruitment strategies and most retention strategies need to be implemented at the UIC campus because of the widely diverse class schedules of the students. The high school counselors play a highly significant role in the local schools and help make students accessible to the I'M READY staff.

High school students are more independent in relation to transportation. However, for some of them, bus fare has been a problem for summer activities. The majority of the students have expressed a need to work during summer months. Therefore, short-term summer programs or half-day summer programs appear to best meet the needs of this population of students.

The positive aspect of the mentoring component causes a special bonding between the student and mentor. This serves as an added nurturing factor.

The high school students in the I'M READY program tend to apply themselves better in the academic setting as they progress from one grade level to another. The social development has been phenomenal as a result of the Future Nurses Club and the related activities. The students take leadership roles in the organizational structure of the club while the staff member serves as facilitator.

One of the most important factors that has been learned is that caring, sharing and nurturing in a supportive academic environment motivates the students to strive toward excellence in developing their potential.

The aggregate high school students' medium percentile scores range on the Test of Achievement Proficiency (TAP) were as follows:

	Year 02	Year 03	Year 04
Reading	21 - 30.5	18 - 49	20 - 50
Math	15 - 32	15.5 - 59	16 - 60
Science	15 - 22	22 - 58	24 - 60

The analysis of the data reveals a percentile range that reflects success of recruitment as well as retention in year 03 and year 04.

For LAS pre-nursing students, retention strategies include a variety of activities such as academic counseling, tutoring, monitoring progress, and identifying financial aid opportunities. Similar strategies are implemented for the College of Nursing (junior and senior students) in addition to the following: 1) opportunity for elected membership in CON Student Council; 2) paid membership in local Chapter of National Student Nurses Association; 3) paid, voluntary, or academic credit based research opportunities with UIC CON faculty; and 4) additional community service opportunities. Senior nursing students are involved in career counseling workshops in preparation for their first nursing job. A 15-week review for the NCLEX-RN licensing examination is conducted in addition to NLN Pre-licensure Readiness Test. An information session on graduate nursing education opportunities at UIC is conducted in an effort to promote education as a life-long experience.

A mentor program was established and maintained to provide a long-term mentoring relationship between each student and a health professional. The I'M READY project staff held several mentor recruitment sessions in local hospitals, schools, and community agencies. In addition, mentor data forms were sent to hospitals, local nursing organizations, school nurses, nursing sororities, College of Nursing faculty, nursing students and related health agencies requesting participation in the I'M READY mentor program. With an overwhelming positive response from these various sources, a follow-up mentor data form was mailed to match a mentor with a student of his/her choice based upon age, grade, sex, and ethnic background. Student/mentor/parental connection was made via letter and telephone. There are now 175 mentors supporting the personal, social and academic development of the I'M READY students. Mentor recruitment is most successful with current undergraduate and graduate students, alumni and nurses who work in health systems trying to recruit minority nurses.

A one-half day workshop is conducted twice a year for new and continuing mentors. The workshop covers the following areas: 1) mentoring process, 2) roles and responsibilities of the mentors, 3) establishing rapport and relationships with mentee and family, 4) shadowing work experience, 5) activities of mentor/mentee, and 6) guidelines in the mentoring process.

In an effort to maintain relevancy to the project, the I'M READY program established a Community Advisory Board. The board supports and participates in identifying the goals and objectives of meeting the health care needs of an urban community. They serve as partners and liaisons between the UIC-College of Nursing and the community at large. The membership of the board is comprised of business leaders, community leaders, educators, health professionals, local school council presidents/members, and parents.

The total student enrollment in the I'M READY program increased from 179 in 1990 to 722 in 1994 as depicted in Chart 2.

Chart 2

University of Illinois at Chicago
College of Nursing – I'm READY Program

Student Enrollment

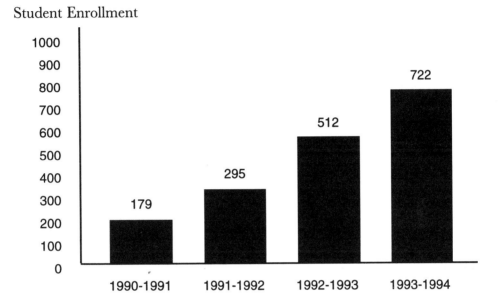

In the fourth year of the project, there were 384 students in the seventh and eighth grade, 188 students in grades nine through twelve, and 150 students in UIC LAS currently involved in the I'M READY program. The total enrollment in the program was 722 students. These students will be academically supported by UIC College of Nursing throughout their educational, social and professional development.

The major accomplishment in the past four years as a result of the I'M READY program (and several other external and internal concurrent influences) is the extent to which the college has transformed its philosophy, mission, undergraduate and master's curricula and organizational structure. The college has shifted to a strong commitment toward defining nursing within the context of a primary health care framework: as community-based care provided for a diversity of communities. The success of the I'M READY program at recruiting young African American and Hispanic youth into a program to support their preparation for success in nursing school has encouraged faculty to believe that minorities can successfully prepare as nurses to assist in changing nursing services to be constructed within the dimensions of need unique to individual communities.

With this spirit, the undergraduate curriculum was revised over the last two years from an upper division entry to a four-year nursing and liberal arts curriculum that admits students as freshmen as well as transfers into the sophomore/junior level. This change reflects the faculty's new commitment to developing students throughout their college education rather than just screening upperclassmen to enter nursing based on demonstrated success in liberal arts and sciences requirements.

The I'M READY program, as well as several other campus programs providing support for pre-college and college students, were critical to shifting the College of Nursing faculty's belief about their role in preparing nurses to practice in a wide variety of service settings with more diverse client populations and broader scope of services. Content revisions in the undergraduate curriculum were also influenced by the I'M READY program and its staff.

Introductory nursing courses begin in the second semester of the freshmen year and continue in the sophomore year, concurrent with liberal arts and science courses, to help students identify with the college and understand how liberal arts and science knowledge is utilized in nursing. A much larger portion of students' clinical practicum experiences will occur in non-hospital settings, with a high priority on community-based services - the ultimate goal is to provide close to fifty percent of students' clinical training outside of the intense/acute care hospital environment. To support this goal, the college is working with existing community-based services and community organizations in other neighborhoods where community-based services do not exist to expand training sites.

The I'M READY program's acceptance and support within African American and Hispanic communities, and the potential nurse-trainees being developed by I'M READY within these communities, has encouraged the faculty to believe these are realistic goals. The campus level "Great Cities Initiative" to redefine the mission of the university as its contribution to the redevelopment of urban life has added commitment and resources toward this effort.

Additionally, the newly revised undergraduate curriculum has a course early in the sophomore year approved by the university as meeting the cultural diversity requirement for undergraduate students. This course, "Cultural Health Issues Through the Lifespan," provides foundational knowledge and skills expanded upon in subsequent clinical nursing courses. People grow and develop within their cultural context of the client, and they have expanded their own knowledge and skills in cultural competency to prepare for this curricular change.

A new student advising structure was implemented with the undergraduate curriculum revision, based on faculty feedback. Each of the five departments is "adopting" an incoming cohort of students for academic advising and professional and social development. An individual faculty advisor from the department is an individual student's academic advisor and the class advisor is from this department. Faculty proposed this new structure to foster student collegiality and improve faculty advising by reducing the range of their students' program plans and status to a single level of student who can be advised in groups, as well as individually. To assist with faculty advising with the doubling of student enrollment, the College Academic Affairs staff, which includes the I'M READY staff, provides individual student advising during the freshmen and sophomore years and turns the students over to faculty for advising when students enter their clinical courses.

The faculty has just revised the master's curriculum to prepare graduates for advanced practice roles in nursing. This curricular revision and the marketing plans under development to support the new programs are also reflective of the spirit of the I'M READY program. Community-based practice sites across a widely diverse range of communities are a high priority for nurse practitioner students' clinical training. Marketing plans being developed for each of the nurse practitioner programs (family, pediatric, school, occupational health and nurse-midwifery) include "grow our own" programs which use independent study, cooperative education/work-study, faculty mentoring and post-BSN structured work experiences to recruit and prepare undergraduate students for the MS program. This specific plan under development places a high priority on minority students who otherwise are at risk for admission denial or subsequent failure in the master's programs.

Over a four-year period, the I'M READY program has helped the college change its entire approach to minority recruitment and retention. Prior to I'M READY program, the college had a very traditional minority support program: one recruiter/counselor position was dedicated to minority recruitment and retention. This was put upon a single individual, who was an African American master's prepared nurse — the entire responsibility for recruiting and retaining minority students. During the past four years with the I'M READY program, the college has additional project-funded I'M READY staff to assist with this responsibility.

The College recently restructured the Office of Academic Affairs (OAA) to incorporate the I'M READY staff and make minority and non-minority recruitment and retention everyone's responsibility. The I'M READY project director is permanently funded as the college's director of minority student affairs, and as urban health coordinator to coordinate minority recruitment and retention programs between the college and other campus units. All college recruiter/counselors work with the I'M READY students and events as well as all other college recruitment and advising programs.

A new position, coordinator for retention program was created this year to dedicate one Office of Academic Affairs staff position to develop and evaluate strategies to improve all students' success, with special attention to any student with risks due to academic and/or socio-cultural factors. Faculty and administrators in the college are much more attuned to looking for ways to incorporate into their programs and plans specific strategies which could provide additional assistance for minority students at risk. As an example, the college is the coordinating office for Chicago's AmeriCorps project. The staff asked if they could target I'M READY students finishing high school to provide them with health-related work experience and financial support during their first year in college or for a year after high school graduation as preparation for college entry.

In summary, the I'M READY program addresses two major social problems: 1) increasing the supply of nurses to better meet the increasing demand; and 2) increasing minorities in nursing to more closely approach the racial composition of the population in need of health services. By supporting the academic, social and professional development of minority children in metropolitan public schools, from seventh grade through college graduation and career placement, as well as developing a sense of mentoring among professional nurses to bring others into the profession, the I'M READY program is improving nursing's ability to meet the demand for its service in an ethnically diverse metropolitan population.

—Dr. Katie M. McKnight (R.N.) is Assistant Professor and director of Minority Students' Affairs in the College of Nursing at the University of Illinois in Chicago, Illinois.

References

Feagin, J.R. (1992). The Continuing Significance of Racism: Discrimination Against Black Students in White Colleges. Journal of Black Studies, 22: 4 (June) pp 546-578.

Fleming, J. (1984). Blacks in college. San Francisco, CA: Jossey Bass.

Keller, G. (1988-1989). Black students in Higher Education: Why So Few? Planning for Higher Education, 17, pp. 50-56.

Lang, M. (1986). Black student retention at predominantly black institutions: Problems, issues and alternatives. Western Journal of Black Studies, 10(2).

Lang, M. (1988). The black student retention problem in higher education: Some introductory perspectives. In M. Lang & C. Ford (Eds.), Black student retention in higher education. Springfield, IL: Charles C. Thomas Publisher.

Academic Intrusion: Key to Minority Student Success

by Quincy L. Moore

Overview:

The comprehensive collection of services offered by the Office of Academic Support (OAS) is a critical ingredient of Virginia Commonwealth University's (VCU) thrust to significantly improve the access and retention rates of minority students and others who have been historically underrepresented in higher education. The development of this office in 1989 was an emphatic demonstration of VCU's concern about diversity, access to higher education, and commitment to promoting excellence in student retention services throughout the university. Ultimately the benefits will reach beyond the VCU educational community and contribute to the enrichment of society as a whole.

This paper describes a multifaceted retention program at the Office of Academic Support at Virginia Commonwealth University in Richmond, VA. The author reviews the historical perspective involved in the development of the Office and identifies problems and barriers to increasing retention rates for all students while continuing to focus on minority students' needs.

A discussion of strategies for decreasing attrition among college students is provided, as well as ways to implement these plans. The usefulness of the OAS model for other campuses is enhanced by virtue of the institution's commitment to providing services to an ever evolving urban population.

"One of the quiet revolutions of our time..., [has been] the equipping [of] thousands of young minority people with the skills and the capacity to make more profound assessments of their lives." –Samuel Proctor

Introduction

Cage (1989), contends that more and more state governments and university systems are shifting the emphasis of their programs for minority students from recruiting them to keeping them in college until they graduate. T. Edward Hollander, chancellor of the New Jersey Board of Higher Education says, "If we don't deal with the total environment in which students study, simply removing economic obstacles just provides a revolving door."

The transition from home to college life is generally considered to be a stressful one for most young adults (Pascarella, E. T., & P. T. Terenzini, 1991). Specifically, one of the first concerns that new freshmen may experience is simply learning their way around the college campus and understanding the university environment. Next, concerns about academic performance appear common. However, if adjustment to college life is stressful for students in general, it is likely to be even more so for black students in particular. Pounds (1989) reports that black students describe predominantly white institutions as unfriendly, unfair, and generally not supportive. Problems faced by new students are often intensified for minority students in that they face additional difficulties associated with racial differences. These stressors can include racial discrimination, social isolation, a lack of student peers, language barriers, few or no minority role models, and a lack of understanding among staff of these problems.

A study on minority student stress (Smedley, Myers & Harrell, 1993), concluded that intervention programs designed to address minority student retention should focus on assisting minority freshmen in understanding the interaction between social and academic stresses they face from peers as well as faculty members.

The programs in the Office of Academic Support (OAS) at Virginia Commonwealth University are designed to intervene in the development of its participants. The goal is to ensure that students aspire not only to obtain a college education, but possibly obtain graduate and professional degrees as well. The design of this office (OAS) is centered in building the skills necessary to achieve these goals.

The mission of Virginia Commonwealth University, a comprehensive, urban, public university, is to provide a fertile and stimulating environment for teaching, learning, research, and service; to promote the pursuit of knowledge; and to disseminate professional skills. Further, the university's mission includes, among others, the provision of:

  • a scholarly climate which inspires students to lifelong commitments to learning so that they will develop competencies to work toward the fulfillment of personal and community potentials;

• an environment of educational excellence which values diversity and enables faculty members to serve as exemplary role models; and educational services for the adjacent urban community through flexible scheduling and through continuing education programs;

• research and educational activities in all disciplines to improve the quality of life and to promote the best use and general understanding of human and environmental resources; and

• establishment of the university as a planning and resource center which is devoted to resolving problems confronting Virginia's communities and to identifying emerging societal needs.

The Office of Academic Support at Virginia Commonwealth University is an educational assistance program that aids academic development of special populations by providing services designed to meet their educational needs. These services include: individualized advising, personal and career counseling, tutorial support, academic adjustments and auxiliary aids as well as social and cultural adjustment opportunities. Students are admitted to the program because of their potential to benefit from its various services.

The Office of Academic Support encompasses several support systems:

(A) Academic Advising and Counseling;

(B) Summer Institute of Learning;

(C) University Tutorial Services and Outreach Activities; and

(D) Services to Students With Disabilities.

Evolving over a period of years, these programs have proven effective in enhancing the success and retention of specifically targeted populations.

Historical Origins and Program Development

The Office of Academic Support was developed out of a Special Services Grant. The federally-funded Special Services Program was implemented at VCU in 1972. The focus of this program was to increase the enrollment of black students at VCU. Many black students admitted to VCU were required to participate in a summer developmental program which focused on the elimination of academic and cultural "deficiencies". These students spent the summer improving skills in English, mathematics, and reading in non-credit classes. Black students who participated in this program were "segregated" from the general population in special classes and in the dormitories. During the academic year, although "integrated" into the mainstream of the university, these "specially selected" students continued to receive support services through a program identified as providing services to a black student population. These services included academic support such as advising and tutoring as well as social activities. (See Chart 1)

Chart 1

Virginia Commonwealth University's Special Services Program Academic Year Organizational Chart

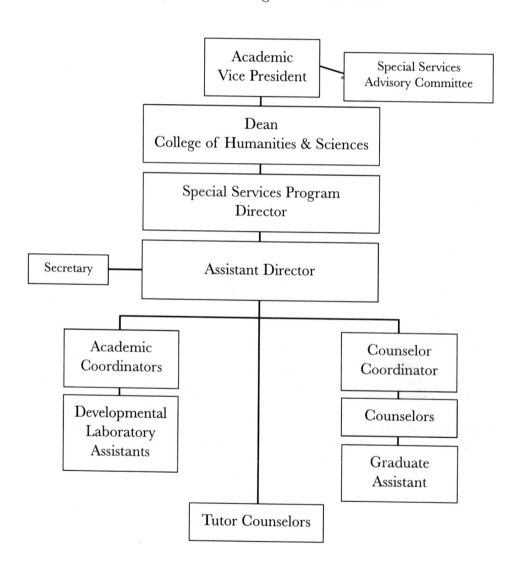

During the 1970s many services offered through Special Services were integrated into the mainstream of the university. For example, basic reading classes became a credit class — Reading and College Study Skills — offered through the School of Education; the self-paced mathematics laboratory developed by the mathematics department was adopted as the major mode of offering freshman level mathematics to all university students. With the integration of these courses into the university's curriculum, Special Services students were offered an opportunity to take placement tests for summer classes and, if indicated, enroll in credit classes during the summer program. At the same time, these students were integrated with other university students in the dormitory. The university also increased its financial support of the program so that enrollment could be increased and a more diverse population served. The program became Educational Support Programs. This program continued to direct the special services project in addition to providing those same services to other identified students.

By the end of the 1970s an average of 180 new students were invited to participate in the program each year. Approximately twenty percent of these students were white or other minority race. Additionally, the university fully supported academic services to these students throughout the academic year.

In 1985 the university elected to fully fund Educational Support Programs. The program was no longer dependent on federal funding for any of its efforts. During the next few years the program focused on opening its services to all university students with special emphasis being given to serving freshmen, sophomores and students experiencing academic difficulty. Of course, the special focus on encouraging the enrollment and retention of minority students was still a major goal.

In 1989 the program became The Office of Academic Support (OAS) and initiated plans to offer services to university students from entry to graduation. Additionally, the Program of Services To Students With Disabilities was made a component of this Office and the tutorial component was expanded to serve a larger number of university students. The summer developmental program became The Summer Institute of Learning. The office was moved from the College of Humanities and Sciences and placed in the Academic Affairs Division under the provost's office. This was a major move in institutionalizing the office. (See Chart 2)

Chart 2
Academic Affairs Division

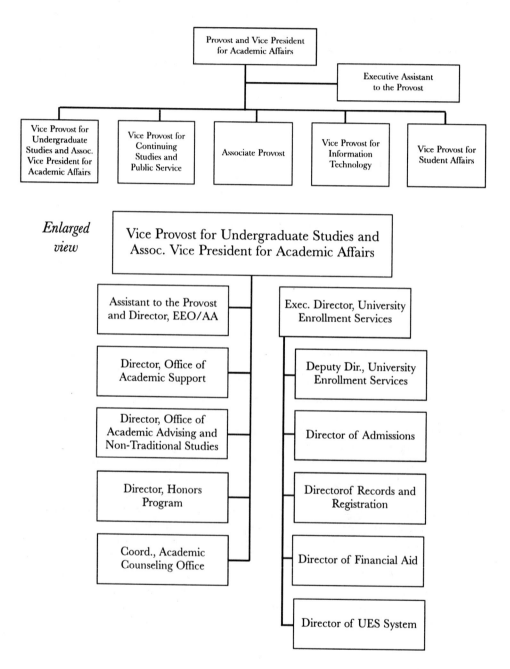

The Office of Academic Support is committed to increasing the retention of students at VCU by offering a variety of services which have been demonstrated as effective in enhancing academic success. Because of the downshift in the economic situation for the university and the state, the Office of Academic Support streamlined its services to provide tutorial support for freshmen and sophomore level classes only. Limitations were also placed on the total number of students the office could serve effectively with these economic constraints. As a result, the office could never fully implement its plan to serve the total population of students at VCU who demonstrate a need for its services. Also, many planned activities could not be implemented as designed.

Academic Advising And Counseling

First-generation college student, minorities, older students needing refresher classes each possess characteristics linked to low retention and high attrition rates. Intrusive advising and counseling support services are critical in ensuring students success and increasing retention rates.

The academic advising and counseling component in OAS is strongly rooted in a philosophy of holistic and intrusive counseling. The counseling/advising process utilized by OAS is successful because counselors are able to build quality and meaningful relationships with their students. In OAS, academic advising is more than an identification of specific courses needed for the completion of degree requirements. These services allow ease of access, broad-based training, knowledge of programs university-wide, monitoring and recordkeeping, and continuous opportunity for evaluation. The OAS model allows continuity of contact as well as frequent contact with advisers. OAS counselors are provided with an opportunity to build relationships which facilitate the successful interaction with students at a critical time in their academic development.

Tinto's (1987), research on student retention focused on models of student persistence and on measures of student growth and satisfaction.

Counselors assist students in identifying and reaching their academic goals and in adjusting to the university environment. The counselor utilizes individual, as well as small group sessions to facilitate student growth and development. Counselors use individual counseling sessions to educate students about their responsibility in a counselor/counselee relationship; to disseminate as well as collect information; and to establish rapport with students. Because of this one-to-one relationship, many students begin to develop the self-confidence and self-awareness needed to succeed in a university environment. This aspect of the counseling process contributes to the successful transition from high school to college and is a significant factor in the student's personal adjustment.

Another counseling technique employed is contract counseling. The student and counselor establish a written contract for academic and personal progress for each semester. This contract states, in detail, specific activities for student involvement during the year. Academic advising has been identified as an important contributor to academic success. The counselor provides individualized advising based on each student's preparation and demonstrated academic performance as well as curriculum requirements. This approach to advising creates a close coordination with departmental advisors which eases the transition of students into the required departmental curriculum.

Effective self-assessment is a crucial aspect of the counseling activity. Counselors use an academic report form developed by the OAS staff to predict academic achievement and then compare those predictions with the actual performance. In this way, students are assisted in more accurately accessing their strengths and weaknesses and in developing academic plans geared to success. (See Chart 3)

Chart 3
Office of Academic Support (OAS)
Academic Report

Name: _____ Date: _____

SSN: _____ Semester Reported:_____

Course no. and name	Credit	Grade Anticipated	Midterm	Final Grade
_____	____	_____	____	_____
_____	____	_____	____	_____
_____	____	_____	____	_____
_____	____	_____	____	_____
_____	____	_____	____	_____
_____	____	_____	____	_____
_____	____	_____	____	_____
_____	____	_____	____	_____
_____	____	_____	____	_____
_____	____	_____	____	_____
_____	____	_____	____	_____
_____	____	_____	____	_____

Comments:

The counselor also provides intensive services in career orientation. Students interests are evaluated through interviews and, where indicated, through referral to the University Career Planning and Placement Center. Activities are planned to broaden career awareness and to help establish career goals. One such activity is the annual career fair sponsored by this office. Students are also given opportunities to participate in career workshops and conferences, and to interact with prominent professionals in their chosen fields.

Counselors interact with the family of each participant to maximize the involvement and support of family members in the students' educational experience. This involvement may include increasing the family's awareness of educational and financial opportunities as well as informing them of the stresses involved in pursuing academic goals. The academic counseling and advising component links the students to academic and support opportunities both within the program and within the university.

An orientation class specially designed by the program offers an opportunity to ensure that each student becomes knowledgeable in the following areas: how to study effectively; test taking skills; education and career planning; interpersonal relationships; adjusting to and/or negotiating the university environment; utilizing campus resources to maximum advantage; and other special interest topics as determined by student interest and need. Consultants from university and community resources are utilized in planning and facilitating these classes. Program counselors, however, are directly responsible for the development and implementation of the classes.

Peer counseling and mentoring support the counseling relationship through formalized interactions with other university students,and provides new students with successful student role models. These continuing university students are employed to live in the residence halls during the summer and assist new students with their transition and adjustment to the university. During the academic year, successful upperclassmen are paired with students who are experiencing difficulty in academic or social adjustment.

Summer Institute Of Learning

An alternative admissions process is provided for selected students who marginally meet or fall below the university's requirements for admissions as full-time degree-seeking students. Students who are accepted through the Office of Academic Support alternative admissions process have demonstrated potential for academic achievement that is not always indicated by their SAT scores. Students admitted to the program may be required to attend a developmental program during the summer prior to their university enrollment.

This experience allows students to ease into the rigorous demands of the university life by improving basic academic skills and personal confidence. The summer program is designed to bridge the gap between high school and college for students who have demonstrated academic weaknesses. Past experience has demonstrated that intensive work in the basic skills areas before attempting the regular university curricula has yielded a more confident, better prepared, and more successfully competitive student.

Summer program activities include:

1. university classes—English, mathematics, reading/college study skills;

2. counselor-taught orientation class;

3. group study sessions and individual tutorial sessions;

4. special focus workshops including: science interest focus seminar, black male discussion groups, study skills and test-taking workshops, utilizing campus resources, identification of community resources; career fair, and learning styles assessment; and

5. social and cultural activities.

The Summer Institute of Learning provides an opportunity to assist students in understanding their role on a university campus and ultimately in life. An intrinsic component of academic success is attitude. Although attitude can't always be "externally" controlled by outside forces, it can be modified to allow students to develop their own "internal" controls. During the summer program orientation sessions are conducted each week by the OAS staff. The first orientation session is always conducted by the director. Expectations and students responsibilities are highlighted during this first program. A campus police officer, who highlights campus safety regulations and policies, usually accompanies the director.

To eliminate tardiness and assist students in establishing their own sense of responsibility, students are told (at the first orientation session) when to arrive for future orientation classes. It's stated to them that soft music will be playing fifteen minutes prior to the beginning of each orientation session. They are expected to make an effort to arrive within that time period. After this first session any student who arrives after the music stops, is escorted to the front of the auditorium and placed in a chair (next to the speaker at the podium) for the entire program.

This form of behavior modification has proven to be very effective in assisting the students in understanding their responsibilities as young adults. Throughout the years VCU professors and instructors often talk to the staff about papers their students write in English class about their summer experience. They always ask about particular papers entitled, "When the Music Stops," because of the impact of that experience. This method has proven to be very effective and creates a positive retention experience for students in the program.

Academic Year – Retention Component

With the beginning of the fall semester, the summer participants enroll in regular university classes, mingle with the larger population of university students, and are subjected to all of the adjustment problems which may affect any new student. The continuing upperclass participants also need continued support designed to enhance their success at VCU and to further develop academic and career plans. It is during the academic year that counseling, tutorial and peer mentoring components of the program play the most significant role.

Through individual interaction between the students and counselors, peer mentors, and tutors, the overall goals of the program are achieved. The academic year component emphasizes a holistic approach to learning within an integrated and structured program. To support this holistic approach, the project continues to provide counseling services to all program participants. This includes upperclassmen as well as new summer admit students.

Using the students' summer performance and other academic records, counselors assist each student in developing an individualized academic plan suited to skills and career goals. Program counselors meet regularly with students in individual as well as small group sessions. Special workshops on study skills are conducted for those students who are continuing to experience academic difficulty. Additionally, time management and stress management seminars will be offered for these students, as well as for students who have jobs.

For upperclassmen, counselors also provide information on career and graduate or professional school opportunities. Program students are given opportunities to participate in several career and leadership conferences during the academic year. These include the Minority MBA Conference, the Mass Communication Conference, the Conference for Potential Graduate Students and the Black Student Leadership Conference. Students are given information and assistance with preparation for graduate examinations and application for financial aid through sponsored workshops and seminars. Workshops and seminars on careers are designed to reduce anxiety and provide information on career decisions. A study by Newman, Fuqua, & Seaworth (1989) identified a variety of variables that are correlated with career indecision anxiety.

Tutorial services available during the academic year will include not only tutors for the basic skill areas, but for the majority of the liberal arts, science and business courses in which freshmen and sophomores traditionally enroll. Individual and group tutoring sessions are available to any program participant who requests such support or is recommended for this support by program counselors. Additionally, tutors assist students in forming and effectively utilizing study groups.

At the end of each semester, the counselor and program administrator conduct an academic review session to examine the status of all program participants. Each staff member discusses the students on their caseload and review their progress or lack of progress for the semester. Staff member welcome comments from other counselors and staff administrators regarding methods and solutions to issues that can impact their students retention and graduation. This review serves as a basis for academic advising, individual assistance plans and special workshops and seminars for the following semester. This review also provides data for continuing program evaluation.

University Tutorial Services

Tutorial services are provided free of charge by the Office of Academic Support. These services are intended to provide additional assistance outside the classroom to undergraduate students who have difficulty grasping specific course skills. The subjects for which assistance is offered are core courses normally taken by freshmen and sophomores. The tutorial services also include intensive study skills workshops and assistance in establishing study groups. Tutors and group leaders provide systematic feedback to counselors on student progress. This interaction between components allows realistic monitoring of "self-reported" progress and self-assessment by students.

The tutorial program provides peer tutors each semester in more than twenty five subject areas. The program focuses on providing assistance with freshman and sophomore level classes. Additionally, the tutorial component provides readers, scribes, note takers, proctors, and other classroom/library assistants requested through the Services For Students With Disabilities Component. Tutorial services may employ as many as seventy-five student workers each semester.

Outreach Activities

The outreach component coordinates training and professional development for the program staff as well as providing specialized experiences for program participants. This component focuses on some of the specific needs of minority students who have successfully completed their sophomore year. Outreach encourages minority students to consider continuing their education beyond the four-year degree by providing information on graduate and professional degree programs.

Experts such as Mr. Silas Purnell of the Ada S. Mckinley Program present seminars on graduate and professional school opportunities. Workshops on time management for working students, stress management and leadership are offered through outreach services. Additionally, outreach sponsors and/or coordinates student travel to special interest conferences including Mass Communications Careers for Minority Students, Minority MBA Conference; National Black Student Leadership Conference; and Virginia State Conference for Potential Graduate Students. The Outreach also coordinates a Graduate Opportunity Workshop for participants in the McNair Space Program at Virginia Union University.

Results And Outcomes For Students And/Or The Institution

Over the years, the program has been shown to be effective in its delivery of service to the targeted populations. The following list briefly details the program's accomplishments:

1. A statistical study by Dr. Robert Johnston, a mathematics professor at VCU, in the early 1980s indicated the ten year graduation rate for students who participated in this program was higher than that of other VCU students.

2. A statistical study conducted by VCU's Survey Research Laboratory in 1985 indicated that students who were participants in the Office of Academic Support's programs presented graduation percentages that were slightly higher than those of the general student population.

3. Yearly data collected by VCU's Office of Institutional Studies and the Office of Academic Support show retention rates over the past several years which compare favorably with the retention of other VCU students. The data indicates the overall retention impact of the Office of Academic Support on the student population at VCU is a positive one.

The retention for OAS participants is higher than that of the general VCU population, as well as the national population. The data from VCU's Report on Academic Advising, Retention and Graduation Rates Among Undergraduates, presented to the Board of Visitors in January 1994, indicates the overall retention impact of the Office of Academic Support on the student population at VCU is a positive one. The retention of OAS participants for the first two years, during which time they receive more intense program support, is similar to rates for non-program students. These statistics are especially significant when recognizing that OAS students have lower SAT scores and high school GPAs than other students admitted to VCU. (See Charts 4 and 5)

Chart 4

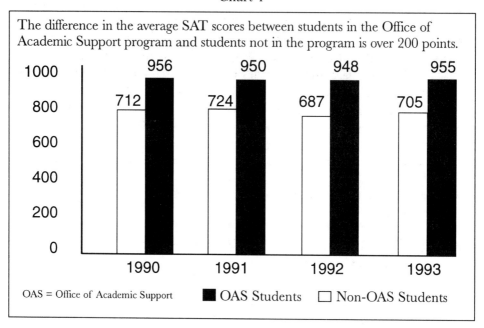

The difference in the average SAT scores between students in the Office of Academic Support program and students not in the program is over 200 points.

OAS = Office of Academic Support   ■ OAS Students   □ Non-OAS Students

Chart 5

One and Two Year Retention Rates
OAS Students and Non-OAS Students

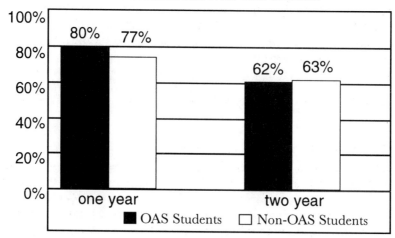

■ OAS Students   □ Non-OAS Students

One year rates are based on seven freshman classes.
Two year rates are based on six freshman classes.

The consolidation of services under The Office of Academic Support in 1989 has had a positive impact on its participants and its retention strategies are being felt at VCU. Although it is too early to fully examine the graduation rates, a six-year longitudinal study on persistence and graduation will be soon released.

4. Surveys of student opinion and program evaluations indicate that students who are involved with this program are satisfied with its services.

5. These surveys and evaluations also indicate that students perceive program services as contributing to their academic success and comfort with the university's environment.

6. University faculty and administrators have evidenced their respect and support for the program through referrals of students for services.

7. The program contributes significantly to the university's efforts to increase minority enrollment by serving an average of 150 new freshmen each year.

Specific Goal And Objectives Of The Retention Program:

1. To increase the number of minority students entering and graduating from VCU;

2. Tto enhance retention rates for VCU students by providing services specifically designed to enhance adjustment of first and second year students;

3. To enhance the likelihood of academic success by providing an opportunity for the development or enhancement of basic skills;

4. To provide personal and academic services which might increase motivation and provide encouragement for success;

5. To assist students in developing coping skills necessary for success in the college environment;

6. To increase students awareness of career opportunities; and

7. To increase students awareness of post graduate and professional school opportunities.

Use Of Resources

Initially the program was funded by the federal government as one of the TRIO programs. Virginia Commonwealth University now completely supports the program. The only exception is limited outside resources for the Summer Institute of Learning, which receives approximately fifteen percent of it funds from the State Council of Higher Education for Virginia (SCHEV). The university has incorporated all of the programs under OAS into one operating budget. This includes professional personnel, tutorial assistance, clerical support, supplies and other related expenses. The university has demonstrated its commitment to the retention of students and has provided resources to fulfill this commitment.

Potential For Adaptation By Other Institutions

The design of the program and its integration within the university's structure makes it easily adaptable on other campuses. In fact, many of the services offered through The Office of Academic Support are available on most campuses. Effective coordination of these services through a unified administrative structure is the key to the program's success. Visible support for the program from key administrators is essential in gaining program recognition and respect throughout the university. Once services are coordinated and the value of these services is recognized, the program can successfully serve the needs of its identified populations.

Evaluation and Assessment

Evaluation of VCU's Transition Program is best expressed in (1) comparison of pre- and post-test scores during the summer; (2) grade-point averages; (3) retention percentages; and (4) graduation rates of program participants. An academic review is conducted at mid-semester and at the end of each semester to assess the academic status of each student. The program has computer access to university records which allows immediate access to all student records. Counselors maintain complete files on every student, documenting their participation and progress. Exit interviews are conducted by counselors and administrators when students leave the university, either for academic, personal or financial reasons, or to transfer to another institution.

The effectiveness of the counseling and tutoring activities is monitored by student usage of the service; student evaluation of counselors and tutors; success of tutored person in courses for which they were tutored; and academic progress of students.

Additionally, program administrators maintain data to generate research and reports detailing overall academic achievement of all program participants, retention rates, academic progress and graduation rates for the program. Access to the necessary numerical data is organized by close cooperation and coordination with the director of university records.

Evaluation of project activities is an on-going process. Program reports are prepared at the end of each academic year and at the close of the summer program. Counselor evaluations are formally done by the program director each spring semester. This evaluation process provides a basis for improving existing program components as well as the development of new program directions.

In its 1990-94 recruitment and retention plan, Virginia Commonwealth

University acknowledges the importance of diversity among its students and commits to including minority Virginians as a significant representation among its students. The university's plan clearly states its support of minority recruitment and retention efforts by committing to sponsor programs such as The Better Information Project, Virginia Transfer Grant Program, Virginia Student Transition Program, and other student recruitment programs.

Conclusion

Intrusive advising and counseling is the "cornerstone" of building and maintaining a successful retention program. Mentoring, academic review, counseling, advising, are all important elements in the ability of colleges and universities to attract and graduate students of color. At no time is this more important than today. Universities are increasing the recruitment budget while decreasing retention efforts. When the difference between the number of students enrolling and the number of students graduating is a negative, then an alarm should be sounded. It is fruitless to make significant attempts to improve recruitment of minority students if there is not also the effort to help them succeed once they are on campus. Emphasis should be shifted from recruitment to retention. There are numerous things that can be done to address this concern:

1). Universities and colleges must develop a "retention" mission statement.

2). The whole university community must be committed to the philosophy of retention.

3). Resources must be allocated to supporting those retention efforts proven effective.

4). The university must demonstrate a commitment to retention programs.

5). The university must continue to design, implement, and evaluate retention programs that provide support for all students which directly impact students' academic success.

The Office of Academic Support program's success suggests that administrators, faculty members, and students have important roles in shaping the interest students have in learning. Finally, successful programs should examine the interconnected relationships of a number of variables in predicting the effect of college on students. Universities should consider the relatedness of academic and non-academic activities as they plan and develop educational programs.

—Dr. Quincy L. Moore is the director of the Office of Academic Support at Virginia Commonwealth University in Richmond, Virginia.

References

Cage, M.L. (1989). More Minority Programs, More Emphasis, Efforts to Keep Students Enrolled in College. Chronicle of Higher Education, 1-24.

Newman, J.L., Fuqua, D.C., & Seaworth, T.B. (1989). The role of anxiety in career indecision: Implications for diagnosis and treatment. Career Development Quarterly, pp. 37; 221-231.

Pascarella, E.T., & Terenzini, P.T. (1991). How College Affects Students: Findings and Insights from Years of Research. San Francisco: Jossey-Bass.

Pounds, A.W. (1991). The Freshman Year Experience: Helping Students Survive and Succeed in College. San Francisco: Jossey-Bass.

Smedley, B., Myers, H., & Harrell, S. (1993). Minority-related Stresses. Journal of Higher Education.

Tinto, V. (1987). Leaving College: Rethinking the Causes and Cures of Student Attrition. Chicago: University of Chicago Press.

Access and Retention Strategies for Underrepresented Minority Students at the University at Buffalo

by Muriel A. Moore

Overview:

Historically underrepresented minority students enrolled in institutions of higher education in the 1990s face challenges qualitatively different from those experienced by their predecessors.[1] Efforts to recruit and enroll minority students into post-secondary institutions during the 1980s were relatively successful. According to the 1993 American Council on Education report, every state in the nation except Washington experienced a growth in total enrollment of minority students in post-secondary institutions between 1980 and 1990. In addition, throughout most of this period, both public and private institutions intensified their efforts to attract more minority students to their campuses by offering substantial financial aid and attempting to make the campus climate more receptive to minority students, faculty, and staff.

While minorities made significant progress in college and university enrollment during the 1980s, these gains have been offset by measures that continue to limit access to higher education in the 1990s and, concomitantly, contribute to increased attrition rates for African-American, Hispanic-American and Native-American students. Since 1990, decreased funding for higher education by state governments, coupled with overt attacks on affirmative action, have led to a decline in the enrollment of historically underrepresented minority students in many public colleges and universities.

Many institutions of higher education throughout the country adopted distinctive approaches for addressing issues related to minority student access and retention as early as the 1970s. This chapter explores the access and retention model utilized by the State University of New York at Buffalo (UB) for the last decade. Although the UB model has not been empirically tested against those employed at other institutions of higher education, evidence suggests that UB is ahead of national trends regarding underrepresented minority student enrollment and retention.

"It is clear ... that, while minority students are enrolling in college in larger numbers, many are not completing degrees. Institutions need to consider the range of factors that contribute to students remaining in college, from financial issues to environmental considerations, in crafting better retention strategies." – Deborah Carter, ACE Office of Minorities in Higher Education

Background

The literature indicates that a comprehensive and holistic approach is essential to the successful recruitment, retention, and graduation of minority students. Brown (1991) identified seven components that are critical to the success of such an approach. First, an attractive financial aid program must be offered. Universities must provide financial aid packages that include grants and scholarships if they intend to have an impact on minority student recruitment. In addition to the traditional funding channels (i.e., state and federal government programs), the local business community and private foundations can serve as important sources of financial aid for minority students by offering scholarships fellowships, and internships. The number of loans offered should be minimal, as African American, Hispanic American, and Native American students historically have had a diminished economic capacity to repay loans.

Second, universities must make their environment attractive to minority students, encouraging a multicultural and pluralistic atmosphere. Minority students must be presented with a climate in which their opinions are well-represented and viewed as important to the growth and development of society. Providing a multicultural environment includes not only ensuring a diverse student population, but also increasing the number of minority administrators, faculty, and staff. Indeed, the presence of minorities in these positions not only improves the educational experience, but also provides cultural and social awareness for white students as well (Brown 1991). In addition, the university curriculum must reflect the contributions of African Americans, Hispanic-Americans, Native Americans, and individuals from other ethnic groups. Universities also must take steps to illustrate the contributions of underrepresented minority students, faculty, and staff to campus life in general.

In conjunction with offering a multicultural environment, a third component of a successful strategy concerns the social climate of the university. The social climate should be comfortable and provide an array of activities that are multi-cultural in nature and beneficial to all students. The student affairs division at universities should be at the forefront in providing diverse cultural activities which help in the intellectual development of the entire student body.

Fourth, institutions of higher education must provide effective retention programs that are clearly articulated and reflect a high degree of institutional commitment and faculty support. An effective retention program must, of course, provide comprehensive services to minority students; develop mechanisms that allow for the systematic collection of data; and monitor the academic progress of program participants—all without stigmatizing the groups in question. For example, without counseling and tutoring programs, many minority students fall through the cracks, as they tend not to use traditional counseling and academic retention services when they require assistance. Academic retention programs can serve as tremendous vehicles for helping minority students expand their intellectual frontiers outside of the classroom setting.

The fifth component of a successful recruitment, retention, and graduation strategy for underrepresented minority students involves sensitizing faculty. Faculty members must make underrepresented minority students feel comfortable, and be available to meet with them and show enthusiasm when advising and answering questions. Faculty members are responsible for ensuring a conducive climate for learning and, therefore, must actively engage underrepresented minority students in classroom discussion and provide them with the analytic tools and discipline that will contribute to their overall success (Ayes 1983).

Sixth, universities must establish and maintain open lines of communication with guidance counselors in predominantly minority high schools. University-community engagement is critical to improving minority access to higher education. A number of initiatives can be implemented to increase underrepresented minority enrollment in college, including campus visits, pre-college programs, special visitation privileges, and close collaboration between college administrators and high school counselors. In addition, campus administrators can visit high schools, providing lectures and offering career days.

Last, and perhaps most important to the success of underrepresented minority recruitment, retention, and graduation, campus administrators must be firmly committed to increasing the total presence of minorities on campus. This support must permeate every level of institutional hierarchies: governing boards, presidents, vice presidents, deans, directors, and faculty members. Thus, not only should emphasis be placed on recruiting underrepresented minority students to campus, but, as mentioned above, a commitment to hiring and retaining minority faculty, administrators, and support staff must be demonstrated as well.

The UB Model: Summary and Achievements

The State University of New York at Buffalo (UB) is a large, diverse, and complex institution. For more than 100 years, UB was a private, regional university primarily serving residents of the Western New York area. In 1962, UB became part of the State University of New York (SUNY) system, and by the mid-1980s, had become the largest of its sixty-four units. Ranked among the premier public research universities in the country, the University at Buffalo encompasses fifteen divisions that offer a broad array of degree programs. The university has over 4,000 full-time and affiliated faculty members, and more than 25,000 undergraduate and graduate students.

As was the case at predominantly white public research universities in the early 1980's, UB's recruitment efforts and retention rates for underrepresented minority students, faculty, and staff did not reflect the representation of those groups within the larger society. In the past decade, however, UB has implemented a model that reflects an institution-wide commitment to providing educational access and opportunities to students from underrepresented minority groups. Within the past decade, the number of historically underrepresented minority students enrolled at the university has consistently increased, with African American, Hispanic American, and Native American students now comprising over ten percent of the student population, the highest percentage in the SUNY system. This steady increase at UB is particularly significant, given that the number of minorities enrolled in higher education — especially African American students — has declined significantly in the last several years (Carter and Wilson 1994, 11).

Believing the current problems of minority representation in higher education cannot be addressed solely at the graduate and undergraduate levels, UB's involvement in programs for underrepresented minority students begins at the elementary school level with a program designed to fight mathematics biases in minority children. At the secondary level, the university offers students a chance to improve academic skills and attitudes toward education through a number of programs. For undergraduate students, academic and financial assistance is coordinated to provide the kind of support services that will improve chances for success, e.g., developmental instruction, tutoring, mentoring, and counseling. Instruction at the graduate level is supported by academic mentoring and financial assistance — often the most sought-after and elusive commodities for underrepresented minority students.

The university has taken a pro active leadership position within New York State by offering a diverse and fulfilling experience for minority students. At UB, the educational access network not only provides minority students with a direct route to and through the university, but offers academic and extracurricular assistance to help them succeed as they advance. It is important to note these programs are not mutually exclusive; rather they are complementary, and allow for synergistic relationships that offer an educational pipeline beginning in elementary school and continuing through graduate and professional studies.

The UB Special Programs model was conceived and instituted in 1982. Prior to the creation of this model, campus efforts to attract and retain underrepresented minority students tended to be scattered throughout different divisions and were unfocused and poorly-managed. The new office, an initiative led by the president, provided a single reporting structure and encouraged a new vision for growth and development. All existing campus programs and activities involving minority student recruitment and retention were assigned to the vice president for academic affairs, who instituted an Office of Special Programs. An associate vice president was appointed to oversee policy development and the day-to-day operations of the new office.

Initially, the programs within this office included a federally-funded Upward Bound program, an adult Educational Opportunity Center, and a state-funded undergraduate Educational Opportunity Program and on university funded undergraduate Urban College Program. The objective of the UB model was to consolidate and expand institutional efforts to enhance the recruitment and retention of minority students. Over the past decade, the Special Programs model has been expanded to include three major areas of support with more than twenty-five individual programs. The three areas include: (1) pre-college programs, (2) undergraduate programs, and (3) graduate and professional fellowship programs. The programs support well over 5,000 students annually, from the pre-college to the graduate level, and receive over seven million dollars annually from a combination of institutional, federal, state and private funds.

The specific mission of the office is to provide leadership, and oversight for a pipeline model to recruit and retain minority students. In addition, the office is responsible for developing and monitoring policy and programmatic issues related to the success of minority students, as well as working with the community-at-large. The unique structure of the office promotes a cohesive support system for the sharing of human and financial resources, provides administrative expertise and leadership, and establishes a forum for supporting and recognizing the multitude of special talent exhibited in the various programs.

Administrators of the various programs meet on a regular basis to explore ways to impact institutional policy, develop curriculum, improve student life, and enhance staff development. Students enrolled in graduate and undergraduate programs serve as mentors and role models for younger students in the pipeline. Academic seminars and student development activities are organized throughout the year to enhance student success. As the literature suggests, these meetings are important for minority students enrolled in predominantly white institutions (Fleming 1985).

Pre-College Programs

All programs for pre-college students are clustered under the Office of University Preparatory Programs (OUPP). Each of these programs offers a variety of educational services to students to increase the awareness, motivation, academic preparation, and personal, and social skills essential for success in college. These programs specifically target youth in grades four through twelve, and are housed in an easily accessible and centrally-located urban campus facility.

In 1992-93, the Office of University Preparatory Programs served over 700 students. Annual retention rates for the five largest pre-college programs ranged from eighty-six percent in the Upward Bound Classic Program to 100 percent in the Upward Bound Math/Science Program. Both of these programs are designed to increase the number of underrepresented minority and/or economically and educationally disadvantaged students enrolled in post-secondary education. The Science Technology Enrichment Program (STEP) offers academic and support services for underrepresented minority students who are pursuing a college major in the scientific and technical areas. To address the high school drop-out rate, two "in-the-school" programs — the School Community University Program (SCUP), and the Liberty Partnership Program (LPP) — were conceived to serve underrepresented minority students. Annual retention rates for these three programs were ninety-one percent, ninety-three percent, and ninety-four percent, respectively. The graduation rates for Upward Bound Classic, Upward Bound Math/Science, STEP, and LPP were seventy-one percent, 100 percent, 100 percent, and, eighty-five percent, respectively.

Buffalo Prep, Inc., a university affiliated private/public partnership is an innovative program which recruits academically talented, underrepresented minority seventh graders from low-income backgrounds to participate in a fourteen-month academic program which prepares them to enter local independent high schools on a full scholarship. This academically rigorous program maintains a retention rate of seventy percent. The high school graduation rate is 100 percent, with graduates admitted to some of the most prestigious colleges and universities in the nation.

Undergraduate Programs

While all of these programs have been successful in increasing the number of historically underrepresented minority students at the undergraduate level, the performance of six programs in particular, is very impressive. The Minority Academic Achievement Program (MAAP) provides academic tutoring, personal counseling and advisement services, as well as financial aid in a small residential setting for academically-talented underrepresented minority undergraduate students. With a ten-year retention to graduation rate of eighty percent, which far exceeds comparative rates for the entire university population, MAAP has been highly successful in retaining its students. The Collegiate Science Technology Enrichment Program (CSTEP) offers academic support services and internships for economically disadvantaged or underrepresented minority students to increase their enrollment in and graduation from programs of study in the scientific, technical, and health-related professions. the eight-year retention to graduation rate for this outstanding program is seventy-two percent. The Collegiate Achievement Program (CAP), is a newer program providing academic advisement and counseling support for underrepresented minority students who have demonstrated the potential for academic and personal success, but who may require more individualized attention at a large research university. CAP uses supervised guidance as its primary intervention strategy. CAP has not yet graduated its first class. The Educational Opportunity Program (EOP), the largest in the SUNY system, provides students from financially and academically disadvantaged backgrounds with a three-tier support system. The system is synergistic and includes personal and academic counseling, mandatory tutoring, and financial aid. Most students entering the program attend an intensive, residential program the summer before their freshman year. The 900 students enrolled in EOP are required to maintain close, personal contact with program counselors and free tutoring is available to them in all subject areas. As a very selective program, EOP admits approximately 250 freshman and transfer students each year, less than ten percent of all applicants. EOP graduates about 150 students annually, or approximately sixty percent of the number in each year's incoming class.

Two federally funded programs that also target underrepresented minority and first generation undergraduate students at UB are the Ronald McNair Post Baccalaureate Achievement Program and the Special Services Program. The two programs are designed to provide students with intense and or sustained academic support services that include supplemental academic advisement, tutoring, and mentoring. The Special Services Program provides a comprehensive support program to first generation and economically disadvantaged college students. In addition to the services mentioned above, students participate in special seminars and enroll in academic credit-bearing courses to supplement their undergraduate experience. While the yearly retention rate is ninety percent, the cohort graduation rate for this program is eighty percent. The Ronald McNair Program prepares low income, first generation college seniors for graduate and professional study. Students are matched with a faculty mentor to engage in year long research projects. They are enrolled in two research methods courses, attend a six week GRE preparation course and weekly graduate school seminars. The program concludes its eight week summer program with a regional research conference, where students present their academic research. The percentage of McNair students who go on to graduate and or professional study significantly exceeds the national average for this population at sixty-eight percent.

Graduate Programs

Retention for graduate students is often directly related to the amount of financial support they receive. Like many graduate students, minority students often have significant personal and financial responsibilities, but, unlike some other students, many do not have personal or institutional support. Without such support, minority students may be unable to attend graduate school or to fully concentrate on their studies due to external job responsibilities. Minority students, for example, are less likely to receive assistantships or other types of financial aid awarded by colleges and universities for a number of reasons (Phillip 1993). Lack of awareness of graduate financial aid resources and how they work may also decrease the number of minority graduate students while weak recruitment strategies undoubtedly also contribute to the low number.

At the graduate level, the impact of the UB Special Programs model has increased the number of minority students enrolling in and graduating from graduate and professional schools. This is evidenced by the fact that UB ranks first among public state universities in New York in terms of total number of minority doctoral degrees conferred in 1991-1992 (Black Issues in Higher Education 1995).

This success is due, in part, to the number of financial aid awards granted to minority students. Each year the university awards over two million dollars in financial support to more than 200 minority graduate students through its four specially designated fellowship programs. Institutional data indicate the increase in minority graduate enrollment has followed the increase in the number of fellowships awarded. The number of fellowships awarded has increased by more than one thousand percent since 1985, as has the total amount of financial assistance awarded to minority students at the graduate level. It is important to note graduate fellowship programs have a retention rate of ninety-nine percent. During the period from 1987 to 1994, the Underrepresented Minority Graduate Fellowship Program funded 342 graduate students, and awarded degrees to 145 graduates. The distribution includes seventeen Ph.D. degrees awarded in eight academic fields: including anthropology, comparative literature, education, English, psychology, and statistics; thirty-three J.D. degrees; and sixty-eight master's degrees in such disciplines as architecture, business administration, library science, and social work. In addition to the J.D., professional degrees also have been awarded in medicine and dentistry. Outstanding graduates of this program include assistant professors in universities and colleges across the country, and others who hold high-level administrative positions.

The Patricia Roberts Harris Fellowship Program has an equally impressive record of funding historically underrepresented minority graduate students at UB. From its inception in 1987 until 1994, this federally funded program, reserved for historically underrepresented minority students in scientific and technical disciplines, has awarded eighteen degrees at the master's and doctoral levels. Outstanding graduates of this program include a Ph.D. in molecular and cellular biology who currently holds a research post-doctoral fellowship at a prestigious Midwest university, and another who holds a Ph.D. in mechanical and aerospace engineering and is an assistant professor at a major southern university.

Impact

The UB Special Programs model has had a significant positive impact on both the enrollment and retention of minority students and on the university's value system as a whole. Indeed, although the UB model has not been empirically tested against those employed at other institutions of higher education, anecdotal evidence suggests that UB is ahead of national trends regarding minority student enrollment and retention.

The UB model has also had a significant impact on student recruitment. To meet this challenge, the Office of Admissions expanded its professional staff, intensified its recruitment programs, and revised its publications to target minority students and to present them in active roles at the university. In terms of strengthening retention among minority students, counseling and mentoring services provided by units throughout the university have helped students come to terms with academic or personal problems they may encounter. Thus, due to strengthened academic and personal support systems, student retention and graduation rates have significantly improved.

Institutional policies have been developed and promulgated that embrace diversity as a much valued ideal of the university community, and the hiring of minority faculty, staff, and administrators in key positions remains a university priority. Two of the five university vice presidents are African American, and the university is participating in state-wide minority faculty hiring programs. In addition, workshops are regularly held that explore the benefits of a multicultural academic environment and workplace. The university strives to maintain a campus climate that allows for open and candid discussions regarding the personal and academic development issues of minority students, faculty and administrators.

Equally important, minority interests and issues represented are addressed within planning groups and committees, as well as in university publications. Underrepresented minority students, faculty, and staff are expected and encouraged to engage in active roles and to provide leadership in the university community to ensure that campus policies and initiatives do not adversely impact the needs, interests, and concerns of underrepresented minority students. Additionally, more academic departments, and individual faculty members are developing programs, identifying funds, and providing support to minority students within their disciplines. Taken together, these measures have led to a vast improvement in the institutional climate and a greater commitment to diversity as an institutional goal.

Problems

A prominent concern common to all these programs is the instability of funding. Programs that provide access and support for underrepresented minority students continue to rely on specially designated state and federal funds. More than seventy percent of the special program funds presented in this model come from external resources. To protect these programs a stable funding floor must be guaranteed through legislation at the state and federal levels and a renewed national commitment must be made to ensure educational opportunities for underrepresented minorities.

A second area of weakness is the relatively small increase in the number of historically underrepresented faculty and graduate teaching assistants at UB. A focused, systematic emphasis is needed to guide and increase underrepresented minority students' awareness of the availability and critical role that teaching assistantships have in relation to graduate study and entry into professorial and professional roles within the academy. The university's recently appointed Vice Provost for Faculty Development has been charged with assisting department chairs in leadership initiatives to recruit, identify, and retain underrepresented minority graduate teaching assistants and faculty.

Conclusion

Through a decade-long initiative led by its presidents, the University at Buffalo has employed a very successful model of minority recruitment and retention. Minority students who are admitted to one of the institution's special programs tend to experience greater academic success and have higher retention and graduation rates than the university as a whole. In some programs, the over-all graduation and retention rates are higher than those of the university honors program or any other cohort of undergraduate students. A few students have also been able to complete their studies within three years, and at least sixty percent attend graduate or professional school after completion of the baccalaureate degree.

The University at Buffalo recognizes that a corrective to the problem of underrepresentation of minorities in higher education does not rest with any one institution; however, it does acknowledge that one institution committed to diversity and willing to develop both immediate and long-term solutions can make a difference. As a major public research institution, the university will continue to develop and refine its recruitment model to ensure that viable opportunities and avenues for the academic and personal success of underrepresented minorities are maintained.

—Dr. Muriel A. Moore is Vice President for Public Service and Urban Affairs at the University at Buffalo, Buffalo, New York.

Bibliography

American Council on Education. 1993. Eleventh Annual Status Report on Minorities in Higher Education. Washington, D.C.: American Council on Education.

Ayers, George. 1983. "Critical Issues: The Illusion of Equal Access." Planning and Changing. 14. 49-55.

Brown, Charles. Spring 1991. "Increasing Minority Access to College: Seven Efforts for Success." NASPA Journal. 28. 224-30.

Carter, Deborah J. and Reginald Wilson. 1994. Thirteenth Annual Status Report on Minorities in Higher Education. Washington, D.C.: American Council on Education.

Fleming, Jacqueline. 1985. Blacks in College: A Comparative Study of Students' Success' in Black and White Institutions. San Francisco: Jossey-Bass Publishers.

Phillip, Mary Christine. July 1993. "Enhancing the Presence of Minorities in Graduate Schools: What Works for Some Institutions." Black Issues in Higher Education. 10. 33-35.

Sherman, Thomas M. Spring 1994. "Assessment and Retention of Black Students in Higher Education." Journal of Negro Education. 63. 164-80.

"The Top 100 Rankings." Black Issues in Higher Education. 12:7. 38-73.

[1]Historically underrepresented minorities are defined as African-American, Hispanic American, and Native American students

A Program to use Black Musical Traditions to Retain Black Students

by Kevin J. McCarthy

Overview:

A new program instituted at the University of Colorado at Boulder allows black students to study the traditional musical styles found within the black community over the past 200 years. It is hoped that the result will be a strengthening of traditions within the black community by assisting the black folk musicians in transferring their musical skills and knowledge to a younger generation of black musicians. The basis of this program is the performance of black folk music, whether it is in the person of a blues shouter, a gospel singer, a stride piano player or another folk musician. The university becomes the vehicle through which black students learn the culture of their own community. This activity is seen as a way to increase interest, motivation and retention on the part of talented black students.

The university has arranged to hire older blacks who learned their musical art by ear at the foot of some other folk musician, long since dead. These older black folk musicians teach individual lessons to young black students who attend the program. The students learn their musical culture, the community trains young musicians for the culture, and the students receive a degree from the university. This article details the program and how it helps retain students in the university while they complete a degree.

Introduction

The role of music departments in universities is seen too often as a bastion of western European culture, and that only in a limited way. Music students spend many years studying the works of "dead, white, male composers" and pass along the traditions found in those works. Presently this role is changing in that many colleges and universities have recently included works of composers of other ethnic backgrounds and some women composers in their Music Appreciation and Music History classes. Often, however, the works included are those that match the standard musical repertoire in genre and instrumentation. So when a black man or a female writes a symphony or an opera, it stands a chance of being included. The only works that are included but do not match this standard are in the field of jazz, where many black musicians have excelled.

The University of Colorado at Boulder houses, in its Music Library, the American Music Research Center. This unit contains books, scores, sheet music, and recordings of many compositions that do not fit the above-mentioned standard. Much of the printed music and many of the recordings represent American folk music in its broadest sense, and includes over two hundred scores and tapes of music of black women composers, possibly the only collection of its kind in the country (Walker-Hill, p. 23). The inclusion of this music in the library has assisted the university in redefining and broadening the mission of the College of Music to include all forms and styles of folk music. Using this resource as a starting point, the College of Music has defined a Bachelor of Arts in American Folk Music. The basis of this degree is the study of and performance of traditional music from many different subsets of the American culture. It is this newly defined program that is discussed in this paper.

For many years, American universities have forced students from many different backgrounds into the same pattern of study, and that pattern reflected a narrow view of the national culture. At the same time, younger generations from all backgrounds have traditionally spent much of their time revolting from the older generation in styles of dress, music, social activities, religion, and recreation. Perhaps this is the appointed role of the younger generation, but the fact is that many of the rich traditions, used for many years within individual cultures, are being lost as the older generations that know these traditions die. If a university defines its task to include the preservation and maintenance of a nation's culture, then its task includes all portions of that culture, not just the portion that looks or sounds like nineteenth century Vienna.

Thus the program presently undertaken by the University of Colorado assists both the university in its task and the older generation of blacks in preserving the rich musical culture associated with the many activities of the black community over the years. The foundation of this program is the performance of black folk music, whether it is in the person of a blues shouter, a

94

gospel singer, or the next Ella Sheppard (pianist for the Fisk Jubilee Singers in 1866 in Nashville). The university will become the vehicle through which black students will revisit and learn the culture of their own community. This activity is seen as a way to increase interest, motivation, and retention on the part of talented black students.

How Will This Program Increase Retention?

Many years ago an author named Andrew Billingsley wrote of the "screens of opportunity," not doors, open to blacks. His point was that those who were successful had a support system that relied on four points: the individual, the family, the community, and the wider society (Billingsley, 1968, p. 97). The first of these, the individual, includes the talents and determination that the student is born with and develops. This program selects students on the criterion of their musical talent as displayed at their audition. Billingsley's second point, the family, will be a part of the student's successes thus far in music and can be counted on to continue the support in the future partially because of Billingsley's third point - the community. Denver does not have a thriving blues tradition and has had an excellent jazz tradition only revolving around a few well-known artists. In the Denver area, the best traditional black music is found in the churches in black neighborhoods. Here, both the family and the community join together to support and encourage those young adults who sing or play piano/organ in these churches. The student feels part of the congregation and supported by it.

The final point brought out by Billingsley is the wider society. In a later work (Billingsley, 1992, p. 171), he speaks of the importance of the value of a strong, supportive family and a strong supportive college. Here is where the University and the College of Music can play a role. The College of Music, in recognizing the student's talent and inviting the student's admission, is committing itself to the success of this student in time, scholarship monies, tutoring, and private lessons from the best black church musicians in the Denver area. Therefore all four of Billingsley's points for success are present in the program.

One needs only to look around a high school to see whose parents and communities are almost always involved. It is the parents and friends of student athletes and student musicians. Therefore, these students tend to have higher achievement scores and fewer average days absent than the other students regardless of ethnicity and economic level (McCarthy, 1993). The program being presented today strives to take advantage of and increase the parental and community involvement in order to strengthen student retention. Since this is a new program, the situation of the student-athlete will be examined for keys to success in retention.

There seem to be four factors in the student athlete situation that can be borrowed for the program presently under discussion: parental involvement, self-esteem and motivation, selection by a college, and continued support and success. First, the student athlete usually has strong involvement from his or her parents.

Further, the community from which the student comes is involved in the student's success. According to a recent report from *Child Trends*, students whose parents are and remain actively involved in the student's activities "tend to do better in class and take part in more activities" (Parental, p. 58A). Recently, the U.S. Department of Education has begun a campaign to promote more parental involvement in children's education (ibid.). If the new program will select from those high school students who have achieved in a legitimate area of black folk music, then one can be assured that the student has already garnered the support of family and community, for that is where the folk music begins and continues.

The second factor is self-esteem and motivation. When one speaks of the student athlete, one can be assured of the student's self-esteem. The student is defined by the successes in athletic endeavors and this success builds self-esteem. The student has accepted the challenge to compete and trains to be prepared once the contest starts. In the same way, a musical performer remains and continues as a performer not because of failures but because of successes in the musical situation. The student in each case is rewarded by the self-knowledge of a job well done and by the adulation of peers, parents, and others within the community. Just as the athlete prepares for the responsibility of the game, the musician prepares for the performance, with knowledge, understanding, and especially, with practice. The student understands the performance situation and is self-motivated to improve in order to present the best musical rendition possible.

The third factor is selection by a college or university. In the case of the student athlete, college coaches search far and wide for those students who will succeed in their programs and who will enhance and improve the program. The most important selection factor is not the student's SAT or ACT score. It is not even the student's GPA at the high school level. The coach is only minimally interested in them. The most important selection factor is the athletic ability of the student. Other parts of the equation can be assisted through tutors, further learning during a red-shirt year, or careful selection of classes to insure success at the campus.

So too, when a student is selected for the College of Music at the University of Colorado, the most important selection factor is the musical audition. Since the college has the right to set admission standards, the other admission criteria are the lowest on the Boulder campus. This is not true because the College wishes to admit non-achievers. Rather, the College of Music feels that the SAT, the ACT, and even the high school GPA have not measured a future music student's major talent. Only the musical audition can do that. Therefore, in this new program, the crucial element in the admission of a student is the audition. At this audition, the student is expected to demonstrate his or her musicianship and at least rudimentary understanding of the black folk music style he or she will be studying. This can only be done by someone who has already achieved a measure of success in performing the style. This leads to the fourth and final factor.

The fourth factor from the student athlete situation is continued support and success and here the college must rely again on the community. The support must come from the black community that sent the student to the college. It is felt that this will exist because this is one of the best ways the community has to save and continue its traditional music. Further, the success of the student becomes another success for the community itself. For example, take the case of a young black female who is a gospel singer. She would audition as a gospel singer, be accepted, and study to become an even better gospel singer. In addition, she would select classes that would broaden and deepen her understanding of the black Community within the larger national community, including the long road that her community has traveled historically. This, along with her lessons and practice, should help to make her an even better gospel singer while continuing the tradition of the style.

In his article dealing with cultural diversity and learning, John Ogbu (1992) identifies nine secondary strategies that black students can use in a predominant white academic atmosphere. Some of these are useful in promoting school success, others are not. The helpful strategies include: accommodation without assimilation, camouflage, involvement in church activities, attending private schools, mentors, and remedial/intervention programs. The music program under discussion emulates each of these positive strategies as follows. The program allows the black student to remain black, since he or she is studying black music and its heritage. There is no question of the student attempting to emulate white students (or cultural passing as Ogbu calls it).

The program encourages the black student to adopt camouflage under the guise of "musician." This means the student is acceptable because of a talent, not because of a birthright. Since the community and church are involved directly in the student's studies and successes, a third strategy is fulfilled. At the College of Music, although there are 25,000 university students on the Boulder campus, there are only 312 undergraduate students in music. This number emulates the numbers and personal attention of a private college. The black student has mentors on the faculty, since each student is given a personal advisor who understands the program and seeks to understand each student. In this program, the advisors will be black members of the music faculty. Finally, the remedial and intervention programs are in place from early identification through the private lessons to the tutorial and financial help available to the students in the program.

Who Will Teach This Music?

A crucial question arises: Who will teach the music? There is only one reasonable answer: the authentic folk musicians from the black community. Therefore, the College of Music has arranged to ask this community to identify the best folk musicians. The answers are expected to be older blacks who learned their musical art by ear at the foot of some other folk musician, long since dead. The older black folk musicians will be hired by the College of Music to teach private lessons in their musical art to individual students who choose to attend this program. This is where the unique standing of the College of Music comes into play. The College of Music can do this although the older black folk musician may or may not have a college degree, that musician understands and performs the authentic music of the black community.

Thus the College can hire these musicians on a professional level even without formal training because their expertise is authentic and needs no certification by a college degree. Therefore, in this program the students learn their own musical culture, the community trains its young musicians for the preservation of the culture, and the students use these studies to work toward a degree from the university.

What Other Courses Will These Students Take?

Since this degree program leads to a Bachelor of Arts in American Folk Music, the students will be expected to register for and complete a number of courses both within and outside of music. The coursework can best be detailed in three sections: music courses, core curriculum courses, and other coursework outside of music.

In the music courses, the students will take five semesters of Music Theory and Aural Skills, five semesters of Music History (including both Western Music and World Music), at least four semesters of lessons from the black folk musicians identified from the community, at least two semesters of some musical ensemble, including a World Music Ensemble which performs every kind of folk music, from gospel to rap, and then the student will either write a thesis about their musical culture or take an additional course in Music Theory or Music History of the student's own choosing (including such courses as Jazz Theory, Ethnomusicology, Music of Africa, Music of Latin America, Oriental Music, etc.). It is hoped that some of the students will select the thesis option in order to further document the richness of the black folk music they have studied.

The selection of classes presented to the students as a core curriculum includes many courses that students might choose in order to learn more about their black culture, including such classes as: Introduction to Black Studies, Exploring the Regional Cultures of Africa, African American Family in U.S. Society, Black Politics, U.S. Race and Ethnic Relations, Afro-American History, the African American in the Arts, Black Religious Life in America and many others. Further, students may select classes that do not appear on the core curriculum list and petition for them to be included in their core because of the special program or special project that interests them.

In the final section of the student's curriculum, the student selects an additional twenty three to twenty five credits outside of music that may or may not be in a single field. For example, a student might put all these in the field of Sociology and end up with a Bachelor of Arts in Music Degree with a double major in Sociology. In the College of Music at the moment, we have 314 undergraduate students including seventy eight double majoring in music plus another field. Of these, about thirty two are doubling in Engineering, another twenty five in Business, and another eleven in Pre-Medicine or Pre-Law. These students are sure to go on either in music or in their other field to be successes and contribute to society because they have learned to achieve.

We at the College of Music at the University of Colorado have every hope that this program will prove effective and will serve as a model for others in the field. If the university can successfully unite the forces of a talented student, and a caring, supportive extended family, a black community willing to support and nurture the talented youths and to continue their most cherished traditional music, and a university that can continue and increase the support to the student, then one wonders how such a program could not succeed.

Why Should This Program Succeed?

Many theories of student achievement revolve around the presence or absence of parental involvement. It is seen as a necessity in order to motivate students and bring the positive force of the home into the students' life at school. However, the strategies devised to create parental involvement should be based on the internal motivation of the parents to be directly and positively connected with students' behavior. If this is true, then the parents of students involved in activities should be motivated to be involved with the school and the students of those parents would achieve at the school. In addition, these students will stay in school.

Thirty years ago, Lucius Cervantes (1965, pp. 198-199) identified twenty characteristics that were commonly found among potential or actual dropouts. He divided these into eight dealing with school, six with family, three with peers and three with psychological orientation as he measured it.

Those dealing with school were:
1. Two years behind in reading or arithmetic at seventh grade level. Majority of grades are below average.
2. Failure of one or more school years (1st, 2nd, 8th, 9th grades most commonly failed; 85% of dropouts behind one year; 53% two or more years).

3. Irregular attendance and frequent tardiness. Ill-defined sickness given as reason.
4. Performance consistently below potential.
5. No participation in extracurricular activities.
6. Frequent change of schools.
7. Behavior problems requiring disciplinary measures.
8. Feeling of "not belonging" (because of size, speech, personality development, nationality, lack of friends among schoolmates or staff, etc.).

The characteristics that dealt with family were:
9. More children than parents can readily control.
10. Parents inconsistent in affection and discipline.
11. Unhappy family situation (common acceptance, communication, and pleasurable experiences lacking; family solidarity minimal).
12. Father figure weak or absent.
13. Education of parents at eighth grade level.
14. Few family friends; among these few, many problem units (divorces, desertions, delinquents, dropouts).

Among the factors listed under peers were:
15. Friends not approved by parents.
16. Friends not school-oriented.
17. Friends much older or much younger.

The factors listed under psychological orientation were:
18. Resentful of all authority.
19. Weak deferred gratification pattern.
20. Weak self-image.

What is striking about these characteristics is that so many of them deal with the circumstances involved with co-curricular and extracurricular activities. For example, usually there is a requirement that a student must be attending school and doing acceptable work before that student can participate in interscholastic competition. This requirement is traced to the National Collegiate Athletic Association, to State Activities Associations, and to local school districts, the famous "no pass, no play" approach.

In the case of instrumental music students, they usually learned their early music skills in an elementary "pull-out" program wherein the student could not leave the home classroom for instrumental music unless that student was working at or above the class average. Thus both athletics and instrumental music act as an external motivator for students who wish to participate in the activities. Further, athletics and music participation eliminate the six of the eight factors Cervantes mentions dealing with the school.

A seventh school factor, frequent change of school, is often eliminated because of residency requirements in athletics and a feeling of belonging in music groups. The eighth factor, behavior problems requiring disciplinary measures, is usually eliminated because of the threat of being forced off of the team or out of the music group.

A further look into Cervantes' factors show that all three of the factors listed under peers are met by the joining of a team or a music organization. The three factors listed under psychological orientation, resentful of authority, weak deferred gratification pattern and weak self-image, are directly combated by membership on a team or in a music group. The authority of the coach or director is unquestioned (or the student does not stay with the group) and in both athletics and music, the hours spent training and practicing in order to perform well at game or concert strengthens the deferred gratification pattern. Being a member strengthens and focuses the self image.

However, equally as striking is that Cervantes does not mention co-curricular and extracurricular activities in his proposed solutions. Without reproducing his entire book here, suffice to say that he proposes many solutions which deal with appropriate tracking of students into college or non-college orientations, with Minneapolis Comprehensive High School as the model (Cervantes, 1965).

A further series of suggestions deals with empowering counselors and teachers to become more understanding of the students and have more testing available to better direct the student. This, even after Cervante's own twenty characteristics list lack of involvement in extracurricular activities as number five. In a later study by the National School Public Relations Association (p.6), the seven-point profile of potential dropouts includes, "is not interested in extracurricular activities."

In the same study, the questionnaire given to students from Poudre Colorado R-1 District included the response "none" given to the question "Extracurricular activities in school" in eighty six percent (p.7) of the cases of dropouts, the highest single negative response on the questionnaire. Wells (1990, p. 32) makes the recommendation that to prevent dropout, schools should "involve students in extracurricular activities and school projects."

Almost every author who writes on dropout mentions the factor of absenteeism. Reid (1986, pp. 26-27) describes the absentee student as one who comes from an unsupportive background, has low self-concept because of constant, unrewarding school experiences, and tends to be a loner, having fewer friends in school than good attendees. Often schools will enter into alternative programs for truants that are short term because they rely on special funding from federal or state monies (Farrar & Hampel, 1989).

What seems to be missed here is the rather rudimentary concept that the student who does not drop out is the student who wants to go to school. There may be various reasons for this motivation, but by studying the dropouts, we cannot arrive at the reasons a student stays in school, only the reasons some dropouts will state for their action. To prevent dropout, we would do well to concentrate on why students stay in school (as well as why others drop out).

Equally missed in much of this literature is the fact that students have motivations of their own, and do not readily and automatically accept what adults believe their motivation ought to be. Thus, a student who has little or no success in school and is contemplating leaving school will be advised and taught that dropouts make barely a living wage, without a high school diploma (Berenbeim, 1993). This solution assumes that the student will take the dropout's lack of money and the problems associated therewith and use it as motivation to overcome the original problem of little or no success in school. It is possible, however, that the offered solution simply will induce stress into the student's life over his or her lack of success and engender further academic problems.

The adult logic of the connection between dropping out, lack of money, and future unhappiness is not felt by the student in the stressful situation of the moment. A better solution would be to help this student find some kind of success somewhere in school. If the student can achieve success in sports or instrumental music, then the "no pass, no play" motivation is immediate and direct. That student will tend to focus on whatever it takes that allows him or her to continue success in the school activity. And in these cases, school takes on a new connotation. It is no longer the place where the student fails, but it is the place that has the team or band that allows the student to succeed, and success in one area can breed success in another. For a student's higher level of self-esteem is built on successes, not the lack of them.

When a student is involved in activities, that student's parents are often involved as well. A glance at the audience at a game or concert confirms this observation. To complete the circle, the recent report from *Child Trends* (Zill and Nord, 1994) contends that students do better in school and are involved in more activities when their parents are involved in school related activities. The report decries the fact that many of today's parents yield influence to a student's peers and that schools do too little to encourage the continued involvement of parents.

Here, again, athletic and music activities can be seen as a method for schools to keep parents involved in schools where their offspring are doing well and succeeding in the activities. Parents can take pride in the accomplishments of their offspring, leading to further parental involvement, perhaps in "booster groups" and to greater self-esteem on the part of the student. This fulfills the recommendation of Farmer and Payne (1992, p. 81) when they call for the schools to "get parents involved in school."

The Colorado High School Activities Association, in conjunction with the Colorado Department of Education and the present writer, joined forces in the spring of 1992 to produce a major study (McCarthy, 1993) comparing high school students who participate in activities with high school students who do not participate. A stratified random sample of high schools was drawn to reflect the urban, suburban, rural, mountain, and plains communities in the state. Each school was contacted to supply data on student gender, ethnicity, at-risk status, socioeconomic status, absenteeism, cumulative grade point average, standardized test scores, and participation in activities. Data was collected on 6,799 students from fourteen high schools.

The study found that those students who participated in CHSAA sponsored activities (including athletics, instrumental music and choral music) have significantly higher (.001) cumulative grade point averages and a significantly lower (.001) rate of absence from school. These results are not affected by the students' socioeconomic level, ethnicity, or at-risk status. Preliminary analysis of the data gathered in a 1994 replication of the study shows exactly the same results, that students involved in athletics and instrumental music earn significantly higher GPA (.001) and standardized test scores (.01) and significantly lower absenteeism (.01).

According to the study, a participant missed school an average of 3.59 days in the two quarters reported while a non-participant missed 5.92 days (39 percent more days absent), a significant difference at the .05 level. High absentee rates are normally an indication that a student may be susceptible to dropping out of school and are listed by Cervantes in his characteristics of potential dropouts (Cervantes, 1965).

Further, the results were analyzed to compare at-risk students who participated in activities with the at-risk students who did not participate. In each school, the at-risk students who participated had higher GPAs and lower absenteeism than those who the school identified as at-risk but did not participate in activities.

The studies reviewed here show a direct relationship between student participation in instrumental music and athletics and the student's success in academic achievement. Further, the study demonstrates a strong relationship between these activities and attendance. Finally, the relationships mentioned here do not seem to be affected by the student's socio-economic level, gender, or at-risk status. In identifying characteristics of potential and actual dropouts, authors have consistently referred to the student's lack of involvement in activities. Yet the solutions brought forth in the literature have not centered on activities as an important element in the dropout problem. The authors consistently write about lack of involvement in activities, poor self-esteem, and lack of school friends, yet the same authors look outside the present system to create new programs to cure the dropout problem. (Finn, 1993) also reports that students engaged in extra-curricular activities are more likely to complete homework assignments, to pass grade level, and to have higher academic performance, regardless of gender or ethnicity.

This author contends that the solution to many dropout problems is already available in most schools. Involve students in an activity where students can succeed and involve them early, in the elementary grades if possible. The parents and parental involvement will naturally follow. The student will stay in school and succeed. Why would this be true? Because a student who commits to being the member of a team or the member of an instrumental music group is more than just a casual dilettante. The member of the team or group prepares for practice and rehearsal by doing added exercises and practice patterns. Further, the student who participates accepts the responsibility of being prepared for the game or concert. This is much different than the student who "hangs out" on a basketball court or "messes around" with a rock or rap group.

The students who take on the appearance of successful athlete or musician are the subject of Solomon's work on black students who drop out of academics and drop into a sports subculture. In his work, the students are not team members, but only seeking to fit an image. "If I don't have gym, I'm spaced out; I'm bored to death" (Solomon, 1993).

The lack of balance between the activity and academics, which could be brought into the situation by a full complement of school activities and a "no pass, no play" rule, causes students to believe they can succeed immediately by simply wishing to look like they have succeeded. In other words, they do not accept the responsibility of competition and regulation, but rather they accept only the non-threatening, outward appearances of successful athletes and musicians. If they can wear the correct basketball shoes or carry the correct music case, they can imagine themselves to be successful. But they accept no responsibility for their missing large basketball contracts or recording contracts.

In the eyes of these students, it is always someone else's fault, and usually has an element of prejudice or favoritism. These students are convinced that their talent is enough, but the world has yet to allow their success. These students are not accepting reality and should not be confused with the students who are accepting the responsibility of school team or music group membership.

Finally, many authors have written about the slide from school failure to disaffection to delinquency (Wehlage, et al., 1992, Polk and Schafer, 1972, and Wells, 1990). However, a recent interview with a Boulder, Colorado Juvenile Court Judge sheds light on the problem. Judge McLean stated that "in my court, I never have high school sport players nor band members brought up before me for sentencing " (McLean, 1995).

Perhaps the best statement of the value of co- and extra-curricular activities was stated by Bert Green (1966, p. 153). In his plan for preventing dropouts, he wrote that these activities often represent "the one and only part of school life that would provide any challenge and satisfaction to the student." When the student becomes engaged in the process involving sports or instrumental music, the student experiences what Wehlage, et al (1989, p. 186) call "the best innovations in curriculum" because the activity provides "both extrinsic and intrinsic rewards and provides for a broader range of opportunities for students to develop competence." But new programs are not necessary, they already exist within the school. These programs for preventing dropout, engaging at-risk students, and involving the parents are the instrumental music and interscholastic sports programs.

The ideas presented in this paper suggest ways in which to encourage black youth to remain in school and graduate from public school. When this reasoning is applied to the college situation, the resultant program, a Bachelor of Arts in Music with a major in folk music is the natural extension. The University of Colorado has led the way among state universities in developing this program. In this program, the students can combine their love of music, their authentic black music traditions, and their support from family and community to help them succeed.

—Dr. Kevin McCarthy is the Associate Dean for Music at the University of Colorado in Boulder, Colorado.

Bibliography

Barnes, Annie S. (1992). Retention of African-American males in high school. Lanham, Maryland: University Press of America.

Berenbeim, Ronald E. (1993). Corporate support of dropout prevention and work readiness. New York, The Conference Board.

Billingsley, Andrew (1968). Black families in white America. New York: Simon & Schuster, Inc.

_____ (1992). Climbing Jacob's Ladder. New York: Simon & Schuster, Inc.

Cervantes, Lucius F. (1965). The dropout: causes and cures. Ann Arbor: University of Michigan Press.

Farmer, James A. and Yolanda Payne (1992). Dropping out: issues and answers. Springfield: Charles C. Thomas Publisher.

Farrar, Eleanor and Robert L. Hampel (1989). Social services in high schools. In Lois Weis, Eleanor Farrar, and Hugh G. Petrie (Eds.). Dropouts from school: issues, dilemmas, and solutions. Albany: State University of New York Press.

Finn, Jeremy D. (1993). School engagement and students at risk. Washington, D.C.: National Center for Education Statistics.

Green, Bert I. (1966) Preventing student dropouts. Englewood Cliffs: Prentice-Hall, Inc.

LeCompte, Margaret Diane and Anthony Gary Dworkin (1991). Giving up on school: Student Dropouts and Teacher Burnouts. Newbury Park, Cal.: Corwin Press, Inc.

McLean, Richard. (1995). Interview with Judge McLean by Kevin J. McCarthy on March 3, 1995 at The Med, Boulder, Colorado.

McCarthy, Kevin J. (1993). Activities and academic achievement, The demonstrable line, in Creating the Quality School. Norman, OK. University of Oklahoma, 279-281.

Ogbu, John U. (1992). Understanding Cultural Diversity and Learning. Educational Researcher. November, 1992. p. 5-14.

Parental involvement urged. (September 5, 1994). Rocky Mountain News. p. 58A.

Reid, K. (1983) Retrospection and persistent school absenteeism. Educational Research, 25, 2, 110-115.

Reid, K. (1984) Some social, psychological and educational aspects related to persistent school absenteeism. Research in Education, 31, 63-82.

Reid, K. (1986) Disaffection from school. London: Methuen & Co., Ltd.

Sheffield, Anne and Bruce Frankel (eds.) (1988) When I was young and loved school: dropping out and hanging in. New York, Children's Express Press, Inc.

Solomon, R. Patrick (1989). Dropping out of academics: black youth and the sports subculture in a cross-national perspective. In Lois Weis, Eleanor Farrar, and Hugh G. Petrie (Eds.). Dropouts from school: issues, dilemmas, and solutions. Albany: State University of New York Press.

Tyerman, M.J. (1958) A research into truancy. British Journal of Educational Psychology, 28, 217-225.

Tyerman, M.J. (1968) Truancy. London, University of London Press.

Walker-Hill, Helen. (1992). Music by black women composers at the American Music Research Center. American Music Research Center Journal, 2, 23-52.

Wehlage, Gary G., Robert A. Rutter, Gregory A. Smith, Nancy Lesko, and Ricardo R. Fernandez (1989). Reducing the risk: schools as communities of support. New York: The Falmer Press.

Wells, Shirley E. (1990). At-risk youth: identification, programs, and recommendations. Englewood, Colorado: Teacher Ideas Press.

Zill, Nicholas, and Christine Nord, "Running in place" report from Child Trends, financed by Robert Wood Johnson Foundation and Nord Family Foundation, Rocky Mountain News, Mon. Sept. 1994, p. 58a.

The Preparatory Division

by J. Blaine Hudson

Overview:

In 1975, the University of Louisville established the West Louisville Educational Program (WLEP) to provide developmental instruction and academic support services to one hundred academically underprepared African-American freshmen each year. In 1982, because of the effectiveness of WLEP and the dramatic growth of the University's underprepared student population, the WLEP model was expanded into an academic unit—the Preparatory Division—with a service capacity of over one thousand students.

The Preparatory Division offers a structured program of placement testing, academic advising and counseling, developmental instruction in the basic skills, individual and small group tutoring. While the division serves students from the general university population, students admitted to the division usually remain enrolled for one year before transferring to a degree-granting unit. Between 1982 and 1990, 2,146 students, or 61.9 percent of all students admitted to the division, achieved eligibility to transfer to a degree-granting school or college. African-American students represented roughly 25 percent of the division's aggregate population and were 26 percent of the transfer population.

The Preparatory Division represents a comprehensive freshman admitting unit that evolved from a successful minority retention program. Although no longer a minority retention program, per se, the division is the only academic unit of the university from which African-American students derive equal or greater benefit than do students from other racial groups. Redesignated, "the Division of Transitional Studies" in 1993, the division continues to serve several thousand students each year.

Introduction

Virtually any educational policy, program or practice can be organized and oriented to the benefit or detriment of students of color—to expand or restrict their access and/or to enhance or limit their retention in American colleges and universities. Consequently, because all students can benefit measurably from the same mix of programs and services, many of the most effective "minority retention" programs are curricula and services that simply work well for students in general. Conversely, merely designating a program as a "minority retention" effort does not guarantee that "minority retention" is the actual purpose of the program or, even if so, that "minority retention" will be achieved.

Of course, the fact that few programs, regardless of how broadly or narrowly focused their missions, promote the achievement of these objectives reflects how higher educational institutions choose, often unwittingly, to perpetuate structural race and class inequalities. This need not be so—as exemplified by the Preparatory Division of the University of Louisville (renamed the Division of Transitional Studies in 1993). The Division belongs to the long history of initiatives to democratize the access and enhance the outcomes of students of color, primarily African-American students, in American higher educational institutions—and represents a comprehensive freshman admitting academic unit that evolved from a "minority retention" program.

The Evolution of the Preparatory Division

The University of Louisville traces its origins to the founding of the Jefferson Seminary in 1798. Although the university existed primarily on paper until 1840, and operated as a collection of professional schools until 1907, it was closed to African-American students until 1931—when, as a result of organized political pressure from the local African-American community, the university established Louisville Municipal College for Negroes as a "black branch" of the larger institution (Cox, 1980).

Real and threatened legal action by the NAACP prompted the Kentucky General Assembly to amend the Commonwealth's educational segregation statute in 1950, which resulted in the end of legal segregation in Kentucky higher education and the closing of Municipal College in 1951 (Hudson, 1994). A comparatively small number of "very traditional" and well-prepared African-American students attended the university through the mid-1960s. However, in the late 1960s, student and community activists pressured the university successfully to create an office of Black Affairs (now Minority Services), a Pan-African Studies Department, and special scholarship and support programs for African-American students. These actions, and the adoption of an "open admission" policy when the university became a fully public institution in 1970, caused a dramatic upsurge in the enrollment of African-American and other "non-traditional" students (Hudson, 1992).

110

While many of these "new" students were reasonably well-prepared, a great many were not and a disproportionate segment of the underprepared population was comprised of African-Americans, other students of color, and poor students of all races. Clearly, this phenomenon was not specific to the university. To illustrate using national data, during this same time period, between twenty and thirty percent of all first-time freshmen were academically deficient in at least one basic skill (i.e., literacy or numeracy) area (Lederman, et al., 1983; U. S. Department of Education, 1985)—and two-thirds of the African-American high school graduates who later attended college were academically underprepared (Weinberg, 1983; Willie, et al., 1991).

Without special attention and assistance, the "open door," using the metaphor common in the 1970s, all too often became a "revolving door." Because African-Americans were overrepresented among the academically underprepared, the issues of racial equity, access, developmental education, and retention became merely different aspects of the same problem. More often than not, African-Americans became the intended or unintended beneficiaries of programs designed to assist academically underprepared students, while underprepared students, regardless of race, usually benefitted significantly from programs to assist students of color.

By 1974-1975, the higher incidence of academic underpreparation, and the high failure and attrition rates of African-American students at the University of Louisville prompted the Kentucky General Assembly to create the West Louisville Educational Program (WLEP). WLEP targeted students predominantly from the "West End" of Louisville, where roughly forty percent of the entire African-American population of Kentucky resided, and was based administratively in University College, the academic unit through which the university's open admission policy was implemented. WLEP was structured, initially, along lines similar to those proposed originally (1969) for the academic support component of the Office of Black Affairs, i.e., as something of a "hard-money" special services (now Student Support Services) program for 100 African-American freshmen each year. WLEP offered intensive academic counseling and advising, individual and small group tutoring, an intensive six-week "summer program", a university orientation course, and remedial/developmental instruction in reading, writing and mathematics (Hudson, 1978a; Hudson, 1978b; Hudson, 1980).

WLEP developed and implemented innovative service delivery and instructional systems—and proved extremely effective. For example, WLEP students outperformed and persisted at higher rates than did underprepared students in general and even well prepared white and African-American students not served by the program (Hudson, 1980). However, even with the establishment of a federally-funded special services program in 1978 and several other scattered service and instructional offerings, the burgeoning population of underprepared

111

students still far exceeded the combined service capacities of these programs. Consequently, by 1980, nearly half of all freshmen and more than two-thirds of all African-American freshmen admitted to the university (well over 1000 students each year) required academic assistance and there was no comprehensive, organized approach to meeting their academic and non-academic needs (Hudson, & Fitzpatrick, 1982).

In essence, the university had first failed to anticipate and then failed to adapt to the implications of becoming a fully public institution in 1970. These failures, moreover, were magnified when, after Kentucky was included under the Adams ruling in 1980, the university was assigned specific targets for increasing African-American student enrollment, retention and graduation rates, and increasing the representation of African-American faculty and staff (Hudson, 1992).

By 1981, these fundamental problems, along with the impact of recurrent budget reductions, prompted a comprehensive reorganization of the university, which included the disestablishment of University College, a decision to end open admissions, attempts to eliminate the Office of Affirmative Action and the Department of Pan-African Studies. These crises created a "window of opportunity" to propose what was then considered a radical solution to the dilemma of how best to serve underprepared students: the consolidation of all remedial/developmental instructional programs, all tutorial programs for under-graduates (excluding student athletes), and all other compensatory educational programs under one administrative superstructure. Because of the long record of effectiveness of WLEP, this consolidated unit would expand the WLEP program model into that of a bona fide academic unit—which would serve a university-wide population, but to which underprepared freshmen would be admitted formally, and in which they would remain until eligible for admission to a degree-granting unit.

After considerable debate, the university president and board of trustees accepted this proposal, in principle, and voted to establish the Preparatory Division, effective July 1, 1982. However, the trustees and the president assumed that, given the national emphasis on "back-to-basics education" in the early Reagan era, developmental education would have a "sunset date", i.e., would soon become unnecessary. Consequently, the division was to be a transitional unit that would be absorbed by a new academic unit, the Basic College, within two years (Hudson, & Fitzpatrick, 1982).

Organization and Administration

Most of the critical choices in the history of the Preparatory Division were made in the months immediately preceding and following its creation. In retrospect, the most important strategic decision made by the leadership of the division was to proceed as though the unit was "permanent," although it was created as a temporary expedient. Given this strategy, administrative autonomy, programmatic viability, and budgetary self-sufficiency were critical and controversial issues surrounding the origins of the division.

With respect to administration and the "place" of the Preparatory Division in the university hierarchy, it was proposed and accepted that the director of the division would report to the chief academic officer of the university (i.e., initially, the vice president for academic affairs and, after 1983, the university provost). Although not a "dean," per se, the director of the division had an equivalent status. Similarly, the Preparatory Division was assigned the status of an administrative academic unit, i.e., a non-degree granting admitting unit with far-reaching service responsibilities. Because faculty could not hold regular appointments in the division, the Preparatory Division Educational Policy Advisory Committee (PREPAC), comprised of faculty from the undergraduate degree-granting units, was created to serve in an advisory role to the director and the provost.

The Preparatory Division was organized into two major internal subdivisions: instructional programs, with separate units for English, reading, mathematics and developmental education (i.e., critical thinking, et al.); and academic support services, with separate units for academic counseling/advising, special services, Upward Bound and university tutorial services. The director was responsible for overall administration, instructional programs and Upward Bound. An associate director shared overall administrative responsibilities with the director, and was responsible for daily operations, planning and budgeting, academic support services, special services and research. Each internal unit was headed by a coordinator who reported either to the director or associate director. Part-time instructors, clerical staff, graduate assistants, tutors and student workers reported to the appropriate coordinator or administrator.

While the Preparatory Division represented one of the earliest large scale efforts to address the needs of academically underprepared students, its existence threatening to more traditional faculty-centered units and strained relations ensued between the division, other academic units and even the university administration were problematic for many years. One source of this dynamic tension, as suggested earlier, was the conflict between those who wished to exclude poor students and students of color from, or marginalize them within, American higher education—and those who wished to democratize access to and equalize the outcomes of enrollment in higher educational institutions. These tensions reflected the conflicting "racial projects" of the Civil Rights and post-Civil Rights eras in the larger society—and shaped much of the early history of the unit.

A related source of this tension was rooted in the racial composition of the Preparatory Division's service population—and, for that matter, the administration, staff and part-time faculty of the division. To illustrate, although African-

American students were never more than thirty-five percent of the students enrolled in the division, they were less than seven percent of the remainder of the university, and the Preparatory Division was perceived by many as the university's unit for black students. Moreover, the division was the only major academic/budgetary unit of the university with African-Americans and/or women in virtually all significant administrative positions.

Consequently, many hoped the division would fail and others merely accepted the necessity of its presence for pragmatic reasons, e.g., maintaining enrollment (given that the university had a funding formula that was enrollment driven). Others, as the Preparatory Division proved successful, waited eagerly for the Basic College to emerge—which became less likely as the division became more firmly institutionalized. Thus, creating the Preparatory Division was a major victory, but making it work and preserving it were equally challenging.

Strategies: Programs, Policies and Practices

The transition from program status to the status of a major academic unit required that a complex process of evolution be compressed into only a few months. Planning and budgeting, facilities management, administrative and clerical support systems had to be devised. A far more elaborate system of internal coordination, control, and program interfaces, which had been the key to the effectiveness of WLEP, had to be organized and implemented. As an academic unit, policies had to be developed and implemented governing testing, course placement, academic advising, student records, academic progress (i.e., probation, dismissal, transfer), cross-registration in college level courses, and transfer to a degree-granting unit. Moreover, all policies pertaining directly to students had to be publicized to meet legal requirements.

The resolution of these critical policy and programmatic issues resulted in the implementation of a systematic approach to developmental education and academic support services. This "system" involved the following essential elements:
1) "open" or reasonably open admission standards which permitted students several options with respect to establishing their admissibility;
2) initial placement testing in reading (using the Nelson Denny Reading Test), writing (using a writing sample evaluated by the Division's English unit) and mathematics (using a local test developed by the Division's Mathematics unit and the Department of Mathematics);
3.) a comprehensive and sequenced developmental curriculum in the basic skills areas, i.e., reading, writing and mathematics (open to all university students);
4) specific placement guidelines for developmental and college level courses;
5) required academic advising;
6) a required, two-semester sequence of university orientation courses (taught by division counselors);

114

7) regular academic, personal and career counseling;

8) easy access to individual and small group tutoring (open to all university students); and

9) an academic assessment phase following each semester in which staff and administrators reviewed all student records, entered appropriate academic actions (i.e., transfer, probation, dismissal), and communicated these decisions to the university registrar and to the students.

The counseling/advising unit, with its responsibility for the orientation course(s) and through a series of interfaces with the instructional and tutorial components, was the linchpin of the division. Consequently, the presence of a strong contingent of competent, dedicated, student-oriented and diverse (by race and gender) student personnel professionals was a key to operationalizing and sustaining the Preparatory Division model.

In essence, students admitted to the Preparatory Division received all division services. Students admitted to other academic units had access to services as needed or based on unit requirements (e.g., based on ACT sub-test scores or placement test scores, they may have been required to take one of the English or mathematics courses offered through the division as a prerequisite to a college-level requirement). Division policies, requirements and unit descriptions were communicated to students, the university community and the larger community through documents, press releases and interviews, meetings and, eventually, a separate "catalog" for the unit.

Finally, the on-going outcomes assessment process developed in WLEP, which entailed end-of-semester quantitative and qualitative evaluations of the performance of each internal program component, had to be adapted to the Preparatory Division. This continuous feed-back loop would produce a wealth of data and several major studies of division operations and outcomes over the ensuing decade. Moreover, the creation of an information-rich environment enabled the division to track enrollment and performance trends over time and to identify, and correct, areas in which race or gender differences in performance and retention may have surfaced. Thus, from its inception and by conscious design, the Preparatory Division was a student-centered, as opposed to a faculty-centered, academic unit.

Outcomes

The most crucial measure of success for Preparatory Division students, and of the effectiveness of the division itself, was the rate at which students admitted to the division achieved eligibility to transfer to a degree-granting unit. Students were allowed only the equivalent of one year of full-time enrollment in which to accomplish this task and, in this limited context, transfer was synonymous with short-term retention. Beyond this, long-term retention was possible only for students who had crossed this first threshold and was a second crucial measure of effectiveness, i.e., of how well the Preparatory Division's services prepared students to move through their college careers.

To summarize the results of several evaluative studies (Hudson, 1985; Hudson, 1986; Hudson, 1991c), between the end of the spring of 1983 and the end of the spring of 1990, a total of 2,939 students achieved eligibility to transfer from the Preparatory Division to a degree-granting unit. This total represents 61.9 percent of all students admitted to the division during this period.

Table 1
Preparatory Division Enrollment and Transfer Patterns: 1983-1989 (Fall Semester data)

Semester	First-Time Students Admitted	Students Who Transferred	%
Fall 1983	782	449	57.4
Fall 1984	629	357	57.8
Fall 1985	501	309	61.7
Fall 1986*	391	263	67.3
Fall 1987	326	251	77.0
Fall 1988	387	264	68.2
Fall 1989	451	253	56.1
Total	3,467	2,146	61.9

* implementation of selective admission standards.

There were no statistically significant differences by race or gender in these transfer patterns over time. African-American students had comprised roughly twenty-five percent of the Preparatory Division's population between 1982 and 1990—and represented 26.0 percent of the aggregate transfer population. Similarly, women had been roughly half of the Division's population and represented 56.2 percent of the transfer population.

Obviously, the connection between the Preparatory Division and its former students becomes attenuated over time and the long-term performance and retention of division students can be defined as the cumulative effect or confluence of a number of contributory factors:

• the quality of academic preparation received in the division;
• the quality of instruction and support received in the degree-granting unit(s);
• the personal motivation of the students; and
• the external circumstances of the students' lives—over which neither the university nor often the students themselves have much control.

Consequently, long-term retention patterns were far more complex. However, the aggregate patterns are reflected in Table 2:

Table 2

Aggregate Retention Pattern: 1983 - 1989 (Fall Semester data)

Students who could have:*	#	Transfers Retained	%	%**	Cumulative Attrition
Completed Year 1	3,467	2,793	80.6	90	- 10%
Returned Year 2***	3,016	2,190	72.6	80	- 20%
Returned Year 3	2,629	1,398	53.2	55	- 45%
Returned Year 4	2,303	873	37.9	38	- 62%
Returned Year 5	1,912	597	31.2	31	- 69%

* Cumulative total of first-time students admitted 1983-1989, Fall semesters only.

** Estimated adjustment to include non-transfers who were also retained.

*** Years of attendance need not be consecutive, i.e., stopouts are included.

Through the spring of 1990, 309 Preparatory Division students had graduated from the university, primarily students admitted between the fall of 1982 and the fall of 1985. This represented roughly twenty-five percent of the students transferred during that period—with many transfers still enrolled. Both the aggregate retention figures and the graduation data were comparable to similar statistics for the university as a whole.

It is important to note that the division did not build its record of effectiveness by serving well-prepared students "in disguise." Apart from the racial and gender breakdowns noted above, these transfer students, and Preparatory Division students in general, were genuinely underprepared and non-traditional. For example, using the "old" ACT, the mean ACT English sub-test score for the Preparatory Division transfer students was 12.26, while the mean ACT mathematics sub-test score was 9.35 and the mean ACT composite score was 12.23. The mean cumulative high school grade-point average was 2.40. Virtually all students in this population were required to enroll in at least one developmental course in reading, English and mathematics prior to transfer. Moreover, nearly sixty percent of these students received some type of financial aid, nearly sixty-five percent worked full- or part-time, and nearly sixty-five percent were first-generation college students.

In addition, as a third component of the assessment of unit effectiveness and as part of the Preparatory Division's on-going research effort, each internal component of the division was studied in-depth at least once between 1982 and 1992. The results of these studies were consistently positive, particularly as they related to academic outcomes for students of color and women (Hudson, 1991a; Hudson, 1991b; Hudson, 1989; Hudson, 1987a; Hudson, 1990; Hudson, 1988; Hudson, 1987b; Hudson, 1987c; Hudson, et al., 1993).

In the spring of 1992, on the strength of this record, the National Center for Developmental Education recognized the Preparatory Division as one of the best (top five percent) programs of its kind in the nation.

Conclusion

No educational program is ever a finished creation. As a postscript, neither the establishment of the Preparatory Division in 1982 nor its existence thereafter were uncontested. The more politically and racially conservative faculty remained suspicious and often hostile toward the unit, and continually challenged its autonomy and policies. Colleagues whose racial and class biases had convinced them the Preparatory Division could do nothing other than fail, because division students were assumed to be innately incapable, were not at all happy when division students succeeded. Rather than question their racial/class stereotypes, they assumed the Preparatory Division was something of an "outlaw unit," flooding the degree-granting units with students who were still "unfit." Fortunately, because the Preparatory Division engaged in constant self-assessment (at a time when few programs in higher education did), ample data were available—for defensive or offensive purposes—with which to affirm the effectiveness of the unit and the legitimacy of the achievements of its students. Still, to many colleagues, the Preparatory Division, left to its own devices, was working too well.

At the heart of the interminable controversies between 1982 and 1991 was the question of the ends the Preparatory Division was expected to serve—i.e., its original mission and vision, or another more conservative and exclusionary ("cooling out") purpose—and the type of division leadership best suited to this task. However, in 1985, once the notion of creating a Basic College was finally shelved, a plan, supported by many traditional faculty members, to place the Preparatory Division under the administrative control of either the School of Education or the College of Arts and Sciences was rejected by the president of the university.

Other challenges and responses followed. In 1986, despite the record of the Preparatory Division, the university adopted moderately selective admission standards which restricted access to the institution and thereby constricted the flow of students into the division. African-American students were affected disproportionately by these new standards. However, the new policy allowed students to establish their admissibility on the basis of ACT scores, high school grade-point average, or basic skills competency tests. Consequently, the

Preparatory Division initiated special efforts (e.g., letters, telephone calls) to encourage students to avail themselves of the basic skills testing admission option if their ACT scores and high school grades were low (Hudson, 1986; Hudson, 1990).

Finally, in 1991, the College of Arts and Sciences was permitted to redefine its admission policy, making transfer from the Preparatory Division more difficult and transforming the division, potentially, from an "avenue of educational opportunity" into something of a "holding unit" for underprepared students—which still included the bulk of the African-Americans in each entering freshman class. On the other hand, in 1993, the Preparatory Division absorbed several retention programs for "better prepared minority students" (after their budgets had been drastically "downsized") and was renamed the Division of Transitional Studies. Although the service population of the division expanded as a result, the full impact of the totality of these changes cannot be evaluated as yet.

Several lessons can be gleaned from the history and current status of the Preparatory Division. With respect to minority retention programs and higher educational programs in general, any one of the following mutually exclusive propositions can be true of a particular program at any given time:

1) a program designed to serve "all" students may serve "all" . students effectively;

2) a program designed to serve "all" students may serve only "some" students effectively, i.e., usually more affluent students of European descent;

3) a program designed to serve "some" students may serve both its target population and other students effectively, i.e., it may assist both its intended and many unintended beneficiaries;

4) a program designed to serve "some" students may serve only its target population effectively; and, finally,

5) a program designed to serve "some" students may serve no one effectively.

The best or most favored of these programs have evolved, as had the Preparatory Division by 1985, from programs characterized by proposition #3, which may have evolved themselves from the status referenced in proposition #4, into the status reflected in proposition #1.

At this stage in its history, the role of the Preparatory Division as an academic unit remains intact although diminished in importance. Its role in offering developmental instruction remains significant and its role as an academic support services unit has been enhanced somewhat. Students of color are still well served by the division and the division remains a model for other programs. However, as the university's commitment has shifted subtly from a concern for providing comprehensive services to academically underprepared students to a preference for providing minimal services to the underprepared and assisting smaller numbers of better prepared students, the role and orientation of the division have shifted as well.

A clearly conceptualized and workable model, competent leadership, genuine institutional commitment and sustained community/regional need are common to the most effective minority retention programs. Based on these criteria, WLEP and the Preparatory Division embodied what works best, both in the short- and long-term, with respect to the retention of academically underprepared students and students of color.

—Dr. J. Blaine Hudson is the Director of the Pan-African Studies Institute for Teachers at the University of Louisville at Louisville, Kentucky.

References

Cox, D. (1980). A brief history of the University of Louisville. Louisville: University of Louisville Archives and Records.

Hudson, J. B. (1991a). Access and African-American students: The impact of selective admission standards. Unpublished manuscript, Preparatory Division, University of Louisville.

Hudson, J. B. (1991b). The achievement of college-level status by developmental students. Unpublished manuscript, Preparatory Division, University of Louisville.

Hudson, J. B. (1989). An analysis of ACT scores, placement tests, and academic performance in reading, English, and mathematics. (ERIC Document Reproduction Service No. ED 3 3 4 916).

Hudson, J. B. (1994). The establishment of Louisville Municipal College: A case study in racial conflict and compromise. Manuscript accepted for publication in the Journal of Negro Education.

Hudson, J. B. (1987a). Follow-up contacts with Fall 1987 minimum admissions students. Unpublished manuscript, Preparatory Division, University of Louisville.

Hudson, J. B. (1990). The impact of minimum admission standards: 1986 - 1989. (ERIC Document Reproduction Service No. ED 334 917).

Hudson, J. B. (1991a). The long-term performance and retention of Preparatory Division transfer students: 1983 - 1990. (ERIC Document Reproduction Service No. ED 334 918).

Hudson, J. B. (1980). The long-term persistence rates of West Louisville Educational Program students. Unpublished manuscript, University College, University of Louisville.

Hudson, J. B. (1988). The operations and outcomes of the University Tutoring Program: 1986-1987. (ERIC Document Reproduction Service No. ED 334 915).

Hudson, J. B. (1985). Preparatory Division: 1983-1984 retention study. Unpublished manuscript, Preparatory Division, University of Louisville.

Hudson, J. B. (1991d). The Preparatory Division: Continuity and Change. Minority Voices, 13 , 63-64.

Hudson, J. B. (1992). The status of minority students, faculty and staff at the University of Louisville: 1987 1991. Unpublished manuscript, Minority Advisory Committee, Office of the President, University of Louisville.

Hudson, J. B. (1987b). A study of the academic performance and progress of students placed in remedial mathematics: 1985-1986. (ERIC Document Reproduction Service No. ED 334 914).

Hudson, J. B. (1986). A study of the academic performance and retention patterns of Preparatory Division transfer students, 1983-1985. Unpublished manuscript, Preparatory Division, University of Louisville.

Hudson, J. B. (1987c). The performance and progress of students placed in English 098 and English 099: 1985-1986. Unpublished manuscript, Preparatory Division, University of Louisville.

Hudson, J. B. (1978a). West Louisville Educational Program: Research reports I-XVII. Unpublished manuscript, University College, University of Louisville.

Hudson, J. B. (1978b). West Louisville Educational Program Student profile and data analysis: Conclusions and summary. Unpublished manuscript, University College, University of Louisville.

Hudson, J. B., and Fitzpatrick, R. (1982). Preparatory Division: Planning Abstract. Unpublished manuscript, University College, University of Louisville.

Hudson, J. B., McPhee, S. A., and Petrosko, J. M. (1993). The relationship between tests, course placement, and the academic performance of college freshmen. NACADA Journal: The Journal of the National Academic Advising Association, 13, 2, 5 - 14.

Lederman, M., Ryzewic, S., and Ribaudo, M. (1983). Assessment and improvement of academic skills of entering freshmen students: A national survey. New York: Instructional Resource Center, CUNY.

U.S. Department of Education. (1985). Many college freshmen take remedial courses. National Center for Educational Statistics.

Weinberg, M. (1983). The search for quality integrated education: Policy and research on minority students in school and college. Westport, CN: Greenwood Press.

Willie, C. V., Garibaldi, A. M., and Reed, Wornie L. (1991). The education of African-Americans. New York: Auburn House.

Project BEAM – Being Excited About Me

by Horace E. Belmear

Overview:

Being Excited About Me (BEAM) is a program that was established at West Virginia University to assist students of color in gaining admission to WVU and then succeeding academically once they matriculated.

In addition, the program also has the grave responsibility of influencing students' self-esteem and to act as a motivator keeping them in school, with optimal excitement and involvement started early. BEAM focuses on the development of the whole student: physical, spiritual, intellectual, social and emotional. BEAM is premised on the importance of first establishing a one-to-one relationship with the prospective students and their parents, getting to know them, establishing trust, and gaining their commitment to the program beyond the admission to the university.

Top administrators recognized at the outset that BEAM represented a complete change from the established program for recruitment and retention of African-Americans and other students.

In this article, the author provides a detailed account of BEAM's programming components, services and goals.

Introduction

The struggle African-American and other students of color face in gaining admission to institutions of higher learning, and then to attain academic success at those institutions, is an issue every college and university must deal with if they are to hold true to their mission of providing equal educational opportunity for all.

To encourage and support the successful matriculation, retention and eventual graduation of African-American students, it is imperative that recruitment and retention efforts are linked. Early intervention is paramount to the success of effective recruiting/retention.

At West Virginia University, the first effort toward that end was to develop a systemwide state newsletter and disseminate it to the feeder schools of the community. This acted as a messenger to families and key community-spirited people, expressing concern about minority students' preparation for, admission to, and retention in college.

From this humble beginning, the West Virginia University "Being Excited About Me" (BEAM) program was developed. BEAM is a strategic program designed to improve African-Americans' coping abilities at predominately white colleges and universities.

Program Components

Although many facets of the BEAM program were already in use in 1980, it was not until 1982 that a retention program was incorporated as part of the recruitment efforts at West Virginia University.

The program has evolved over the years into its present comprehensive form. The heart of BEAM is found in its promotional activities and support services. The following is a closer look into what comprises the BEAM program:

Satellite Office:

This office is part of the Admissions Office located at the Charleston Medical Center, Charleston, WV. This site was chosen to be in close proximity to the largest population of African-Americans in West Virginia. The office is staffed by a director and a secretary; the office reports to the director of BEAM.

Academic Majors Clubs:

These clubs were originally used as a means of getting minority freshmen to meet and know each other; all freshmen were invited to join the club of their major. One drawback was that many freshmen were not positive of their intended major. Another drawback was that many stopped attending these clubs after their freshman year.

After a few years, freshmen were not invited to join the academic clubs, but rather, after being advised at one of the pre-enrollment seminars, they were asked to join the now-existing Pass Key program—a program sponsored and funded by the counseling center. This program is staffed with a director and a number of peer counselors, the number depending on how many minority freshmen were enrolled.

The Academic Majors Club is reserved for sophomores and up; upperclassmen act as mentors and give counseling. For this program to be successful, counselors should be trained and paid for their services.

Mentoring Program:

The mentoring program started with having black faculty, administrators, directors, staff employees, and community people willing to serve as mentors. These people would pull names of students from a basket, and they would contact those students. Although this was not the best way to organize a mentoring program, it served to show concern. Later, a task force was organized to study the mentoring program, and from that, there are now trained mentors, and the matching-up process is more developed. This program works well now.

Annual Report:

This report is a complete report of the year's work in recruiting and retention, with statistical numbers and evaluation of all programs.

The report was distributed to the president, department heads, the state board, some clubs and organizations, and community organizations throughout the state to include Inroads, Upward Bound programs, and other selected organizations.

Admission Seminars:

These seminars are conducted on campus and in the communities. Staff travel extensively in recruitment/retention efforts. A videotape was produced for these seminars to highlight campus support services with much action and appeal. The seminars are announced in local church and school bulletins.

Pre-Enrollment Seminars:

These programs are conducted either in churches, hotels, or libraries for students admitted to the university. Their friends and parents are invited to attend. The seminar addresses the final concerns of the students and parents regarding such things as class scheduling, financial aid, organizational involvement, residence and roommates.

Retention Workshops:

The West Virginia State Governing Board, showing a great concern for retention and the role of secondary schools, colleges and communities of the state, established a committee to explore these issues. The chancellor appoints two university representatives, two college representatives, and two State Board representatives to serve on the committee. Their task is to organize and plan for workshops each year.

The committee invites the presidents of every college in the state; high school and college counselors; Upward Bound directors; community leaders, parents, and students to attend these workshops.

Campus Visitation (African-American Student Information Day):

Admission counselors identify small groups of African-American students to bring to campus, and they provide bus or van transportation throughout the year. Efforts are also made to provide on-campus housing for the groups through the Housing and Residence Life Department.

In targeted areas, out-of-state community organizations and college awareness programs are asked to sponsor campus visitation day. Visits are emphasized on Hype Day, which is specifically designed to provide information to African-American students and their families.

Cultural Center:

The Center for Black Culture and Research was established in 1987 to contribute to the quality of life of African and African-American students on campus. The center assists students in a wide range of areas, including adjustment to university life, problem-solving, and general academic advising by providing a variety of support services and programs. One center outreach effort is the Health Science Seminar for middle school students.

Office of Student Life:

The Office of Student Life is committed to serving the black students in all aspects of campus life, just as it is to the general student population.

Financial Aid Office:

The Financial Aid Office reserves campus-based funds for late African-American applicants. This department's staff participates in various information sessions for pre-college African-Americans.

Career Services Center:

This center assumes the responsibility for ensuring that programs, resources and internships are extended to African-American students.

University Advising Center:

The University Advising Center incorporates minority student advising into their training program. Twice yearly a professional staff person presents a training workshop to academic advisors addressing the issues involved in advising minority students.

Counseling and Psychological Services Center:

This center is very cooperative in rendering services to African-American students with respect to their counseling needs. It also conducts research on the African-American student experience.

Pass-Key I AND II:

This program is specifically designed to facilitate African-American student retention. Pass-Key I provides mentoring, support and facilitation for African-American freshmen (students receive one hour of course credit).

Pass-Key II is a three-credit hour course offered in cooperation with the Department of Psychology; it focuses on the unique adjustment tasks that African-American students face in a predominantly white society (both on campuses and in the broader society).

President's Visiting Committee on African-American Affairs:

This committee's membership consists of alumni and professional leaders from the community. The membership term is at least two years.

The committee's mission statement includes

- identification of African-American issues and concerns
- development of recruitment and retention strategies
- promotion of a sense of community
- establishment of a positive climate for the African-American community
- evaluation of institutional efforts in this area
- acting as liaison with the African-American community beyond campus, and with key African-American leaders
- assisting in recruitment and career placement of African-American students
- supporting development efforts on behalf of the African-American community

Black Community Concerns Committee:

The purpose of the University Black Community Concerns Committee is to promote and encourage institution-wide activities and initiatives in conjunction with the Social Justice Council, a council supported by the president of the university and other organizations. Their goal is to increase and retain the number of African-American students, faculty and staff on campus. This committee's membership is made up of faculty, staff, and students; fourteen of its twenty-one members should be black.

Special Assistant to the President for Social Justice:

This office serves as the permanent chair of the Social Justice Council and is a member of the university cabinet.

Social Justice Council:

This council is a coalition charged with responsibility for providing coordination of the work and activities of the various protective groups.

The Division of Student Affairs:

In 1990, the Division of Student Affairs established African-American student retention as its number-one priority. The deans, directors, and key staff of the Division of Student Affairs suggested a task force on the issues and problems of African-American student retention in April 1990. The task force indicated the university's current efforts on African-American student retention were insufficient and uncoordinated and warranted improvement. Consequently, the committee recommended that a coordinated approach be undertaken to improve student retention, and this approach manifested itself in BEAM.

Senior Administrators:

Senior administrators regularly monitor information about progress in increasing retention and graduation rates of students. Senior administrators meet regularly with pre-college institutions, promoting the efforts of the BEAM program.

BEAM Operating Plan
(Academic Year – July Through June)

- Promotion: July through June
- Data Base Manager: July through August
- Student Selection and Scheduling: July through August
- Orientation: July, August and September
- Pre-College Programs: July through June
- Assessments and Referrals: July through June
- Mentoring: September through June

Specific Activities:

- Identify feeder high schools and other related schools
- Establish contacts with the outreach Programs
- Promote workshops in feeder communities on college experiences for students and parents
- Visit the feeder schools and other community helpers at least two times a year
- Promote a "parent-school" relationship organization
- Seek financial assistance
- Establish an alumni network to initiate an African-American mentoring program
- Conduct graduate and professional workshops

BEAM Development Plan

(Submitted to associate provost for student activities and director of admission and records.)

The plan includes:

1. Promotion

2. Database Management

3. Feeder School Selections

4. Student Selection

5. Documentation

6. Assessments

7. Mentoring

Plan Elements Examined:

1. Goals: the BEAM goals are to influence students' self-esteem and to motivate students to stay in school with optimal excitement and involvement. This influence speaks to the following needs of minority students:

- physical

- spiritual

- intellectual

- social

- emotional

Paramount to this is a successful pre-college program. The preparation received at the pre-college stage should include:

- psychological

- social

- economic

- academic

- emotional

- discipline

- diversity sensitivity

2. Promotional principles include:

- seeking institutional and state commitments;

- making personal contacts with students and families;

- setting up conferences and interviews with high school administrators, faculties, and counselors;

- conducting systematic data collections on students seeking admission to the college; and
- developing programs for admitted students.

3. Group orientation: exploration of strengths and weaknesses, academic preparations and community activities and achievements, including special skills and talents.

4. Database management: much care must be given to the database for each of the following— high school records, program office, and Office of Admission and Records.

5. Feeder schools: over a period of years, BEAM has established feeder schools in the two major cities in the state; and has carried the program to these schools and received outstanding support for those efforts.

6. Student selection: some of the selections are made by the high school counselors, some by interested community people, and others are taken from those seeking information about the program and from those on the admitted list.

7. Assessments: a constant assessment/evaluation of the strategies used is vital; add to that the year-by-year progress of the students involved.

8. Documentation on the students and the program are paramount. Assessment and documentation must be done carefully with valid measures.

9. Mentoring: most retained and graduate students, recently, credit a mentor as being the guiding force in their successful college life and their careers. A mentoring committee is needed to secure available faculty and staff people to serve as mentors.

BEAM Program Steps:

I. Group orientation: identification and explanation of goals of the program.

II. One-on-one: designs to promote persistence, problem-solving, and processes that will emphasize—

- self-reliance
- self-respect
- industry;
- perseverance

III. Exploration: inclusive of—

- academic strengths and weaknesses
- background preparations
- performance skills
- community activities and achievements

IV. Assessments and referral: inclusive of—
- faculty
- support services
- student organizations
- resources
- mentoring program, etc.

V. Compulsory adherence: compulsory regular interview sessions scheduled with each student with a professional counselor. During these sessions progress assessments of their academic and psychological responsibilities are documented. At these sessions, the students are referred to the following support services according to their problem needs:
- Learning Center
- Study Skill Program
- Mentoring program
- Student organizations
- Pass-Key Program
- Reading and Writing Labs
- Advisory Center
- Career Services Center
- Math Learning Center
- Library
- Pre-Professional Clubs
- Health Services
- Counseling and Psychological Services Center

PROGRAM EVALUATION: success of these steps of the program after admission, as with the entire BEAM program, requires:
- communication
- planning
- cooperation
- commitment
- coordination
- evaluation
- placement

Staffing and Support Resources

The staff includes: a director, assistant director, graduate assistants, a secretary and volunteers.

Support resources include: Provost for Student Affairs; deans and directors; student organizations; career counseling services; psychological services; feeder school counselors; community leaders; President's African-American Advisory Committee; and admission and records offices.

—Mr. Horace E. Belmear (retired) is the former Assistant Dean of Admission and Records, at West Virginia University in Morgantown, West Virginia.

The Comprehensive Academic Program in Nursing

by Roy Ann Sherrod and Lynda Harrison

Overview

The Comprehensive Academic Program (CAP) was a multifaceted program developed at The University of Alabama Capstone College of Nursing (CCN) to increase nursing education opportunities for individuals from environmentally or financially disadvantaged backgrounds. In 1988, the program was funded for three years to improve recruitment and retention of minority students as well as non-minority students who were from disadvantaged backgrounds. This article is a description of CAP as a model program for recruitment and retention of minority and other disadvantaged students. Evaluative data regarding the effectiveness of strategies implemented to achieve objectives are presented. Recommendations for future programs are included also.

Historical Origin

The Comprehensive Academic Program was implemented through the initiative of Dr. Norma Mobley who was dean of the University of Alabama Capstone College of Nursing (CCN). Early in her tenure, Dr. Mobley noted with concern the disproportionate number of minority and other disadvantaged students who actually attended and graduated from the CCN. In a bold move, Dr. Mobley allocated time to faculty member Lynda Harrison to develop a proposal for a program to increase the recruitment and retention of disadvantaged students at the CCN. A grant was submitted to the Division of Nursing within the Department of Health and Human Services for $375,496. In 1988, the program was funded for three years with the objectives to:

1. recruit and select at least twelve qualified students per year who were from environmentally or economically disadvantaged backgrounds;

2. facilitate the entry of at least twelve qualified disadvantaged students per year into the Capstone College of Nursing;

3. provide counseling, academic, and social support services to assist disadvantaged students to complete the Capstone College of Nursing program successfully;

4. provide preliminary education for disadvantaged students prior to their entry into upper division nursing courses, which would assist them to complete the Capstone College of Nursing program successfully; and

5. provide disadvantaged students with stipends of $200 per month while they were enrolled as full-time students at The University of Alabama (Sherrod & Harrison, 1991).

Program Evolution

The program evolved from a needs assessment which included a review of relevant literature and a survey of faculty, students, and campus services. Results of the initial needs assessment indicated that there was not a sufficient database at the institution or college for recruitment and retention information. The needs assessment provided the basis for development of such a database for the program.

The faculty were surveyed to assess their perceptions of what supportive services would be helpful to students; to gauge their awareness, perceptions, and use of campus support services; and to collect their ideas regarding sources of student academic and non-academic problems. Similar assessments of students were made. Results indicated that stress, financial problems, inadequate preparation, limited awareness and use of support services, and poor study skills were some of the primary sources of student difficulty.

A survey of campus resources indicated that many services such as tutoring and assistance with test-taking were already available. Thus the intent of the

134

grant proposal was to supplement these services as needed rather than duplicating them. The background information indicated that awareness and use of these services should be enhanced. The results of the needs assessment thus provided useful information to assist in identifying academically high risk students so that appropriate services could be developed and offered to them.

Program Introduction

Several aspects of CAP were introduced to CCN faculty prior to its implementation. Many of these CAP activities were introduced as a result of proposal development. For example, faculty were introduced to the CAP concept in a faculty meeting early in proposal development to solicit support and provide information. Later, the needs of the faculty in terms of how to advise and teach disadvantaged students were discussed, as well as the methods for collection of baseline data for evaluation of program effectiveness. After initial introduction, updates were presented at each faculty meeting. Faculty were encouraged to share ideas and concerns from the very beginning.

Once funding was received, a consultant conducted a two-day workshop for faculty to address issues related to advisement of at-risk students. A second one-day workshop was conducted a year later to provide follow-up and address areas of concern. One of the most helpful measures in program introduction was the total unconditional support of the administration. There was a clear message from the dean that this was an important, worthwhile project and faculty were encouraged to provide their full cooperation.

Implementation Strategies

The strategies designed to accomplish each of the CAP objectives were diverse. Many of the services offered through the CAP project were offered to all nursing majors rather than only to disadvantaged students. In this way it was hoped that there would be no negative stigma associated with the project which might limit students' willingness to take advantage of project services. This section includes a description of the strategies used to address each program objective, as well as the indicators that were used to evaluate the extent to which each objective was accomplished.

Objective 1: To recruit and select at least twelve qualified individuals per year who are from environmentally or economically disadvantaged backgrounds.

Implementation Strategies. The focus of this first objective was to encourage qualified disadvantaged students to apply for admission to The University of Alabama as potential nursing majors. One method for achieving this objective included the establishment of a Future Nurse Club (FNC) in at least one high school in each of eleven counties in west Alabama. The project director served as a facilitator to the advisors of the FNCs, and the advisors were invited to attend an initial orientation session at the College of Nursing. During this session advisors received packets of information about suggested club activities and resources, as well as information about nursing careers and the educational program at the College of Nursing. During the course of the project over 200 FNC members visited the College of Nursing. Students who participated in the FNCs also could purchase special T-shirts to wear on club meeting days or for other activities.

A second strategy to increase the recruitment of disadvantaged students to the university included the development of a community advisory council consisting of members from parent, social, religious, and educational groups. Members of this council participated in meetings with the project director during which they learned about the educational program at the College of Nursing and also learned about career opportunities in nursing. Council members then disseminated information provided by the project director about nursing career opportunities to high school students and others in their respective communities.

A third strategy involved collaborating with the Macy Bioprep Project, a program funded by the Macy Foundation which had been established several years prior to initiation of the CAP project. The Bioprep program was designed to enhance recruitment of rural students into health careers. Nursing faculty taught workshops on basic nursing skills for Bioprep students, and presented programs about nursing over the Bioprep satellite network. Flyers about nursing careers and educational programs also were distributed to counselors in high schools through-out the state of Alabama which participated in the Bioprep program.

A final strategy to enhance recruitment of disadvantaged students to the university involved working with local radio, television, and newspaper sources to increase media coverage about nursing and career opportunities. The project director and the director of the Office of Student Services (OSS) for the CCN also distributed brochures about the CAP project to guidance counselors and students in high schools throughout the state.

Evaluation. Evaluation of the effectiveness of the CAP program was based on comparison of four groups of students. Group A students entered the CCN program as freshmen during the year preceding project implementation. These students served as a control group for project evaluation purposes. Group B, C, and D students entered the CCN as freshmen during the three years of project funding. These students represented the "treatment group" for project evaluation purposes. Because most project activities were available to all students regardless of whether or not they were disadvantaged, this aspect of the evaluation provided a comparison of students who entered the university before the CAP services became available with those who entered after the services were initiated. In addition to comparing "control group" (Group A) and "treatment group" (Groups B, C, and D) students, the evaluation also included comparisons of students who did and did not receive stipend support. Stipends were offered as part of the CAP grant to 32 of the most financially disadvantaged students over the course of the project.

Students in Groups A, B, C, and D completed a Personal Data Form (PDF) during their freshman year. The PDF was based on an instrument originally developed by Watts and Wollridge at the State University of New York in Buffalo (Watts, 1984). The PDF was designed to evaluate the extent to which each student might be considered educationally or financially disadvantaged. For example, one of the indicators of educational disadvantage was an item in which students had to rate the extent to which they believed that their high school backgrounds may have made it difficult for them to succeed in college.

Approximately 43 percent of the students in all four groups indicated either "not sure," "possibly hard," or "definitely hard" in response to this question. Stipend students were rated as significantly more "educationally disadvantaged" in their response to this question than were non-stipend students (t=2.64, p=.009).

In order to evaluate the extent to which various recruitment strategies initiated through the CAP project were effective in recruiting disadvantaged students to the College of Nursing, several items were added to the PDF during the second year of the project. These items required students to indicate their sources of information about the College of Nursing. Over the three years of the project there was a significant increase in the number of students who indicated that they had learned about the nursing program through Future Nurse Clubs, College of Nursing faculty members, University of Alabama representatives, or College of Nursing brochures.

Objective 2: To Facilitate the Entry of at Least Twelve Qualified Disadvantaged Students Per Year into the Capstone College of Nursing

Implementation Strategies. The second project objective focused on helping students to achieve academic success during their first three semesters at the university so that they would qualify for promotion to upper division nursing courses in their fourth semester. A key strategy used to accomplish this objective included expanding the faculty advisement program that was already in place in which students are required to meet with their faculty advisors at least once a semester usually during pre-registration.

A consultant with expertise in working with disadvantaged students provided two workshops for faculty to help them learn about ways to identify and address students' academic and non-academic problems. Faculty also learned about the many existing campus resources that were available to provide academic, financial, and psychological support as needed.

The college also instituted a Mandatory Academic Counseling Program for students whose grade point averages fell below a 2.0 (on a 4.0 scale). These students were required to meet with their faculty advisors or a mandatory advisement counselor (MAC) on a monthly basis, to develop contracts and plans for improving their academic performance.

Another strategy included developing a special section of a study skills course (the "Academic Potential" course) for nursing students. The course provided information on note-taking, test-taking, and time management.

Evaluation. Students who follow the nursing curriculum as outlined in the university catalog are eligible to apply for promotion to upper division nursing courses during their third semester and take their first clinical nursing course during their fourth semester. For a variety of reasons (e.g. academic or financial problems), many students do not apply for upper division promotion until later than their third semester.

Only 44 percent of Group A students who were still enrolled at the university during their fourth semester had applied for promotion to upper division nursing courses, compared to 58 percent of Group B and C students (who entered the university after the CAP project was initiated). These data suggested that the support services provided through the project helped more students progress through the program following the timetable outlined in the catalog.

In order to evaluate the faculty advising system, faculty advisors recorded all contacts with their advisees on a faculty advising process record. This record included information on the date of each student contact, student problems identified, actions taken, and referrals made. Total scores were computed to document the number of student problems identified, the number of actions taken, and the number of referrals made by the advisor.

Independent sample t-Tests were computed comparing the advising activities reported for Group A students and students in Groups B, C, and D during their freshman year. There were significant differences between the two groups in the length of advising sessions, number of problems identified by the advisor, number of actions taken and number of referrals made by the advisor, and the advisors' ratings of their effectiveness (see Table 1).

Table 1—Results of t-Tests comparing faculty reports of advising activities for Group A with Group B, C, and D Students

Dependent Variable	Group A	Mean Group B, C, and D Combined	tValue	Degrees of Freedom	PValue
Length of advising sessions (mins)	48.41	66.26	-3.50	133.2*	0.001
No. of problems identified by advisor	2.23	3.44	-2.99	89.4*	0.004
No. of actions taken by advisor	2.98	3.76	-1.98	101.7*	0.050
No. of referrals made by advisor	1.07	2.35	-3.67	137*	0.000
Advisor's rating of effectiveness	1.85+	1.35	3.69	164	0.000

* Separate variance estimate of t used because assumption of homogeneity of variance was not met.

+1 = very effective; 5 = definitely ineffective

Similar differences were found when comparing stipend and non-stipend students. Faculty reported spending more time during advising, identifying more problems, taking more actions, and making more referrals with "treatment group" students compared with "control group" students, and with stipend students compared with non-stipend students.

Another measure of the effectiveness of the advising program was to compare awareness and use of campus support among students in the "treatment" and "control" groups (see Table 2).

Table 2 - Results of t-Tests comparing Group A, B, C, and D Students' awareness and use of campus services

Dependent Variable	Group A	Mean Group B, C, and D Combined	tValue	Degrees of Freedom	PValue
Awareness of campus support services	4.95	4.68	0.61	189	0.544
Use of campus support services	0.82	1.73	-4.0	98.08*	0.000

* Separate variance estimate of t used because assumption of homogeneity of variance was not met.
Copyright J.B. Lippincott Co. 1994. Sherrod, R.A. & Harrison, L. Nurse Educator, 19(6), p. 29-33.

Table 2 indicates that although there were no differences in the awareness of support services, students in Groups B, C and D reported using significantly more of these services than did students in Group A. This finding suggests the enhanced advising program was effective in encouraging students to use services that could facilitate their entry into upper division nursing courses.

The outcomes for the Mandatory Advisement Program (MAP) were less positive than were the outcomes for the overall advisement program. During four semesters in which the MAP was instituted, a total of 179 students had grade point averages (GPAs) less than 2.0 and received letters outlining the program requirements (e.g. that students were required to meet monthly with their faculty advisors to develop contracts and plans for improving their academic performance). Only 118 of these students fulfilled the requirements of the program and met with their advisors. Because there were no penalties associated with failure to comply with the mandatory advising requirements, faculty perceived this aspect of the project to be ineffective.

Objective 3: To Provide Counseling, Academic, and Social Support Services to Assist Disadvantaged Students to Complete the Capstone College of Nursing Program Successfully

Implementation Strategies. Strategies for accomplishing this objective included establishing a Registered Nurse Mentor Program, a Big Brother/Big Sister Program (in which upper division nursing students were paired with lower division students), and a Peer Support group. Additional services included the development and purchase of appropriate remedial programs and materials and the provision of faculty tutors for upper division nursing students. Other tutors for chemistry, math, and biology courses were also provided.

Evaluation. Problems were encountered in maintaining the Nurse Mentor

Program, the Big Brother/Big Sister Program, and the Peer Support Program. Nurse Mentors and Upper Division Big Brothers/Sisters often had problems making contact with their assigned students. Although some students reported that these relationships were helpful, many indicated that finding time to meet with mentors and upper division students added additional stress to their already crowded schedules. Similarly, attendance at the monthly support group meetings was generally low. The use of faculty tutors was high, however, and students rated the tutoring programs as extremely helpful.

One outcome measure used to evaluate the extent to which the third objective was accomplished was comparison of retention rates for students in Groups A, B, C, and D, and of those for stipend and non-stipend students. The retention rates for Group A, B, C, and D students at the end of their first year in the program were 90 percent, 88 percent, 86 percent, and 89 percent, respectively, suggesting the CAP program did not have a significant effect on general student retention. However, the students in Groups B and C who received stipend support from the project had significantly higher retention rates than did students who did not receive stipends (56 percent and 62 percent for non-stipend students compared to 75 percent and 100 percent for stipend students).

Another method used to evaluate the extent to which the third objective was accomplished was to conduct qualitative interviews with a total of 36 students (from Groups A, B, C, and D). When asked to identify positive aspects of their academic experiences, students identified a number of grant-supported activities including the special study skills class, the RN Mentor Program, the Big Brother/Big Sister Program, and the Peer Support Group. When asked to recommend additional services that the university might provide to help students with academic and non-academic problems, students made the following suggestions:

1. Be more directive and require students to use support services if they are having problems.
2. Provide more frequent quizzes in selected classes.
3. Encourage students to study in groups.
4. Have clinical nursing faculty available to help students in the clinical practice lab during designated study hours.
5. Encourage students to get involved with campus activities.
6. Promote more group meetings for lower division nursing students.
7. Promote more social integration of black and white students.
8. Increase student awareness of campus support services.
9. Match roommates with common interests (Sherrod et al., 1992).

A final strategy used to evaluate the third objective was to send surveys to all Group A, B, C, and D students who did not continue to enroll in university courses. Although the response rate was low, the 38 students who returned the surveys indicated the factors that influenced their decisions to withdraw from the nursing program included: (a) academic problems with non-nursing courses; (b) low vocational interest in nursing; (c) disappointment in prenursing and nursing classes; and (d) insufficient financial support.

Objective 4: To Provide Preliminary Education for Disadvantaged Students Prior to their Entry into Upper Division Nursing Courses, Which Will Assist Them to Complete the Capstone College of Nursing Program Successfully.

Implementation Strategies. Many of the strategies used in addressing the other project objectives also related to the fourth project objective. An additional strategy included instituting a one-credit hour "Introduction to Nursing" course that was offered to first semester nursing majors. The course included content on nursing, the role of the nurse, upper division nursing courses, and campus support services. A second strategy included establishing a Cooperative Education Program in which nursing students could receive assistance in finding part-time employment in a health care facility. It was hoped that if students needed to work in order to meet their financial obligations, having a job in a health-related field might help students in their nursing courses as well.

Evaluation. Evaluations of both the Introduction to Nursing course and the Cooperative Education program were extremely positive. The data related to student retention which have already been presented also relate to this fourth objective.

Objective 5: To Provide Disadvantaged Students with Stipends of $200 per Month While they are Enrolled as Full-Time Students in the College of Nursing

Implementation Strategies. In order to identify students who were financially disadvantaged and who might qualify for stipend support from grant funds, Personal Data Forms were mailed to all students who were admitted to the university and who declared nursing as their major. Students whose family incomes were below the federal poverty guidelines (as stipulated by the grant) were eligible to receive stipend support. A total of 32 students (fourteen Black and eighteen White) received stipend support during the three years of the project.

Evaluation. Students who received stipend support frequently commented that they were able to devote more time to their studies because the stipend support decreased their need to work at paying jobs, although there was not a statistically significant difference in the mean number of hours worked per week by stipend and non-stipend students. The benefits of the stipend support can be inferred from previously reported data indicating higher retention rates for stipend students.

Organizational Structure

The organizational structure of CAP was quite effective. The overall project implementation was the responsibility of the project director who devoted 100 percent of an FTE (full time equivalent) to the project. The director of research (DR) served as the CAP project evaluator and CCN director of special projects at that time. This person, in turn, answered directly to the dean. In addition to the project director and program evaluator, the CAP staff consisted of a secretary and two part-time counselors. The counselors and secretary were under the direct authority of the project director. The program evaluator, with assistance from the project director, was responsible for the assessment and analysis of program effectiveness. The secretary performed clerical duties and assisted with data entry for program evaluation. The two part-time counselors were responsible for tracking and meeting with project students whose grade point average fell below a 2.0 on a 4.0 scale. These counselors were employed to address student non-compliance and faculty inability to track students or closely monitor their progress because of time constraints.

Program Impact

Many of the services instituted during the CAP project have been continued by the College of Nursing. The faculty advising program continues, although faculty no longer complete advising process forms documenting their actions during each advising session. A college Student Affairs Committee evaluates student and faculty perceptions of the advising system every two or three years, and these evaluations continue to be positive.

The Future Nurse Clubs were continued for a time in many of the high schools in West Alabama, with faculty serving as advisors and sources of support to these clubs as needed. The director of the Office of Student Services continues to make contact with area high schools for recruitment.

During the last year of the CAP project, the project director secured funding from the Chatlos Foundation to provide a summer residential program for 15 disadvantaged high school students. These students participated in a number of activities designed to enhance their understanding of nursing career opportunities and educational programs. The project director also was successful in obtaining federal funds (each year since the CAP project ended), to provide scholarships to financially disadvantaged students.

The director of the Office of Student Services provides an informal peer assistance program in which he connects upper division students with lower division students whom he identifies as needing additional support. This program, which is individualized and based on identified student need, appears to be more effective than the Big Brother/Big Sister program which was developed during the CAP project.

Many of the tutoring programs that were initiated during the CAP project (e.g. chemistry and math tutors) also have been continued through the campus Center for Teaching and Learning.

The College of Nursing continues to maintain a strong commitment to retaining disadvantaged and minority students in the program. Although data are not available to identify trends in the numbers of financially or educationally disadvantaged students who have enrolled in the program since the beginning of the CAP project, Table 3 illustrates the percentage of African-American students who have been enrolled in the University of Alabama and in the Capstone College of Nursing during the fall semesters each year since 1986. The CAP project was initiated in April 1988, and was funded for three years. These data indicate the College of Nursing continues to enroll a significantly higher percentage of African-American students than the university as a whole.

Table 3

Percentage of Capstone College of Nursing and University of Alabama Students by Race

	1986	1987	1988	1989	1990	1991	1992	1993	1994
African-American									
CCN	2.1	23.3	24.7	2.2	22.2	17.6	17.1	17.3	18.7
UA	9.1	8.8	8.6	8.7	9.0	9.6	9.8	10.2	10.7
Non-African-American									
CCN	8.0	76.7	75.3	78.0	77.8	82.4	82.9	82.7	81.3
UA	90.9	91.2	9.4	9.3	9.1	90.4	90.2	89.8	89.3

Problems

To undertake such a project is worthwhile, but it can be difficult as well. The greatest difficulty is providing continuity of program services if they are initiated with soft monies such as with a grant. Once the money is gone, in many cases, so is the program. Discontinuing such programs can send a negative message to the university community about the institution's value of and commitment to such programs. Most people's perspective is that if it is important, the institution will find a way to support it. In the case of CAP, the program was approved for another two years by the division of nursing, but no funding was received. So, the CCN supported continuation of some services, but not all. For example, tutoring for chemistry was continued, but the $200 a month stipend for students could not be continued.

One other great difficulty in implementing a project of this nature is students' compliance and use of services. Often, students who need services the most are the least likely to use them. Many students fear being viewed negatively if they use support services. If there are no serious valued consequences for failure to access and use services then many students will not comply. For CAP, it was necessary to engage the services of mandatory advisement counselors (MAC) to assist with follow-through and assess compliance. The issue of whether to require students to participate in programs and use certain services is one that faculty members must debate further. While some argue that students should be required to access services, with sanctions if they fail to do so, others hold that students should be able to decide on their own. If they decide not to use the services, then they must bear the consequences of that choice, even if it is failure. To demand or require students to participate may not be treating them as adult learners, some say.

Faculty support is vital. With all their other responsibilities, faculty members may find it difficult to devote time to such a project if they do not value it. To assist with the additional time disadvantaged students might need and to relieve faculty, mandatory advisement counselors might be employed with graduate training in counseling.

Insights

As a result of experiences with CAP, many insights were gained. Increasing the recruitment and retention (R&R) of minority and disadvantaged students will enhance the social and economic status of all segments of society. R&R programs require sustained efforts with an awareness of the need to minimize any negative stigma of R&R activities and promote their benefit to the institution and society.

There must be administrative and faculty support or the program will have very limited success. Administration will most likely have the best opportunity to impress upon the faculty the importance of and need for their cooperation. Because faculty may have more opportunities to impact students in terms of meeting objectives and using the services of the program, their support is crucial.

When developing services, it is helpful to remember that no matter how wonderful project staff, faculty, and/or administration think the services are, if the students won't use them the program will have little value. Thus, the development of an R&R program should begin with assessments of what students in the target population believe would be helpful and useful. Once services are identified and decisions are made regarding required use of services by students, effective sanctions should be incorporated for students who fail to comply with program requirements. If there are no effective sanctions for failure to use services, then there should be no requirement to use the services.

Ongoing reminders to faculty about available resources and additional types of activities they may engage in may extend the supportive role of advisors.

With the CAP project, a form was included in each student's academic record with a checklist of available resources and advisement interventions. These activities were checked after each student's visit with the faculty member.

In closing, when and if special funds are no longer available, such as with a grant, someone should be designated with the administrative responsibility for maintaining and following through with program activities rather than leaving various aspects up to individual faculty or groups. Also, R&R goals should be an integral part of the strategic plan for the institution and/or division. This strategy will ensure that the original program goals remain a priority for the institution or division.

—Dr. Roy A. Sherrod is an associate professor, and Dr. Lynda Harrison is a professor in the Capstone College of Nursing at The University of Alabama in Tuscaloosa, Alabama.

References

Crawford, A. & Olinger, B. (1988). Recruitment and retention of nursing students from diverse cultural backgrounds. Journal of Nursing Education, 27(8)(8), 379-381.

Jones, S. H. (1992). Improving retention and graduation rates for black students in nursing education: A developmental model. Nursing Outlook, 40(2), 78-85.

Reed, S. B. & Hudepohl, N. C. (1983). High-risk nursing students: Emergence of remedial/developmental programs. Nurse Educator, 8, 21-26.

Sherrod, R. A. & Harrison, L. (1991). Comprehensive program for disadvantaged nursing students. Nursing Special Project Grant Final Report. United States Department of Health and Human Services, Health Resources and Services Administration, Division of Nursing. Grant Number 5D19NU24271.

Sherrod, R. A. & Harrison, L. (1994). Evaluation of a comprehensive advisement program designed to enhance student retention. Nurse Educator, 19(6), 29-33.

Sherrod, R. A. & Harrison, L. L.; Lowery, B. H.; Wood, F. G.; Edwards, R. M., and Gaskins, S. W. (1992). Freshmen baccalaureate nursing students' perceptions of their academic and non-academic experiences: Implications for retention. Journal of Professional Nursing, 8. 203-208.

Watts, W. (1984). Professional Nursing Career program for disadvantaged students: Striving for professional achievement in nursing (SPAN). Journal of the New York State Nurses' Association, 15 (2), 34-41.

Retention of African-Americans in Engineering
by Forest D. Smith

Overview:

Louisiana State University (LSU) is the flagship institution of the state of Louisiana. It is a nationally-recognized research institution, rich in history and tradition, which offers diverse educational, recreational, and cultural opportunities, and helps shape the future through education, research, and public service. The enrollment of the university is 25,000, graduates and undergraduates. The College of Engineering is a main component with 2,500 engineering students; of these, 300 are minority students.

The recruitment of minority students has been a major commitment of the College of Engineering for the past sixteen years. From programs designed to attract high school students to the field of engineering, to fellowships for graduate students, many opportunities are available to minorities. As a result, the College of Engineering has substantially increased the number and ability of minorities enrolling in this field of study. More recently, however, the question has been: "Why aren't more African-American students graduating?"

Hence, the goal of the Minority Engineering Program (MEP) is to increase the number of African-American engineering graduates from the class of 1990 by twenty percent, and improve the grade point-averages to equal those of the average engineering student. The results of these efforts has proven successful such that of the thirty-eight students in the class of 1990, ten are graduating this year. This is an increase of 30 percent.

This article will discuss a development and implementation process that can be used as a university-wide or college retention plan.

Introduction

The successful retention of minorities has generally been hindered by inadequate recruitment and retention policies in higher education; an insufficient supply of minority faculty role models and mentors; and government policies that reflect the administration's unwillingness to commit the resources needed to improve the education of all its citizens (Halberstam, 1991; Reich, 1991). Hilliard (1978) agrees that, "the issue of academic failure by minority groups can be characterized as methodical, ideological, permanent, and an essential element in the way the whole society is organized, and it is racial" (p. 10).

In light of this, the Minority Engineering Program (MEP) was established at LSU. The initial goal of the MEP was to increase the number of African-American engineering graduates from the entering class of 1990 by twenty percent, and improve their grade-point averages to equal those of the other students. To reach this goal, the following three objectives had to be met: (1) the number of students entering the college from the Junior Division had to be increased by fifty percent; (2) those students had to participate in seventy-five percent of the freshmen orientation activities; and (3) counseling, advising, and academic tracking had to continue throughout the sophomore, and junior years. These efforts have proven successful in that of the thirty-eight students in the class of 1990, ten are graduating this year. This is an increase of thirty percent. Furthermore, the GPAs of all students are as follows:

	African-Americans	All Students
Seniors	2.69	2.78
Juniors	2.78	2.79
Sophomores	2.87	2.95

Given the success of this program, a more in-depth look at the MEP is warranted. Inclusive in this article will be information on: (1) developing and implementing this retention plan; (2) establishing a resource base; (3) presenting the orientation course; (4) setting up the database and evaluation procedures; (5) working with the alumni and community resources; and (6) presenting the plan to the institution.

Historical Origin/Development of the Program

The College of Engineering at LSU has aggressively worked to improve its efforts to retain minority students. During the spring of 1988, a full-time retention coordinator was hired, funded by a grant from the ARCO Foundation, to work with the students, faculty, and staff. This was the result of an enrollment evaluation that was requested by the new dean. This report showed very little discrepancy between the ACT scores, GPAs or schools that students were coming from; yet, there was a major discrepancy in retention rates between white students and African-American students.

A retention coordinator who reported to the associate dean of undergraduate activities began to work on this problem. After numerous surveys and retention research, a proposal to establish the MEP was presented to the College of Engineering. The following research includes theoretical perspectives and research studies on retention.

Theoretical Perspective

In the areas of administrative policy, instruction, and faculty/staff orientation, the university's ultimate goal of teaching, research and service can only be attained through the deliberate attempt to become a multicultural educational entity. Theories that concentrate on student retention suggest reasons for this emphasis.

Three theories which seem to be the most revered in the area of student retention support the change to multicultural education. The theories are: Tinto's Student Integration Model (1975), Bean's Industrial Model of Student Attrition (1983), and Weiner's (1985) Attributional Theory of Achievement Motivation (1985). In addition, there are several studies that discuss addressing the needs of students in a multicultural environment.

Student Integration Model

Tinto's Student Integration Model includes two domains, social and academic. Social integration occurs on a continuum that includes degrees of involvement in campus activities and campus life. The academic integration reflects the direct relationship between higher education and future occupational attainment. This model explains how different persons can perceive the same situation in different ways.

Bean's Industrial Model takes an individual's model of turnover in work organization and applies it to colleges and universities. He assumes that students and employees leave their respective organization for similar reasons. He suggests twelve determinants that impact the two variables of satisfaction, resulting in retention or departure. The twelve determinants in the theory are: grades, practical values, personal development, routinization, communication, participation, personal integration, courses, fair treatment on campus, involvement opportunities, and marrying.

The Attributional Theory by Weiner suggests that students' beliefs about the causes of their success or failure are a valid determinant of their success in college.

None of these three theories has been completely operationalized, so more research and more discussion are necessary.

Retention Studies

In addition to these models, there are many studies that seek to explain why minority students are not retained as well as whites. The studies on retention in higher education can be grouped into three major categories: student qualities at the time of matriculation; institutional traits; and student experiences at the institution.

Student Qualities At Time Of Matriculation

In dealing with student qualities at the time of matriculation, one also needs to consider the attributes the student brings from high school. Pre-college factors affect student retention in college. Ramist (1981) reports that high school GPA and class rank are good indicators of student persistence. The higher the GPA and class rank, the more persistent the student. He also suggests, "income level of parents, the pre-college environment, student personality characteristics, and ability affect student's preparation for the college environment" (p.92). Astin (1976) and Freters (1977) report the educational level of the parents is more influential than the income.

Several studies demonstrate that minority students are generally more likely to drop out of college than whites (Astin, 1975; Lenning, Sauer and Beal, 1980; Pascarella, et.al, 1981; Ramist, 1981). Astin's (1975) research additionally shows that differences between races disappear as the socioeconomic level and ability are controlled.

Discussing the non-cognitive factors as they relate to retention, Tinto, in his book, Leaving College (1987), says:

> *"Beyond the existence of possible discrimination, minority students, generally, and black students, in particular, may find it especially difficult to find and become a member of a supportive community within the college. Beyond the issue of "critical mass," there is the relative question of the range of supportive communities available to minority students. Sharing a common racial origin (or any other single attribute) is no guarantee of the sharing of common interests and dispositions, producing more of a likelihood of isolation (p.71)."*

He further notes that black students are more likely to drop out of predominately white colleges than at predominately black colleges. Tracey (1985) and Pascarelli (1985a,1985c) also support the idea of non-cognitive factors greatly affecting minority student retention. Several other researchers (Smith, 1982; Britt, 1975; Smith and Baruch, 1980) discuss the validity of student qualities as contributing to black student retention. Sedlacek (1987) summarizes his non-cognitive factors for minority retention as: (1) positive self-confidence; (2) realistic self-appraisal; (3) understanding and dealing with racism; (4) demonstrated community service; (5) preference to long-range goals; (6) availability of strong support system; (7) successful leadership experience; and (8) knowledge acquired about college (p.245). These factors are highly correlated with persistence (Cope and Hennah, 1975; Pantage and Creedon, 1968).

Additionally, a nine-year follow-up on the persistence among black and white students in more than 350 four-year colleges and universities suggest that black students are also more concerned with belonging to formal institutional associations than white students, and are, therefore, additionally concerned with isolation as a non-cognitive factor (Tracey, 1985).

Institutional Traits

Institutional characteristics include a complex array of physical, academic, social, and psychological attributes that make up the campus environment (Hossler, 1984, p.70). The positive alignment of these characteristics with the students improves retention. This research is supported by other authors who also promote redesigning the campus environment to enhance the "student-integration" (Creager, 1968; Painter and Painter, 1982; Pace, 1980; Moos, 1974; Astin, 1978; Noel, 1978; Lenning, Sauer, and Beal, 1980; and Blocher, 1974).

The size of the institution does not seem to affect minority retention. Female students generally are retained at higher rates than males (Astin, 1975). More important to retention is the discipline the student pursues, and its importance to the mainstream mission of the institution. It goes without saying that faculty and staff influence the experience of students in college.

Student Experiences After Matriculation

The students' experience after matriculation is positively influenced by: (1) a good GPA and academic programs; (2) discovery of significant others; (3) a high level of involvement in student activities; (4) living on campus; and (5) satisfying financial needs through aid/scholarships.

Even when a supportive social, intellectual community is found, a question remains as to the degree to which that will be central to the mainstream of institutional life. National evaluations of special services support programs (eighty percent minority) indicate that the success of a program, and that of its students, hinge upon the degree to which both administrators and students perceive themselves as central to, rather than marginal to, the daily life of the institution (Tinto, 1987, p.71).

A major component of the program is an orientation course for African-American, Hispanic and Native American students. This credit course was accepted by the College of Engineering and then the university. It is designed to be part of a comprehensive retention effort that includes follow-up throughout the students' college careers, and will be required as a condition for scholarship, aide in community building, and maintaining student self-esteem. Students will be tracked throughout their college careers. The positive benefits of such a course are well-documented in retention research. Surveys and interviews with LSU engineering graduates, and continuing students also suggest that transition information, a sense of community, and skills training are definitely needed.

The graduation rate of the engineering department is similar to that of the university at about thirty-three percent. The history of minority students in the College of Engineering reflects a one-in-ten graduation rate among minority students. The largest attrition occurs between the entry date and the sophomore year. In 1986, there were 105 African-American students in the freshman class and seventy students in the College of Engineering. But in 1987, there were only seventy-seven students in the College, a lost of ninety-eight students. Of course, some of that change was due to career indecision, but this large discrepancy occurs systematically each year.

Major Events and Milestones in the Program's Development

According to the Office of Budget and Planning at LSU (1992), retention rates averaged, over the previous ten years for all students, thirty-eight percent, and sixteen percent for black students. While neither figure approaches the national average, there is a marked difference for blacks and whites, as blacks make up only ten percent of the student population of 23,000. Looking closer at what these figures mean, let us consider the freshman cohort of 1984. The data from the freshman class of 1984 indicate there were 4,457 white and 456 black freshmen students. The Office of Budget and Planning reports that of this group, 2,865 white (64.3 percent) and 223 black (48.9 percent) returned for their sophomore year. The junior year for this cohort shows that 2,290 white (51.4 percent) and 157 (34.4 percent) matriculated. The fall 1988 data shows 1,982 white (44.5 percent) and 123 black (27.0 percent) approaching graduation. To date, 1,660 white (38.3 percent) and 80 black (17.5 percent) students in the 1984 cohort have graduated from LSU. These data were utilized when the task force was engaged by the new chancellor in 1988 to review undergraduate education at LSU.

In his article, Rice (1989) discussed his findings of a retention survey administered in 1987 to 186 continuing black students (ten percent of total enrollment) during registration, and of an attrition survey mailed to 176 students who did not return from the previous fall's group of students. Important to note here is that 100 of the students were in good academic standing; thirty-one percent returned the survey. The surveys were divided into two sections. The first section asked general demographic data about students and their families; the second section asked students to rate eighteen statements on the academic, financial, and social environment at the university. A final question asked the students to rate their overall experience at the university.

Mitchell's (1989) recommendations to deal with student concerns center around redesigning the university in six areas: (1) entry or admissions support; (2) departmental support; (3) personnel support; (4) financial support; (5) program and technical support; and (6) cultural heritage support through a comprehensive institutional unit. As the retention rates of black students are so low, consideration of alternatives, and more research are appropriate.

Looking specifically at the College of Engineering, recruiting efforts have kept the number of African-American students constant over the decade. The disturbing statistic is the lower proportion of African-American students in the College as compared to those entering Junior Division. While some of that drop can be explained by longer residence time for some, it also reflects a greater drop-out rate. With similar credentials among African-American and white freshmen students, this rate is not readily explainable. There is no university minority affairs office that might be able to answer these questions. Hopefully the data with engineering students as a model can be used toward this end, as well as to increase understanding among the engineering faculty.

For African-Americans in particular, the retention rate of students who enter the College of Engineering was less than half what it was for all students. The students in the engineering department average 6.7 percent African-American, whereas the graduating classes average only 2.1 percent African-American.

Looking back on the origins of the MEP, first, the Recruiting into Engineering of High Ability Minority Students (REHAMS) program began in 1976 with a corporate grant. It continues to be a viable recruitment effort. Over 400 students have participated in this summer residential program administered from the MEP. The retention component of the MEP has three-fourths of its budget provided through grants, from foundations, and corporate investors. The college provides the balance of the funding. A decade ago it began to intensively recruit minority students into engineering. Initially this program centered on the REHAMS program. The goal, now, is to increase the graduation rate of minority students to match that of all students.

It was difficult to get the orientation course offered for credit. The first two years, students met with the coordinator from 6-7:30 p.m., voluntarily. During this period, the syllabus for the course was defined and the academic communities began. The course was approved in 1990 as a two-semester course for all students. The MEP held one section for its students. Presently, this is the only section of the course being offered.

It was difficult to get the students to meet a second time to work on the academic groups, but many of them did. Throughout this time, brochures, manuals, and program procedures were established.

The coordinator worked hard to make the MEP a high-profile entity by giving presentations at conferences, participating on university and engineering committees, and producing literature and publicity for the program in every available media, local, regional, and national.

A major boost for the program came when the coordinator was appointed to the NSBE Regional Advisory Board after making a presentation at their national conference. Another spurt of notoriety came when the coordinator was co-founder of a group whose purpose is to increase the skills of professionals on college campuses in Louisiana in the area of recruitment and retention of African-American students.

During 1991, the MEP established a corporate advisory board to assist with resource development and program planning needs. This group consists of corporate investors, faculty, staff, and students. The members promote the work of the MEP within their companies, and give a lot of credibility to the program. They are instrumental in providing additional resources to the program. The university chancellor agrees the MEP should be institutionalized, but cannot fund it in the midst of state budget cuts. During the spring 1995 meeting of the advisory board, the dean of engineering restated his commitment to maintaining the MEP.

Some of the most recent progress is the result of so many of the engineering students having a GPA of 3.0 or above. During the Spring of 1994, 34 of the 120 African-American students honored at the university were from engineering. This prompted the faculty to request these students to work in their laboratories. The MEP has also enabled several students to become involved with summer research programs, and the Ron McNair Post-Baccalaureate Program to increase the number of students entering graduate school.

The MEP continues to work on improved faculty relations by getting them involved with student design projects, working on the advisory board and scholarship committee, and making presentations with graduate students.

Implementation Strategies

The university was introduced to the MEP during the summative review by Dr. Landis during the fall of 1990. The university participants in the presentation were from the chancellor's office, Office of Academic Affairs, Office of Student Affairs, the Junior Division, the Career Planning and Placement Center, the Enrollment Management Office, engineering department chairman and faculty, engineering student leaders and corporate investors (the advisory board was formalized during the spring of 1991). The program design was presented as a five-year plan, with the fifth year showing improvement in retention rates.

The MEP proposal is designed to work with 250 students, a staff of three professionals, a graduate student, and fifteen student workers. The budget has never allowed for any additional professionals. Consequently, the refinement of many of the program's components is still to come. The coordinator has made adjustments, such as utilizing graduate students in the assistant, workshop coordinator, and data maintenance positions. Increasingly important as the program matures is good relationships with university offices. The MEP does not duplicate any existing services. Students are required to learn, and be a part of university departments, which is most important during the first two years.

Faculty members are on the advisory and scholarship boards. Students are also directed to work in laboratories. Through the Junior Division, minority students are directed to participate in MEP.

The program has expectations of the students and they are aware of it. The coordinator interviews each student in the class to find out why they are at LSU; and to explain the mission and legitimacy of the MEP. The students understand what the motto means when it says, "Not a hand-out … just a hand." The MEP is implemented, based on its established mission to increase the graduation rates of underrepresented minority students, by: (1) increasing the pool of students qualified to pursue engineering by providing academic and career exposure to precollege students; (2) providing the resources to ensure student success in college; (3) assisting the students in reaching career goals; (4) working with the faculty and staff to create an environment to attract and graduate minority engineering students; (5) maintaining communications with alumni for continuity; and (6) continuing strong collaborations with corporate and community representatives.

Programmatic Operations

This plan is a comprehensive one that involves changing the entire system. This program involves seven components, based on the "Community Building Model" (Landis, 1985). Those components are: (1) a precollege program; (2) a student orientation course; (3) scholarships, academic excellence workshops, and clustering of students; (4) a student newsletter; (5) academic tracking; (6) increasing student involvement to maintain self-esteem; and (7) a parent and corporate advisory council.

The precollege component of the program is first, and revolves around a summer residential program. This is a four-week opportunity for students to learn about the university through an experiential approach to learning. They are taught mathematics, English, and computer science by college faculty. They are exposed to all the departments on the campus and spend time with high level administrators, faculty, and students. They also participate in career-oriented hands-on activities in the engineering laboratories and at industry offices.

The college component of the plan includes precollege students and other first-time freshmen students. The student orientation course is probably the most important. Most of the variables contributing to student success are addressed during this time. This two-hour credit course is designed to assist students in their transition from high school to college, and emphasizes the importance of group work and institutional involvement. During these classes the students are provided with information on: study skills; time management; improving communication skills; financial aid and scholarships; racism; understanding what employers want; test-taking skills; career exploration; the resources and organizations available at LSU; understanding the college catalog; how to meet professors; and how to make new friends. The students also do hands-on career-related design projects, oral and written reports, and interact with corporate representatives. Most of these interactions are forced requirements of the course. The class meets weekly throughout the semester for two, one and one-half hour sessions. Additionally, students are required to meet with faculty during the first two weeks of school and biweekly throughout the semester. To evaluate the effectiveness of the program, students and faculty are asked to note what they think they need to know in the beginning of the class, and at the end of the semester an evaluation validates that the class met their concerns, as well as its designed goals.

Students participate in academic excellence workshops as a third component. During these workshops, students experience and learn the value of "the art of group study." An academic relationship develops between students and faculty that supports clustering in courses, and highlights the value of research.

These sessions are facilitated by graduate students and faculty. Students are encouraged to use the techniques taught in the workshops for all courses. Additionally, students are given extra credit for attending academic enhancement workshops provided by the Learning Assistance Center on study skills, career decision-making, reducing anxiety in mathematics, etc.

A fourth component of the retention plan is a newsletter, the "Future Engineer." Through this medium, students are reminded of the preparation needed for entering the workforce, and excerpts from the orientation course syllabus are included for the parents' information. Through this newsletter, details of the program successes are available to parents, faculty, and corporate employers.

The fifth component is academic tracking. Progress reports are sent to all the students' professors after four to five weeks of school. The academic progress that is reported by the professors is compared with the self-report of the students, and adjustments are made as needed. The students are also counseled individually to help them re-evaluate their study techniques, and begin planning for the mid-term exams. Actual data is maintained on student progress in mathematics courses; as this is the course used in the academic excellence workshops for demonstration.

The sixth component of the program, and, by far the most important, is maintaining the self-esteem of students through getting involved with campus activities; serving as mentors to other students; representing the College of Engineering at various events; increasing the rapport with faculty and staff; and increasing their responsibility for their academic performance. Students are selected as representatives at engineering programs, conferences, and when recruiting is done at high schools. Expectations are high and recognition is a big part of this component.

On a day-to-day basis, students are given responsibility for various projects involving recruiting strategies for other students, and task-force duties for retention, involving academic excellence activities and career development opportunities. They also select academic department offices, laboratories, and other high-visibility offices throughout the campus in which to perform their work-study duties. These experiences provide them with an opportunity to interact with faculty, administrators and staff on career-related concerns.

The students are always encouraged to run for student officers in engineering and campus-wide organizations. They are referred to the office of minority service as resource persons. They also offer tutoring to high school and other college students.

The seventh component of the program includes the Parent Advisory Council (PAC) and the Corporate Advisory Board (CAB). The purpose of the PAC is to provide parents with information on college services, so they can encourage participation by the students. This council provides a legitimate link between the College of Engineering and parents. The council meets during registration each semester. Throughout the year, the retention office communicates with parents about their students' progress. The Corporate Advisory Board is a working arm of the MEP in regards to resource development, providing professional engineers, technical assistance, planning, and working with faculty and administrators. The Corporate Advisory Board assists with recruitment, retention and resource development in a variety of ways. As a part of their involvement, CAB members provide mentors from their companies to work with the students. The provost requires each college to be represented on the board. Students at each class level are also selected to serve on the board.

The final aspect of this multicultural education plan involves the total university redesign efforts. Representatives from the JD Deans Council, PAC, and CAB participate on the curriculum and budget committees. They are involved in all scholarship decisions on the college level, and several departmental decisions. They attend all department faculty meetings, which allows an opportunity to promote multicultural concerns.

Through this program, the students' cognitive and non-cognitive issues are addressed. The multicultural trend at the university works toward a holistic model (Taylor, 1985, p.13). As Taylor's model also suggests, "the program attempts to have: (1) recruiting outcomes that will attract both sexes to all disciplines; (2) better knowledge of ways to lessen cultural conflict; (3) humanistic, sensitive counseling and career guidance; (4) peer support within and among minority group members; (5) proponents of multicultural education on the counseling staff, faculty, and in the administrative ranks; (6) access to academic skills; and (7) access to career and placement services and (8) research and service components."

The retention program is in its fifth year. Continuing students meet with the coordinator individually and in groups. Presently, the freshman classes of 1988 and 1989 have been organized into their own group to promote a community spirit. It is interesting to observe the dynamics of these groups as they develop.

Junior and senior students also are seeking assistance in improving interpersonal skills, career planning, time management, finances, and preparing for interviews and plant visits. The program's credibility with these students is steadily increasing. They also serve as mentors to the younger students. Many have been instrumental in developing and supporting the group study concept.

The MEP has an annual awards program to honor students in the spring, providing them with personalized plaques, certificates, scholarships, etc. During December, the college will recognize graduating seniors at the NSBE banquet. Additional awards and accolades are planned throughout the year, such as the REHAMS summer scholarship.

The MEP works closely with the student engineering organization. The LSU NSBE chapter is a viable, ongoing organization. Delegates have been assisted in attending regional conferences. Biweekly meetings and several social functions are held during the academic year. An advisory board links the students to local industry and business. The chapter sponsors regular study sessions during midterm and final exams. The regional chairperson and precollege chairperson are LSU students. The MEP was instrumental in assisting the Hispanic students in forming a Society of Hispanic Professional Engineers (SHPE) chapter at LSU. The two societies have faculty advisors who assist them in understanding the faculty, and serve as ombudsman for the students.

Organizational and Institutional Administrative Structure and Staffing

The coordinator serves as autonomous administrator of the program. This position, similar to all undergraduate college programs, reports to the associate dean of undergraduate activities, who reports to the dean. The staff consists of a part-time assistant coordinator, two graduate assistants, three part-time instructors, an administrator for the REHAMS program, and twenty student assistants.

The assistant coordinator is responsible for supervising the management of the office and the staff. One of the graduate students coordinates the experiential section of the orientation course. The other graduate students are responsible for the mechanization of office data.

Indicators of Program Success

Objective One: To Increase the Number of Students Entering the College by Fifty Percent.

Presently, the regular attendance of the orientation course has peaked at seventy five percent of the entering students. At least sixty percent of the group attends some portion of the program. Finally, before the end of the freshmen year, eighty percent of the students have at least come in for counseling on a voluntary basis. By making this course mandatory for the students, it is ensured that they will then be exposed to the other components of the retention program. The actual numbers can be determined through the enrollment and tracking process.

Objective Two: To Increase Student Involvement in all Orientation Activities to Seventy-Five Percent

By requiring the students to attend this course twice a week, there is a far greater chance of advising them of the other orientation activities and assuring their attendance. There is more opportunity for personal contact and to monitor their involvement in all activities. The attendance in this class is ninety five percent. Additionally, the more the students attend, the more likely they will carry out the assigned task.

Objective Three: This Course Will Establish a Routine of Counseling, Advising, and Tracking That can Easily be Continued Throughout Their College Careers

Academic tracking began with the freshman class of 1988, with concentration given to scholarship students who had to maintain a good average. This number represents seventy five percent of the students. This figure reflects that many students do not decide on their college until after scholarship deadlines have passed. This year it is planned that all minority students who come to spring/summer registration will sign up for this course.

The tracking involves a report from instructors in math, science, and English one month after school starts. Midterm and final grades are recorded and adjustments are discussed and implemented as needed for each student. The instructor also provides updates a month after midterm grades. Course attendance is monitored, as is that of counseling sessions and review sessions. Numerous personal follow-up activities go on throughout the semester (calls, mailings, visits to dormitories, student union, etc.).

This tracking continues throughout the students' careers. Follow-up counseling sessions also continue on all minority students. Data is being collected and compared on these scholarship students and the non-participants. Presently, the retention of African-American engineering students is equal to that of all students as reported by the Associate Dean in the 1994 Annual Report.

The graph clearly shows the students who have taken the orientation course are remaining in engineering in greater numbers than those who did not take the course. That is, twenty nine percent of the students taking the course in 1990 are still in engineering compared to only eighteen percent of the students that did not take the course. Similar findings can be seen throughout the three other groups; forty three percent who took the course are still in engineering compared to twenty one percent of non-participants in the 1991 class; fifty three percent compared to thirty one percent in 1992; and seventy seven percent compared to sixty three percent in 1993.

Retention Of Minority Students In MEP Freshman Orientation Class

FALL 1990

Students Enrolled in ENGR 1051		Students Not Enrolled in ENGR 1051	
Number	Percentage	Number	Percentage
35	51%	28	49%

	Students Enrolled in ENGR 1051		Students Not Enrolled in ENGR 1051	
	Number	Percentage	Number	Percentage
Still in ENGR	10	28.6%	5	17.9%
Changed Major	9	25.7%	13	46.4%
Not at LSU	16	45.7%	10	35.7%

FALL 1991

Students Enrolled in ENGR 1051		Students Not Enrolled in ENGR 1051	
Number	Percentage	Number	Percentage
28	34.6%	53	65.4%

	Students Enrolled in ENGR 1051		Students Not Enrolled in ENGR 1051	
	Number	Percentage	Number	Percentage
Still in ENGR	12	42.9%	11	20.8%
Changed Major	5	17.9%	19	35.8%
Not at LSU	11	39.2%	23	43.4%

FALL 1992

Students Enrolled in ENGR 1051		Students Not Enrolled in ENGR 1051	
Number	Percentage	Number	Percentage
47	56.6%	36	43.4%

	Students Enrolled in ENGR 1051		Students Not Enrolled in ENGR 1051	
	Number	Percentage	Number	Percentage
Still in ENGR	25	53.2%	11	30.6%
Changed Major	9	19.1%	10	27.8%
Not at LSU	13	27.7%	15	41.6%

Retention Of Minority Students In MEP Freshman Orientation Class

FALL 1993

Students Enrolled in ENGR 1051		Students Not Enrolled in ENGR 1051	
Number	Percentage	Number	Percentage
39	59.1%	27	40.9%

	Students Enrolled in ENGR 1051		Students Not Enrolled in ENGR 1051	
	Number	Percentage	Number	Percentage
Still in ENGR	30	76.9%	17	63.0%
Changed Major	6	15.4%	7	25.9%
Not at LSU	3	7.7%	3	11.1%

FALL 1994

Students Enrolled in ENGR 1051		Students Not Enrolled in ENGR 1051	
Number	Percentage	Number	Percentage
32	.52.5%	29	47.5%

	Students Enrolled in ENGR 1051		Students Not Enrolled in ENGR 1051	
	Number	Percentage	Number	Percentage
Still in ENGR	32	100.0%	29	100.0%
Changed Major	0	0.0%	0	0.0%
Not at LSU	0	0.0%	0	0.0%

Impact on Increasing Minority Students' Presence/ Participation at the University

The MEP students have had a positive impact on LSU in several ways: (1) these students are being utilized to recruit other students to undergraduate and graduate programs; (2) Region V of the National Society of Black Engineers (representing thirty three engineering schools) is the LSU chapter and has the third highest GPA in 1995; (3) one of the MEP students was selected as the "Top Black Student" by the U.S. Black Engineers Conference and the National Society of Black Engineers; and (4) minority engineering students are now the leaders in many more student organizations. This local, regional, and national notoriety has greatly improved the university's image throughout the country.

Additionally, the MEP has been awarded "Most Outstanding Program" by the National Association of Minority Engineering Program Administrators, the African-Americans in Higher Education, and the National Society of Black Engineers, and has earned several local awards. Faculty, staff, and graduate students have co-presented papers to the American Society of Engineering Educators and other groups.

Students now see the same kinds of successes they were accustomed to in high school as being possible in college. This reality is very powerful for the student's sense of self. African-American engineering students are the leaders in all aspects of university life—athletic to student government.

Lastly, the academic community that has developed equips the students to better manipulate the culture at a predominantly white university.

Implications for the Future

This program was initially designed to retain more minority students in engineering. In addition, it provides psychological support to students enabling them to maintain the high self-esteem with which they enter the institution. The realities of the twenty first century dictate that educators reform their philosophy to one that better reflects the needs, and the means to properly educate the majority of students in the education pipeline, including minorities and women.

Never before in U.S. history has education meant more to the growth and progress of individuals and the nation. In addition to providing the human capital that administers the operation of the government, the corporate world, and the professions, the educational system also trains the future work force that will revitalize its own faculty. Consequently, the survival and growth of higher education is dependent on the retention and graduation of its students.

The fate of U.S. economic development is in the hands of administrators in higher education. Demographic trends indicate a more diverse, and smaller pool, of high school graduates. Never before has the plight of these students been more critical to the security and economic development of the nation.

The theories on retention and multiculturalism need to be operationalized and more research needs to be done. This research must be translated into the language that administrators deal with, and that is money. It must discuss how improved retention impacts saving, allocating and investing money.

Successful efforts are difficult to mount, if only because of the continuing inability to make sense of the variables and characteristics of retention. Issues of congruence and integration are common to all who find themselves different from the mainstream. As becoming educated is a process, efforts can begin at any time to improve interactions, and the experiences of students. What is needed are plans to use the information to do those things deemed in the best interest of students. For example, improvement in African-American student educational opportunities on college campuses would translate into an improved environment for all students, since retention of all college students is so low.

To make some sense of it all on a local level, it seems necessary to focus on the mission of the university. Some specific remedies might include answering these questions: (1) Why do students come to this institution? (2) What are the characteristics of the matriculants? (3) What are the salient characteristics of the campus environment? (4) What are the characteristics of the persisters? (5) What are the characteristics of the dropouts? (6) How do students benefit from attending this institution?

In conclusion, after these questions are answered, and the information is shared with the campus community, some specific methods of then moving toward retention include:

(1) organized efforts with sample programs and services as with minority engineering;

(2) an evaluation and review of what is being done in regards to minorities;

(3) working toward refinement of existing programs;

(4) sharing of information with administrators, faculty, and staff concerning retention, demographics and campus redesign to eliminate stereotypic thinking;

(5) centralizing efforts without losing the institutional responsibility to all the campus community; and

(6) finding a way to translate multicultural education into savings.

Shared Insights

The challenges for enhancing and promoting this environment are still ahead. The MEP is looking, not just to add numbers of underrepresented minorities to the college "mix", but to create a microcosm of society. This way the student will get a head start on living and working with a variety of groups, and reap the benefits that accrue to those who learn early that cooperation yields more than conflict.

The MEP has made laudable strides toward institutionalization of this program, and has been most successful in providing students, faculty, and staff with the tools to reach mutual goals.

Administrators should not expect too much, too soon. Much effort should be placed on establishing liaisons and partnerships throughout the campus, the community, and the corporate world.

—Ms. Forest Dent Smith is the Coordinator of the Minority Engineering Program College of Engineering at Louisiana State University at Baton Rouge, Louisiana.

Bibliography

Astin, A.W. (1976). Preventing Students From Dropping Out. San Francisco: Jossey-Bass Publishers.

Astin, A (1978). Four Critical Years. San Francisco: Jossey Bass Publishers.

Banks, J. A. and Banks, C. A. (Eds.). (1993). Multicultural Education: Issues and Perspectives (2nd ed.). Boston: Allyn and Bacon.

Bean, J.P. (1983). The application of a model of turnover in work organizations to the students attributions process. Review of Higher Education. (6), 129-48.

Blocher, D.H. (1974). Campus learning environment and the ecology of student development. In J.H. Banning (Ed.). Campus ecology: A perspective for student affairs. Cincinnati, OH: NASPA.

Creager, J.A. (1968). Use of research, results in matching students and colleges. Journal of College Student Personnel. (9), 312-19.

Freters, W.B. (1977). Withdrawal from institutions of higher education: An approach with longitudinal data involving diverse institutions. National Center for Educational Statistics. Washington, D.C.: U.S. Office of Education.

Hossler, D. (1984). Enrollment Management: An Integrated Approach. New York: College Entrance Examination Board.

Landis, R. Ed. (1984). A Model Retention Program. Improving the Retention and Graduation of Minorities in Engineering. pp. 27-35. NACME: New York.

Lenning, O.T.; Saver, K.; and Beal, P.E. (1980). Student Retention Strategies. AAHE-ERIC/Higher Education Research Report no. 8. Washington, D.C.: American Association for Higher Education.

Louisiana State University Office of Budget and Planning Statistics, October, 1992.

Louisiana State University Report Concerning the Status of Minorities at the LSUBR campus from 1964-1979.

Louisiana State University Task Force Report on Undergraduate Education, 1988.

Mickey, R. (1988) Counseling, Advising and Mentoring as Retention Strategies for Black Students in Higher Education. Black Student Retention in Higher Education. Lang, M. and Ford, C.Eds. Illinois: Charles C. Thomas

Moos, R.H. (1974). Systems for the assessment and classifications of human environments: An overview. In R.H. Moos and P. Insel (eds.), Issues in Social Ecology. Palo Alto, CA: National Press Books.

Noel, L., ed. (1978). New directions for Student Services: Reducing the dropout rate. San Francisco: Jossey-Bass Publishers.

Pace, C.R. (1980). Assessing diversity among campus groups. In L.L. Baird, R.T. Hartnett, and Associates (eds.). Understanding Student and Faculty Life. San Francisco: Jossey-Bass Publishers.

Painter, P., and Painter N. (1982). Placing students for stability and success. In W.R. Lowery and Associates (eds.). College Admissions Counseling. San Francisco: Jossey-Bass Publishers.

Pascarella, E.T., and Terenzini, P.T. (1980). Predicting Freshman persistence and voluntary dropout decisions from a theoretical model. Journal of Higher Education. (51), 60 75.

Ramist, Leonard (1981). "College student attrition and retention." College Board Report no. 81-1. New York: College Entrance Examination Board.

Rice, Mitchell and B. Alford (1989). A preliminary analysis of black undergraduate students' perceptions of retention/attrition factors at a large, predominately white, State Research University in the south. Journal of Negro Education 58 (1) ,68-81.

Smith, F. (1993). Retention of Minority Students into Graduate School. Proceedings: Centennial Meeting of the Gulf-Southwest Section of ASEE. (1) pp. 74-81.

Tinto, J.V. (1975). Dropout from higher education: a theoretical synthesis of recent research. Journal of Educational Research. (45), 89-125.

Weiner, B. (1985). An educational theory of achievement motivation and emotion. Psychological Review. 92 (4), 548-573.

Other Suggested Readings

Anderson, Edward (1978). A retention design applied to an equal opportunity program. In Lee Noel (Ed.), Reducing the Dropout Rate. San Francisco: Jossey-Bass, Inc.

Britt, Maurice W. (1975). Blacks on White Campuses. Minneapolis: Challenge Production Inc.

Brown, Shirley (1988). Minorities in the Graduate Education Typeline. GRE-ETS.

Clark, Robert (1973). Black students/white university: different expectations. Personnel and Guidance Journal. (51), 463-469.

Cope, R.G. and Hannah, W. (1975). Revolving College doors: The Causes and Consequences of dropping out, stopping out and transferring. New York: John Wiley and Sons.

Engineering Manpower Report. Oct, 1989. #97. AAES.

Halberstan, D. (1991). The Next Century. New York: Morrow.

Hartigan, J.A. and A.K. Wigdor, eds. (1989). Fairness in employment testing. Washington, D.C.: National Academy Press.

Hilliard, Asa (1978). Equal educational opportunity and equality education. Anthropology and Education Quarterly. (9), 110-126.

Keller, George (1988). Review Essay: Black students in higher education. Why so few? Planning for Higher Education. (17), 3-21.

Lomotek, K. (1991). The Racial Crisis in American Higher Education. Albany; State University of New York Press.

Nettles, M.A., ed. (1988). Toward Black Undergraduate Student Equality in American Higher Education. Greenwood Press.

Pantager, T.J., and Creedon, C. (1968). Attrition among college students. American Educational Research Journal. (5) ,57-72.

Pascarella, E.T. (1985). Racial difference in the factors influencing bachelors' degree completion: A nine-year follow up. Paper presented to the annual meeting of AERA, Chicago.

Reich, R.B. (1991). The work of Nations: Preparing ourselves for 21st century capitalism. New York: Knopf.

Sedlacek, R.W. (1987). Black students on white campuses: 20 years of research. Journal of College Student Personnel. (11), 484-511.

Smith, Donald H., and Baruch, Bernard M. (1981). Social and academic environments on white campuses. Journal of Negro Education.50 (3), 299-306.

Taylor, Charles A. (1985). Effective Ways to Recruit and Retain Minority Students. Wisconsin: NMCC, Inc. Publications.

Tinto, V. (1987). Leaving College: Rethinking the Causes and Cures of Student Attrition. Chicago: The University of Chicago Press.

Tracey, T. and Sedlacek, C.W. (1985). The relationship of non-cognitive variables to academic success: A longitudinal comparison by race. Journal of College Student Personnel. (26), 405-10.

Genuine Commitment and Key Strategies for Student Success

by Clifton A. McKnight

Overview:

Retention programs abound in our colleges and universities and many new strategies are becoming common knowledge. With the general emphasis on program outcomes, McKnight suggests that administrators and faculty should look at the uniqueness of individual students as a barometer of retention success. To encourage this shift, he suggests a new paradigm to measure student success that considers the personal outlook and life experiences of students. In this article, the author mentions comprehensive strategies that reinforce small and progressive steps of students throughout their education, and emphasizes both physical and personal support for students' success.

The author discusses the critical impact of committed faculty and staff in improving the academic environment of students. He outlines special strategies to further enhance their effectiveness, giving special attention to new students and student-athletes. He describes the All-Pro Partnership at Montgomery College of Maryland that has a comprehensive approach to student retention and development, in collaboration with existing college programs.

Introduction

Many may be familiar with the story of the stroller on the beach who committed himself to the arduous task of returning beached starfish to their ocean home. The starfish stretched for miles along the shoreline, yet the compassionate stroller reached down again and again to rescue each stranded creature and flung it back to safe waters. Onlookers were intrigued by this stroller who persisted in a laudable effort that, nonetheless, seemed futile. As it goes, someone stopped to inquire of him, "Why are you doing this? There must be thousands of starfish stranded along this shore. Your efforts could not possibly make a difference with so many lost." In response, the stroller looked at his admirer and looked at the starfish in his hand. Then with a glimmer in one eye, the stroller exclaimed, "It will make a difference to this starfish!"

When examining successes and failures in student retention, this story is significant and timely. The stroller did not allow the demise of many starfish to sway his unrelenting dedication to each one, and each lifesaving gesture was emphasized and deemed a priceless success. But in many student retention programs today, individual successes are often overshadowed by general program outcomes. Most often, student success is rated by retention or graduation rates. Some institutions may further rate student performance by grade point average. "Cutting edge" institutions may even include student goal achievement in individual success. But while all of these measures have their place, efforts must go further to broaden the picture of what is considered student success. The stroller's aphorism is a welcome correlation for retention success today, and it speaks volumes to the ongoing commitment to individual students that should be made in student retention programs. Making a positive difference in students' lives often happens one student at a time.

The time is ripe for a paradigm shift. As students grow, their skills, goals, and perceptions change. As they exercise the power of thought, their world expands. To measure whether a student has reached his/her original goals or not may be to measure the smallest success that a student experiences. For example, some students may seek college education only as a means to an end. That end may be to get a job, a career, a promotion, a spouse, or just to get away from home. Others come to learn how they can make a difference for themselves and their communities. The new paradigm for student success should be based on understanding students' individual experiences in college and then determining whether the students' thoughts and actions, as influenced by those experiences, take them to a "better place" both subjectively and objectively.

The first step to establishing this new paradigm is to begin redefining institutions and the goals of educators. Education and service need not take place only when a student is on campus. Students' "coming of age" (including returning adult learners) can be assisted through pre-college outreach in the communities. Furthermore, students can continue to benefit even when they drop out of school or stop benefitting directly from the resources of their higher educational institutions. An institution that endeavors to function in such a comprehensive manner and accommodate individual differences is never likely to be short of students or involved alumni.

The Comprehensive Approach

Retention programs abound. Every day someone comes up with a new slant or a new twist to an old solution. This is a good thing in the sense that varying approaches provide a representation of change toward progress. Different factors in retention programs should be examined for a comprehensive approach to retention success.

Adequate resources and financial assistance are crucial components to help ensure retention. For example, financial assistance, academic assistance, and organized opportunities for debate, discussion, scholarship, socialization, competition and collaboration are all outstanding building blocks for an education. However, resources and programs, by themselves, are lifeless instruments. Occasionally, self-assured and self-directed students can take full advantage of these fine instruments of learning. But often the complexities of life can confuse and discourage even the best students, and an abundance of programs alone becomes ineffective in their success.

Fortunately, these instruments can be brought to life by educators whose efforts are directed with a learned mind, an insightful eye and a sincere heart. A critical focus in retention programs should be the continued identification and nurturing of supportive and effective administrative faculty and staff. The educator as practitioner must not only be informed, but also inspired. He/she must be much more than capable, he/she must be committed. These personal characteristics are important to the success of retention.

During the Tenth Higher Education Conference on Black Student Retention, renowned psychologist and keynote speaker, Dr. Asa Hilliard III, eloquently pointed out that intention, or the sincere desire to facilitate student success, is a prerequisite for retention. Colleges should identify those educators that earnestly promote student success and those that perpetuate failure. They can also help students identify "high risk" instructors that have no intention to facilitate their students' success. Little research is needed to note the role that educators with vision, determination and commitment played in the success of African American students, young and old, during the oppressive era of segregation. One example is Mary McLeod Bethune who laid the foundation for thousands to become more than just "retained." Starting with less than one dollar and fifty cents in her pocket, she persisted with her dream of raising the station of slave descendants by providing them with quality learning.

Times are different now, but persistent dedication and sacrifice is still crucial. Some students today must be concerned with just getting to school alive and worrying about school expenses. These are issues that cannot be ignored, and serious battles must be waged. It is critical, however, that these abhorrent issues do not become so distracting that the care of students is left at the mercy of apathetic or malicious educators. Those educators who have the ability to inform and inspire must remain on the front lines to advocate for and ensure the success of these evolving leaders of tomorrow. Students often respond to genuine interest and will put forth the added effort to reach the expectations of a caring instructor.

Attention to the humanistic and professional development of educators is a sure way to improve the academic environment for students. Eagerness, respect, and preparedness are contagious qualities. An instructor who is excited about a topic can bring that topic to life for students. The following strategies are suggested to enhance the overall effectiveness of educators in retention programs:
- identify key personnel by their commitment as well as their proficiency;
- establish a means for these educators to network and synergize;
- develop professional enhancement opportunities internally and facilitate access to conferences and workshops externally;
- create mechanisms for attracting and retaining the most dedicated and brightest educators;
- reward creativity and commitment;
- assign resources to support planning, assessment and evaluation; and
- establish formal and informal outreach and feedback efforts.

Often discussions about retention are based on student problems and identifying the shortcomings or needs of students. Justifiably, the true focus sometimes lies in the respective institution and its culture. Lower retention rates may generate questions concerning whether something in the institutional structure inherently ostracizes certain students or otherwise limits their potential based on inappropriate indicators. Finding answers to these questions and seeking solutions to student problems can contribute substantially in improving persistence.

The cultural integrity of institutions is essential to long-term enhancement of student success. Institutions must be relevant to, and up-to-date with the demands of the times. Resources to address the ever-evolving demands of society must include social "laboratories" within the institution that mimic global perspectives. Extra-curricular and co-curricular activities which provide a safe place to consider new thoughts and meet new people—to expand one's horizons—must be prevalent. Students learn about various cultures through personal interactions and textbooks. Interactions are significant from student to student, and from educator to student. One educator impacts many students over extended periods. It follows that an effective retention program would employ educators who are effective when dealing with students and with each other. The culture of the institution should be inviting, encouraging and far-reaching.

Overall, the secrets to fostering student success are not secrets at all. They are strategies which may be observed in varying degrees, at a variety of institutions. Circumstances where comprehensive approaches are especially useful involve recent high school graduates and student athletes.

New Students

The transition from high school to college is often traumatic for new students. Learning how to balance freedom and responsibility, for example, is a feat few adult citizens have mastered, let alone recent high school graduates. Leaving the familiar for the unknown, saying goodbye to friends and family, and establishing new relationships can be difficult. Finding a comfortable niche in a strange environment is tough when one has not identified where or, more likely, "who" their new "inside" is. This psychosocial isolation is magnified by uncertainty.

New students coming into a new environment are introduced to an alien culture articulated by the brand of higher education practiced by the administrators, faculty and staff of that particular institution. Learning the rules of this new game is filled with pitfalls. All too often, academic insufficiency is confirmed after the first exam and academic preparation and study habits that may have been ideal in high school are severely questioned as an undergraduate.

Life problems the student faced prior to coming to college do not just disappear after arrival on campus. With such a burdensome load to bear, how can the student succeed? Completing high school and having the vision to enroll and attend college, marks a level of individual tenacity in and of itself. The willingness to make new friends and to strike on new paths are the bold and courageous undertakings of a pioneering spirit. This can be a mark of success. Many students need a structured opportunity to connect with and to support one another while strengthening study habits and learning about the ways of the institution and the history of higher education in the United States.

Student-athletes

All students want to feel and be successful. Even the student who believes he/she only wants to play sports wants to be successful, and like most, he/she tends to focus on those areas where success has been achieved before. Student-athletes who attend community colleges often have not performed well enough academically to attend a four-year institution that would provide them with an athletic scholarship. Many of these students were shunted through high school without developing the requisite skills needed to graduate. Students participating in athletics do not corner the market in this regard, but the demand for their athletic skills offers the "system" an added incentive for "social promotion" that supersedes academic performance. Social promotion grants these students eligibility to continue subsequent seasons in their respective sport(s). Students in turn measure their success in part by excelling in athletics.

Like the general student body, students participating in sports come from various cultures and socioeconomic backgrounds. African Americans are among the many groups overrepresented in difficult financial and social circumstances. Some students have the arduous task of negotiating limiting resources at home, treacherous neighborhoods and malicious instructors. Arguably, a large percentage of these students pursue sports as an outlet. Sports represents one of a very limited number of avenues to escape grave conditions, whether solely perceived by the student or readily apparent to society.

Sports participation also represents a valid reason to stay in school. Student-athletes are far more likely to put up with practice than with class, however, since their experience of success and reward on the playing field is more pronounced. They readily experience success, affirmation and confirmation while participating in their sport, whereas they may feel further and further isolated in the classroom. Programs designed to facilitate athletes' success and retention must take careful steps to reinforce experiences outside that which is directly and immediately in their realm (sport). Important areas in coursework and life goals can be creatively linked to the athletic experience and significantly impact the student's success over time with his/her sustained and challenging efforts.

The Montgomery College Approach

At the Rockville, MD campus of Montgomery College, the All-Pro Partnership was developed to address a variety of the hurdles and obstacles student-athletes (many of whom are African American) face, including those that are self-perpetuated. The All-Pro Partnership was developed in a team effort supported by the Dean of Students, and consists of the athletic director and several coaches and counseling faculty. Athletes participate in the general student programs, but they receive specialized counseling and advising to enhance their success. As an important component, first-year student-athletes participate in the general advising program provided to all degree-seeking and potential transfer students. This advising programs is called the Montgomery College Advising, Planning Program (MAPP). Student-athletes attend special sessions where information is covered regarding resources, institutional guidelines, important dates, curricula and transfer, etc.

As part of their course load, student-athletes enroll in an eight-week course entitled "College Survival." This one-credit course, available to all students, is customized to relate the successful attitudes, habits and experiences of the athlete to classroom success. The students are encouraged to carry one notebook in which classwork for all classes may be found, examined, and utilized to help formulate new academic strategies. Attitude and performance are further stimulated by guest speakers and video presentations featuring former students and student-athletes as well as professional athletes and others.

The All-Pro Partnership project is augmented by a mentoring program called Project S.U.C.C.E.S.S. which is a pilot effort geared to the retention of all African American students, including student-athletes. Project S.U.C.C.E.S.S. describes the following components: Support, Understanding, Caring, Commitment, Education, Sensitivity, and Skills.

Project S.U.C.C.E.S.S. mentors include administrators, faculty and staff interested in student success. Students and student-athletes who are referred to the project are assigned mentors with whom they interact for various types of support. Students can contact their mentors for conversation, tutoring, and accessing various resources.

Research shows that African American students demonstrate more extreme attrition than the overall student population. The strategies and programs described above can maintain the commitment, caring, and comprehensive programming needed for academic success.

—Mr. Clifton A. McKnight is in the Office of Student Development at Montgomery College in Rockville, Maryland.

A Retention Model for University of Massachusetts-Dartmouth Paul Cuffe Institute

by John E. Bush

Overview:

Many black students who attend college are often underprepared because they have not had the benefit of experiencing a cultural lifestyle that contributes to a successful college experience. Unless they have come up in a solid middle class experience, they tend not to do well because the demands of college are too much for their ability to meet them; consequently, many of the students drop out before they attain a degree.

With adequate concern, commitment and legitimate help, most of the potential dropouts would remain to get a degree. This has been demonstrated time and time again in many higher educational institutions throughout the United States. University of Massachusetts-Dartmouth is no exception. The Upward Bound, College Now and START programs have all been successful in increasing retention.

This article argues that a collaboration of students, faculty and staff, working in a formal organization (Paul Cuffe Institute), dedicated to establishing educational programs and support systems of various kinds, will do much to raise the retention rate at the university, primarily because committed participation will enhance the desire to achieve and therefore remain until graduation.

Introduction

Colleges and universities have always been interested in the retention percentages of the students whom they have recruited. In the late 1960s and early 1970s more black students began to attend white colleges and universities. From that time until the present, researchers throughout the United States have been studying the retention problems of black students in white colleges and universities. Such studies continue today as there are now fewer black students attending predominantly white universities than there were in the seventies and the eighties, and their rate of retention has decreased.[1] There are several reasons for the reduced attendance and retention; primary among them are financial concerns, followed by disillusionment (usually caused by racial incidents) with social life at white universities.[2]

Even with fewer blacks in attendance at white schools, it is increasingly difficult to keep them there until graduation. This is particularly true at the public universities and colleges. Some of the retention studies have suggested the black students who tend to remain until graduation are black students who have backgrounds which are comparable to white students who graduate, e.g., a strong commitment to middle class values (which puts much stress on achieving higher education), adequate finances, a strong desire to achieve which emanates from parents who have received college degrees, and of course the ability to study successfully for four years.[3]

Even with such positive attitudes, many black students who attend white colleges and universities, do not get degrees from those institutions. Again, retention studies have discovered there are several reasons for the black student's failure to complete their studies. These reasons may be subsumed under the heading "lack of institutional support," i.e., support from deans and other administrative officials, faculty, various service departments, programs, financial aid offices and counselling departments.[4] This is not to suggest anything sinister; the bottom line is that white institutions tend to function primarily for white students, that is, white students who "know the ropes" and know their ways around the institutions and their various offices. For these students, the institution is merely an extension of the high schools from which they have come, and the social organizations and social life are also continuations of something they have known in the past. The landscape, the faces and the programs are familiar, which enable them to function more successfully without feeling so alienated.

On the other hand, black students are attempting to function in a completely different social climate. Unless they have lived in integrated situations and experienced life as middle class whites have experienced it, they begin their educational experience in a very different and challenging social situation. Their chances of getting through the experience are significantly reduced, primarily because they come from different cultural perspectives.[5]

For the student of color, everything is essentially based upon white cultural instrumentalities. In addition to a curriculum which is generally focused on the Western European tradition, all the student organizations, which tend to be managed by white students, focus upon programs which reflect their interests, such as the music groups and speakers brought to the campus, as well as social entertainment, such as movies, plays and comedy nights, etc. Moreover, because there are far more white students than blacks who run for student offices (which tend to control the social and political life of the campus), white students easily manage to win, thus giving them power and control. The resulting configuration almost automatically forces black students to form social groupings of their own (which is what most of them tend to do), or decide not to participate in anything.

Support Groups

At the University of Massachusetts-Dartmouth, the students of color tend to be members or associated with United Brothers and Sisters. This group, which was formerly the Black Student Union, is now composed of Latinas, Latinos (mostly of Puerto Rican ethnicity), Cape Verdeans, Africans, African Americans and students of color from the Caribbean. There are also students of mixed parentage, (white and black) who may or may not belong to the group. Those who do not tend to either remain isolated or associate with white students.

Although the students of color comprise only 7.5 percent (including Asian and Pacific Islanders) of the student body, the men have managed to establish two black fraternities. There is also a Men of Color discussion group which was established by a faculty member in 1990. More recently a Women of Color discussion group was established. These two groups do not have officers and are only loosely organized, solely for the purposes of discussing common problems and making friendship connections. In addition to these groups, there is a faculty staff group, the Black Coalition, which was established in 1974. In 1993, another group was formed, The Young Black Caucus, made up of younger staff members who have various staff positions in the university. Of course, all of the organizations are volunteer organizations, designed to increase political and social awareness.

Aiding Matriculation and Retention

UMass-Dartmouth has three groups designed to help students of color matriculate and receive degrees from the university. These groups are financed by the university, with directors appointed by university officials.

One such group is Upward Bound. Its responsibility is to tap high school students in the tenth grade and enroll them in a pre-college program, with the purpose of getting them interested in attending college after graduation from high school—any college, not necessarily UMass-Dartmouth.

The second program is the College Now Program, created to give older students, that is, students who may have been out of high school for some time, a second chance to get a college degree and thereby, hopefully improve their lives and opportunities to make a decent living. This program, which has been in operation since 1968, has managed to consistently graduate students who are often in the top ten percent of the graduating class. The program has a high retention rate, usually 80 to 85 percent (the first year), which is considerably higher than those students admitted through the regular admission process. In 1994-95, their rate of retention was lower than usual. In January 1995, they had a retention rate of 65 percent. It is not known at this point why this rate was lower than usual; however it may have occurred because the program admitted approximately 100 students, which is about forty more than they admitted in 1993-94. Research may reveal that the additional students may not have been as motivated or as well-prepared as past students.

The final university program instituted for minorities is the START program (Steps to Abstract Reasoning and Thinking) which is similar to College Now, but is geared specifically toward recruiting and supporting students who will study in the areas of science and engineering. This is a more recent program, which has demonstrated some promise. Like Upward Bound, students are also recruited in the high schools.

The aforementioned high retention rate of College Now students may be attributed to several factors. As has been mentioned, motivation is very important, and of course, previous preparation contributes significantly. However, students who are admitted under a five-year program must meet certain obligations. The program is very structured. The students are assigned counselors and they must report to them regularly. They also attend group study sessions and they must take advantage of the tutoring sessions available in the Reading and Writing Center and the Math Center.

In addition, professors are provided with forms wherein they document the progress of the students. Those reports are returned to the College Now office. The structure of the program is well- devised. The monitoring of progress is a very serious endeavor and the students seem to like the program very much. Most of them speak highly of the program. This regimented program produces positive results. It certainly helps College Now students get involved in the larger university programs. Traditionally, they have been successful in taking leadership roles and have made outstanding contributions to the university; having acted in plays, served as members and officers of several student organizations, served as peer counselors, members of the Student Senate, and in one case, one of the students became president of the Student Senate. In addition, many have graduated with honors. Elements of this program should be incorporated in the retention efforts provided for students who are admitted through regular admissions.

Having discussed the various programs on hand that are designed to increase retention, it is now necessary to discuss briefly, why retention efforts and various programs in general tend to lack effectiveness; however to a lesser extent in the College Now and START examples.

Lack of Effectiveness Examined

The following assumptions regarding the retention efforts are made on the basis of experience gained from long service at the university. Many of the faculty of color as well as staff have agreed in informal discussions that the following factors contribute to lack of retention of students of color:

(1) The students of color lack political knowledge necessary to survive in college—"the survival game."

(2) They do not feel good about themselves as people of color.

(3) They do not feel comfortable being in a basically all- white environment.

(4) They do not readily form study collaboratives.

Briefly stated, students must be taught how to play "the survival game". They must be taught that to enroll in a course and study only to pass it, does not contribute to their overall success, unless they also learn how to get a good grade after they have studied hard. They must also be able to establish dialogue with the professor and make themselves known to him/her. Research has revealed that those students who sit near the front, participate and attend regularly tend to do best.[7] Students of color must be taught they must participate, ask and answer questions, visit the professors in their offices, and get to know the professors and department chairpersons as well as deans and higher-ups.[8]) Students have to be taught how to become more than a name. Associated with this process is getting to know their advisors. Students have to know they should visit with advisers on a regular basis. The more information a student has concerning the process and rules of the game, the more likely he/she will achieve success in the university setting.

Regarding the second observation, that students of color do not feel good about themselves; it has been observed, particularly by professors of color, that black students know practically nothing about their historical past; what they do know leaves them with negative feelings. These feelings tend to contribute to their avoiding each other and also contribute to a lack of success in the larger scheme of things. James Baldwin made the observation that black Americans tend not to want to look into the faces of other African Americans and Africans, because it reminds them too much of their past.[9] This avoidance causes many black students not to get involved in the activities of black student organizations, such as United Brothers and Sisters, as well as other student groups on campus. These estrangements contribute to the drop-out rate.

The third point states that students of color are not comfortable in an all-white environment. It is difficult for black students, who for the most part, have matriculated from black neighborhoods and often from predominantly-black high schools, to suddenly be thrust into a white environment and be expected to integrate and do well. This new social situation requires a period of adjustment, which some of the students do not successfully make.[10] Those who might have lived in integrated neighborhoods and who might have attended primarily white high schools tend to have a little easier time adjusting, but nevertheless, they must choose friends carefully. It has been observed that such students tend to align themselves with white students, perhaps because of "successful" past experiences in their integrated hometown situations. Their coming together might be an attempt to reduce the feelings of alienation which occur in the large university setting.

The college lives of black students are generally not organized in ways which tend to guarantee success. At UMass-Dartmouth there were about 203 students of color in September 1994. Although the registrar's office reported there were 212 students of color registered in the spring term of 1995, that number is suspect. It seems the loss of thirty-five College Now students had not been included. The total number of black students represents 3.5 percent of the student body. (The total undergraduate student body is approximately 5,000). As of January 1995, approximately 100 of the black students had not registered for the fall semester of 1995. The reasons for this phenomenon is not known at the present time. It is believed that many students experienced financial difficulties and could not register at that time.

Those students who remain must be organized and instructed in ways to increase their chances of survival. They can improve their chances of getting a degree in many ways. Individually and collectively, they must be encouraged to take courses from black professors. They must take courses which give them a clearer and more correct picture of the African diaspora. They should also share their experiences with their peers, and be encouraged to join black student organizations, as well as the regular university student organizations. By getting involved, they will gain "know-how", and political savvy and experience, which will help decrease the degree of intimidation they experience in a basically white environment. They will (in the long run) learn to manipulate the environment, so that it more readily serves their own needs.

In addition to the above, black faculty must encourage students of color to join in collaborative efforts which will be of benefit to both parties. Faculty can help black students survive and flourish, primarily because they themselves have done so. They can use their knowledge and experience to help the students, and the students can use their political power (once they have gained it) to help the faculty and themselves get some of the things they want and need from an administration often insensitive to the needs of blacks. This idea has been discussed informally, and in formal meetings among black faculty and staff. Related ideas have often been discussed in Black Coalition meetings. Basically, the discussions usually end with the question: "What can we do to get the students of color more involved in university life?" The faculty and staff feel that if students are involved, they will be more likely to remain at the university until graduation.

Umbrella Organization

In formal discussions, during the early part of the 1994 fall term, it was realized that an umbrella organization was needed to represent all the students of color and faculty-staff organizations. Discussions began to focus on how to make the idea a reality. These discussions were tedious and sometimes acrimonious, because they involved attempting to do something which had never been done in a college or university setting, that is, create an organization of students, faculty and staff, wherein all parties would have equal representation and equal say, not only in how the organization would function, but more importantly, in how it would serve as a retention effort. It was not feasible to simply establish another organization, which would develop yet another retention program, and that was not the goal. Instead we looked to the successful College Now and START programs. In addition, the Office of Multicultural Affairs also provided an example of ways to serve multicultural students, and thereby help them to remain in school.

The basic assumption was that by forming an umbrella organization with representation from all groups, and especially by getting the students involved in various university activities, more of them would remain in the university. If the students became immersed in various programmatic efforts to structure a more exciting university life, they would develop a sense of self-assuredness and a sense of achievement. They would have the opportunity to develop a sense of pride because they would be working alongside faculty and staff in various common endeavors; they would be working with their role models as well as their peers in an effort to achieve a common good.

The idea is even more exciting and compelling because all the participants would be involved on a voluntary basis. This is particularly true of all of the faculty and most of the staff, because they have positions which are not directly related to student services; they are paid for doing a job in the university which, in most instances, is not affiliated with the retention effort.

When the basic idea was created, the organization was conceived as an unofficial college within the university; an unofficial college structured just like the regular colleges, with deans, etc. The chancellor was of the opinion that it would create some confusion by calling it a college, so it became an institute. The forthcoming Unity House took the name of Frederick Douglass; thus the new organization became officially known as Paul Cuffe Institute, named after the great sailing captain, entrepreneur and educator born in Cutty Hunk, MA; and who lived in Dartmouth.

Paul Cuffe Institute

The objectives of Paul Cuffe Institute have been delineated and discussed from time to time, and have changed in the process, but are now more clearly defined as the following:

(1) to bring all the student faculty and staff groups under one umbrella in order that they can share knowledge and work to achieve common goals (which is best defined in objective number four below);

(2) to work together to establish a warm, welcoming and friendly environment, especially for students of color, so they will be encouraged to remain in the university until graduation;

(3) to encourage all of the organizations to list the dates of their program activities with the institute in order that cooperative efforts can be established to support each other's programs;

(4) to work as a unified group (however, specific political concerns would still be addressed by the Black Coalition) in order to ensure that the affairs of people of color receive serious consideration and action in the university hierarchy;

(5) to present educational and cultural programs for the organization and for the larger university; and

(6) to establish and encourage social relationships between and among faculty, staff and students.

It is assumed that in carrying out these objectives, a significant contribution will be made to keep students at the university and, (in the long run), attract other students to the university.

The following organizations send delegates to be members of the governing board of Paul Cuffe Institute:

1. The Black Coalition;

2. Young Black Caucus;

3. Alpha Phi Alpha fraternity;

4. Iota Theta fraternity;

5. Men of Color discussion group;

6. Women of Color discussion group;

7. United Brothers and Sisters;

8. established offices which deal with multicultural affairs, e.g., Office of Multi Cultural Affairs, College Now, Upward Bound, Affirmative Action/ Cultural Diversity, staff members and dining hall employees of color, particularly managerial staff.

The organizational structure of the institute is made up of representatives from each of the above groups, who serve as delegates. Co-directors have been elected. Students will take other official positions. Some of the specific responsibilities of the institute are to coordinate the following annual events: Black History Month, the annual scholarship banquet, and the Martin Luther King observance. The institute also presents its own programs, such as the presentation of Dr. Asa Hilliard, who gave a university-wide lecture on the bell curve, the day the Paul Cuffe Institute was officially announced to the university community.

There have been many meetings to discuss and formulate this concept. The meetings have been productive, but there has been a great sense of frustration for several reasons, one of the primary ones being that the Institute has not received regular or consistent support from the students. Many of them fail in their basic responsibilities as students operating in a university setting.

Although there are many existing problems, the efforts to organize the Paul Cuffe Institute have brought the people-of-color community closer together, resulting in the hope that continued planning and more dedicated organization will produce not only a more viable representation of the people-of-color community, but also, more importantly, will make a substantial commitment to retention.

It is believed the organization will work well in a university of this size, essentially because the population is not too large and it is appropriate to institute and carry out the objectives. Past activity, meetings, etc. have given evidence, that it would be more difficult to work with larger groups. People of color in a larger university would have a more difficult time establishing such a group, because there would be so many more students, and perhaps not a substantially greater number of faculty and staff who might be recruited to take part in the organization. The program can only work if faculty and staff in the university setting have established some particularistic relationships with each other and with students, and have decided they not only accept the idea of being role models, but also are willing to become personally involved with the students.

Naturally, the results of all efforts must be monitored. If there is a significant rise in retention rates, monitoring will allow for more specific identification of the reasons for the increase. It is hoped, of course, such research will reveal it was due to the efforts of the Paul Cuffe Institute.

—Dr. John E. Bush is Professor of Sociology and Special Assistant to the Chancellor for Multi-Cultural Affairs at the University of Massachusetts, in Dartmouth, Massachusetts.

Notes

1. Arrington & Scott discuss this notion in their piece reported in the National Retention Project (1993), reported in The National Retention Project of the American Association of State Colleges and Universities.

2. The Chronicle of Higher Education has reported on such incidents recently, at such schools as University of Pennsylvania, Rutgers and UMass-Amherst. Astin writes "that the mix of widely differing characteristics, needs, etc. makes it difficult to create community". He reported the above in his article "Forging the Ties that Bind" in College Board Review.

3. Reducing the Drop Out Rate by Robert G. Cope, especially page 4, which discusses "individual characteristics."

4. See Anderson's discussion of this idea in Organizing the Campus for Retention. He discusses promoting persistence and academic achievement. The idea is also discussed by James B. Rose in Reducing the Dropout Rate, p. 57.

5. Issues and Problems in the Retention of Black Students in Predominantly White Institutions of Higher Education. In this piece, by Barbara Love, factors attracting retention are catalogued. The focus is on African American students who do persist and what is needed to establish a climate of inclusion. The idea is also discussed by Richardson and Young. See bibliography.

6. This idea is regularly reported in the literature. See especially the study by Anderson, In Organizing the Campus for Retention.

7. In order for the student to get more involved in the academic experience, he/she must develop positive internal forces e.g., motivation, academic skills, joy of learning, etc. Anderson discusses this in depth under the topic "Decision to Attend College" on page 11-19 in Organizing the Campus for Retention.

8. David S. Crockett discusses the importance of advising in his piece "Academic Advising: Cornerstone of Student Retention," in Reducing the Dropout Rate. He suggested that much advising is perfunctory, and also tends to be ineffective. Perfunctory advising tends to be discouraging to students, especially students of color.

9. James Baldwin has discussed and analyzed blacks' relations to other blacks in many of his writings. In The Price of the Ticket, he writes about this phenomenon in "Encounter on the Seine" p. 35-39 and "White Man's Guilt," p. 409-414. His main theme is that blacks tend to have internalized negative feelings which whites have directed toward them. This negativity is often directed toward other blacks.

10. See Edward Anderson in Promoting Persistence and Academic Achievement Among Minority Undergraduates.

Classroom Techniques for Black Male Student Retention

by John F. Gardenhire

Overview:

The goal of this article is to present specific techniques that any teacher could use to keep black male students from dropping out of their classes. To achieve this goal, the author focuses on twenty ideas and approaches that he has used successfully for many years. These ideas are accessible to teachers who work in a classroom setting and they are free of institutional budgetary considerations. The basic concept of the article is that humanizing the educational experience is effective in meeting the needs of black males.

Their needs are unique in that they grow up through an educational and social system which tends to marginalize them. According to the author, the rewards of humanizing instruction for these students are rich and varied. One reward lies in the improved mental health of the teacher who will feel empowered to make changes in the lives of students. When these ideas are internalized by the students, it empowers them as well. That empowerment frees students to explore their potentials.

These techniques, the author says, if applied daily, will make the classroom an exciting place for black males to study.

Introduction

Several years ago, at Laney College in Oakland, CA, it became obvious that action was needed on the retention front, when statistics came to light indicating the college was losing an inordinate number of "at-risk" students, even though they had demonstrated both ability and skills. Too many of these students were dropping out, just disappearing, without even bothering to "drop" officially.

The problem was attacked on the classroom level. The plan, presented below, is based on the philosophy of an experimental program that existed on the Laney campus years ago. Although that experimental program is no longer in place, its concept was a good one for the students it served: at-risk students.

The program focused on "humanizing" the curriculum. The effectiveness of that Experimental College can still be shown by looking at the statistics for any semester during its tenure. For example, the 1971 spring semester found 250 students enrolled; 241 of those students finished the semester. The ideas of that program can be incorporated into the plans of any instructor.

Traditionally, instructors work alone in the space of the classroom struggling to share information in ways that enable students to learn. The key word here is "alone." In the face of modern demands requiring a multicultural workforce by the next century, it is paramount the isolation of teacher and student no longer be the model for teaching any students, especially at-risk students. Twentieth-century success demands the production of a skilled workforce. Thus, the institutions of higher learning must focus on new ways to serve all students, in particular those at risk. When the formula that works for the at-risk student population is found, it will be that formula that will serve all students, because the kinds of classroom experiences that benefit at-risk students are the kinds of experiences that benefit all students.

The research shows the ideal retention programs are those which are institutionally-based, campus-wide, and highly structured. Why aren't there more successful programs "modeling" on more campuses? Is there a leadership vacuum? Even without strong leadership, many effective things can be done to enhance at-risk student retention. Whatever the cause of the paucity of programs, the at-risk student retention problem ultimately falls on individual instructors.

Teachers are the answer for many reasons. First, the teacher is the closest to the problem. Second, it is easy for them to start a specific program because they have the autonomy necessary to meet the individual needs of each student.

Techniques

Any classroom teacher can use these techniques, listed below, to foster student retention:

1. learn every student's name;
2. assign specific office hour visits;

3. use "calling cards";

4. touch each student each day;

5. use peer tutors and counselors;

6. use collaborative learning frequently;

7. use five-minute "get-acquainted" sessions;

8. encourage students to join clubs and campus activities;

9. walk students through the campus;

10. take field trips;

11. vary instructional mode;

12. make very short-term assignments;

13. set very short-term goals;

14. include everyone in classroom discussions;

15. make a scrapbook about successful role models;

16. be fair, firm, demanding, consistent, and predictable;

17. provide all materials from the beginning;

18. be animated in the instruction;

19. teach a memory skill; and

20. make self-esteem an aspect of every assignment.

These techniques can be applied at once and should be, beginning the first day an instructor meets the class. It is not as formidable as it might appear to be. The explanation that follows illustrates the ease with which this plan can be implemented:

The Explanation Of Techniques

1. *Learn Their Names.* This might seem obvious to an experienced teacher, but it needs to be said again. Call students by their name when referring to them, especially when referring to African American males. If possible, memorize their names on the first day; if not, learn the names as quickly as possible. Issues of self-worth, "specialness," and identity are addressed in a positive way by utilizing this first technique.

2. *Assign Specific Office Hour Visits.* These should begin during the first week of each semester. This will take a lot of time during the first weeks, but the pay-off is wonderful in its effect upon retention. These visits can be very informal, consisting of a simple discussion of where they went to high school and what plans they have for their future vocation. At the beginning of each visit, always ask questions which allow the students to bring up issues that concern them. Frequently, this will yield information and

facts they would not tell their parents or their best friends—about health or drug problems, issues of abortion, financial or relationship problems, and thoughts of suicide—the revelations unfold as a trusting relationship is established. These discussions reveal the many factors weighing upon students that affect their ability and willingness to complete courses. When the problems are addressed, students who were contemplating dropping out often will reconsider and make great efforts to finish the course work. Students want to succeed and they want to please. Given the chance, they will.

3. *Use Calling Cards.* These are five-inch by eight-inch index cards folded in half to make a four-sided four-inch by five-inch index card. On each "page," students write the name and phone number of four classmates, whom they must call twice a week, recording the time and date of each call. This "networking" establishes class bonding and greatly reduces feelings of isolation and loneliness. Monitor these cards weekly. Students who use the calling cards not only finish the course but do the best work, in most cases.

4. *Touch Each Of The Students.* This technique might seem dangerous, but it can be accomplished in a non-threatening way, in a number of ways. Unobtrusively make a hand-to-hand contact while passing out materials, or brushing or touching a hand or shoulder while "working the room." The same technique can be applied in a very clear and overt way, too. Shake hands with the students as they leave the classroom. This eliminates charges for the door at the end of class periods. Of course, shake hands when students come to the office for a visit. This technique humanizes the learning experience.

5. *Use Peer Tutors And Counselors.* Students will hear from peers what they cannot "hear" from instructors. Choose former students who have achieved well or utilize effective learners in the current class. With a little training—i.e., making clear what is needed—these students can be a wonderful resource for both the students and instructor.

6. *Use Collaborative Learning Frequently.* Collaborative learning is what used to be called "small group" learning. Use it. It works. Students share questions and information in these small group sessions that foster their learning-skill development. These groups provide a comfortable place for at-risk students to explore ideas in a rather safe, less-exposed way than would occur in a discussion held by the entire class. Safety is the key here. Since so many of the students served by these programs are at-risk students, this safety factor is important. The at-risk student, by definition, is one who has been wounded by school experiences so that he/she needs

lots of protected spaces to work on developing his skills and confidence. This technique provides that security. In the instructional plan, this technique can be used in reading, discussion, test preparation, and brainstorming. These are just a few ideas for this technique's employment.

7. *Use Five-Minute Get Acquainted Sessions.* At the beginning of each semester, structure five minutes for students to ask each other specific questions about themselves: their name; one thing they like about themselves; and one thing about themselves they would like to improve. Use this technique for two weeks. Encourage inclusiveness by having students talk with others they don't know. This is another form of networking and reinforces the concept of making connections with fellow students to reduce the feelings of isolation.

8. *Encourage Joining Clubs And Campus Activities.* Research on student retention shows the persistent students are those who participate in some out-of-class activities. These students are more likely to finish course work than those "parking lot-classroom-parking lot" students, for which the junior colleges are famous. Commuter institutions have a particularly difficult time holding students. The reason for this is that students who are without connections lack reasons for "sticking around" when there are problems or when there are difficulties of any kind.

The solution to that problem lies in the club and group activities that can be found on any campus. Introduce students to them. Since they won't know about most opportunities, be their resource person, perhaps take them to a meeting. Schoolwork becomes more of a balanced activity when students are involved in extracurricular projects that connect them to the greater campus life. An involved student is a retained student. Some examples include:

a. swim club;

b. The Black Student Union;

c. drama club;

d. photography club;

e. dance groups;

f. volunteer groups;

g. music groups;

h. art groups; and

i. sports groups.

9. *Walk Them Through The Campus.* Make no assumptions about what at-risk students know about the campus. Take them on a walking tour of the grounds, naming the buildings and features they need to be familiar with

in order to function on campus. Use a map, but be sure the students know how to read a map. If need be, teach them that skill on the first walk they take. Be detailed in descriptions of campus and its special qualities and problems. Access for all students should be a part of this presentation. Special places for students to gather after class should be highlighted and emphasized. Unique aspects of the campus should be focused upon. When students discover there is more to the campus and school than books and classes, they are given yet another reason for staying with the program. The more reasons they can find for staying the better.

10. *Take Field Trips.* Students report the most memorable school-connected learning experiences occur on field trips. This is true at all levels. With the at-risk students, field trips are especially useful since these students are less likely to have been exposed to the experiences offered by the field trip. A broadly experienced student is a better prepared student, with more to think about, to talk about, and to write about.

11. *Vary The Instructional Mode.* Lecture as little as possible. Use video. Use collaborative learning techniques. Use short student presentations. Avoid classroom arrangements that have students looking at the back of each others' heads. Sit in circles so students can see each other and the instructor as well. Avoid sitting behind a desk. Sit with the students. Use films. Use TV. Use guest speakers. Avoid boring these students.

12. *Make Very Short-Term Assignments.* Make short-term assignments which are clear and easily monitored, easily tested and assessed, and for which students are held accountable. Make these assignments at the beginning of each class period; never shout assignments to students as they head for the door. Make short-term assignments which provide students with immediate gratification when they are completed on time and well. Make short-term assignments which allow you to give frequent compliments.

Use the following:

a. In ten minutes…

b. In twenty minutes…

c. By the end of the hour…

d. For tomorrow…

e. For next week… (rarely)

f. By the end of the semester… (never, or not until students are really clear in understanding academic time.)

When possible use "a" and "d" and avoid the rest!

13. *Set Very Short-Term Goals.* This way at-risk students will not get over-whelmed by academic time. They need to learn how to use their time; teach that concept through the use of goals-setting. The assignments are on the instructors terms, the goals on the students'. Ask them:

    a. "What do you want to learn during this hour?"

    b. "What do you want to learn by tomorrow?"

    c. "What do you want to learn by the end of the week?"

    d. "What do you want to learn by the end of this unit?"

    e. "What do you want to learn by the end of the semester?"

    d. "What do you want to learn to get a good job?"

    f. "What do you need to learn to have the kind of life that you want?"

    Here, ask students one other question: "What are you doing now to achieve what you want?"

14. *Include Everyone In Classroom Discussions.* Using this technique will help students feel they belong to the group and that their ideas, feelings, and values are important and respected. The comfort level of the at-risk students correlates highly with their willingness to complete the course. When appropriate, use ideas that students bring up as a part of the instruction. Encourage divergent thinking by pointing it out and complimenting it. To allow the participation of each student during each class period, the instructor must be vigilant and avoid the trap of allowing two or three highly verbal students to monopolize the discussion.

15. *Make A Scrapbook About Successful Role Models.* Make a scrapbook featuring successful black role models so students can build an ongoing tower of models they can learn from and plan to emulate as they progress through the course. This technique is very easy to use and students get excited about the persons they want included in their scrapbook. Sports figures might be their first choices, but their tastes will broaden as other kinds of models are introduced and as their sophistication grows. This represents an inexpensive means to "consciousness raising." Use of this technique provides students fresh ways of thinking and rethinking their choices of the kinds of lives they want to lead. This technique "pushes back horizons" for them in that it opens new areas of possible achievement that most will not have known about and therefore, never considered. Another unexpected consequence of this technique is the fun added to the program by the energy and interest generated. Sometimes, this technique takes on the feel of a competition if it is assigned as a collaborative learning or small group activity.

16. *Be Fair, Firm, Demanding, Consistent, And Predictable.* Be fair, firm, demanding, consistent and predictable when working with at-risk students. They need a place where fairness is a given in their lives. Much of what they have experienced is not fair and has never been fair and looks as if it is never going to be fair. Since many of their experiences have been in households where there are few rules which are adhered to, firmness keeps them from testing the limits of their behavior.

17. *Provide All Materials From The Beginning.* The students will feel better if they have everything they need from the beginning. If the institution cannot provide money for duplication and such, spend some; it will be worth the price—and can always be included on your income tax.

18. *Be Animated In The Instruction.* Use techniques of professional performers. Move around the room. Use other voice tones than the school teacher tone. Avoid looking and being boring. Remember, with the at-risk student, it's a competition for the attention of the right-brained, visually-oriented student (it is called TV), so use all the energy possible. Energy is central to being the center of their focus. Get their attention and keep it by being animated.

19. *Teach A Memory Skill.* During the first or second class meeting, teach the rhymed number skill because it is easy to learn and it works for students instantly. Students love having at their command a real learning tool they can use in their schoolwork and elsewhere, too. If unfamiliar with these techniques, buy one of the pop memory books and learn to use these ideas, then teach one to the students.

20. *Make Self-Esteem An Aspect Of Every Assignment.* Since self- esteem is a major missing factor in the lives of too many at- risk students, instructors can quickly build that quality in their students by carefully planned assignments. Think of ways to make assignments that every student will feel empowered by doing. The careful phrasing of assignments will accomplish this goal for instructors and enhance the educational experience of their students at the same time.

—Dr. John F. Gardenhire is the director of Black Male Mentoring at Laney College in Oakland, California.

Black Ombudsman Program Model
by John F. Reid, Jr.

Overview:

In a July 2, 1993 article in the USA TODAY newspaper, California State University at Fullerton (CSUF) was categorized as having one of the twenty five worst rates for graduating African American male student-athletes among Division I schools. More than 90% of these athletes were special students, considered high-risk academic students. Their academic performance ranged from failure to below average, and they had a history of low retention and graduation.

The Black Ombudsman Program (BOP) was established to address these problems. One of the ways it does this is through administering a questionnaire that measures non-student athletes' versus student-athletes' levels of contentment, retention rates and graduation rates. The questionnaire also examines demographics, academic integration and social integration indicators relating to attrition.

As a result of this annual survey, BOP has used the findings to guide the development of its program; to improve organization; and to improve the retention rate of its African American student-athletes since the spring of 1994. This article examines the evolution of the program and how it contributes to African American student-athlete retention.

Historical origin and development of program

The Black Ombudsman Program began when it was discovered, through a tutoring program for student-athletes, that some, even at the senior level were nearly illiterate. Their command of the English language was elementary. Their elementary and secondary educational institutions had apparently failed to prepare these students for academic success. The purpose of this project is to generate awareness of this problem at CSUF by systematically describing the experiences of high-risk students. African American males have the highest drop-out rate and all athletes are at risk due to their high incidental special admit classification and drop-out rates.

Clearly, there is a need to improve the self-esteem of this troubled population and provide improved access to academic and social support systems. Since most of the problems are enduring and normative, it will take a great deal of compassion and teamwork to wipe away denial and apathy currently prevailing.

In addressing this issue, the following questions acted as a starting point: Is there a relationship between isolation, discontent and African American student attrition? Do isolation and discontent rank higher among reasons for African American student athletes leaving CSUF?

Cal State-Fullerton, founded in 1959, is a public comprehensive university, the largest four-year institution of higher education in Orange County, CA, and one of the largest campuses in the twenty two-campus California State University system. Despite CSUF's good overall minority graduation rate (the university ranks twelfth nationally in its graduation of minority students), it shares with many of its sister campuses a difficulty in retaining and graduating African American male student-athletes.

Student attrition is defined as students leaving institutions of higher learning. It has been an ongoing concern of administrators and researchers. The most recent studies of attrition tend to be more longitudinal in nature, and attempt to explain behavior. More contemporary models employ complex interactions that synthesize a student's perception of the college experience into an interactive model where the university and its members have a "measurable effect" (Serpe, 1991).

According to recent statistics extrapolated from the Chronicle of Higher Education, fifty seven percent of scholarship athletes who entered Division I institutions in 1987 graduated within six years. CSU schools averaged forty seven percent during the same period. Furthermore, CSU white male student-athletes' graduation rate averages nearly 2.5 to 1 when compared to African American male student athletes' graduation rate (Blum, 1994).

Most academically successful high school athletes are preferentially taken by the top-ranked schools. Retention and graduation rates have, therefore, become one of the major criteria established recently by the accreditation board for the university's athletic department.

In the fall of 1993, Richard Serpe's Report on Survey of Student Attrition (1991) was put into use and replicated through a random sampling of the general population. The project was named the Black Ombudsman Program (BOP). Its objectives are to serve the African American student-athlete population by:

- increasing recruitment of academically qualified candidates;
- increasing their graduation rates;
- assisting them in their transitions from college to the real world of work; and
- engaging participants as mentors to elementary school-aged African American males.

The primary concern of the program is the academic success of CSUF's African American male student athletes. The program provides motivation and resources to ensure that all of these students place proper emphasis on their academic programs, and assists those on academic probation to improve their grade-point averages. The program coordinator serves as the participants' ombudsman and advocate with various offices on campus, and coordinates advising, tutoring, counseling, and campus services. The major component of the program consists of special tutors to assist BOP students to persevere in their studies and complete their degrees.

While academic success is the primary objective of the program, Afrocentricity is its philosophical cornerstone. The failure of African Americans to develop an Afrocentric culture is a major source of psychological, social, political and economic dysfunction among African American males. The BOP's weekly Afrocentric training workshop (readings, guest speakers, group sessions) addresses the program's objectives by reinforcing key characteristics necessary for success:

- self-efficacy, which builds the participants' belief in their ability to success-fully complete a task or behavior, i.e, a course of study;
- self-esteem to increase participants satisfaction, confidence and pride in themselves; and
- mastery, which replaces reactive or impulsive behaviors with the appropriate coping skills needed to feel successful in social or academic situations.

Pretest and post test surveys were conducted in the spring semester of 1994, using all African American basketball players. The surveys' outcomes were analyzed to determine areas of weaknesses and strengths. The players were given an opportunity to give their views specifically in regards to addressing their needs. As s result of players' responses, BOP has increased its tutorial effort;, started acting as advocates to secure university support services for student athletes (academic advisement, financial aid, etc.); started weekly Afrocentric didactic training; brought mentors onto campus from the community (judges, lawyers, bankers, business leaders, etc.); and taught study and time management skills.

Key to the BOP approach is the extended family concept. Because academic and social integration in the university setting is arduous for most African American male students, the involvement of role models, mentors, and advisors can make a marked difference in their success as students. The BOP provides participants with these human resources through a corps of African American community leaders who work with the participants on a volunteer basis. In addition, the BOP Advisory Council, composed of African American members of the faculty and staff, foster important communication and cooperation links throughout the campus.

To further implement the extended family concept, BOP participants themselves act as mentors to younger African American males. They are "Big Brothers" to K-6 grade students from single-parent households. In the first year of its operation, BOP established partnerships with Walter Knott Elementary School (Buena Park) and Ruby Drive Elementary School (Placentia) to create these important mentorships and foster meaningful educational and social interactions among the participants. These real-life experiences allow both university and elementary school students (twenty so far) to acquire the self-esteem necessary to succeed in school.

With the extended family concept at the program's core, the BOP's objectives create symbiosis among the university, the student athletes, the elementary school students, and the community advisors. Together, all of the BOP participants work to ensure that Cal State-Fullerton's African American male student-athletes develop the skills and commitment necessary not only to persist and succeed as college students, but also to become community leaders.

The original mission of the BOP was to help more African American male basketball players graduate. The current mission includes working with both African American male and female athletes participating in all sports.

Major Events/Milestones

Community outreach to elementary school-aged African American students is an important component. BOP outreach has select student athletes and CSUF staff committed to excellence. This process maintains the university's role as an extended family member by introducing and supporting participants in various hosted on-and off-campus African American activities. Cooperative real-life experience on campus and in the surrounding communities are explored. Activities include campus tours and games. Off-campus activities include excursions to tide pools, museums, and scientific (at-sea) shipboard experiments. These experiences are mutually motivating and educational. Since the majority of student-athletes and K-6 students are products of single-parent households, CSUF hopes to provide BOP services to fulfill needs in both groups of students.

On October 14, 1994. the Hafif Family Foundation in Claremont, CA, awarded the BOP a grant to specifically support these outreach efforts. BOP is committed and continuing to expand on the extended-family concept by increasing activities providing exposure and learning experiences in the arts and sciences.

CSUF had graduated only three African American male basketball players the past eleven years. In the spring of 1995, five black student-athletes graduated. Among the five graduating seniors were two male basketball players. The spring of 1995 semester was precedence setting, representing the first time in CSUF's thirty eight-year history, that more than one African American male basketball player graduated simultaneously.

Implementation Strategies

During the fall of 1993, CSUF's director of Educational Equity was approached to obtain funding for a graduate assistant and student assistant to support the coordinator. The funds were provided to conduct a pilot study during the 1994 spring semester, that included group counseling sessions, time management training and study skill development classes, motivational training, and identifying and assigning faculty mentors.

Next the program expanded under the auspices of the vice president of academic affairs. More programs and services to include female African American student athletes were begun. Another female student assistant position was added to the administrative staff.

The program continued to grow and the director of athletics assumed responsibility for the overall program, in the spring of 1995. Funding was provided to pay a graduate student assistant which had been a volunteer post since initial implementation in the program.

Programmatic Operations and Activities

The BOP current philosophy that guides the operation comes from affirmative action and organizational development theory. At the beginning of each semester, pretests are given to black student-athletes. These measure self-esteem, mastery, self-efficacy, social and academic integration, racial self-esteem and African American self-consciousness. Respective GPAs are monitored throughout the semester.

During the semester, Friday sessions are held, focusing on the program components previously described. Tutorial sessions are held as requested. At the end of the semester, post tests using the same instruments are given, to measure outcomes of the program. Areas are targeted for program development, and courses are identified that typically prove difficult for students. Appropriate improved modifications are applied in the next semester. A different combination of student services is continually evolving, based on this outcome data.

Organizational and Administrative Staffing

There are a total of four individuals working in this program. The director of the Black Ombudsman Program reports to the athletic director, and is assisted by one graduate assistant and two student assistants, all of whom report directly to the director of the BOP.

Indicators of Program Success

During the 1994 spring semester, more than fifty percent of the BOP participants demonstrated improved GPAs of 2.5 or higher. Two students made the Dean's list. The fall of 1993 vs. the spring of 1994 GPAs show a range of increased GPAs from +.22 to +1.07. The aggregate increased GPA totaled +.54. Two participants' GPAs increased by a point. The program was recently given authority to conduct an independent study course, conjointly with the Speech Communication Department, to teach library and computer skills and enhance writing abilities. None of the BOP student-athletes have dropped out of CSUF since the program began in 1993.

Impact on Increasing Minority Retention

The Black Ombudsman Program Advisory Council was formed in February 1994. The council is comprised of African American faculty and senior staff members. The chair of the council reports directly to the president of the university. They meet once a month and receive a report on all program activities. Council responsibilities include advocating and mediating for the program with the university's administrators and the university at large; planning and coordinating campus-wide social functions; and establishing faculty mentorship.

Recently a collaborative effort has been established between the president, the athletic director and the Advisory Council. This group also meets monthly to distribute information on program activities to the entire university community. The program's growth has spawned these advisory councils, resulting in networking all university support services to improve BOP students' integration.

Problems, Vision for the Future, What the Program Needs

The program's major problem is funding, which is woefully inadequate. None of the staff positions are full-time, even though the coordinator works more than forty hours per week. All other staff members work more than twenty hours per week. All of the staff positions are paid for only twenty hours per week. Work space is adequate for only one person, yet all staff members share the same desk. The Program director designed and maintains program activities on a personal home computer. None of the staff have personal computers on campus.

With continued program success, it is envisioned that BOP will include all student-athletes eventually, even though black student-athletes have the most serious problems. Black student graduation rates are so far behind the general undergraduate student rates. One of the goals is to help as many as possible achieve honors' grades; student-athletes need to be seen as more than "dumb jocks" and to have the university expect them to graduate.

In order for the program to be more viable, awareness of the unique problems to African American student athletes must be fostered. The "shackles" of denial must be broken and this type of program must become proactive in resolving identified problem areas. Here at CSUF, the prospects for recognizable changes are realistic based on university support from the top down.

Shared Insights and Advice to Others

Most black student athletes have been socialized since high school to depend on their immediate environment to solve their problems, thus making them dependent people. Dependents have trouble making decisions and rely too heavily on others. Feelings of worthlessness, insecurity and fear of abandonment predominate. Their self-fulfilling prophecy projects a self-defeating "self." Self-defeating types choose acquaintances and situations that lead to disappointment, failure, and mistreatment by others. They often reject attempts to help them or make sure that such attempts will not succeed.

The focus for recovery is in stressing talents, alternative life choices and the behavioral consequences of sabotaging themselves. It is important to reinforce strengths and to act as a support for these student-athletes' concerns without becoming critical of them or accepting responsibility for their lives.

Attempt to instill the virtues of self-empowerment through taking the initiative in resolving their own problems. It is also important to instill the notion associated with power that is acquired through education: knowledge is power!

—Mr. John F. Reid, Jr. is the Founder and Director of the Black Ombudsman Program at California State University in Fullerton, California.

Reflections of the College of Arts Retention and Enhancement Services (CARES) Program

by Reed Markham

Overview:

CARES (College of Arts Retention and Enhancement Services) at California State Polytechnic University-Pomona is a nationally recognized college based equity program for underrepresented minority students who have declared a major in the College of Arts. The CARES Program provides students with the comprehensive support services they need to succeed in their college life and future careers. The CARES program provides faculty mentoring, career mentoring, study skills courses, tutoring, academic excellence workshops, social events, a study room, and financial aid resources.

Over 60 volunteer faculty members assist students in the CARES program. CARES has implemented a planned mentoring system that involves a one-to-one relationship between a faculty member in the College of Arts and a student mentor. Planned mentoring is a systematic process which helps people develop their capabilities through relations between mentors and mentees. CARES faculty mentors are great resources for academic advice, career networking, and support service references. Faculty mentors help build self confidence, assist students with personal problems, offer quotable quotes, trigger self-awareness, share critical knowledge, offer encouragement and inspire their mentees.

The CARES student tracking system indicates over 90 percent retention of CARES participants. Over 200 students utilized the CARES services during the last academic year. This article describes the CARES program in detail.

Introduction

Henry Adams, the educator wrote: "A teacher affects eternity; he can never tell where his influence stops." The faculty mentors in the College of Arts Retention and Enhancement Services (CARES) program have influenced the lives of hundreds of students from disadvantaged backgrounds.

CARES has gained national recognition due to its planned mentoring process. In a letter recently written to the CARES faculty mentors, Vice President Albert Gore observed: "In the previous seven years, you have provided numerous students access to the resources necessary to succeed in their education and careers. Not only is this important for the futures of those that you help, but it also serves as an example that I hope other schools choose to emulate."

The underlying philosophy is that the quickly changing technological and human environment requires competent college-educated citizens of all ethnic backgrounds who can work together in creative problem solving groups. The transition from high school to college is difficult for all populations, and particularly for those persons who do not have family histories of college success and who are not demographically similar to most college faculty and staff.

Planned mentoring is a systematic process which helps people develop their capabilities through relations between mentors and mentees. While informal mentoring of ethnic minority college students occurs on every college campus, planned mentoring programs extend the power of mentoring.

Planned mentoring involves a one-to-one relationship between a faculty member in the College of Arts and a student mentee. A recent study indicated that most students graduate from college without ever visiting a faculty member. Yet these faculty members are great resources for academic advice, career net-working and references. More than sixty faculty members in the College of Arts volunteer their time to assist students in the CARES program.

The values represented in the mentoring program include: equal opportunity for all parts of the population; strength through diversity; faculty-student relation-ships; organizational structures which empower students, faculty, and staff to make a difference in society; and the value of liberal education, fine arts, and social and behavioral sciences in society.

Great mentors offer challenging ideas. Great mentors provide students with opportunities for growth experiences. Great mentors help build self-confidence; assist students with personal problems; offer quoteable quotes; trigger self-awareness; share critical knowledge; offer encouragement; and generally inspire their mentees. Many academicians measure their success by seeing their name in print on a published article, or by the number of memos they distribute, or by how many meetings they attended during the year. The success of CARES faculty mentors can be seen in the lives of students they have inspired.

What are the traits of great mentors? great professors? I agree with Joseph Epstein, author of *Masters: Portraits of Great Teachers* who said that outstanding teachers have three common characteristics: "a deep love for their subject and an ability to arouse a similar love and earnestness in their students; a charisma, glamour, or personality that enables them to ignite their audiences; and the talent and depth to inspire their students to reach beyond themselves to attempt what seems impossible."

Although CARES faculty mentors are underpaid, overworked, and sometimes unappreciated, they receive great joy from knowing that from their efforts will come the doctors, teachers, and leaders who will decide the destinies of this state and nation.

History

CARES, the equity program in the College of Arts, was established in the fall of 1987 to increase the number of African American, Latino, and Native American students graduating from Cal Poly with degrees in the arts. The CARES program was developed in response to the CSU Chancellor's educational equity mandate. This mandate is based on the state master plan for higher education (March 1989) which documents the changing realities of demographics in the work force. Dramatic population growth is fueled primarily by growth in persons of color.

Between the years 2000 and 2010 a majority of California citizens will be nonwhite; with Latinos comprising over thirty percent of the population, Asians thirteen percent and blacks eight percent. One sixth of the current elementary student population is born outside the United States. At the same time, there is clear evidence that ethnic minorities are not able to take full advantage of the public education provided by the California school system. Minority students drop out of the educational system at higher rates.

For every 1,000 white California ninth-graders, fifty-six will graduate from a public university. For every 1,000 black and Latino students, sixteen and fourteen, respectively, will receive a baccalaureate degree. While this ratio is higher in general for Asians (176 of 1000), Asian students are underrepresented among College of Arts disciplines. The College of Arts is unique in its organizational function as the liberal arts component in a polytechnic university. At Cal Poly 17.5 percent of all majors are in the College of Arts. About thirty percent of the majors are self-identified ethnic minorities.

The idea for the CARES program was generated in a grassroots effort in 1987. A retreat in the fall of 1988 resulted in the first mentee/protege social affair, held in the spring of 1989. A lottery-funded retreat at the beginning of the fall of 1989 was conducted to train the twenty-eight faculty mentors in attendance. Recruiting efforts in 1989 resulted in forty-eight faculty mentors and 159 proteges.

In 1994 the CARES program operated with constrained resources. The major problems faced by CARES students include increasing tuition and unavailability of courses. Despite the restricted resources, the CARES program received a strong level of faculty and administrative support during a difficult year. During the 1993-94 academic year the student enrollment increased 166 percent from the 1992-93 academic year. In 1994, the CARES program provided mentoring to 160 students in contrast to sixty in 1993. In 1995 the CARES program increased student membership to 240 with sixty faculty members continuing service to the program.

Major Events and Milestones

During the 1993-94 and 1994-95 academic years, CARES participants refined program goals and procedures. CARES' mission is oriented toward supporting changes in students (behaviors, cognitions, and feelings), faculty, and the university in an effort to help ethnic minorities reach parity in society.

Mentor/Protege Recruitment and Matching

One hundred proteges were recruited to join a group of sixty proteges from the 1992-93 academic year and were matched with sixty faculty mentors. Membership in CARES increased 166 percent from the previous year. The typical protege was a female Latina majoring in liberal studies.

1993-94 Proteges:

Latino	67%
Asian	19%
African American	13%
Native American	1%
Male	24%
Female	76%

Majors:

Behavioral Science	6%
Communication	13%
English	5%
History	1%
Liberal Studies	34%
Philosophy	1%
Physical education	5%
Political Science	5%
Psychology	17%
Social Work	6%
Sociology	6%
Theatre	1%

Faculty Mentors:
Forty new mentors were recruited to join a group of sixty mentors for the 1993-94 academic year. Faculty participation increased 200 percent over the previous year. Due to faculty members on leave and the departure of some faculty members, faculty participation remained constant for the 1994-95 academic year.

Faculty mentor major field of study:

Behavioral sciences	12%
Communication	25%
Economics	8%
English	13%
Ethnic/women studies	6%
HPER	13%
History	5%
Philosophy	6%
Political Science	6%
Social Sciences	6%

Recruitment was successful this year due to a strong recruitment drive during the SOS orientation program last summer. Faculty recruitment was successful this year due to a strong CARES telephone survey program. Ninety percent of the faculty mentors reported strong participation in CARES mentoring and activities. Ten percent of the faculty mentors reported their proteges did not visit with them.

Mentor training:
One hundred percent of the mentors received instruction through the CARES publication, Faculty Mentor Notes. All mentors were contacted by phone each quarter to provide mentoring assistance. During the 1994-95 academic year faculty mentors were added to the internet system. The CARES staff sent faculty members announcements and messages through the campus e-mail system.

Information exchange:
The CARES director played the role of hotline respondent. The CARES director supervised the publication of CARES information publications and the CARES section of HOME BASE, a college-based program publication.

Protege contact hours:
Faculty mentors spent an average of ten hours per quarter on CARES activities. The CARES director provided students with twenty-four contact hours per week each quarter.

Protege retention 1993-94:
The following indicates the percentage of students who were retained during the fall, winter and summer quarters of the 1993-94 academic year.

CARES Proteges:

Male	99%
Female	98%
Overall	99%

Program Goal Completion for the 1993-94 and 1994-95 Academic Years:

The goals completed during the 1993-94 and 1994-95 academic years give insight into the CARES program activities and services:

Major goal completion 1993-94:

1. Recruited forty new faculty mentors through phone messages and personal recruitment letters.
2. Distributed two issues of the mentoring newsletter, Faculty Mentor Notes.
3. Increased student membership to 160 through regular recruitment drives.
4. Provided daily opportunities for CARES student advising. The CARES program provides students with assistance with learning resources, testing, financial aid, evaluations, re-entry, admissions, tutoring, advising, housing, health, and psychological services.
5. Held two CARES social and two CARES academic excellence workshops. Workshops focused on success in the classroom and financial aid resources.
6. Updated SA299: Success Skills for College of Arts majors course materials with a focus on financial aid resources.
7. Developed a financial aid database. The financial aid office resources are inadequate for our purposes; consequently, a CARES database was developed.
8. Acquired a new CARES study room. This room provides students with a centrally-located place to study.
9. Provided daily access to the study room.
10. Developed a CARES study room library with the donation of more than a thousand books and publications that students can utilize to write papers and complete research.
11. Assisted students in preparing for annual local, state and national scholarship competitions, teaching students how to locate resources and prepare competitive applications.
12. Presented two professional papers on retention topics—at the Cal Poly Fall Academic Forum and Cal Poly Spring Academic Forum. The Faculty

Center for Professional Development offers two forums a year for the presentation of academic research—CARES presented research on learning styles analysis and video- based supplemental instruction.

13. Developed a CARES mentoring-writing project with elementary school students; worked with El Sereno Elementary School in East Los Angeles.

14. Developed a public speaking contest for International Polytechnic High School. Ten students presented speeches on the value of education.

15. Chartered a College of Arts Leaders Club.

16. Compiled a list of potential grant resources and publications.

17. Increased community visibility through appearances on two television talk shows and articles in local, state and national news and education publications on retention topics.

18. Participated in the 1994 National Higher Education Conference on Black Student Retention. Served as a conference facilitator.

19. Furnished the new study room through donations from faculty and students including a sofa and refrigerator.

Major goal completion 1994-95:

1. Recruited new faculty members and replaced those leaving: sixty faculty mentors.

2. Distributed four issues of the mentoring newsletter, Faculty Mentor Notes.

3. Increased student membership to 240—a sixty-six percent increase from last year.

4. Provided daily opportunities for CARES advising.

5. Held three CARES socials and three CARES academic excellence workshops on financial aid, career success and developing communication skills.

6. Developed a textbook for the SA 299 course to be published by Simon and Schuster. This publication provides students with financial aid and campus resources and advice on how to improve grades, communication, and leadership skills.

7. Located additional financial aid resources to add to database. California State University tuition increases continue to be a challenge to financially-strapped CARES students.

8. Added additional furniture to the CARES study room.

9. Provided daily access to the CARES study room.

10. Continued the development of the CARES study room library through annual book drive.

11. Assisted students in preparing for local, state and national scholarship and leadership competitions, several students are scholarship and leadership finalists.

12. Presented two professional papers on retention topics—at the National Higher Education Conference on Black Student Retention and Cal Poly Faculty Center for Professional Development. The focus of this year's research was on developing mentor programs.

13. Continued mentoring writing project with low-income elementary school students at El Sereno Elementary School.

14. Continued developing College of Arts Leaders Club.

15. Completed a proposal for a U.S. Department of Education grant for an Upward Bound program. Also, completed drafts for two grant proposals.

16. Increased program visibility through speeches about the CARES program on local cable television.

17. Increased program visibility through articles in campus and local publications, including articles on Black History Month.

18. Participated in the 1994 National Higher Education Conference on Black Student Retention. This conference provides retention educators and practitioners with information about the nation's foremost retention programs and resources.

19. Acquired computers for use by CARES students. Cal Poly is moving forward with its goal to get on the superinformation highway. Computer literacy is essential for today's college student. Due to a limited number of computers on campus, CARES is attempting to provide students with additional computer resources.

Implemenetation Strategies

The CARES program was introduced to the campus by the College of Arts in response to the mandate from the chancellor of the California State University, encouraging the development of equity programs. Cal Poly-Pomona is a comprehensive institution with a current enrollment of 17,050.

The College of Arts has the most academic departments of any college on the campus with thirteen BA degree offerings and six BS degree offerings. The college has now focused on the development of multicultural and international education programs.

College-wide support of the program is encouraged through a strong public communications program including newsletters, open houses, special programs and regular phone, e-mail and message contact.

Programmatic Operations and Activities

The CARES program works to achieve its mission by offering the following services:

Faculty mentors: volunteer faculty mentors in the College of Arts who assist students with academic planning and support services.

Career mentors: graduates of Cal Poly-Pomona who provide students with assistance in making important career decisions.

University success course: SA 299: Success Skills for College of Arts Majors provides students with instruction on improving grades, locating financial aid resources, and improving communication and leadership skills.

Tutoring: through the Educational Opportunity Program (EOP), CARES students are provided with tutors who assist with most academic subjects.

Academic Excellence Workshops: dynamic speakers provide up-to-date information on academic topics of importance to CARES students.

Social activities: quarterly social activities provide students with the opportunity to interact with faculty mentors and students.

Financial aid information: Students can gain access to the latest scholarship and financial aid opportunities.

Study room: Students can complete research, hold meetings and study in a study room centrally-located on the campus.

Mentor Selection

The research on mentoring college students indicates that effective faculty mentors possess the following qualities:

1. They are people-oriented and secure. They like and trust their mentees.
2. They share expertise, encourage mentee ideas and help them gain self-confidence.
3. They encourage vision and challenge to the mentee.
4. They provide guidance for the achievement of specific goals.
5. They educate mentees about the political machinery of the campus.

The following faculty mentor checklist was issued in the recruitment program:

1. What are the basic characeristics we want mentors to have?
2. How will we reward mentors?
3. How will we recruit mentors?
4. How will we use promotional materials to attract mentors?
5. What systems do we have or need to record and maintain the mentor pool?
6. What will we include in the description of the mentor's role?
7. How will we orient mentors to the role?

Student surveys indicate that students want the following from faculty mentors:

1. concrete and direct suggestions;
2. information about courses;
3. assistance in locating information;
4. sharing information about common interests; and
5. encouragement and motivation.

Organizational Structure

The CARES program is located in the College of Arts. The CARES staff consists of a director and two student assistants. The CARES program also receives some administrative tutoring support from the Educational Opportunity Program and some program development support from the College-Based Programs.

The director reports to the dean of the College of Arts. The president of the university has delegated the oversight for retention programs to the vice president of academic affairs. The dean of the College of Arts reports to the vice president.

Indicators of Program Success

The major accomplishments of the CARES program include the following:

- The retention of students in 1993-94 academic year was ninety-nine per-cent. Retention of students in the 1994-95 academic is predicted to be over ninety percent.
- A dramatic increase in the number of students participating in the CARES program—more than 240 students in 1994-95.
- More than 200 students utilized the CARES support services, including academic excellence workshops, social events, and the study room.
- More than ninety percent of the students enrolling in the SA 299 course report increases in their grade-point averages.
- More than 1,000 books have been donated to the CARES study room library.
- The CARES study room provides access to thirty student study spaces.
- The SA 299 course: Success Skills for College of Arts Majors has served over 100 students.
- CARES retained sixty faculty mentors for the 1994-95 academic year.
- CARES received recognition from several local legislators and community leaders.

Problems, Solutions, and Visions of the Future

In 1993, the CARES program was housed in an obscure small office on the roof of Building 94. Very few students (and faculty) knew that there even were offices on the roof of that building; faculty and student participation was dwindling. Today, the CARES program has high campus visibility and the students have a "home" in a large, centrally-located office in the old administration building.

The major problems facing the CARES program in the future are:

1. limited financial resources: The program operates on a budget of $5,000 and the director receives 6.0 units of released time; the program receives twenty hours of support per week from student assistants contributed from the Educational Opportunity Program (EOP).

2. increasing workload demands: The program is struggling to deal with the dramatic increase in student participation; at the same time, the program is finding difficulty getting students to visit their mentors on a regular basis.

3. increasing need for strong database management: The program is getting on the information superhighway this year with the implementation of two tracking systems; prior to this year, statistical data was difficult to track.

The solutions to the above mentioned problems include:

• writing successful grants (currently working on two major grant proposals);

• continuing to be visible with strong campus publications and regular communications with faculty and students;

• encouraging the donation of computer equipment and expansion of the CARES staff; and

• Increasing student/mentor interaction through holds on records and mentor incentives.

As the CARES program expands, it will continue to search for new ways to meet the ever-changing needs of students. The CARES program faculty and staff are enthused about the opportunity to help student goals become reality.

—Dr. Reed Markham is the Director of the College of Arts Retention and Enhancement Services program at California State Polytechnic University in Pomona, California.

Facilitating Opportunity and Climate for Underrepresented Students

by Barbara Evans

Overview:

At majority institutions the discrepancies between African-American and white student graduation rates can be staggering. Research indicates that in many cases there has been about a 25 percent gap in the rates. Nationally, the graduation rates for African-American students is about 32 percent compared to about 56 percent for white students. At the University of Pittsburgh, after a six-year period, African-American students' graduation rate is 39.6 percent while the rate for white students is 65.3 percent.

As the United States continues to evolve into a country that is becoming primarily populated by people of color, higher education institutions must rethink current policies and the campus climate to examine what messages are being sent to students of color and how to eliminate substantial graduation rate gaps between the races. The University of Pittsburgh is trying to ameliorate the discrepancies in graduation rates with the implementation of a multi-layer mentoring program called Facilitating Opportunity and Climate for Underrepresented Students (FOCUS). African-American and Hispanic freshmen automatically become FOCUS participants and are involved in a series of academic and social support activities. The students are placed in small groups of ten comprised of undergraduates, a graduate student leader and a faculty member.

The following article discusses the impact of FOCUS and the lessons learned after the first year of operation. Also mentioned is the University of Pittsburgh's relationship with African-American students in the past and its current retention efforts. Two frameworks, Vincent Tinto's theory of student departure and Kofi Lomotey's cultural theory are discussed as paradigms to explore the reasons why some students opt to stay at majority institutions, while others choose to leave.

INTRODUCTION

> *"It wasn't until I took some classes in the Black Studies Department and heard the perspectives of some of the black professors that things started to click for me. This university focuses on certain cultural needs and black culture is not one of them. It needs to be more diversified. There's nothing to do. There's not one place for blacks to congregate. Culturally, that's not sound."* –African-American male student at Pitt

Theoretically, a central mission of universities is to educate all of their students. One of the stated missions of public universities is to teach students using all the techniques, resources, and personnel at their disposal. However, many universities appear to have lost sight of this basic tenet which should guide their operation (Allen, 1988). The low graduation rates of African-Americans at predominantly white institutions indicate the translation of the core mission to educate all students, in practice, is not so evident.

Nationally, African-American students' graduation rates are about 32 percent compared to 56 percent for their white counterparts. The University of Pittsburgh's graduation rates reflect the national trends by having about a 25 percent gap between the rates of these two groups of students. Pitt's graduation rate is 39.6 percent for African-Americans over a six-year period, compared to 65.3 percent for whites (McLaughlin, 1994).

Educational experts vary in their interpretations about why African-Americans tend to have low retention and graduation rates at predominantly white institutions. Success in college is not only a matter of intellectual ability (Boyer, 1984). It is also a matter of achieving a sense of membership, belonging, or integration within a college's academic and social communities (Boyer, 1984). Black students who attend predominantly black colleges have less difficulty attaining a sense of membership within their academic community and, consequently, experience less stress than their peers who attend predominantly white colleges. (Fleming, 1984) The failure to achieve a sense of membership or integration within an academic community may provide a basis for understanding why black students who are not in academic jeopardy still leave predominantly white college campuses (Allen, 1987; Tinto, 1988).

Consequently, quantitative data such as surveys containing closed-ended questions generating only descriptive statistics may not be able to detect certain aspects of the campus climate. Campus climate involves the culture, habits, decisions, practices, and policies that make up campus life. It is the sum total of the daily environment, and is central to the "comfort factor" that minority students, faculty, staff, and administrators experience on campus (American Council on Education, 1989). Consequently, nonquantitative variables, such as professors' attitudes and racism, in the university environment may send signals of acceptance or rejection to African-American students.

214

Theoretical Explanations

Vincent Tinto, who is a theorist and researcher on student departure, based his theoretical model of dropout behavior on Durkheim's theory of social suicide. That theory was important to social psychologists because of its relevance to individual suicide. The likelihood of suicide in society increases when two types of integration are lacking — namely, insufficient moral (value) integration and insufficient collective affiliation (Tinto, 1975).

Due to similar underlying themes in Durkheim's theory of social suicide, Tinto was able to draw a link between the suicide that occurs in society to students dropping out of college. Presumably, lack of integration into the social system of the college will lead to low commitment to that social system and will increase the probability that individuals will decide to leave college and pursue alternative activities (Tinto, 1975).

Tinto differentiates between dropouts who are dismissed because of poor academic performance and those who are voluntary withdrawals. Although academic dismissal is most closely associated with grade performance, dropout in the form of voluntary withdrawal is not (Tinto, 1975). Such withdrawal, instead, appears to relate to the lack of congruency between the individual and both the intellectual climate of the institution and the social system composed of his peers (Tinto, 1975).

Consequently, Tinto devised a conceptual schema for dropouts from college that included individual and institutional commitments. It indicates how a student's intellectual development is affected by academic integration and social integration with both peers and faculty. These commitments are examined at the beginning and the end of the schema and indicate how a student progresses through the system.

Tinto espoused that college dropout can be viewed as a longitudinal process of interactions between the individual and the academic and social systems of the college. The student's experiences in those systems, as measured by his normative and structural integration, continually modify his goals and institutional commitments in ways which lead to either academic persistence or dropout (Tinto, 1975).

Basically, dropouts do so because of either low goal commitment or low institutional commitment. A student's level of commitment within the system can have its origin in the student's background. If he/she comes from a family with high expectations of the student to graduate, and that student has been socialized to attend college and graduate, then that student will enter college with a high level of commitment. The reverse is also true. Specifically, children from lower status families exhibit higher dropout rates than do children of higher status families, even when intelligence has been taken into account (Sewell & Shah, 1967). The authors state that students who persist in college often have parents who are more affluent and more educated. In addition, the relationship that a student has with his/her family is germane to college completion. College persisters tend to come from families in which the parents tend to enjoy more open, democratic, supportive, and less conflicting relationships with their children (Congdon, 1964).

If a student's parents do not have high expectations for him/her at the time of college entrance, there is a high probability that the student will drop out if the campus climate at a predominantly white university does not provide that student with support. Once in college, the student has to interact with other students and faculty. If those interactions are not positive, they can influence a student's decision to continue or withdraw from college, particularly if that student is African-American.

Some researchers (Shade, 1982) contend that African-Americans stress social rather than instrumental cognition. If Shade's observations are correct, we would expect African-American students to fare better in settings that provide opportunities for self-expression, creativity, and innovation rather than in settings that stress traditional forms of teaching and learning (Allen, 1991).

Black students attending predominantly white colleges apparently experience considerable adjustment difficulty. Many of the adjustment problems are common to all college students, but African-American students also experience additional problems. For instance, many of these students often find it necessary to create their own social and cultural networks given their exclusion (self-and/or otherwise imposed) from the wider university community (Allen, 1986). Of all problems faced by black students on white campuses, those arising from isolation, alienation, and lack of support seem to be most serious (Allen, 1986).

Although Tinto focuses on the theoretical reasons for student dropout, which include the student's background, goal commitments and institutional characteristics, Claude Steele, (1992) a social psychologist, argues that the problems of African-American dropouts do not have anything to do with "innate ability" or "environmental conditioning."

Steele states that 70 percent of African-Americans at four-year colleges drop out compared to 45 percent of white students. "The culprit I see is stigma, the endemic devaluation many blacks face in our society and schools. This status is its own condition of life, different from class, money, culture. It is capable, in the words of the late sociologist Erving Goffman, of 'breaking the claim' that one's human attributes have on people. I believe that its connection to school achievement among black Americans has been vastly under appreciated" (Steele, 1992).

Steele cites African-American students' progression through the educational system to support his devaluation claim. He states that African-American students enter into the schools with test scores that are close to the scores of white students. However, by the time the African-American students get to the sixth grade, their achievement levels begin to lag behind those of white students.

He notes this pattern of decline continues through high school and college. In 1980, for example, 25,500 minority students, largely black and Hispanic, entered high school in Chicago (Steele, 1992). Four years later only 9,500 graduated, and of those only 2,000 could read at grade level. The situation in other cities is comparable (Steel, 1992).

Steele cites the various culprits that act as agents in devaluing many African-Americans, such as "a history of slavery, segregation, and job ceilings; continued lack of economic opportunity; poor schools; and the related problems of broken families, drug-infested communities and social isolation." However, in view of those factors, Steele indicated that the achievement deficit persisted even when African-American students came from middle class and wealthy families that were not affected by the above deficiencies. Steele attributed the poor achievement of African-American students to "something else." Doing well in school requires a belief that school achievement can be a promising basis of self-esteem, and that belief needs constant reaffirmation even for advantaged students. "Tragically, I believe, the lives of black Americans are still haunted by a specter that threatens this belief and the identification that derives from it at every level of schooling" (Steele, 1992).

Steele purports that stigmatization and racial vulnerability are the causes of devaluation that are perpetuated by the school system. When a student is not recognized for his/her talent in a school system, those memories are locked into that student's mind (Steele, 1992). Thus, from the first grade through graduate school, blacks have the extra fear that in the eyes of those around them their full humanity could fall with a poor answer or a mistaken stroke of the pen (Steele, 1992).

Consequently, students learn that acceptance into the school system will be hard won and learn to "disidentify" with that school system. In this way, African-American students on majority campuses who feel alienated by the campus climate, may opt to "disidentify" with anything that is representative of achievement. These actions may take the form of "psychological insulation" where the students disengage themselves from the academic climate in which they are supposed to excel. In many cases, dropping out of college is the end result.

Cultural Framework

A second theoretical explanation of high attrition among African-American students at majority institutions is a cultural perspective. Lomotey (1990), in his study "The Retention of African-American Students: The Effects of Institutional Arrangements in Higher Education," emphasized the importance of cultural influences to attrition and retention. Lomotey sought to explore how Oberlin College was able to assuage the alienation that African-American students experienced at Oberlin, which is a majority institution.

Lomotey focused on the idea that culture influences how new members are socialized into an organization. This occurs through the development of cultural artifacts such as a historical, image, organizational climate, sacred norms and institutions (Lomotey, 1990). Culture is a dynamic expression of a collective view of the world (Goodenough, 1971). It is a shared way of thinking, based on agreed upon norms, values and beliefs (Siehl and Martin, 1981).

Lomotey's study focused on three entities: the Afrikan Heritage House (a dormitory for African-American students), the Black Studies Department, and ABUSUA (the African-American student association). He interviewed 31 people (eight students, eleven faculty, six staff and six administrators), regarding the benefits of these to African-American students. Lomotey coded the information into four categories: support, cultural enrichment, status and political advantage.

Support encompasses helping African-American students get through Oberlin on an emotional, social or spiritual level. It includes things like offering a sense of community/family, offering a sanctuary, and being a resource (Lomotey, 1990).

One Oberlin student in Lomotey's study voiced the importance of African-Americans having support on a majority campus:

"Not many of us today have reached the desired level of self confidence and level of self assuredness. I feel, as a young, black American growing up in this country, places like Afrikan Heritage House are necessary. If not for political reasons, then at least for the sense of family. I think Afrikan Heritage House appeals to black students for different reasons. For myself, I feel very comfortable there. I don't need to put on any airs. I want to be myself."

Cultural enrichment helps the students learn about their heritage and helps to develop self pride and confidence. To encourage this, Oberlin holds a Friday Night Lecture Series and sponsors other discussions facilitated by ABUSUA. Students surveyed felt they derived status from the Black Studies Department, which serves as a good resource with its national reputation and strong faculty.

Lastly, political advantage is gained when the students are able to voice their political views and activism on campus. Lomotey's study illustrates the need for institutions to consider the culture of the organizations and the students represented. The concept of organizational culture provides a useful way of thinking about the kinds of changes institutions need to make and a process for making them (Kuh & Whit, 1988). The culture of any organization consists of the assumptions and beliefs shared by its members (Kuh & Whit, 1988).

It's important that we not only look at the campus culture, but that we look also at the symbolic representations of that culture—the cultural artifacts (Lomotey, 1990). Artifacts such as campus climate, sacred norms, and historical image offer insight into how African-American students are treated on a given campus and can play a role in the retention of African-American students (Lomotey, 1990).

These two previously discussed frameworks set the possible infrastructure to explain student retention and interactions on college campuses. The following section will address the institutional considerations that must also be included in the overall assessment.

Institutional Characteristics

It is fairly clear that public institutions of higher education tend to have higher attrition rates than private institutions, if only because much of the student selection process takes place before entering private colleges, whereas the selection process within the public institutions normally takes place after entrance (Astin, 1972). Also, institutions that have a higher quality because of a greater number of faculty with doctorates and higher incomes per student, tend to have larger numbers of graduates.

One approach to determining why retention discrepancies occur is to examine the policies of institutions that have implemented successful retention programs at their schools. The University of Pittsburgh has recently taken some steps to ameliorate the huge discrepancies between African-American and white student retention and graduation rates.

The University of Pittsburgh

The University of Pittsburgh is an urban, state-related, public research university located in the Oakland section of Pittsburgh, PA. Oakland is a working class neighborhood with a potpourri of ethnic groups. It is also a neighboring community to the Hill District, which is a predominantly African-American community of mostly low income residents, with a small presence of middle class residents.

The university, which was founded in 1787, also has four satellite campuses located in Greensburg, Johnstown, Titusville and Bradford. The University of Pittsburgh has about 90 academic, research and administrative buildings and resident halls spread over 132 acres. Pitt's enrollment is about 34,000 students, of which 28,000 attend the Pittsburgh campus. The university, which offers about 400 degree programs, is also Pittsburgh's largest employer with about 10,000 employees.

Meeting The Needs of Diverse Populations: The Past

The University of Pittsburgh has a history of confrontation when dealing with the specific needs of particular students while under the auspices of previous chancellors. For example, Robert Alberts indicated in his book, *The Story of the University of Pittsburgh*, that in 1968 during Chancellor Wesley Posvar's tenure, members of the Black Action Society (BAS) supplied Dr. Posvar with a list of demands. Those demands included the establishment of a Black Studies program replete with African-American instructors, a black history research center in the library, and efforts to recruit more black faculty, staff and black students. (The BAS originally demanded that at least 51 percent of the next freshman class be black, but it dropped that point) (Alberts, 1986). When the BAS did not get any responses to their demands, eight months later in January 1969, 70 African-American students converged on the chancellor's office and requested to meet with Dr. Posvar. The students were informed that the chancellor was not in and they said they would wait. They placed two guards dressed in dashikis and carrying spears outside the chancellor's office. When the chancellor returned, the students gave him a list of the grievances and demands. After some discussion, the students left, but not before telling Dr. Posvar that if he did not heed to their demands "something terrible was going to happen" (Alberts, 1986). Before leaving, the students demanded the chancellor commit to declaring January 15 a university holiday in honor of Dr. Martin Luther King. Dr. Posvar said he could not do so at that time without deferring the request to the appropriate deans and department chairs. He did allow the BAS students to have the rest of the day off without penalty. The students left and circulated throughout the campus, demanding that students be allowed to miss class in honor of the holiday.

After that incident, Dr. Posvar initiated some changes on campus, including hiring African-American recruiters and implementing a program called Project-A that was aimed at providing "high-risk" students with academic preparation during the summer. The chancellor also stepped up measures to recruit African-American faculty by offering higher salaries. In 1968, the groundwork for the Department of Black Studies was laid. But in 1969, the university had only 230 black students in a freshman class of 2,100, only 20 black faculty members in a full-time faculty of 1,400 and only ten black students among 404 in the School of Medicine (Alberts, 1986).

On January 1969, on the anniversary date of the BAS students' march on the chancellor's office, 30 students took over the university's computer center in the Cathedral of Learning. They blockaded the elevator doors, barricaded the glass door of the center and settled down for a "lock-in" (Alberts, 1986).

The students occupied the computer center for six and a half hours and negotiated for another five hours. They left peacefully after being assured that no punitive actions would be taken against them.

One year later, January 15 became a university holiday in honor of Martin Luther King; and the Black Studies Program, which was chaired by Jack Daniel, had 16 courses, a faculty of ten instructors and 270 students. (Alberts, 1986) More recently, the Management Information and Policy Analysis Department indicated that there were eight black, tenured faculty in the Black Studies Department as of 1992.

Nearly a quarter of a century later, of the 550 faculty in the Faculty of Arts and Sciences who are tenured or in the pipeline for tenure, the percentage who are black or other minorities has increased slightly. From 1985 to 1988, those numbers rose from 7.9 percent to 10.1 percent, but have changed little since then (University Times, 1992).

The numbers and percentage of black tenured and tenure-stream faculty are low and, although small in numbers, have shown a decline over the last five years. During this period, the number of black tenured and tenure-stream faculty has ranged from a high of 52 in 1989 to a low of 47 for the fall of 1992 (Chancellor's Annual Affirmative Action Report, 1993).

On the Pittsburgh campus in the fall term of 1992 there were 93 African-American full-time faculty and 2,390 white full-time faculty. There are 802 African-American students enrolled in the College of Arts and Sciences compared to 8,719 white students. Additionally, The School of Medicine had two African-American graduate students and 51 African-American first professional students (The University of Pittsburgh Fact Book, 1993).

Although 25 years has elapsed since BAS made their demands, improvement in the number of African-American students and faculty is still forthcoming.

Retention Documentation at Pitt

The Institutional Research Office of Budget, Planning and Analysis published an information document in November 1993 charting the retention rates of students by race, gender and residence. The document covers cohorts for 1985-1991 and includes first-time, full-time freshmen who matriculated during those years. This researcher requested data on years prior to 1985 and was told that data was unavailable. Additionally, the researcher was informed that data available for the cohorts 1985-1991 was being incorporated into a new system. The new document (Number 190) was released to the public in November 1993. In July 1994, an updated version, document (Number 197) was released.

Based on the new document, the average retention rate for Asian American students three years after the initial enrollment is 77.7 percent compared to 72.8 percent for white students, 55.2 percent for black students and 54.6 percent for Hispanic students. The average graduation rate for Asian American students six years after the initial enrollment is 66.9 percent compared to 65.3 percent for white students, 51.4 percent for Hispanic students, and 39.6 percent for black students (Institutional Research, 1994).

The above results indicate a 25.7 percent difference in the graduation rates of white students and African-American students. History is cyclical. Although a quarter of a century has elapsed since the BAS made demands for increases in African-American faculty and students, time appears to be repeating itself. Proportionally, African-American faculty and student representation in 1994 mirrors the numbers of the late 1960s. In many cases, the numbers are worse.

One administrator who has been at Pitt for more than 25 years stated his observations over the last two decades:

> *"Administratively, most of what we have at this university for African-Americans is a result of the 60s. There has been no new major initiative at this university that was not a product of the 60s. I'm not talking about one student here and one faculty member there. The biggest initiative is the recent thing we just did to announce the new Helen Faison scholarships, the K. Leroy Irvis scholarships, and the 30 new Challenge scholarships. That is the first major initiative approaching almost $1 million in expenditures that we have done in at least the last two decades."*

Meeting the Needs of Diverse Populations: The Present

More recently, the university has initiated several activities such as the creation of a new position (Assistant to the Chancellor for Minority Affairs), several scholarships, the Chancellor's Diversity Task Force and the multi-layer mentoring program, Facilitating Opportunity and Climate for Underrepresented Students, (FOCUS).

FOCUS, a mentoring program for first-year minority students, was implemented in the fall of 1993. There are ten freshmen, an upperclassman, one graduate student and one faculty member per group. The purpose is to render a support mechanism and activities for the undergraduates to assure their successful integration into the campus environment by providing:

- an opportunity to explore issues of transition and
- adjustment to Pitt's campus;
- peer and faculty mentoring opportunities; and
- a feeling of connectedness in small groups combining
- scholastic and social objectives.

FOCUS evolved out of a mentoring program called EXCEL which was implemented eight years ago. EXCEL was designed for "regular admit" students who were not part of any student support service programs. The purpose was to provide freshmen students with mentoring opportunities with faculty and upperclassmen.

Programmatically, EXCEL students were mailed information and asked to acknowledge their participation in the program by mailing in their responses. When the Assistant to the Chancellor for Minority Affairs position was created, additional resources were made available and EXCEL evolved into FOCUS in the fall of 1993. FOCUS materials are mailed to all incoming African-American and Hispanic students, and those who do not want to participate in the program have the option of selecting out of the program. Whereas EXCEL was managed by committee, the responsibility for managing FOCUS is shared by the Assistant to the Chancellor, and the Director and Assistant Director of New Student Programs in the Division of Student and Public Affairs.

Currently, 255 freshmen students participate in FOCUS. The leaders are upperclassmen in the College of Arts and Sciences, the College of General Studies, The School of Nursing, The School of Engineering and the School of Pharmacy. The leaders attend an orientation program and several workshops to learn mechanisms to assist new students with acclimation to Pitt. The leaders also learn how to be supportive to the students by listening to their needs and concerns; referring students to learning skills facilities; having small group discussions on pertinent issues; and participating in a variety of social and academic activities.

Prior to the fall semester, the groups are encouraged to get together and share information. They also meet once a month to exchange ideas about coursework, faculty or university activities. Several times throughout the year, the groups mingle as a total group in cultural and social activities.

A newsletter and calendar of events that describe a plethora of activities geared toward African-American and Hispanic students provides a linkage to FOCUS participants.

Since the program's inception, several milestones have occurred. The program is working to become a line item within the university, several foundations have expressed interest in supporting the program, and FOCUS has been cited in the Pennsylvania Commonwealth Report. Additionally, the American Council on Education is also going to cite the program as a model for helping to increase the number of minority applications.

Additionally, in the fall of 1995, the group leaders participated in a weekend retreat to learn how to be effective group leaders. The format consisted of a brainstorming session, in which participants examined campus-wide retention efforts and developed linkages to every branch of student life in the university. The Council on Minority Support (COMS) is a university-wide committee that has the shared goal of providing quality support services for students. That committee, which consists of administrators, faculty, staff and students, assists FOCUS with its efforts.

Some of the problem areas associated with FOCUS involve students' concern that the program only concentrates on the freshman year. However, some African-American alumni have expressed an interest in becoming involved with the program. Another dimension may be added that would allow alumni to provide nurturing past the freshman year. In addition, the option of FOCUS alumni returning to the program as group leaders to assist incoming freshmen with their acclimation to the university is also on the horizon.

The concept that students were "chosen" to participate in the program may have negative connotations. Sometimes students perceive their inclusion in programs such as FOCUS as indications of some type of deficiency. In an effort to move beyond the negative perceptions associated with some student support programs, FOCUS administrators plan to improve the training for group leaders and get a firm commitment from students prior to the fall semester. FOCUS personnel intends to have a reception and/or some other type of an event during the summer bridge programs. During the advising sessions Graduate student leaders can develop contact with the undergraduate students and get them to sign a contract that stipulates their commitment to the program.

FOCUS administrators indicate the success of the program depends on having a "personal element." They stress the importance of administrators getting personally involved with the students and developing a caring rapport with them. Small gestures such as telephone calls to inquire about the student's progress in class or financial aid status can send a strong message to students that they are not just a number in a large institution.

It is evident that the University of Pittsburgh has taken some measures to improve the retention rates of African-American students. Since a majority of these are fairly recent, formative and summative evaluations of the efforts must be incorporated into the programs to assess the impact. Programs such as FOCUS must be effective, operationally, and not just theoretically. The best way to determine the impact is to complement quantitative data such as pre- and post-program GPA scores with qualitative data from the participants themselves. Ask them about their perceptions, and the impact of the specific programming on their college experiences, and for recommendations. Administrators can then focus on the business of retaining African-American students by meeting their specific needs as opposed to "perceived needs." Perhaps, this will translate into higher retention and graduation rates.

—Dr. Barbara Evans is the Assistant Dean of Student Academic Services at the Graduate School of Public Health at the University of Pittsburgh in Pittsburgh, Pennsylvania.

References

Alberts, Robert C. (1986). Pitt. The Story of the University of Pittsburgh. Pittsburgh. The University of Pittsburgh Press.

Allen, Walter, Epps, E. and Haniff, N. (1991). College in Black and White. African-American Students in Predominantly White and in Historically Black Public Universities. New York. State University of New York Press.

Allen, Walter. (1987). "Blacks in Higher Education: The Climb Toward Equality. Change. May/June.

Allen, Walter. (1988). "Black Students in U.S. Higher Education: Toward Improved Access, Adjustment, and Achievement." The Urban Review, Vol. 20, No. 3.

Allen, Walter. (1986). "Gender and Campus Race Differences" in Black Student Academic Performance, Racial Attitudes and College Satisfaction. Atlanta: Southern Education Foundation.

American Council on Education. (1988). Minorities in Higher Education. Washington, D.C. Office of Minority Concerns, American Council on Education.

Boyer, Ernest. (1984). College: The undergraduate experience in America. New York: Harper & Row.

Carter, Deborah, & Wilson, Reginald. (1989). Eighth Annual Status Report. Minorities in Higher Education. Washington, DC. American Council on Education.

Fleming, Jacqueline. (1984). Blacks in College: A Comparative Study of Student's Success in Black and in White Institutions. San Francisco: Jossey-Bass.

Goodenough, W. H. (1971). Culture, Language and Society. Massachusetts. Addison-Wesley.

Green, Madeleine. (1989). Minorities on Campus: A Handbook for Enhancing Diversity. Washington, DC. American Council on Education.

Kuh, George & Whitt, Elizabeth. (1988). The Invisible Tapestry: Culture in American Colleges and Universities. College Station, TX. Association for the Study of Higher Education.

Lomotey, Kofi. (1990). "Culture and Its Artifacts in Higher Education: Their Impact on the Enrollment and Retention of African-American Students." Spencer Foundation.

McLaughlin, Eileen (1993). Retention and Graduation Rates at the University of Pittsburgh, Information Document Number 190. University of Pittsburgh. Institutional Research, Office of Budget, Planning and Analysis.

McLaughlin, Eileen. (1994). Retention and Graduation Rates at the University of Pittsburgh, Information Document Number 197. University of Pittsburgh. Institutional Research, Office of Budget, Planning and Analysis.

Shade, Barbara. (1982). "African-American Cognitive Style: A Variable in School Success?" Review of Educational Research. 52 (2): 219-244.

Siehl, C. & Martin, J. (1981). Learning Organizational Culture. Paper, Graduate School of Business, Stanford University.

Steele, Claude. (1992). "Race and the Schooling of Black Americans." The Atlantic Monthly. April. pp. 68-78.

Tinto, Vincent. (1975). "Dropout from Higher Education: A Theoretical Synthesis of Recent Research." Review of Educational Research. 45 (1): 89-125.

University of Pittsburgh. (1993). Office of Affirmative Action. Affirmative Action Data Report: Students and Faculty By School. Fall 1990-1992.

University of Pittsburgh. Office of Budget, Planning and Analysis. (1993). University of Pittsburgh Fact Book.

Retention of Black Female Graduate Students: A Model of Hope and Coping

by Ann L. Carter-Obayuwana

Overview:

Although most studies related to retention have centered on concerns and attrition rates of undergraduate students, graduate students also are confronted with the formidable tasks of managing the stressors of a rigorous post baccalaureate program as well as coping with personal and interpersonal issues. Though the vast majority of these studies investigates retention of black students on white campuses, retention rates at black colleges and universities are generally far lower. In addition to the lack of research on graduate student retention at black colleges, there has historically been very few publications on African-American female students and the impact of both race and gender on their college matriculation.

The purpose of this article is to discuss the Model of Hope and Coping as used with African-American graduate students at an historically black university. This model examines coping ability and degree of hope as important variables in retention. Specifically, this article includes: (1) An introduction which states the problem of retention of Black female students; (2) A description of the unique challenges that face African-American women students in higher education; (3) A discussion of the relationships between hope, stress, coping, and student retention; (4) A review of a two-part pilot study that investigates level of hope, the ability to cope with stress, grade-point average, and retention among first-year African-American female graduate students at a historically black university; and (5) A discussion of successful models of retention and their implication for the current study and for effective retention of Black students.

Introduction

Many first-year college students experience serious difficulty in adjusting to and coping with the challenges and stressors of university life, as well as the often formidable task of managing their own personal and interpersonal stressors.

In recent years, research has primarily focused on the adjustment difficulties of undergraduate students as they struggle to cope with the challenges and stressors of university life. These difficulties included adjustment to campus life; the rigors of college study; maturity in handling unrestricted time and freedom; interpersonal relationships; separation from family and friends; and juggling the economic realities of college matriculation. For many individuals, these adjustments and responsibilities prove to be overwhelming.

Though university faculty and administration are intent on facilitating students' academic adjustment, personal adaptation, and individual coping skills, they usually only encounter these students in a crisis or an acute situation when their inability to cope with internal and external stressors places them at risk for termination from the university. This termination is due either to substandard academic performance or unaddressed personal problems that preclude their continuation as a student. Ideally a systemic process could be implemented that would accurately predict, and therefore alert, university personnel to these students with low coping skills. Subsequently, these students could be identified early and then receive appropriate, timely, and supportive interventions before their stressors become incapacitating.

Although university personnel try to intervene during these periods of student adjustment and problems, the difficulty in carrying out these proactive interventions has been a systemic inability to accurately and quickly identify those students who, because of poor coping skills and other salient internal and external liabilities, are most at risk for academic failure, personal distress, and attrition. This systemic shortcoming has been due in large measure to the fact that there has not been a reliable assessment instrument or process that could initially identify those students at risk for attrition or those with ineffective coping skills. Usually by the time faculty and administrators are cognizant of students' ineffective coping skills, students are enmeshed in acute distress, disability, and or imminent severance from the university. The lack of students' effective coping skills and the university's inability to promptly identify these vulnerable students inevitably leads to less than optimum academic performance, heightened anxiety, and increased rates of attrition.

Because of college and personal life stressors that all students are faced with today, it is important they have effective coping skills in order to successfully navigate the university environment, their own personal challenges, and the global community. It would seem imperative, therefore, that any model of retention must specifically and clearly address the issue of the degree and level of student coping ability.

Although most studies related to retention have centered on issues of concerns and attrition rates of undergraduate students, graduate students also are confronted with the formidable tasks of managing the stressors of a rigorous post-baccalaureate program as well as coping with personal and interpersonal issues. Additionally, the vast majority of these studies investigate retention of black students on white campuses, (Obiakor & Barker, 1993; Salles, 1993; Sedlacek, 1987; Sherman, Giles, Williams-Green, 1994), with far fewer studies investigating black students attending historically black colleges and universities (HBCUs), although retention rates at black colleges and universities are generally lower (NCAA 1994/1995). Due to this lack of systematic study on graduate student retention at HBCUs, it is important to begin to methodically examine graduate student attrition at predominantly black colleges and universities. In addition to the lack of research on graduate student retention at black colleges, historically there has been very few publications on African-American female students and the impact of both race and gender on their college matriculation.

Taking these underserved populations into consideration, as well as the important links between coping, stress, and student retention, it is important to investigate these hitherto neglected areas.

Challenges Of African-American Women

The struggles and obstacles female students face in attempting to achieve a full and rewarding higher education experience are being increasingly documented (Ehrhart and Sandler, 1990; Hall and Sandler. 1982, 1984; and Nieves-Squires, 1991). For African-American female students, these struggles emerge from the twin dilemmas of race and gender, and pose additional burdens as the black woman student strives for higher education. Carter, Pearson, and Shavlik (1988) capture the essence of this dilemma when they state:

> *"At the intersection of race and gender stand women of color, torn by the lines of bias that currently divide white from nonwhite in our society, and male from female. The worlds these women negotiate demand different and often wrenching allegiance. As a result, women of color face significant obstacles to their full participation in and contribution to higher education. In their professional roles, women of color are expected to meet performance standards set for the most part by white males. Yet, their personal lives extract a loyalty to their culture that is central to acceptance by family and friends...At times, they can even experience pressure to choose between their racial identity and their womanhood...the combined effect of these pressures can be destructive if they are not recognized and if the faulty premises that underlie them are not addressed"* (p.98).

Additional research confirms the double jeopardy and obstacles that African-American college women students face. These women students are often perceived negatively because of the stereotyped characterization of black women. For example, Weitz and Gordon's (1993) research on the images and traits that Anglo college students have about women indicate the traits selected for American women in general are overwhelmingly positive, while those traits portrayed of African-American women are far more negative.

In this study, 45 percent of the sample characterize women in general as intelligent (the most common trait for women in general); but only 22 percent characterize black women as intelligent. The most commonly selected trait for black women was "loud", which did not appear at all on the list of the most commonly selected traits for American women in general. Additionally, Weitz and Gordon state that American women in general are viewed as "sensitive", "attractive", "sophisticated", "career-oriented", and "independent", while black women are perceived as "loud", "aggressive", "argumentative", "stubborn", and "bitchy". The authors state these findings have major implications for black women's ability to succeed. Although their data comes from college students, Weitz and Gordon remark that "it is from the ranks of these students, however, that future teachers, employers, and others who hold positions of authority will be drawn." Extrapolating from this study, therefore, Wietz an Grodon hypothesize that white teachers and supervisors, for example, will less often reward young black women for their successes than reward young white women, and will less often chastise black women for their failures. As a result, black women's incentive to achieve may decline. Moreover, those black women who do achieve, whether in school or the marketplace, will likely find that their achievements either are not rewarded or are even held against them by whites as signs that these black women are stepping out of their 'places' or benefitting undeservedly due to "good luck."

Although the Weitz and Gordon (1993) study was done on a predominantly white campus involving white students, they indicate that further research is needed to clarify to what degree these oppressive and stereotyped images have been internalized by other groups (e.g. black men, black women, and other ethnic groups of color) and to what degree they shape the African-American woman's campus experience. Further, they conclude, it is clear that one cannot assume that ethnic images hold across gender lines or that gender images are robust across ethnic lines.

Other studies have investigated the different experiences of black men and black women in both historically black and white colleges, and their findings provide insight into both the overt and subtle stressors that black women face in academia. The studies by Fleming (1984) and Allen (1986) note the following four interesting findings related to the personal and interpersonal environments of African-American women in higher education: (1) black women become less assertive when they are educated with men; (2) they sometimes believe they are less competent than men; (3) African-American women lose some social assertiveness skills in black colleges, but not in white colleges where black men are fewer in number; and (4) black women often suffer from emotional pain, social isolation, or intensified fears about their competence, especially on predominately white campuses. These fears and negative perceptions certainly take a toll not only upon the academic performance of black college women, but also upon their personal and interpersonal relationships as well.

Moses (1989) investigated stressors in the residential and social lives of African-American female students. In these personal and interpersonal domains, she noted that the quality of the social and residential life that black women students experience often has a profound and lasting effect on their maturity, growth, and self-esteem. On one hand, their experiences often include intense scrutiny or direct attack such as racial discrimination and sexual harassment; conversely, black women students are often isolated, ignored, and dismissed, which can lead to feelings of alienation and lowered self-esteem. Other interpersonal and personal stressors for black women relate to dating. Collings (1987) states that dating can be problematic for black women on both black and white campuses because there are fewer black men on either type of campus, and the ratio of black women to black men is often two to one. This dating issue for black women students is also compounded because, as Allen (1986) notes, black males tend to date interracially more often, while black females do not cross racial lines as frequently.

The importance of a nurturing environment, such as that which exists on many historically black campuses, in countering these stressors cannot be overlooked. However, even on these black campuses African-American women are not free of obstacles and discrimination (Fleming, 1984). Although black colleges and universities have traditionally provided residential and social environments where young black women could develop within a relatively safe environment free from racism, they have not been free from sexism. These oppressive views and behaviors also prevent black women college students from assuming leadership roles. To illustrate, Hall and Sandler (1984) state that most black women often do not take leadership roles because on predominately white campuses and on coeducational black campuses they deal with racial barriers and gender biases. Often leadership roles are fostered only for the very few women students who attend all female, predominately black environments that nurture leadership skills and growth as a part of their daily experiences.

Even when African-American women transcend these personal and interpersonal barriers that impede their undergraduate matriculation and complete their first degree, the paucity of graduate school opportunities looms as another obstacle. Moses (1989) and Chandler (1988) note that black women students often do not receive encouragement from advisors to undertake graduate training, and they may feel isolated and therefore not comfortable enough to ask faculty members to write letters of reference for their graduate admissions. Finally, there is not enough financial aid available to black female graduate students. Their salaries are less than those of white and black men, and therefore black women may be reluctant to take out additional loans to pay for graduate school. Banks (1988) states that black women who do enter graduate school are often still viewed by others and themselves as strangers or outsiders. In another study, Zappert and Stansbury (1987) state that black women (and other women of color) were affected negatively by the sex of the advisor more often than men, had fewer responsibilities in research groups than men, were ambiguous about holding academic appointments, published less than men, and showed less self confidence overall than men. Finally, these authors state that black women have their credentials constantly questioned. Black female graduate students must constantly fight the impression and stigma of being an "affirmative action admission."

It is not surprising, therefore, that at the graduate level of education, European Americans are almost eight times more likely to obtain a master's degree than are individuals from ethnic groups of color; and the percentage of enrollment for African-American graduate students is the lowest of all ethnic individuals (Chronicle of Higher Education, 1991). In recent years, the actual graduation rate is decreased for black women enrolled in graduate study. For example, in 1975-76, black women earned 8.7 percent of the master's degrees; in 1984-85, the number dropped to 6.1 percent as compared to 11.3 percent for all minority women and 82.3 percent for all white women in 1985. Black women earned 5.7 percent of the doctorates in 1974-75 and 5.4 percent of the doctorates in 1985-89, which compares to 10.9 percent for all woman of color and 34.1 percent for white women (Brazziel, 1987, 1988).

Moses (1989) notes that although African-American women have been participants in higher education for more than a century, not only are they almost totally absent from the research literature, but rarely is the impact of racism and sexism on African-American women in academe examined. Racism and sexism are powerful challenges to the academic progress of African-American women and create formidable stressors as well. Therefore, it is important to now examine the roles that stress, hope, and coping play in the academic and personal lives of African-American female college students.

Stress, Hope, and Coping

The double jeopardy of race and gender that negatively impacts the African-American female student clearly places her under a great deal of stress during her matriculation. The formative work on stress and coping and their impact on individuals' health was done by Selye (1974, 1976). In these research studies, it is stated that not only is stress ubiquitous and inevitable, but stress without distress is of questionable clinical significance.

Thus, stress is a "problem" only if an individual cannot effectively cope with

232

the presented stressor and therefore suffers "distress." Therefore, the issue is not if African-American women students are faced with stress—because the literature and personal reports clearly show that they are—but *how* they can effectively cope with and minimize the impact of acute and chronic stress. This "distress of stress" characterizes their campus environment and intrudes negatively upon all aspects of their other life domains. The critical key is to find effective coping strategies that neutralize campus and personal stressors. It is especially important that the degree and level of coping abilities of African-American female students be identified early so that immediate and appropriate interventions can be initiated.

One particularly effective way that an individual can successfully counter these inevitable and omnipresent stressors is directly related to one's degree of coping through hope. The research consensus is that one's level of hope positively correlates with one's overall ability to cope with stressors by reducing fears and anxieties, and by increasing personal coping skills, protective factors, and resilient characteristics. Further, the components of hope are scientifically derived, defined, assessed, and can be used in a variety of settings to help individuals cope with the stressors of life (Beavers and Kaslow, 1981; Carter, 1994; Carter and Obayuwana, 1995, 1994, 1993; Frank, 1968; Korner, 1970; and Obayuwana and Carter, 1982; Obayuwana, Carter and Barnett, 1984; and Obayuwana, Collins, Carter, Rao, Mathura, Wilson, 1982).

From these research studies, two important principles emerged: an individual's level of hope highly and positively correlates with degreee of coping ability, and the components of hope can be empiracally identified, defined, measured, and enhanced. According to Obayuwana and Carter and their associates, (1982, 1984), the five comprehensive components of hope are: Ego Strength, Perceived Human Family Support, Education, Religious/Spiritual Assets, and Economic Assets. Hope, therefore, is operationally defines as that "state of mind resulting from the positive outcome of Ego Strength, Perceived Human Family Support, Education, Religious/Spiritual Assets, and Economic Assets".

Each one of these variables comprises the critical component of hope and is an essential part of an individual's coping resources and assets. These components of hope and coping are formally defined, and their implications for black women college students are briefly discussed:

Ego strength: "The sum of the attributes of an individual which constitute the core of his or her personality, facilitate all desired adaptations, and serve the primary function of self gratification and or preservation."

Perceived human family support: "The degree of perceived availability of moral support, meaningful inspiration, and desired assistance which an individual senses in the process of interaction with the immediate family, relatives, friends, neighbors, and significant others."

Educational assets: "All forms of awareness and knowledge acquired by the individual through formal learning or by experience, which provide a better understanding of the environment, one's immediate plight, and the laws of nature or society."

Religious/spiritual assets: "Those characteristics of an individual which represent or promote a meaningful and satisfying relationship with an omnipotent and loving deity, force or being who is believed by the individual to provide in perpetuity for one's total welfare, especially when prescribed commandments and lifestyle doctrines are followed."

Economic assets: "Money and property, real or anticipated, including all items, arrangements, or situations considered by the individual as contributory to wealth and material sufficiency because they either actually enhance potential buying power or merely confer a perceived relative degree of financial comfort."

For the black female college student, each one of these components of hope are important in assisting her to cope with university and personal stressors. For example, high levels of Ego Strength encourages her to celebrate the uniqueness and strengths of race and gender, regardless of external perceptions or what others may say or do. The asset of Human Family Support enables the student to activate this network for encouragement, nurturance, and positive reinforcement during stressful situations. Educational Assets helps the student to better integrate and cope with new challenges and experiences by employing knowledge gained from past experience and utilizing it to more effectively cope with new realities and stressors. Religious/Spiritual Assets, whether it takes the form of meditation, yoga and/or prayer, provide the coping mechanism that empowers black female students to successfully counter traumatic events by tapping into this powerful spiritual energy resource. Finally, Economic Assets, whether formal (grants, scholarships, loans, personal wealth) or informal (promise of economic assistance from family/friends) facilitates coping skills by more effectively addressing the monetary stress and anxiety associated with student life.

Each of these five components of hope can be objectively assessed on the three dimensions of affect, cognition, and behavior through the administration of the Hope Index Scale (H.I.S.). The H.I.S. is a psychosocial testing instrument designed to objectively assess the attributes of hope in adult individuals without racial, gender, or socioeconomic biases. The scale is a 60 item forced-choice (yes/no) questionnaire which takes about 20 minutes to administer and is easily scored (Obayuwana, Collins, Carter, Rao, Mathura, Wilson, 1982). In clinical settings, one can objectively assess an individual's degree of hope and coping by using the Hope Index Scale, the Scoring and Interpretation Guide and the Diagnostic Chart (Institute of Hope, 1982). An appropriate treatment plan, using Hope Theory (Carter and Obayuwana, 1988) can also be designed and implemented. Hope Theory is a conceptual and clinical framework that maintains and enhances hope, increases one's coping ability, and inproves one's overall quality of life. Taken together all of these components comprise the Model of Hope and Coping.

All tested individuals are rated on a Hope score of 0 – 500, which automatically assigns each person to one of five normed categories of experimentally determined significance (Institute of Hope, 1982). These categories are detailed in Table 1.

Table 1

Score Range	Description
450–500	Optimal Hope Superior Coping Ability
350–440	"Normal" Hope Varying Characteristics
250–340	Mild Hope Deficit Maladaptive Behaviors
150–240	Severe/Moderate Hope Deficit Significant Coping Inadequacies
Below 150	Pathological Hope Deficit Serious Suicide Contemplation

Since the Hope Index Scale has been used to assess degree of stess and coping in various populations under stress, it was felt that this instrument would be useful in assessing degree of stress and coping ability of African-American first-year graduate students. A pilot study was initated that utilized the tenets of the Model of Hope and Coping as well as employed the H.I.S. to ascertain effective and ineffective coping levels of students.

The purpose of this pilot study was to address the following two questions: (1) "Can higher education faculty and administrators accurately, reliably, and quickly identify those students who are at risk because of their inability to effectively cope with stress?" and (2) "can higher education faculty and administrators accurately, reliably, and quickly identify those students who are able to effectively cope with stress?" Since universities have not been able to establish a personal one-on-one relationship with every incoming student so that as they faced difficulties and stressors, mechanisms could be in place to enable them to more effectively cope with stress and to provide these identified students with the needed support, assistance, and resources of the university, it seemed essential that these two questions be explored.

Pilot Study

A pilot study was designed in which fifty incoming first year Black female graduate students were selected. These students were all admitted to a master's level counseling degree program and were all enrolled in counseling classes at a large HBCU on the east coast. A self-report instrument and the Hope Index Scale were administered to all participants to determine their perceived level of stress and their degree of hope and coping. Before administering the psychological instruments, it was important to allow sufficient time for positive interaction so the desired environmental conditions of mutual respect, trust, and empathic understanding could be established. These important conditions have been positively correlated with higher levels of self disclosure, genuineness, and authenticity, which are significant factors in this study (Belkin, 1988; Corey and Corey, 1989; Hackney and Cormier, 1994). It was felt that under these nurturing conditions, students would more likely feel comfortable enough to honestly share their personal and university-related stressors as well as their individual coping skills and abilities.

After the establishment of these conditions of trust , empathy, and respect, an indepth self-report instrument was administered to the sample. This instrument elicited, on a five-point, Lickert-type scale, the students' perceived degree of university-related stressors and their abilities to cope with these stressors. The list of specific stressors and the participants' particular ways of coping with these stressors (both university and non-university) were obtained through open-ended, write-in responses. The Hope Index Scale was then administered to the sample.

The results indicated a positive correlation between the self-reports and the Hope Index Scale. Those "high hope" scoring individuals (H.I.S. = 350 and above) also reported a high ability to cope with their self-reported stressors. The higher the H.I.S. score, the higher the student's self report of being able to cope with university and non-university related stressors. Conversely, those "low hope" scoring individuals (H.I.S. 150 - 340) indicated in their self reports a lower ability to cope with both university and non-university related stressors.

These findings also indicated that even when the stressors were identical—such as a death in the family, interpersonal problems, financial aid difficulties, etc.—the high H.I.S. scorers rated themselves more able to cope with these same named stressors than did the low H.I.S. scorers. The significance of the Model of Hope and Coping is that one can identify the ways and to what degree one copes with stressors. By identifying how an individual copes with stress—that is by determining what combination of specific hope and coping components (i.e. Ego Strength, Perceived Human Family Support, and Spiritual/Religious, Educational, and Economic Assets) an individual employs—a personalized Hope and Coping Profile can be constructed. This Hope and Coping Profile can be used not only by the student to better understand her/his coping style, but also by faculty and administrators for referral and advisement purposes.

One year after this initial study, a follow-up investigation was undertaken to address the following issues: (1) To review the percent of the pilot sample in each of the five coping categories; (2) To establish baseline norms, and to compare it with the scores and norms from other studies and the general population; and (3) To examine the grade point averages (GPA) of the participants after one year to note relationships between GPA and the scores on the Hope Index Scale.

The percent of the sample in each of the five categories of hope and coping are reported in Table 2.

Table 2

Percent of Graduate Student Sample In Five Categories Of Hope

Percentage	H.I.S.	Scores Description
0% (n=0)	450 – 500 =	Optimum Hope Superior Coping Ability
55% (n=28)	350 – 440 =	"Normal Hope" Varying Characteristics
40% (n=20)	250 – 340 =	Mild Hope Deficit Maladaptive Behaviors
5% (n=2)	150 – 240 =	Severe/Moderate Hope Deficit Significant Coping Inadequacies
0% (n=0)	Below 150 =	Pathological Hope Deficit Serious Suicide Contemplation

The distribution of coping scores for this sample on the Hope Index Scale is within the expected range, and is reflective of the H.I.S. scores of the general population as assessed in previous samples. In general populations, a very small percentage of individuals fall within the category of "Optimum Hope", and individuals scoring in the "Pathological Hope Deficit" category are usually institutionalized as patients in psychiatric facilities. This sample distribution falls within the expected middle three categories and provides baseline data concerning the range of H.I.S. scores for African-American female graduate students.

For the majority of the students (55 percent) who are successfully coping with university and personal stressors, no specific university intervention is required although enrichment programs would be beneficial. The second largest category, approximately 40 percent of the first year students, have some "mild" coping deficits. Specific supportive university interventions and referrals, such as personal counseling or academic support, would be desirable not only to prevent further erosion of coping ability, but also to enhance coping skills. Finally, the very small number (5 percent) of students who fell within the severe/moderate hope and coping deficit, require top priority regarding university resources.

Therefore, immediate and intensive university interventions are necessary.

Through examination of each subscale of the five components of hope, specific recommendations can be made. If, for example, it is found that a student is low in the Perceived Human Family Support coping area, a recommendation to increase her social support and networks could be made. An informal support group, therapeutic group, social club, or a sorority would be a possible avenue to explore. Edds (1988) echoes the importance of Human Family Support in coping with the traumas of college life by recommending and describing the benefits of the black sorority in three areas: namely, as a stable and enduring social outlet to counter the personal and interpersonal stressors of black women, a refuge that offers black women psychological strength in an often hostile university and community environment, and as a place providing comfort and purpose.

The significance of the Model of Hope and Coping through the use of the H.I.S. in predicting ineffective and effective coping students and in providing specific intervention and retention guidelines for university faculty and administrators was also underscored by an examination of the sample's grade-point averages (GPA) after one academic year.

Table 3 indicates the GPA of three high scorers on the Hope Index Scale; these individuals are identified as "effective copers." Conversely, the GPA low-scorers are presented and identified as "ineffective copers."

Table 3

Grade Point Averages and Hope Index Scores of
First–Year Female Graduate Students Effective/Ineffective Copers

Effective Copers		
H.I.S. Scores	Sem #1 GPA	Sem #2 GPA
400	3.3	3.6
410	4.0	4.0
430	3.5	3.8
Ineffective Copers		
H.I.S. Scores	Sem #1 GPA	Sem #2 GPA
230	3.3	3.0
280	4.0	4.0
290	2.5	1.3

The basis premise suggested by these findings is that high H.I.S. scores are indicative of above-average to excellent grade-point averages. These two indicators—high H.I.S. scores and above average GPA—strongly resonate effective coping students who are succeeding both academically and in overall coping with the stressors of life. These students, therefore, are at very low risk for attrition.

In looking at the lowest scoring and ineffective coping individuals in Table 3, it is noted that two out of the three individuals have low H.I.S. scores (230 and 290) that correspond to decreasing grade point averages (3.3/3.0 and 2.5/1.3). Initially, it was felt that this finding of corresponding low H.I.S. scores and low and/or decreasing GPA would hold constant across all subjects.

However, a rarely occurring, yet intriguing finding was observed with the third case: a student with a low H.I.S. score (280) nevertheless has a high GPA (4.0). In reviewing the self-report and indepth interview file of this student, a cogent explanation emerges. There is a current and past history of ineffective personal and interpersonal coping ability which is reflected in poor social relationships and ineffective coping with other dimensions of life. While the individual often does well in one aspect of living, as, in this case, the academic setting, other areas of life are very unsatisfactory and overall life challenges are very poorly addressed. Behaviorally, the profile of this student is often manifested in the "straight A" student who inexplicably does harm to self or others. Similarly, this type of individual profile is often seen in the classroom "whiz kid" who unfortunately is unable to positively socialize or interact in any meaningful way with others outside of the classroom. These identified personality characteristics matched the realities of this student's coping ability and indeed seemed to be valid across other samples.

The critically important findings from these studies are that high GPA alone is not sufficient to indicate low risk of attrition, an individual's coping ability or successful adaptation to the university environment. Therefore, it is erroneous for university personnel to only look at GPA and to believe that all high scoring GPA students are exempt from attrition or personal distress. The critical measure is not the GPA, but the degree of coping ability as indicated by the score on the Hope Index Scale. This finding is reinforced by another study which found, in an examination of students' records, that a large percent of students who failed to return had high GPA's (Lee, 1993).

Therefore, in all cases when H.I.S. scores are low,—even if GPA is high—it is indicative of ineffective and inadequate coping in some important areas of an individual's life and should signal immediate attention from and intervention of university personnel in order to reduce student anxiety and increase university retention rates.

In this follow-up study, it was reaffirmed that without effective coping abilities, the personal difficulties and campus-related stressors that incoming higher education students face are overwhelming and often lead to student distress, anxiety, and withdrawal from the university. Specific studies relating to graduate students indicate a dire need to enhance students' coping ability in graduate programs through augmenting social and academic support services, mentoring programs, as well as personal student attributes of effective coping with campus and personal stressors (Adams, 1986; Clewell, 1987; Halcon, 1988; Isaac, 1986; Richardson, 1990; Steele, 1991; & Wilson and Stith, 1993).

From the findings of this two phase pilot study, the following benefits are derived by using the Model of Hope and Coping and the Hope Index Scale as the overall framework for student retention:

1. *Student Retention.* The use of the Model of Hope and Coping, including the administration of the Hope Index Scale to incoming students, is an effective and accurate way to systematically identify those students who have ineffective coping skills and therefore are at greatest risk of attrition. It is strongly suggested this instrument be utilized early in the year at such meetings as student orientations and precollege sessions. This systematic, proactive, and early identification of students' degree of coping can improve retention rates.

2. *Student referral.* Since students with serious coping deficits are identified earlier through their score on the H.I.S. and their Hope and Coping Profile, more timely interventions can be made. These interventions are expressed in better targeted and more focused referrals to university resources (i.e., counseling centers, academic reinforcement) that will support students' needs. These early interventions and focused referrals are efficient in terms of time, personnel, and money.

3. *University Programs.* With the systematic identification of effective and ineffective coping students, needs assessment information is more accurately obtained and thus program planning is enhanced for effective and ineffective coping students as well as university administration. High and low coping students can be specifically and optimally matched in a peer coping and retention program; or, the effectiveness of freshmen and graduate orientations and follow-up programs could be better planned and implemented.

4. *Budgetary efficiency.* The reduction in remedial efforts, reactive programs, and acute crisis interventions for students results in more preventive efforts, proactive programs, and strategic planning and management for student affairs. As an outcome of this proactive and preventive practice, budgetary expenditures are more efficiently planned and utilized.

5. *Maintaining diversity.* Since attrition rates vary among different student populations and seem to intensify based upon racial or gender composition, a retention program that embraces and accurately addresses student diversity is desirable and necessary. Because the Model of Hope and Coping and specifically the H.I.S., does not discriminate based upon race or gender, it is a useful assessment to identify all students, without bias, who are at risk for attrition.

6. *Students' well-being.* As a result of increased student retention, focused

referrals, effective programs, student body diversity, and budgetary efficiency, the overall quality of students' campus experience and personal well-being is enhanced. Additionally, with an awareness of their degree of coping ability and personal knowledge on how to enhance it, these students are better prepared to more capably and productively address the complex issues and challenges of the twenty first century.

While, unquestionably, some useful information and trends was gathered in this initial study, a more indepth and comprehensive approach was deemed important. Such an approach would include a larger sample size, participation of both women and men, increased length of study, comprehensive research design and data analysis, and formal institutional support consisting of both personnel and funding. These broader issues and concerns are employed in the current study.

Successful Models of Retention: Implications for the Current Study

The limitations that were noted in the two phase pilot study necessitated an investigation that would be more comprehensive in concepualization and implementation. In conceptualizing this current study, it was important to first review various successful models and programs of retention, with particular emphasis on their applicability for African-American students. After this review of retention models and programs, the formation and implementation processes of the current study are described.

Many theoretical models have been postulated to explain student retention and attrition. Although the conceptual emphasis of all these retention models vary, they all converge to discuss and include the importance of student's coping ability. Coping ability, when it can be accurately measured, appears to be one very important and critical factor in the retention of students.

The retention model of Kember (1989) finds that students who exhibit "weak" or "high risk" profiles are more likely to drop out of school. Thus, if a student's ability to cope with stressors can be enhanced, the "high risk" profile for attrition is reduced. Another model by Spady (1970) incorporates social integration which arises from shared group values, normative congruence, and friendship support. This social integration, especially as it is expressed through social supports and campus networks, directly increases students' ability to cope and their commitment to the institution which results in higher rates of retention.

Tinto and Wallace (1986) extend Spady's model by including family background characteristics and individual attributes as important variables in increasing retention. These twin concepts of increased individual or ego attributes and enhanced family support are all directly related to augmented abilities to cope. Rowser's (1990) retention model is based upon expectancies for future experiences, or hope. Some of the same, but not all, of the coping components (e.g. Ego Strength, Family Support) that appear in the Model of

Hope and Coping are employed. Griffin (1991) discusses strategies for black student retention that primarily includes an adjustment approach that is similar to Spady's work.

Finally, the retention models of Pascarella (1980) and Bean (1982, 1983) both discuss the importance of students' personal characteristics, such as coping ability or coping style, in interaction with the institution.

A review of literature involving various university and college programmatic efforts to increase retention of African-American and/or other students of color finds that coping ability of students is a central and important variable in reducing attrition (Allen, 1988; Rowser, 1993). The positive relationship among increased coping ability, higher retention rates, and students' well being have been empiracally demonstrated (Baccus, 1993; Carter, 1994; Carter and Obayuwana, 1995; Montoya and Taliaferro, 1993).

Retention studies relating to graduate students indicate a dire need to enhance student's coping ability in post-baccalaureate programs through augmenting social and academic support services, mentoring programs, as well as assessing and enhancing personal student attributes of effective coping with campus stressors (Adams, 1986; Clewell, 1987; Halcon, 1988; Isaac, 1986; Richardson, 1990; Steele, 1991; Wilson and Stith, 1993).

This current study is an ongoing and longitudinal one that examines retention rates of African-American graduate students at Howard University using the Model of Hope and Coping as the overall framework. The study, which began in the 1995-1996 academic year, targets all incoming first year male and female graduate students (approximately 1,000) representing all levels (masters and doctoral) and departments at Howard University.

Institutional support and funding were received from the Office of the Vice President for Academic Affairs to undertake this preliminary one year graduate retention study. Since receiving funding, the Graduate School of Arts and Sciences and the departments with graduate programs also have been actively involved and supportive of this endeavor because of the recognized importance of graduate retention.

Retention of students is one of the most compelling issues facing Howard University today. To begin to address this issue, a University-wide Retention Task Force was created in 1992. The final report of this Retention Committee stated that Howard University is "not succeeding in meeting the needs of the majority of students enrolled; and entering first-time-in-college (FTIC) freshmen are graduating at a rate of 33.4 percent in five years" (Lee, 1993). These rates compare unfavorably to institutions who are effectively retaining students and who have attrition rates as low a 7 percent and graduation rates as high as 83 percent (Taylor and Reece, 1994).

Such an unacceptably high attrition rate results in a tragedy of unfulfilled human potential as well as staggering economic losses. It has been calculaed that on the basis of an undergraduate dropout rate of approximately 21 percent per annum, Howard loses millions in estimated revenue from undergraduate students who drop out every year (Lee, 1993). Therefore it is not surprising that retention is, and must remain for some time, a top-priority issue for Howard University.

The current focus of attention, however, has been on identifying issues, planning strategies, and undertaking remedial interventions related to attrition and retention only for *undergraduate* students. To date, the University has neither systematically gathered information regarding attrition and retention related to graduate students nor included graduate students in any of its current university-wide research and programmatic efforts to increase retention and reduce attrition. This position seems to reflect the retention efforts of other colleges and universities to direct their resources primarily or soley to undergraduate students and programs.

Howard University—as a comprehensive research institution of higher education with a unique and rich history—certainly influences and is influenced by all of its students. However, the character of any comprehensive research university, is greatly influenced by its reputation for scholarly investigations and professional development as exemplified through its graduate students who become highly competent researchers, practitioners, and leaders in their respective fields. Therefore, it is important to ensure that the retention rate of graduate programs remains high.

The latest available data from the Annual Report of the Graduate School of Arts and Sciences (Sadler, 1993) indicate an attrition rate of 20 percent for the 1991-1992 school year. This figure compares to the unacceptably high 21 percent attrition rate for Howard University-FTIC freshmen. However, it is not clear if these undergraduate and graduate rates are comparable since the 20 percent graduate attrition figure does not specifically identify level of graduate study (Masters, Ph. D., etc.), year or semester of student attrition (first, second, etc.) demographics for student dropouts, reasons for leaving, or a comparison with previous attrition rates.

Given this ambiguity regarding the status of graduate student retention data, it is important and necessary to ascertain baseline information and other salient variables in investigating the attrition and retention rate for graduate students. For this current study, the following goals and objectives were identified:

(1) The identification of coping levels as ineffective or effective for all first year graduate students through the administration of the Hope Index Scale.

(2) The construction of a Hope and Coping profile for all students based upon their score on the H.I.S., and their identified coping style.

(3) An examination of the relationships among first-year retention rates and the Hope and Coping Profile.

(4) An analysis of the relationships among first-year retention rates and the following variables: current grade-point average, department and level of study, major academic concentration, gender, race/ethnicity, qualifying admissions exam scores (e.g. GRE), and demographics of post bacculeaureate school attended.

The process employed to achieve these stated goals and objectives was a multi-strategic one. It was critical to attain the necessary support from key individuals in the administration. After noting that retention was a top institutional priority, funding support was sought and received from the Office of the Vice President for Academic Affairs. Next, the Graduate School of Arts and Science was involved in, and actively supported this study. Finally a one-page introductory letter which briefly described the Retention Project was sent to all Deans of Schools and Colleges who had graduate programs. This letter requested support from the Deans in implementing this Project in their Schools/Colleges and requested the identification of their staff person responsible for graduate student enrollment and/or advisement.

To expedite receipt of support and to avoid additional paperwork, this initial letter to the Deans included a signature line and space to indicate their reply to be faxed. A 100 percent return rate and approval response was obtained within the one week deadline. Next, the identified retention designee was sent a letter which indicated the Dean's approval of the Retention Project as well as their designation as the key individual, given a brief description of the Project, and requested their assistance in administering and collecting the Hope Index Scales.

After this administrative approval process, the second phase of the Retention Project, student participation, was begun. In chronological sequence, three forums were held to obtain student participation: (1) Students attending the annual orientation program for new graduate students hosted by the Graduate School of Arts and Sciences were administered the Hope Index Scale; (2) The departmental designee administered the H.I.S. during the Fall registration period to students not previously assessed during the graduate orientation program; (3) A departmental review and follow-up was made for the remaining untested students. At each forum, the Project was briefly described, informed consent was obtained, and the Hope Index Scale was administered and collected.

The third phase includes data analysis and a final report. At the conclusion of this first year, a written report will be published which describes and discusses this study's research findings, interpretation, recommendations, and conclusions. This report will be of value in better defining the relationships among graduate students' retention rate and hope, coping and the other central variables under study in this project. At the conclusion of this one year project, additional funding will be sought so that these students can continue to be followed throughout their entire matriculation at Howard University. From these additional data, it is felt that significant information will be added to the body of knowledge regarding effective retention models and programs for students attending historically black colleges and universities.

The critical significance of better understanding and enhancing graduate student retention is compelling. For as the new millennium with all its bright promises and multifaceted challenges begins to dawn, this new age will belong to those individuals who can effectively and successfully cope in the fast-paced and complex world of the twenty-first century. The Model of Hope and Coping is instrumental in preparing individuals to be successful and effectively coping students of today and accomplished world citizens and leaders of tommorrow.

—Dr. Ann L. Carter-Obayuwana is a Graduate Associate Professor of Counseling Psychology in the Department of Human Development and Psychoeducational Studies at Howard University in Washington, DC.

References

Adams, H. (1986). Minority Participation in Graduate Education: An Action Plan. Washington, D.C.: The Report of the National Invitational Forum on the Status of Minority Participation in Graduate Education.

Allen, W. (1986). Gender and race differences in Black students academic performance, racial attitudes, and college satisfaction. Atlanta: Southern Educational Foundation, 71-84.

Baccus, G. (1993). The impact of social support networks and retention. Proceedings of the 6th Annual International Conference for Women in Higher Education. El Paso: University of Texas at El Paso, 1-3.

Banks, T. L. (1988). Gender bias in the classroom. Journal of Legal Education 38, 142-143.

Bean, J. P. (1982). Conceptual models of student attrition: How theory can help the institutional research. In E. T. Pascarella (Ed.). New Directions for Institutional Research: Studying student attrition, 36, (17-33). San Francisco: Jossey-Bass.

Bean, J. P. (1983). The application of a model of turnover in work organization to the student attrition process. Review of Higher Education, 6, 129-148.

Beavers, W. R. and Kaslow, F. W. (1981). The anatomy of hope. Journal of Marital and Family Therapy, 7, (2), 119-126.

Belkin, G. S. (1988). Introduction to counseling. Dubuque: Wm. C. Brown.

Brazziel, W. F. (1987/1988). Total doctorate degrees by race/ethnicity for selected years (chart). Road blocks to graduate school: Black Americans are not achieving parity. Educational Record, 68/69 (Fall/Winter), 111.

Carter, A. L. (1994). The Hope Index Scale as a predictor of stress and coping ability in first year African-American female graduate students. Proceedings of the 7th Annual International Conference for Women in Higher Education, El Paso: The University of Texas at El Paso, 88-93.

Carter, A. L. and Obayuwana, A. O. (1995). Hope and coping skills of female graduate students: A follow-up study. Proceedings of the 8th Annual International Conference for Women in Higher Education (in press) El Paso: The University of Texas at El Paso.

Carter, A. L. and Obayuwana, A. O. (1994). Health, stress, and hope. Silver Spring, MD: Institute of Hope.

Carter, A. L. and Obayuwana, A. O. (1993). The Hope Model: A survival guide for women in higher education. Proceedings of the Sixth Annual International Conference of Women in Higher Education. El Paso: The University of Texas at El Paso, 20-24.

Carter, A. L. and Obayuwana, A. O. (1988). Hope Theory: A mental health approach to coping and wellness. Silver Spring, MD: Institute of Hope.

Carter, A. L. and Obayuwana, A. O. (1981). The Hope Index Scale, the Scoring and Interpretation Guide, and the Hope Index Diagnostic Chart. Silver Spring, MD: Institute of Hope.

Carter, D. J. and Wilson, R. W. (1991). Ninth annual status report on minorities in higher education. Washington, DC: American Council on Education.

Carter, D., Pearson, C., and Shavlik, D. (1988). Double jeopardy: Women of color in higher education. Educational Record, 69/69, (4/1), 98-103.

Chandler, T. L. (1988). Attracting minority graduate students and faculty in an atmosphere of increasing competition. Council of Graduate Schools Communicator (June 5), 21.

Chronicle of Higher Education Almanac. (1991, August 28). Special issue.

Clewell, B. (1987). Retention of Black and Hispanic Doctoral Students. Part I: Personal and Background Characteristics of Persisting and Nonpersisting Black and Hispanic Graduate Students. Part II: Retention of Minority Doctoral Students: Institutional Policies and Practices. Princeton, NJ: GRE Board Research Report #88-4R, ETS Research Report 87.

Collins, M.N.K. (1987). More young Black men choosing not to go to college. Chronicle of Higher Education (December 19), A6.

Corey, M. S. and Corey, G. (1989). Becoming a helper. Pacific Grove, CA: Brooks/Cole Publishing Company.

Edds, M. (1988). The sorority behind Black feminism. Review of In search of sisterhood. Delta Sigma Theta and the challenge of the Black sorority movement. (Giddings, P., Los Angeles Times, July 31).

Ehrhart, J. K. and Sandler, B. R. (1990). Rx for success: Improving the climate for women in medical schools and teaching hospitals. Washington, DC: Association of American Colleges.

Fleming, J. (1984). Blacks in college: A comparative study of student's success in Black and White institutions. San Francisco: Jossey-Bass.

Frank, J. (1968). The role of hope in psychotherapy. International Journal of Psychiatry, 5 (5), 383-395.

Griffin, O. T. (1991). Strategies for Black student retention: A conceptual review. The Western Journal of Black Studies, 15 (4), 235-241.

Hackney, H. and Cormier, S. (1994). Counseling strategies and interventions. Boston: Allyn and Bacon.

Halcon, J. (1988). Exemplary Programs for College-Bound Minority Students. Boulder: Western Interstate Commission for Higher Education.

Hall, R. M. and Sandler, B. R. (1984). Out of the classroom: A chilly campus climate for women. Washington, DC: Association of American Colleges. Project on the Status and Education of Women.

Hall, R. M. and Sandler, B. R. (1982). The classroom climate: A chilly one for women? Washington, DC: Association of American Colleges. Project on the Status and Education of Women.

Issac, P. (1986, August). Recruitment, Retention, and Graduation of Minority Graduate Students. Paper presented at the Annual Convention of the American Psychological Association, Washington, DC.

Kember, D.d (1989). A longitudinal-process model of drop-out from distance education. Journal of Higher Education, 603, 1278-301.

Korner, I. N. (1970). Hope as a method of coping. Journal of Consulting and Clinical Psychology, 34, 134.

Ladner, J. (1993). As quoted in : Final Report of the Howard University Retention committee, pg 2, Howard University, Division of Academic Affairs, Washington, DC

Lee, C. M. (1993). Final Report of the Howard University Retention Committee. Howard University, Division of Academic Affairs, Washington, DC:

Montoya, A. and Taliaferro, B. (1993). Recruitment and retention: Are we doing only half the job? Proceedings of the 6th Annual International Conference for Women in Higher Education. El Paso: The University of Texas at El Paso, 122-126.

Moses, Y.T. (1989). Black women in academe: Issues and strategies. Washington, DC: Association of American Colleges.

Mow, S. L. & Nettles, M. T. (1990). Minority access to and persistence and performance in college: A review of trends in the literature. In J. Smith (Ed.) Higher education: Handbook of theory and research (Vol VI). (35-105). New York: Agathon.

NCAA (1994/1995). 1994 NCAA division II and III enrollment and persistence rates report. In Retention rates of African-American college students. Journal of Blacks in Higher Education (Winter), 56.

Nieves-Squires, S. (1991). Hispanic women: Making their presence on campus less tenuous. Washington, DC: Association of American Colleges.

Obayuwana, A. O. and Carter, A. L. (1982). The anatomy of hope. Journal of the National Medical Association, 74, (3), 229-234.

Obayuwana, A. O. and Carter, A. L. (1986). Understanding human hope: Current thoughts and trends.

Obayuwana, A. O., Carter, A. L., and Barnett, R. M. (1984). Psychosocial distress and pregnancy outcome: A three-year prospective study. Journal of Psychosomatic Obstetrics and Gynecology, 3, 173-183.

Obayuwana, A. O., Collins, J., Carter, A. L., Rao, M. S., Mathura, C. C. and Wilson, S. b. (1982). Hope Index Scale: An instrument for the objective assessment of hope. Journal of the National Medical Association, 8, 761-765.

Obiakor, F. E. and Barker, N. c. (1993). The politics of higher education: Perspectives for African-Americans in the 21st century. The Western Journal of Black Studies, 17, (4), 219-226.

Pascarella, E. (1980). Student-faculty contact and college outcomes. Review of Educational Research, 50, 545-595.

Richardson, T. (1990). Recruitment and retention of Black students in graduate programs. Educational consideration, 18. (1), 31-32.

Rowser, J. F. (1990). A retention model for African-American students. The Western Journal of Black Studies, 15, (3), 166-170.

Sadler, W. A. (1993). Annual Report of the Graduate School of Arts and Sciences, 1992-1993. Washington, DC: Howard University, 25.

Sailes, G. A. (1993). An investigation of Black student attrition at a large, predominantly white, midwestern university. The Western Journal of Black Studies, 17, (4) 179-182.

Sedlacek, W. E. (1987). Black students on white campuses: 20 years of research. Journal of College Student Personnel, 28, (6) 484-495.

Selye, H. (1974). Stress without distress. New York: Lippincott and Crowell.

Selye, H. (1976). The stress of life. New York: McGraw-Hill.

Sherman, T. M., Giles, M. B., and Williams-Green, J. (1994). Assessment and retention of Black students in higher education Journal of Negro Education, 63, (2) 164-180.

Spady, W. (1970). Dropouts from higher education: A theoretical synthesis of recent research. Review of Educational Research, 45, 89-125.

Steele, R. (1991). Mentoring: An effective tool for retention of minorities. Missouri: Author.

Taylor, O. and Reece, A. (1994). Howard University PEW Retention Grant Proposal. Office of the Vice President for Academic Affairs. Washington, DC: Howard University,

Tinto, V. and Wallace, D. L. (1986). Retention: An admission concern. College and University, 61, (4) 290-291.

Webster's Encyclopedic Unabridged Dictionary of the English Language. (1989). New York: Gramercy Books.

Weitz, R. and Gordon, L. (1993). Images of Black women among Anglo college students. Sex Roles, 28, (1/2), 19-34.

Wilson, L. and Stith, S. (1993). The voices of African-American MFT students: Suggestions for improving recruitment and retention. Journal of Marital and Family Therapy, 19, (1), 17-30.

Zappert, L. T. and Stansbury, K. (1987). In the pipeline: A comparative analysis of men and women in graduate programs in science, engineering, and medicine at Stanford University. Stanford: Stanford University, School of Medicine.

The University of Georgia-Athens Patricia Roberts Harris Felowships: Minority Graduate Student Support for Academic and Career Success

by Maurice Daniels, Patrick Johnson and Louise Tomlinson

Overview:

The University of Georgia Patricia Roberts Harris Fellowship Program (PRHFP) has a long-standing and impressive record in securing fellowships from the U.S. Department of Education for individuals from minority groups who are pursuing masters and doctoral level study in academic fields where they are underrepresented.

This discussion describes the selection, academic and social support, and resources used for purposes of recruiting and retaining minority graduate students. The discussion also delineates the institutional record of commitment and resources that contribute to the successful retention of PRHFP Fellows and underrepresented graduate students in general. Critical components that contribute to the success of the PRHFP include innovative approaches to recruitment, mentorships and peer support, networking opportunities, academic support programs, and the establishment of PRHFP student assistantships and awards.

Strategies for institutionalization, such as supporting non-PRHFP students and linking with other recruitment and retention efforts, are also critical aspects of the strategies for implementation that will be discussed. In addition, an analysis of evaluation factors such as retention, completion and employment rates, and the extent of student presentation and publication of scholarly papers is provided. Finally, the impact of the program, as well as problems, solutions, and insights are shared.

Origin and Development of the Program

The Graduate and Professional Opportunity Program was initiated by Congress in the late seventies. The program was designed to expand the opportunities for women and minorities in the United States to obtain graduate and professional degrees. The program is a highly competitive one in which the best institutions compete to participate. In 1986, the fellowship program was named after Patricia Roberts Harris in honor of her contributions and dedication to the field of public service. Ms. Harris, an African-American female, was born in Mattoon, Illinois in 1924, graduated from Howard University in 1945, and completed a Law degree at George Washington University in 1960.

Although PRHF programs are funded at a number of institutions, the competitive process awards funds to those institutions that present a program design which is tailored to resource capabilities through which they demonstrate the potential to deliver appropriate services. Each program is based on unique visions and creative enterprises that assure academic and social support for minority graduate students.

At the University of Georgia the program was initiated in 1980 by Dr. Jack Jenkins, who was a faculty member in the Department of Psychology. His commitment to expanding opportunities for graduate and professional students and his visionary leadership of the program initially led to funding opportunities in the areas of chemistry, physics, and psychology. Several other disciplines including veterinary medicine and genetics later became involved in the program.

Based on a recommendation from Dr. Jenkins, Dr. Maurice Daniels, an associate professor in social work, was appointed director in 1986 by the vice president for academic affairs. Since 1986, the program has expanded and more than $1,000,000 has been awarded for Patricia Roberts Harris fellowship opportunities to graduate students at the University of Georgia. The 1991 proposal for PRHFP awards received a perfect score, the 1993 proposal for PRHFP awards received perfect scores in two of three academic areas, and the 1995 proposal received a score of 100 in three of four academic areas, based on competitive reviews conducted by the United States Department of Education. Additionally, several innovative recruitment and retention models have been employed that have had a major impact on expanding graduate and professional opportunities for minority students. The creative academic and social support opportunities offered students through the current program are described in this manuscript.

Major Events and Milestones

A critical feature of the PRHF program at UGA is that campus and comn..:nity networking opportunities are carefully coordinated. In addition to support mechanisms such as an orientation and reception, fellows are made familiar with strategic outlets for networking. Such entities include the office of the Department for Minority Student Services, the Graduate and Professional Scholars organization (a peer support group for graduate and professional underrepresented students), and the Annual Black Faculty and Staff Forum which addresses the status of blacks at UGA and presents awards for outstanding contributions and accomplishments by faculty, staff and students.

Academic support programs are designed, targeted, and announced. Academic support is provided in the way of skills workshops on a variety of topics, as well as small grants to support student projects and presentations, and tutoring services. Workshops have been conducted on topics such as "Research and Grant Proposal Writing," "Study Strategies and Test-Taking Skills," "Professional Memberships and Professional Development," and "Computer Literacy Skills." Academic support for fellows has also included workshops that address skills such as getting on-line with the UGA mainframe, using e-mail, library search capabilities, and statistics programs such as SPSS, SAS and others.

Small grants are provided to students who need assistance with expenses for completing research projects, preparing and delivering presentations at professional conferences, and preparing manuscripts for publication. Students are also made aware of the availability of tutoring services provided campus-wide through the Tutor-House staffed by trained tutors.

The PRHF Student Assistant Program is a unique feature of the PRHF program effort. It is an incentive for involvement from non-participating disciplines by offering a PRHF Student Assistantship to students in the departments that have assisted in program development efforts and in securing PRHFP funds—rather than first being open to all disciplines. It is designed to encourage student interest in and exploration of a career in academia—particularly available career paths in a university setting.

Additional institutional funds for Graduate Minority Assistantships bolster the support of PRHFP Fellows and other minority graduate students. An institution-wide recruitment program aims to identify and attract individuals from underrepresented groups by including the designation of institutional funds for graduate minority assistantships for which PRHFP Fellows qualify in specific instances.

Implementation Strategies

Institutional commitment is a necessary cornerstone in the foundation of the PRHF program. The institutional commitment is made evident by the related efforts of the dean of the graduate school, the Presidential Minority Faculty Hiring Initiative (PMFHI), the establishment and operation of the Department of Minority Services and Programs (DMSP), and the financial support of minority students by the graduate school in the form of graduate assistantships. As a result of the graduate school efforts, of the 368 minority students enrolled in graduate study, 178 hold graduate assistantships for the 1994-95 academic year. The total value of these assistantships is more than $1.4 million.

The PMFHI allocates dollars from central administrative resources for the hiring of minority faculty. The initiative has resulted in a net increase of twenty-eight new full-time African-American faculty members during the past six years. The Department of Student Activities created the DMSP in 1990 to facilitate support programs and enhance the quality of life for underrepresented students at the University of Georgia.

The support of specific participating disciplines is critical. The viability of the PRHFP is due in large part to the commitment and assistance of specific disciplines in contributing to the grant proposal and enrolling underrepresented students. The diverse array of areas of study that traditionally have been supported in the past five years include: Mathematics, Microbiology, Political Science, Science Education, Social Work, Sociology, and Statistics.

The PRHF office attempts to institutionalize its effort by inviting administrators and faculty from a variety of departments to support the recruitment and retention of minority graduate students by offering them the opportunity to submit departmental proposals of commitment to academic support and supplementary financial assistance as a part of the yearly PRHF proposal submitted to the U.S. Department of Education, in exchange for the support services that are provided by the PRHFP to every PRHF student and to other minority graduate students.

The PRHF office is diligent in its effort to publicize the grant awards and other achievements in major campus newspapers and at various special interest meetings.

As has been mentioned, the PRHFP reaches out to provide support to minority graduate students in a variety of disciplines who are not PRHFP Fellows. The program constantly seeks to institutionalize its agenda by creating linkages with other campus efforts with which a mutually beneficial interest can be identified. For example, the mentorship component of the PRHFP is now coordinated by the efforts of the University Affiliated Programs (UAP) office that seeks to recruit minority graduate students into various fields of study related to the needs of disabled populations, but has specifically engineered a mentorship program for matching students and faculty in a variety of disciplines. In turn, the Director and Co-Director of the PRHFP have served on the steering committee of the UAP and the PRHF co-director has participated in UAP recruitment at various college campuses where PRHF material was included in the UAP recruitment package.

Programmatic Operations and Activities

Successful recruitment of minority graduate students for participation in the program is attributed to the diligent dissemination of information to predominantly minority-populated colleges and universities and to recruitment visits at these sites. Information is disseminated widely at professional conferences. A Minority Visitation Day is also sponsored on campus in selected disciplines which provides financial support to potential candidates to visit a department of interest and tour the campus. Recruitment is also enhanced by tapping into a network of faculty at traditionally black institutions who serve as resources for identifying potential students. The PRHFP office also benefits in its recruitment efforts by tapping into the campus undergraduate application pool.

PRHFP fellows are initiated into the program with an orientation and reception provided by the campus-wide graduate and professional minority student organization and hosted by the PRHFP office in conjunction with the office of the vice president for legal affairs. Campus and community tours, links with community outreach persons, and other receptions are provided. A schedule of these and other relevant year-long events is provided to fellows. A directory of minority and other community businesses is also distributed to fellows.

Mentorships and peer support is provided for fellows. PRHFP fellows are matched with a faculty member in their area of study. The mentorship program is coordinated through the Office of University Affiliated Programs. A graduate assistantship is funded by the Graduate School for a graduate student coordinator who coordinates student involvement for recruitment and retention efforts including peer academic support groups.

The adequacy of program and campus resources assures that PRHFP Fellows and other minority graduate students at the University of Georgia have access to a variety of resources that facilitate their academic and social pursuits. The PRHFP office is located in the school of social work building where the PRHFP support staff is located as well as student lounges and conference rooms. The PRHFP equipment includes IBM computers, laser printers and software programs made specifically available to PRH fellows as well as duplication services, software check-out, and typewriters. Dispersed across the campus in several departments and locations are facilities and services such as computer laboratories, a mainframe computer system, an institute for behavioral research (which provides statistical services), an extensive video and audiotape collection and video and audiotape duplication services provided by the instructional resources center, and the largest library system in the state. In addition, there is a commitment by the university to supplement expenses for research materials and other needs of PRHFP Fellows related to their scholarly pursuits.

Administrative Structure and Staffing

The PRHFP Advisory Committee has been prudently selected and appointed to include diverse representation in terms of race, gender, institutional status, discipline, and expertise. The committee serves to make policy decisions on the administration of the program, including responses to individual requests and reviews of PRHFP and non-PRHFP student eligibility for supplementary assistance provided through the PRHFP office. The members of the advisory committee possess the kind of expertise which is critical in overseeing the program in terms of negotiating and grant writing on its behalf and providing the kind of input to program support services that matches the students' needs.

Members include the associate dean of the graduate school, the associate director of the division of counseling and testing, the associate director of affirmative action, and an assistant professor of reading in the division of academic assistance who is also the co-director of the PRHFP. These individuals advise the director of the PRHFP who is an associate professor in the school of social work and assistant to the dean of the graduate school.

Program Success and Accomplishments: Formative and Summative Data

The evaluation of the PRHFP operation and success is culled from both formative and summative assessments. Retention, degree completion, employment rates, participation, productivity, and student and faculty advisor perceptions of progress and quality of experience in the program are important aspects of program evaluation. The PRHFP's track record and the track record of respective disciplines in recruiting and retaining graduate minority students who demonstrate productivity and persistence to completion of their chosen degrees, as well as success in career placement is outstanding.

For example, in the school of social work, the graduation rate of African-American full-time MSW candidates is exceptional. In September of 1991, eleven African-American students matriculated into the program and all of them have graduated. Of the twelve that entered in 1992, eleven have graduated. It is important to note that the University of Georgia School Of Social Work has been awarded ten PRHFP Fellowships in the past six years and 100 percent of these students have either completed their MSW and are gainfully employed in careers serving the public interest or are currently enrolled and in good standing with the University of Georgia.

The success of the conduct of the PRHFP is also made evident in the attendance rates of fellows at PRHF sponsored workshops and other scheduled support activities. Workshops have been attended by substantial numbers of PRHF and other graduate students who then requested follow-up sessions on the same or other topics and have provided positive feedback on the coverage and relevance of these units. The extent of minority graduate student involvement in presentations at prestigious professional conferences has been impressive. This evidence is accounted for in the number of students who apply for and receive small grants for partial reimbursement of the costs incurred for preparation of presentations, travel, and lodging.

For example, some of the conference presentations that have been supported by the PRHFP in the past year have been for a student in the Department of Animal and Dairy Science presenting on "Diet Selection and Composition of Gain in Somatotropin Treated Rats", at the Experimental Biology Meeting; a student in the Department of Educational Psychology presenting on "The Impact of Training and Concreteness in Reading Vocabulary Development", at the Southeastern Psychological Association; and a presentation by a student in the Business School on "Brand Repositioning Strategies" at the 24th Annual Albert Haring Symposium. It should also be noted that a PRHF student majoring in microbiology is the recipient of the Southern Council of Graduate Schools Award for Best Masters Thesis of 1993-94.

The positive academic track record of UGA PRHF recipients is also reflected in grade point averages and persistence. Fellows have held an average GPA of 3.48 with a median of 3.61. Seventy-five percent of the students have had a GPA of 3.2 or higher and twenty-five percent have a GPA of 3.9 or higher. The average GPA for male fellows is 3.4, with a median of 3.4, and the average for female fellows is 3.5, with a median of 3.6. The persistence rate of PRHF recipients is commendable at 78% with fourteen out of eighteen fellows completing the program.

Responses to a 1994 survey of faculty advisor and student perceptions of several variables that affect student progress provide positive indicators for the PRHF experience at UGA. The survey included several likert scale items that explored the following factors: computer skills, study and test-taking skills, time management, networking with faculty, mentor-mentee relationships, and networking with students. Each factor was rated on a scale of one (poor) to four (excellent) and corresponding questions were constructed for both the fellow and the advisor.

Responses indicated that both advisors and fellows give high ratings to progress and participation, with students' ratings being consistently more conservative than advisors' ratings across variables. (See Table 1 for a comparison of mentor-mentee ratings.) Overall, fellows' highest ratings were ascribed to the mentor/mentee relationship (a 3.3 average rating), while their lowest ratings were ascribed to networking with faculty and networking with students (a 2.8 average rating). Overall, advisors' highest ratings were ascribed to fellows' networking with faculty and the mentor/mentee relationship (4.0 and 3.8 average ratings, respectively), while their lowest ratings were ascribed to fellows' computer skills and time management skills (3.5 average ratings).

The mean difference between fellows' and advisors' ratings across variables was .6 rating points. The greatest disparity between fellows' and advisors' ratings was found in perceptions of networking with students (1.2 rating points) where fellows were less positive than advisors as to the extent that they were engaged in this activity. The greatest agreement between fellows' and advisors' ratings was found on perceptions of technical writing and research skills (.3 rating points) where fellows were somewhat less positive than advisors.

Table 1
PRHF Evaluations for 1994-95

Comparison of Mentor-Mentee Perceptions of Fellow's Progress

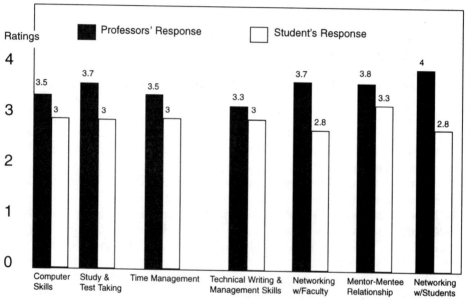

For each of the likert scale items on the factors mentioned previously, there was also space provided for elaborated comments on both the student questionnaire and corresponding questionnaire for the fellows' advisors. Fellows' elaborated responses on their perceptions of their computer skills ranged from indicating limited keyboard agility to familiarity with several word processing and graphics programs, to fundamental knowledge of several statistical software packages. Most importantly, in more than one instance respondents also indicated that classes offered in their department, other students, or the staff had been very helpful with computer literacy challenges.

Fellows' responses did not indicate any concern about study skills in particular, but did acknowledge a challenge in test-taking and room for improvement in this area. Fellows' self-assessments of their technical writing and research skills ranged from good to excellent. They attributed their skills in these areas to either their participation in a research seminar class or to the assistance of department faculty in general.

Comments on their perceptions of networking with faculty indicate a range of involvement emanating from what was described as little initiation on the part of faculty to an "open door" invitation accompanied by positively viewed experiences. Fellows' perceptions of their mentor/mentee relationship indicated that they either had a good relationship with their major advisor or other faculty who have provided positive input to their development and academic networking. There were no elaborated responses on the issue of time management or networking with students.

The survey also included several fill-in items which asked for information on papers presented at professional conferences during time as a PRHF recipient, papers published, memberships in professional organizations and attendance at PRHF sponsored activities and events on campus. Although only three of the respondents indicated any involvement in the presentation of papers at professional conferences and none indicated publications in professional journals at the time the survey was administered, one student was preparing a manuscript to be submitted for publication and a majority of the fellows indicated that they were members of one to three professional organizations.

The workshops and other PRHFP-sponsored events that students attended most were as follows: orientation receptions, department colloquia, department socials, the study skills and test-taking workshop, computer orientation, and the technical writing workshop in descending order of frequency. Graduate tutorials were attended the least.

Impact: Participants and the Institution

The success and productivity of PRHFP Fellows has created a positive and visible image of minority graduate students. Their performance and accomplishments have impacted other potential minority graduate students. Their track record has also convinced numbers of departments and faculty within those departments that the recruitment and retention of minority graduate students is a viable and worthwhile pursuit. The enduring effect of the PRHFP experience has been that many of the same departments have continued to recruit new students and additional departments have become involved in the program.

Visions for the Future

The institution can invest its accumulated wisdom and track record with the PRHFP to generalizing the organization and implementation aspects of the model to continuing recruitment and retention that might be funded by new sources. It is incumbent upon the institution to further diversify and utilize more of their funding resources for such purposes, by looking towards additional grants and to financial support from African-American and other minority alumni. The prospects for such changes to take place are excellent, considering the track record of previous PRHFP Fellows and the potential that has been made evident by some of the shining stars in the galaxy of Historically Black Colleges and Universities-HBCUs that have become highly successful in the way of innovative and enduring fundraising campaigns.

Insights and Advice

Predominantly white institutions and HBCUs have much that they can learn from each other in the recruitment and retention of minority graduate students. This is acknowledged in the aforementioned discussion pertaining to the acquisition of program funds. However, there is also a need for institutions to look toward a new perspective of the concept of retention.

Retention should be defined as the successful maintenance of the same students initially enrolled in a program, such that they complete their degree requirements while developing skills necessary for success in their chosen careers, and such that they are successful in securing meaningful career placement that is relevant to their field of study. Retention is not successful if students complete a program of study but either fail to access or prematurely drop out of the job market in their chosen field.

The national policy for retention standards should call for program designs that are systemic in nature, that provide opportunities for skill development in career-related contexts, that implement carefully targeted formative and summative evaluation processes, and that monitor the success rate of career placements of graduates as a part of their recruitment and retention plan.

—Dr. Maurice Daniels is the director of the Patricia Roberts Harris Fellowship Program and an Associate Professor in the School of Social Work at the University of Georgia in Athens, Georgia.
—Mr. Patrick Johnson is a Patricia Roberts Harris Fellowship Program Graduate Assistant in the Department of Statistics at the University of Georgia in Athens, Georgia.
—Dr. Louise Tomlinson is co-director of the Patricia Roberts Harris Fellowship Program and an Assistant Professor of Reading in the Division of Academic Assistance at the University of Georgia in Athens.

Penn State's Center for Minority Graduate Opportunities and Faculty Development

by Deborah F. Atwater and Catherine G. Lyons

Overview:

Much of what is included in this article is based on seven years of experience working in Penn State's Center for Minority Graduate Opportunities and Faculty Development. The evolution of making the center an effective tool for retention of minority faculty, and retention and recruitment of minority graduate students is documented in the following narrative.

The Center evolved in 1987 out of an expressed need for change. Consequently, the university Faculty Senate approved the Center in July of 1987. One program director and university administrator remembers that "from the start, there were some of us who knew we had better do something to address some disturbing trends in the area of faculty and student recruitment, retention, and development. That something had to be extremely well thought-out in the ensuing effort to define and redefine Penn State's mission and commitment." To address the shortage of professors and the losses of minority students through the educational pipeline, the Center was born. Specifically, the major goal of the Center was to find a way to bring in new minority faculty and graduate students, keep them at Penn State, and see to it that their professional needs were satisfied.

Introduction

The Center is housed at Penn State's University Park Campus, located in State College, PA, which is the administrative hub of the institution. It is the primary site for graduate study and one of twenty two campuses in the Penn State system. Graduate degrees are also awarded at Penn State Behrend, Harrisburg and Great Valley campuses. In addition to the director of administrative affairs and the campus CEO, faculty at the Commonwealth Educational System are responsible to the department and their college deans at University Park. As a result of the complex campus structure, the center serves faculty and, in some cases graduate students at locations other than University Park.

This statewide campus system is an outgrowth of the community-based campuses Penn State established during the economic depression of the 1930s. By literally taking higher education to the students, the university lowered the cost of attending college and enabled many persons to enroll who otherwise could not afford to do so. Today, nine of every ten Pennsylvanians lives within thirty miles of a Penn State Campus. University Park Campus is the hub for graduate work in most fields and enrolled more than 6,600 advanced-degree students in 1992-93. A total of 10,441 students were enrolled for graduate work at all campuses. Penn State, all locations, has about 4,100 full-time faculty and has a faculty/student ratio of 1:19. Of the nearly 1,700 professional faculty at University Park, about eighty eight percent hold doctoral degrees.

A. Goals, Values, and Beliefs

I. Historical Perspective

The Center was born to address the shortage of professors and the losses of minority students through the educational pipeline. The university defines diversity as "the creation of an environment in which all persons of all backgrounds can work, study and live together in ways that expand our collective knowledge of individuals and societies." The center has operationalized that definition to encompass a population that is inclusive regardless of ethnicity, race, gender, age, religion, sexual orientation, and physical capabilities.

The visionaries who designed the center's structure included the administrative staff of the graduate school, minority faculty and staff, and university administrators. It was under their guidance that special care was employed to hire the "right" director and senior faculty mentor to facilitate the implementation of the center's goals and objectives.

The center's vision is to help increase minority presence at the Pennsylvania State University. Our mission is to address pipeline issues related to undergraduates, graduates, and all-but dissertation students and junior faculty. We will help empower students who are underrepresented, first generation and needy to partake of the educational advantages sponsored by Penn State. Our work with junior faculty will empower them to become promoted and tenured within this system. Our work with the university at large helps to promote a climate that is accepting of diversity and conducive for the entire Penn State community.

The major events and milestones in the program's evolution and development can best be addressed by a discussion of the objectives and goals of the center.

Goals and Objectives

The center has two major offices to promote and support underrepresented minority graduate students and faculty at Penn State University. For counsel and strategic planning, the center has a ten-member advisory board that consists of two vice provosts, a department head, a dean and senior faculty in various colleges in the university. The advisory board was instrumental in the development of a university-wide mentoring award. The award of five hundred dollars and a plaque is presented at a university awards ceremony each year. Since its inception, there have also been a number of majority faculty and staff, that have provided ideas and support to the center by reading dossiers or participating in faculty development workshops.

Minority Graduate Students

Each of the university's academic units (Colleges of Agricultural Sciences, Arts and Architecture, Business Administration, Earth and Mineral Sciences, Education, Engineering, Health and Human Development, The Liberal Arts, Medicine, Science, and Communications) has a designated person to direct/coordinate minority recruitment and retention for both undergraduate and graduate students. The college directors/coordinators tailor their recruitment strategies to respond to the needs of their college. The coordinators and directors of recruitment and retention collectively form a council. The council meets monthly to review their status, share experiences, and evaluate performances. The kinds of activities Penn State employs in recruiting graduate students are varied and very diverse, and the center's objectives complement those of the college directors/coordinators, and are listed below:

Below is a listing of objectives and activities to accomplish those goals for both, the Office for Minority Graduate Opportunities and the Office for Minority Faculty Development.

Objective 1. To identify and recruit talented undergraduate minority students. Penn State addresses the need for identification of potential students through an extensive nationwide recruitment program. Examples of recruitment activities include:

1. Attend, and actively participate in the numerous professional and recruitment fairs hosted by colleges and universities throughout the country;

2. Recruit Penn State undergraduates;

3. Attend and participate in professional conferences and forums germane to minority recruitment and retention issues;

4. Purchase and develop resource materials to enhance the marketing of Penn State to potential minority graduates;

5. Purchase information to assist in identifying potential minority graduate students;

6. Provide orientation visits to Penn State campuses for prospective graduate students;

7. Create and devise ongoing exchange and on-site visitations;

8. Nationally distribute informational brochures to advertise minority graduate opportunities at Penn State;

9. Advertise in local and national publications;

10. Participate and assist in planning a state conference on graduate opportunities for Black and Hispanic students; and

11. Network to establish partnership institutions at historically black colleges and universities and historically Hispanic institutions.

Objective 2: To retain students at the university until they have satisfactorily completed all requirements for the enrolled degree. The Office for Minority Graduate Opportunities works closely with the college directors/coordinators in retaining students. These strategies vary from college to college but may include the following:

1. Create opportunities for minority students to interact with minority faculty and staff, with the intention of providing an atmosphere in which mentoring relationships can develop;

2. Counsel and consult with individual students regarding personal needs, concerns, and issues affecting their tenure at Penn State;

3. Work closely with the leadership, and support the activities of the black, Native American, and Spanish-speaking graduate students' associations;

4. Coordinate and facilitate support seminars for minority graduate students;

5. Provide half-time graduate assistantships, to be awarded to minority graduate students working in administrative units;

6. Establish and publish a minority graduate students' newsletter to showcase student achievements and to provide linkages between minority graduate students and alumni; and

7. Provide tutors for students who may experience academic problems.

Objective 3: To provide opportunities for minority graduate students' professional and personal development at Penn State. Support activities include:

1. Minority graduate students' participation at national professional conferences;
2. Professional development workshops and forums for minority graduate students;
3. Opportunities for visits to professional headquarters and offices; and
4. Working with faculty to provide opportunities for students to collaborate with them regarding research, teaching and service (including writing articles).

Minority Junior Faculty

The objectives of the Office of Minority Faculty Development are threefold: Objective 1: To provide mentorship to assist in retaining minority faculty members. The office is designed to serve new minority junior faculty members. When they arrive, junior faculty are inundated with information that can take a long time to process. This office takes the initiative to provide a number of mentoring activities to make sure that new faculty are well-versed regarding the Penn State system. Some of the mentoring activities the office provides include (but are not limited to):

1. Consultation sessions, beginning many instances with an entrance interview, extending to an extensive assessment interview, and continuing with a series of individual, specific consultation sessions throughout the year;
2. Networking receptions to provide opportunities for junior and senior scholars to meet each other to share research ideas and pedagogy;
3. Resource-sharing opportunities which afford the scholars chances to review "request for proposal" guidelines and criteria, including a resource/conference room for faculty to use for meetings, research, and study; and
4. Working with department heads and/or deans discussing formal as well as informal, mentoring by senior faculty.

Objective 2: To promote minority faculty development through professional workshops and seminars. To assist faculty in gaining rank and status within their various departments, each semester a number of critical workshops are provided. The three-and-one-half hour workshops are usually held on Saturday mornings and attendance is on a voluntary basis. Memos announcing the workshops are mailed to all deans, CEOs at the Commonwealth campuses, department heads, and individual minority faculty. The workshop announcements also appear in the Intercom, which is Penn State's faculty/staff newspaper, inviting all interested faculty to attend. The workshops include:

1. Promotion and Tenure - A senior faculty facilitates the session and literally walks the participants through the promotion and tenure process. The workshop is designed to give the participants opportunities to review the requirements for the dossier.

2. Publishing - A senior faculty demystifies the publishing process. The presenter's approach is very practical and concrete suggestions are made.

3. Proposal Writing/External Funding - An experienced grants officer from one of the academic units usually presents the workshop, a senior faculty or the Director of the Office of Sponsored Programs. At the end of each workshop, faculty leave with ample materials to serve as supplemental documentation to help them ease the stresses related to proposal/grant writing.

4. Vitae Preparation - A senior faculty actually reviews and makes recommendations on how to improve and update junior faculty vitae. The emphasis of the workshop is to discuss how to effectively package and market one's experiences on paper.

5. Moving From Associate to Full Professor - A senior faculty offers strategies on dossier preparation according to Penn State's HR23 guidelines in the area of scholarship and research, teaching and service. Newly instituted, this workshop came as a direct result of numerous requests and concerns to increase the number of full professors in the minority pool.

6. Special NSF and NIH Workshops - On a few occasions, special work-shops coordinated with representatives from The National Science Foundation and National Institutes of Health have been offered for interested faculty and students.

    Workshops # 1,2,4, and 5 are regularly facilitated by senior minority faculty, who have gone through the promotion and tenure process and have advanced to the rank of full professor.

Objective 3: To provide supplemental funding for research. To assist faculty in their research endeavors, the following strategies are employed:

1. Funding to travel to workshops, conferences, professional meetings, and

2. Funding to conduct research at special libraries and/or data banks. This office provides both the physical and psychological support services for underrepresented faculty who don't have the traditional internal supports.

B. Assessment and Accomplishments

Evaluation and Program Effectiveness

Minority Graduate Students

All of the activities listed under the Office for Minority Graduate Opportunities have been accomplished with varying degrees of success. The director continues to appraise the center's activities and submits reports to the dean of the graduate school and the director of The Educational Opportunity Planning Committee on a quarterly basis.

Penn State's Center for Minority Graduate Opportunities and Faculty Development works directly with the academic units to assist in the recruitment, retention, and professional development of the underrepresented students enrolled at the university. Listed below are some of the broad accomplishments of the office during the 1993-94 academic year:

Recruitment

- Attended and participated in graduate school fairs throughout the country. At the Council of Graduate School and Graduate Record Examination Forums, the office's representative participated on "Minorities in Graduate School" and "Returning Adults" panels.

- In support the "grow our own philosophy," the center's staff gave workshops for McNair Scholars, Student Support Services, developmental year, minority sororities and fraternities, and other students who indicate an interest in graduate school.

- Made use of minority locator services to locate students nationwide who have indicated an interest in graduate school, including the Committee on Institutional Cooperation Name Exchange.

- Maintained ongoing exchanges and site visitations with predominantly black institutions. We have established partnerships with the CIC Alliance Schools (Jackson State, MS.; Lincoln University, PA; Texas Southern; Coppin State, MD; and Prairie View), as well as with other schools such as Florida A&M University, Virginia State University, and Clark Atlanta University.

- Printed and distributed information about support services and academic programs to prospective students.

- Provided orientation visits to students from predominantly minority institutions located in PA or neighboring states. We have had visits from groups of students from Lincoln (PA), Medgar Evers (NY), Delaware State (DE), University of Maryland, Eastern Shore and Coppin State College (MD).

- Coordinated activities for thirty one young scholars participating in the CIC Summer Research Opportunities Program. Worked closely with the coordinator of minority programs for the Eberly College of Science and the director of minority engineering programs for the College of Engineering in assigning mentors, planning weekly activities and extracurricular activities.

Since the center's existence, the number of minority graduate students has consistently increased. See the following table:

Table 1. Graduate Enrollment of Underrepresented Students from 1987-1994.

	1987	1988	1989	1990	1991	1992	1993	1994
Af Am	224	244	259	256	291	329	326	336
Latino Am.	107	131	129	131	126	132	154	155
Native American	37	45	36	34	36	28	28	34
TOTAL	368	420	424	421	453	489	516	525

Except for 1990, there has been a steady increase in the overall number of underrepresented students.

The center believes not only in recruiting underrepresented students and bringing them to Penn State, but also that the university must then provide a support system and provide professional development activities until the student obtains the degree for which they enrolled. To assist in retaining underrepresented students, the center works closely with the college coordinators and directors. Some of our retention activities include the following:

- Created opportunities for minority graduate students to interact with faculty with the intention of providing an atmosphere in which mentoring relationships can develop.

- Counseled and consulted with individual students regarding personal needs, concerns, and issues affecting their tenure at Penn State. The center's director meets with approximately thirty students monthly.

- Worked closely with the leadership of the African-American, Native American and Spanish-Speaking graduate student associations.

- Coordinated and facilitated support seminars, including "ABD Seminars," for underrepresented graduate students.

- Provided tutors for students who may experience academic problems.

- Instituted a bi-monthly minority graduate student support group. The feedback has been very positive, and continuation of the sessions has been requested.

The following activities are examples of professional development support.

- Supported underrepresented students' participation at national conferences, funding approximately twenty five underrepresented students to attend conferences during the 1993-1994 academic year.

- Sponsored professional development workshops and forums for underrepresented students. During the academic year, hosted bimonthly meetings for those students who needed a support group to aid in their acclimation.

- Worked with faculty to provide opportunities for students to collaborate with them with their teaching, research, and service.

Evaluation and program effectiveness are documented for each of the stated objectives. Recruitment activities are documented by responding to each prospective student, inviting them to apply to Penn State. Fee waivers are granted to all students applying from feeder schools, and to individuals not from feeder schools who request fee waivers. All college directors and coordinators of minority recruitment and retention offices receive, financial support from the center's budget to assist with their recruitment and retention of minority graduate students. In turn, each June they submit a report, outlining their expenditures and evaluating their recruitment efforts. Retention activities are also documented. As an integral part of all workshops, seminars, and on-site visits, participants are asked to evaluate the activities.

This feedback continues to be used as constructive information to modify program activities. Professional development activities for each student who requests moneys for professional conferences are kept on file; in many instances, papers, and abstracts of the student participants. Since the inception, the program has received positive feedback from students, faculty, and staff, as well as administration. Graduate students were especially pleased with individual consultation sessions and the financial support given to attend conferences. The center will continue to document successes and will continuously evaluate programmatic activities to modify the program to better meet the needs of minority graduate students.

Minority Junior Faculty
Results Achieved and Identification of Program Participants

During the academic year 1993-94, the acting senior faculty mentor, a Professor of Agricultural and Extension Education, met with seven faculty members new to the campus, for entrance interviews. Contact was maintained with junior minority faculty if and when needed. It needs to be noted that senior people who transfer to the university need some of the services that the center provides.

A total of seven minority faculty development workshops were held during the academic year 1993-94. The topics included: promotion and tenure, external funding, the publishing process, and vitae preparation. Three of the workshops were conducted by members of the Center for Minority Faculty Development Advisory Board. In previous years, during the spring semester, a round-table or intermediate level workshop has been offered on promotion and tenure, publishing, and external funding. The roundtable workshop participants have individual manuscripts, proposals, etc., critiqued by the workshop facilitator.

A small number of faculty from the Commonwealth Education System attended the workshops.

Summary Data for Spring 1994 Workshops

	Vitae		Publishing		Ex. Funds		Total	
	M	F	M	F	M	F	M	F
African American	2	3	2	3	0	2	4	8
Hispanic	0	3	0	2	2	2	2	7
Native American	0	0	0	0	0	1	0	1
White	1	0	1	0	0	0	2	0
Other	1	1	2	1	2	1	5	3
Total	4	7	5	6	4	6	13	19

The workshop summary indicates the total number of participants by ethnic group and gender for the Spring of 1994. This represents one semester of workshop participants, but it is representative of the participants during the acting senior faculty mentor's tenure.

The acting senior faculty mentor met with a number of department heads and deans who have junior minority faculty in their departments concerning the mentoring process, and maintained the quality of services provided, especially in the category of professional development and counseling. The senior faculty mentor conducts entrance and exit interviews with all new minority faculty.

To enhance communication and networking among the faculty, the office sponsors two receptions, one in the fall and one in the spring. Also, a welcome packet is distributed in the fall to all new faculty. The contents include pertinent information about the town and surrounding areas, as well as the campus. It is interesting to note the welcome packet has increased by some twenty percent in information included since its inception in 1988.

Cost of Program

This office has provided travel and research funds for junior minority faculty (see chart):

Distribution of Minority Faculty Funds
July 1, 1993 - June 30, 1994

	Black	Hispanic	N. Amer.	Total
Total Number Funded	17	14	0	31
Female Faculty	8	7	0	15
Male Faculty	9	7	0	16

C. Proposed Initiatives, New and Continuing

Design for Planning and Preliminary Diversity Goals

During academic year 1992-93, the Graduate School and Equal Opportunity Planning Committee invited an external review team to evaluate the center. The team consisted of: an Associate Vice Chancellor for Academic Affairs from the University of Illinois - Champaign/Urbana; the President of the National Consortium for Educational Access, Inc., Georgia Institute of Technology; and an associate provost and Director of the Center for Multicultural Education for Federal Region II of Baruch College. To enhance the effectiveness of the center, the team made the following seven recommendations: (The starred goals are yet to be completed and are viewed as part of the expanded mission explained in the next section.)

1. The university should include diversity as part of its mission statement. The university has included as part of its vision and mission statement a commitment to diversity.

2.* The center's work with all new faculty should become a part of the center's scope of work. The external review team acknowledges that all new faculty could benefit from the personal attention and workshops that are currently being provided for minority faculty.

3.* The relationship with the graduate school should be established through a permanent funding allocation. Currently the Office for Minority Graduate Opportunities is funded by EOPC and the graduate school yearly. The Office for Minority Faculty Development receives funding from the Graduate School to support faculty development activities.

4. The issue of how to effectively recruit faculty and students from the most underrepresented Hispanic populations needs to be addressed. The faculty recruitment process involves a search committee which generates a pool of attractive candidates from the department's choice. In recruiting graduate students, the center's director along with the directors of college minority programs, generate a pool of applicants from which graduate committees can choose students for admission into academic programs. The senior

faculty mentor and the director are asked on many occasions to meet with prospective faculty or students.

5.* The center should be provided with the necessary funds, space, and staff to address the needs of all entering students from underrepresented groups. When the graduate school reorganized, the center expanded, adding a resource and meeting room.

6.* The issue of diversity should be addressed at the departmental level. The university realizes that diversity has to be addressed at all levels to be effective. During Academic Year 1994-95, each unit was required to write a strategic plan outlining their commitment to diversity.

7.* The institution should provide resources to achieve a "critical mass" of students and faculty from each underrepresented group.

When the center was conceived in 1987 it was expected to grow and prosper. The original staffing called for a staff of five: the director of the Center for Minority Graduate Opportunities and Staff Development; the director of minority faculty development; the assistant director; a secretary/receptionist; and a data analyst/informational specialist. In the fall of 1993, a full-time permanent staff assistant was hired, making the total staffing four. The staff meets monthly to discuss the operations of the center.

The Center for Minority Graduate Opportunities and Faculty Development is a prototype effort designed to expand the accession and enhance the professional development of the university's underrepresented students and faculty. From the beginning it was anticipated that this effort would expand to broader constituencies and that, ultimately would serve as the model for recruitment, retention, and professional development for all students and faculty.

The Office of Minority Graduate Opportunities and Faculty Development has made substantial contributions to the overall university progress. Several ideas introduced by the Center have been adopted by several units across the University. For instance, exit interviews have been conducted by the senior faculty mentor since 1988. Recognizing the value of such interviews, the Office of Human Resources has incorporated exit interviews as a part of the "exit process." In a similar mode several academic units are beginning to provide workshops on promotion and tenure. Since the inception, more than 130 minority junior faculty have attended workshops provided by the center and over eighty three percent of them have become tenured and promoted to associate faculty.

The Center For Minority Graduate Opportunities and Faculty Development is Penn State's centralized mechanism for monitoring the progress of both minority graduate students or faculty. The center provides a place where students and faculty can visit to brainstorm ideas, and formulate strategies to deal with problems that arise while they are at Penn State. The center, when it was conceptualized, was the "politically correct" thing to do; now it has developed and emerged as a critical aid toward graduation and/or tenure.

Where will the Center be five years from now?

The Center's director and advisory board are contemplating that during the next five years an expansion is expected of the center's mission to serve Penn State minority, majority and international graduate students and junior faculty. Since the center's inception, both students and faculty have sought to gain clarity as to why the center was chartered to service only underrepresented minorities. With the onset of recent local, national and international changes, it is critical that the Center's philosophy and mission include the service of majority and international students and faculty.

It has been well-documented that support systems and climate are features that influence the success of graduate degree-seeking students. As the number of underrepresented minority graduate students and faculty increase, the center can take a greater role in conversing with both before offers are made. Sometimes, center representatives are invited to participate in the interviews. At this juncture, it could be highly recommended and strongly encouraged by the deans.

Office for Minority Faculty Development

This document offers a blueprint for expanding the sphere of operation of the Office of Minority Faculty Development. In particular, it consists of a proposal to formally expand the mission of the Office of Minority Faculty Development to serve all non-tenured, tenure-track faculty, and using a developmental or bridge approach to extend support to minority faculty and potential faculty who are not on tenure track.

The Office of Minority Faculty Development, through the senior faculty mentor, has initiated a variety of innovative strategies that have facilitated the recruitment and retention of faculty of color. However, the potential of the Office of Minority Faculty Development has not yet been fully realized because of structural limitations in terms of institutionally imposed constraints on the populations that can be served. As part of the expanded mission, there is a need to upgrade the senior faculty mentor position to assistant dean; and to align it with the creation of the deanship in the graduate school and the elimination of the position formerly entitled "associate dean."

It is recommended further that the senior faculty mentor should hold the rank of full professor. This expanded responsibility for all junior faculty development would fill an existing void in the overall faculty development efforts. It would also reduce some of the perceived stigma associated with seeking support from an office with a presumably focused constituency, which may have unintentionally discouraged some faculty of color from making use of services. The perceived stigma that some ethnic minority faculty attach to the office has not impeded majority faculty from using, to good advantage, the center's services. It would also forestall efforts to duplicate services provided by the center by advocates for other constituency groups, e.g. women. New fiscal resources and human resources would be required to enable the center to succeed in this new responsibility.

Increasing numbers of faculty of color and potential faculty of color are coming from non-traditional channels. These include instructorships for those who have not completed dissertations, fixed-term appointments (which carry no commitment of conversion to tenure track appointments), and professional staff who have decided to pursue terminal degrees with the goal of entering the professorate. The use of these fixed-term appointments varies by college and departments, and thus it is necessary to explore ways to institutionalize the wording of those appointments to ensure mutual benefits to appointees and departments. An example would be in mentorships/preceptorials that sponsored their completion of the doctorate with a way to lessen the probability of exploitation of minority faculty in those appointments. Currently the center is not authorized to provide financial support to these constituencies.

There is a need for a developmental approach that attempts to maximize the opportunities of each individual including conversion to tenure-track appointments where appropriate. As an example, minority faculty hired on a fixed-term basis could be hired for two years with a guarantee of mentorship and research support during the summers of the type provided to SROP students. Individuals could be appointed for one to two semesters pending completion of dissertations, rather than being brought in ABD. It would be advisable to actually introduce these individuals to the "rainbow file" (HR 23 mentioned earlier) and its construction, and to instate a parallel second year review that lowers the tension and anxieties generally faced in the actual tenure-track second year review. There is also a need for new strategies to recruit potential faculty from industry, especially in the sciences and engineering fields, who might want to change careers, obtain a doctorate and enter the professorate. Such an approach will provide a needed bridge for those individuals and will strengthen long-term commitment to PSU.

These initiatives are in keeping with the original charter of the office, which is to provide mentoring, guidance and counseling as well as retaining and increasing the pool of minority faculty at PSU. Penn State recognizes the value of the center and has given its directors the encouragement to start the institutionalization process. The Office of the Vice Provost for Educational Equity, with the support of the university's provost, encouraged each academic and operational unit to write a strategic plan for diversity. These plans were reviewed and each unit was given feedback by which to assist in altering the practices of their unit. On the average, the academic plan reflected and mirrored many activities sponsored by the center. They provided evidence of the success of several center activities and often these activities have been adopted and modified by the colleges. The center also has its strategic plan which calls for increased staffing and permanent funding. The center has the possibility to become a model for other national programs. Over the years, faculty and administrators from several institutions like the University of Illinois at Chicago, Clemson University and representatives from the Council of Graduate Schools have visited Penn State to observe our operations.

The concerns grow out of the national outcry against affirmative action. While Penn State's vision statement revolves around diversity, no doubt the national affirmative action dialogue will impact these efforts, if only through comparisons. The other concerns are of a direct response to the actual operation and they are issues that are currently being discussed.

Many of the faculty that were junior when the center began are now associate professors and tenured. During the same time period, Penn State made a concerted effort to bring in more senior faculty, and as a result of these two aggressive actions, there are very few " underrepresented minorities" in the current junior track. The numbers are remaining constant, and options are being explored to increase those numbers.

Likewise, the numbers for graduate students are slowly increasing due to strong partnerships with HBCUs and HISs. The challenge is to continue recruiting and enrolling students in the nontraditional areas. The goal is to enroll students in multiple numbers so that students can benefit from "in-group" support.

The following is recommended to increase the retention and professional development of minority faculty and students:

1. Diversity must be valued and must be a part of the university's stated mission.

2. The initial proposal should come from senior faculty and administrators.

3. The Faculty Senate and top administrators such as the president, provost, etc., must indicate strong support.

4. The funding must be a permanent part of the university's budget.

5. Adequate space and staffing must be provided along with the necessary equipment.

6. Due to the level of activity, those individuals serving as senior faculty mentors should be full professors.

It has been very exciting to be a part of the start-up of this rewarding venture. With the continued support of Penn State's administrators, faculty, staff and students, these efforts will continue to be successful and beneficial to the populations this university serves.

—Dr. Deborah F. Atwater is an Associate Professor in the Departments of Speech Communication and African/African-American Studies.
—Dr. Catherine G. Lyons is the Director of the Center for Minority Graduate Opportunities and Faculty Development at The Pennsylvania State University, University Park, Pennsylvania.

The University of Florida and Santa Fe Community College Graduate Student/Faculty Development Program

by Karen C. Smith

Overview:

Nationwide, the proportion of minority faculty in institutions of higher learning is minuscule. The representation of full-time minority faculty in higher education is twelve percent and about three percent of these are African-American. Most research studies note the shortage of qualified minorities who aspire to complete Ph.D. degrees, and the shortage of those who, once matriculated, actually complete the degree (Gooden, Leary and Childress, 1994). This is a major concern, given the proportion of minority students already enrolled in college and the ever-increasing growth of culturally diverse student populations. It is projected that by the year 2000, one in three college students will be a person of color (Winbush, 1994). This reality calls for drastic measures in an effort to recruit, train and retain minority faculty members so that students can identify with positive role models in the classroom and the community at large.

It appears the problem (challenge) facing colleges and universities are threefold:

1. the declining numbers of blacks and other minorities enrolled in graduate and doctoral programs;
2. the low number of blacks in teaching and administrative positions in higher education; and
3. recruiting and retaining minority graduates for community college teaching once they receive their Ph.D. degrees (Collins, 1993).

This article examines how the University of Florida and Santa Fe Community College faculty collaborated in addressing these challenges.

Introduction

According to Gooden, et. al., (1994), the scarcity of minority faculty is further compounded by the prediction of a shortage of college professors by the year 2000. Many professors, mostly white males, will soon retire. During the 1990s, over half of the teachers currently in community colleges will be leaving, primarily as a result of retirement (Baker, Roueche, & Gillett-Karam, 1990). Experts caution about assuming minorities will benefit due to the large number of anticipated vacancies, because there has been a decline in the number of minorities entering the higher education "pipeline." Unfortunately, the most dramatic decline can be found among African-Americans entering and completing undergraduate degrees and continuing on to graduate or professional school.

The national research council reports there is a decreasing number of blacks obtaining doctoral degrees, which in the past had been considered the surest route to faculty positions in institutions of higher education. This report also states that black participation in institutions of higher learning has suffered more than that of any minority group in recent years. It is quite evident that if there are not minority graduate students, there will not be minority professors. In many instances, those who do complete their degrees are not attracted to the traditional faculty positions in higher education. Their reasons range from inadequate salaries to a lack of minority support in the local community (National Research Council, 1986).

If colleges and universities are serious about educating, recruiting and retaining minority faculty, they have to move beyond traditional recruiting efforts and apply more creative and imaginative strategies and mechanisms (O'Brien, 1988). Unless significant efforts are made to increase the number of minority applicants and ensure that minority faculty are hired, projections indicate further reductions, which will seriously impact not only higher education, but public and private schools as well (Collins, 1993). In response to this challenge, the Santa Fe Community College/University of Florida Black Faculty Development Project was born.

Historical Origin and Development of the Program

In an effort to recruit more Ph.D. students to the University of Florida (UF) and attract more black faculty to Santa Fe Community College, two institutions of higher education, both located in Gainesville FL, embarked on a cooperative recruiting program. This program originated in 1987 under the cooperative efforts of Dr. Rod McDavis, an associate dean for the graduate school at the University of Florida, and Santa Fe Community College's former president, Alan J. Robertson. A dialogue ensued between President Robertson and Dr. McDavis, concerning Santa Fe's need for black faculty and the use of potential strategies to increase minority representation on Santa Fe's campus. There was also a need for Dr. McDavis to secure more funding sources for minority graduate students pursuing advanced degrees. At the time, there were 322 professors at Santa Fe, twenty-three of whom were black. UF's graduate school had 5,000 students, 200 of whom were black.

Both parties were interested in developing a partnership that could ultimately benefit both institutions and possibly serve as a model program for universities and community colleges nationwide. Their ideas were also shared with Dr. Don Price, past dean of the graduate school, and Dr. Don Bryan, past vice president for academic affairs. Both of them saw merit in the idea and provided their support for the project. Dr. Portia Taylor, the assistant to the president at Santa Fe Community College at the time, was also instrumental in helping to develop the program.

Several meetings occurred between the two parties representing both institutions and a cooperative agreement was made. The joint venture was presented to the Santa Fe Community College Board of Trustees for approval in the spring of 1987. Their approval was overwhelming and the partnership was formed and originally called the Santa Fe Community College Board of Trustee Fellowship for University of Florida's doctoral students.

Impetus for Program Implementation

The motivating forces behind the development of this cooperative partnership were many. Both parties (The University of Florida and Santa Fe Community College) recognized the need to:

A. Redress the steady decline in the number of minority graduate students nationwide. Despite the nation's rising black population, the number of black undergraduates had dropped. During the mid-eighties the number of black undergraduate students dropped 3.4 percent nationally (National Research Council, 1986).

B. Increase minority faculty representation on the community college level.

C. Encourage more inter-institutional cooperation in the Gainesville educational community.

D. Combat the lack of available black faculty members and graduate students.

E. Recruit faculty for the community college from a qualified pool of local graduates from the University of Florida.

F. Provide graduate students with an opportunity to gain teaching experience—an opportunity not offered in the university setting.

G. Identify funding sources to assist graduate students at the University of Florida.

Both schools designed and implemented the Board of Trustee Fellowship
Program in an attempt to address these needs.

Mission Statement

The University of Florida, in collaboration with Santa Fe Community
College, is committed to providing minority students with high quality
educational opportunities that will aid in their personal, social, academic and
career growth. Both institutions are committed to meeting the diverse needs of
the Gainesville community by actively recruiting, training and retaining minority
graduates for educational/teaching careers in the university and community
college setting.

Mission Goals and Objectives

The mission goals of this partnership are to:

A. Assist in the recruitment and retention of minority students in graduate
    programs at the University of Florida by providing a fellowship (offered
    by the community college), that will pay their tuition and fees.

B. Increase the number of African-American faculty members at Santa Fe
    Community College while increasing the number of African-American
    doctoral students at the University of Florida.

C. Develop an ongoing recruitment tool for hiring minority faculty for the
    community college.

D. Attract more minority graduate students to the University of Florida by
    offering a supplemental teaching program at the local community college.

E. Develop and maintain an ongoing professional partnership between the
    two institutions that would provide benefits for both institutions.

F. Attract black Ph.D. students to the University of Florida and simultaneously
    help the community college "groom/develop" its own black faculty.

G. Attract "potential" black faculty to the benefits of teaching in the
    community college setting.

H. Assist in the successful recruitment and retention of the University
    of Florida minority graduates for faculty positions at Santa Fe
    Community College.

I. Allow minority graduate students to apply their academic knowledge
    immediately in various classroom settings at Santa Fe Community
    College. This will provide the graduate students with challenging
    teaching experiences in conjunction with their academic preparation.

J.   Attract minority graduate students to two major institutions of higher learning that are committed to:

    a.   their professional growth and development;

    b.   meeting their financial concerns; and

    c.   providing professional job placement upon completion of the Ph.D.

K.   Provide an interactive supportive learning environment for the recipients of the faculty development program.

Program Changes

The mission statement and goals/objectives of this program, have not changed over the eight-year period. However, the program has undergone a title change from the Santa Fe Community College Board of Trustee Fellowship Program to the Santa Fe Community College/University of Florida Black Faculty Development Project. Two other changes have occurred over the eight-year period. There has been a reduction in the number of classes students are expected to teach.

During the earlier years, minority students were expected to teach a total of four classes per year. However, in an effort to reduce some of their teaching responsibilities, the maximum is now three courses per year. The preference is to teach one course per academic term—fall, spring and one in summer. The other change includes an expansion of discipline areas. Initially, students were recruited from limited discipline areas. During the program's inception, the focus was only on those specializing in English, math, humanities and sociology. Only students in these areas were specifically sought out for participation in the program. During the last three years, all discipline areas have been added. Both institutions agreed that if the university could recommend quality graduates in any discipline area, they would be more than willing to accommodate them. This decision is viewed as a major milestone in ensuring the ongoing success of the program.

Programmatic Operations and Activities

According to the founders, the joint effort works this way:

Step 1: Advertisement

Like other universities, the University of Florida recruits minority doctoral students on a nationwide basis. The assistant dean of the graduate school visits numerous colleges during the course of the year—informing students of the merit of these and other fellowship programs. The university also has in place visitation programs which are held during the fall for seniors and the spring for juniors. The visitation programs provide prospective minority graduate students with the opportunity to learn about the university graduate and professional programs. Housing and meals are paid for by the university and each student is reimbursed up to fifty dollars for travel expenses. The career planning offices at the University of Florida also assist in advertising the program.

Other promotional efforts include advertisements in the Chronicle of Higher Education, Black Issues, and similar educational media.

Step 2: Program Criteria/Requirements)

Those that enroll at the University of Florida are encouraged to apply for the Santa Fe/University of Florida Black Faculty Development Project. Applicants must meet the minimal requirements for this fellowship. The minimal requirements include:

1. They must have a "minority" status. For Santa Fe Community College, the defined minority group remains African-Americans who are United States citizens. The college feels this group has the greatest need for role models for their students.

2. They must have a master's degree in one of the approved areas. To date the disciplines with the greatest need for instructors are English, mathematics, humanities or any of the creative arts, especially the performing arts and physics.

3. Students must register and receive credit for at least nine graduate school semester hours each semester (fall and spring).

4. Applicants must submit their GRE or GMAT scores before an application for admission is processed.

5. Students must maintain at least a 3.0 GPA and understand that their continued participation in the project is dependent upon satisfactory academic progress (3.0 GPA). Participants also must make satisfactory progress toward their doctoral degrees at the University of Florida.

6. Students cannot concurrently hold another University of Florida remunerative position or accept any other fellowship or assistantship without the approval of the associate dean responsible for the Santa Fe Community College/University of Florida Faculty Development Project.

7. A signed contract must be returned to the associate dean for graduate studies and graduate minority programs. (See Appendix I for copy of contract.)

Step 3: Review of Credentials

University of Florida personnel review the applicants and their credentials and make the final decision concerning their appointment as a graduate fellow. At the community college level, a department committee also reviews the candidates' credentials, and interviews qualified applicants. Those whose teaching experience and/or philosophy complement the needs of the department are then recommended for fellowship awards.

Step 4: Receipt of Stipend

Once an agreement has been made to participate in the program, the graduate student is offered a $9,000 stipend paid by Santa Fe Community College. In addition, all tuition and student fees are paid, supplemented with a $1,500 summer stipend. Students can receive these funds for a maximum of four years. Non-Florida residents receive out-of-state tuition.

Step 5: Teaching Responsibilities and Recruitment Efforts

In exchange for this monetary support, the students agree to serve as adjunct faculty at Santa Fe Community College. Participants must teach three courses (one fall, one spring, one summer). The fellows are also expected to assist Santa Fe Community College in the recruitment and retention of minority students in their discipline area over a one-year period. As college faculty, the doctoral students are allowed to apply their knowledge immediately in the classroom.

Step 6: Evaluations

Santa Fe and the University of Florida will continue to provide ongoing evaluations (both verbally and written) and feedback concerning students' overall performance in the program. Information exchange will continue for the duration of the fellowship.

Step 7: Hiring

Upon completion of the Ph.D. degree, fellowship recipients are offered full-time positions at Santa Fe Community College, if openings are available in their discipline area. The college hopes to hire some minority faculty as a result of this program. However, if this does not happen the program has still provided a regular flow of quality minority adjunct faculty teaching at the college.(See Appendix 1)

Organizational Structure

Both college presidents have maintained their commitment to the Santa Fe Community College/University of Florida Faculty Development Project developed by Dr. McDavis and President Robertson eight years ago. Over the years, their commitment has been expressed through monetary support and funding decisions that will ensure the survival of this program through the twenty-first century.

However, the day-to-day operations of the program are overseen by the associate dean of the graduate school and minority program at the University of Florida. He has the responsibility of maintaining all of the information regarding the operation and progress of the program. This includes annual reports, evaluations, conferences, recruitment efforts, policy decisions regarding the program, and a commitment to the program's stated goals and objectives. He is assisted by three secretaries who specialize in various areas of expertise.

Once the applicants have been selected, they are referred to the personnel director of Santa Fe who reviews their files and credentials and provides an affirmative to whether he is accepting them as a likely candidate for the program. Once that decision has been made, and the recipient has identified his/her area of expertise, the file is turned over to the division chair who, along with a screening committee, prepares for an extensive interview with the graduate student. Once the interview is completed, the chairperson informs the personnel director of his/her decision to hire or not hire the student.

During the graduate students' tenure at Santa Fe, they can be assisted in many ways by the other faculty members who are in their discipline area. If they choose, graduate students can also participate in faculty meetings and other functions of the department. Once selected, they serve as full-fledged adjunct faculty and are expected to abide by all of the rules and regulations provided in the SFCC faculty adjunct handbook.

In the unlikely event the recipient is terminated, he/she has an obligation to notify the department chairperson, the personnel director at Santa Fe Community College and the associate dean of the graduate school concerning the decision to terminate his/her contract.

Success Measures

The success of the Santa Fe Community College/University of Florida Black Faculty Development Project is measured by several criteria. These criteria include the following:

A. Graduation Rates

To date, all of the participants in this program have completed their Ph.D. degrees with the support of the stipend and both institutions' commitment to their professional growth and development. While some of them chose not to remain in the Gainesville area, all of them were able to complete their degrees within the time constraints of the fellowship (a four-year maximum).

B. Job Placement

All of the participants in the faculty development program are gainfully employed in institutions of higher learning throughout the United States. With their credentials and the support they received from both institutions, all of the fellows have fared quite well in the workplace.

C. Support of the Program

To date, all of the administrators in charge of the program at the University of Florida and Santa Fe Community College remain enthused about the prospects and the potential this program has for increasing minority representation in institutions of higher education. It is quite evident that good intentions alone will not produce results without the wholehearted support of the presidents, administrators and board members. To date, it appears that each of the "key players" on both campuses appear genuinely committed to the continuation of this program. In spite of the cutbacks and streamlining of various programs, both institutions openly support this successful initiative and will continue to provide the necessary funds for its operational needs.

D. Quality Candidates

Every graduate student who has been recommended by the University of Florida for adjunct placement at the community college has been accepted without hesitation. This is an indication of the quality of students being referred to SFCC for the faculty development program.

E. Positive Role Models

Santa Fe Community college, via this program, has a regular flow of quality minority faculty teaching at the college. In addition to serving in a teaching capacity, they also serve as positive role models in the classroom and in the local community.

F. An Enhancement of Teaching Skills

Many Ph.D. recipients will work in an academic setting upon the completion of their degrees. Under this unique arrangement between the University of Florida and Santa Fe Community College, students are given the opportunity to survive as full-time students, improve their teaching skills, and "grow" professionally. Many of the participants have indicated how this program has enhanced their teaching and interpersonal skills.

G. Annual Evaluations

Each year annual evaluations regarding the students overall performance are submitted to the associate dean of graduate school and graduate minority programs. These evaluations have been exemplary and the various discipline areas have been very pleased with the caliber of graduate students recommended to Santa Fe Community College. Annual reports regarding the success of this program are submitted through the graduate school's office on a yearly basis.

H. Recruitment and Retention

Both institutions are aware that hiring minority faculty is just the beginning. To call their efforts successful, they must retain the minority faculty they hire. One of the participants in the program has been hired as a full-time faculty member since August 1989. She received tenure in 1992. Her employment was a direct result of her participation in the Santa Fe Community College/University of Florida Black Faculty Development Project. She is evidence of a faculty member that was "home grown." She is currently applying for the chairmanship of the Historical and Social Science Department. Both institutions are pleased to announce that at present a few more are "growing."

How has the Program Impacted Both Institutions?

The institutional benefits and programmatic strengths far exceed the short-comings of the program. Both institutions appear determined to increase the number of doctoral students at the University of Florida and full-time faculty at the community college. Both institutions are committed to creating a faculty that reflects the increasing diversity of the student body. To date, both institutions are proud they took the risk of developing a creative approach to increase the cultural diversity of the faculty. They realized (as have other institutions) that adhering to traditional approaches and using the common excuse that "no qualified blacks exist" yields no positive results. Both institutions maintain this program has benefitted them in several ways:

A. This partnership has enhanced both institutions' visibility in the Gainesville community. Through their joint efforts, they have expressed a firm commitment to cultural diversity in higher education. Since the program's inception, both institutions have supported the program verbally and financially. Both institutions recognize this partnership is a positive public relations tool. The community at large is pleased and impressed with their efforts to address the need of educating and increasing minority faculty.

B. As faculty positions become open, Santa Fe has the benefit of selecting from a pool of qualified minority candidates ready to fill the faculty slots—resulting in an increased presence of minorities on the campus.

C. Minority doctoral students are benefiting by gaining teaching experience and developing a professional network on the university and community college level. This interaction will not only benefit them, but will also benefit the institution. Each of the fellows brings to the institution a diverse background, and a plethora of experiences and perspectives that will enhance the entire community college setting.

D. The graduate students in the community college setting have created a minority faculty presence on the campus and in the Gainesville community.

E. Minority graduate faculty serve as positive role models and mentors for the diverse student population. By the turn of the century, two out of three students will be "people of color." Their presence in both institutions of higher learning will be crucial in helping to meet the needs of all students and possibly motivating more students to pursue avenues of higher education.

Concerns and Probable Solutions

The problems plaguing this faculty development program are few. Some major concerns that are being addressed:

Concern 1: Program Selection

Most of the graduate students who apply for the University of Florida and Santa Fe Black Faculty Development Program generally do so as a last resort. This program is seen as a viable option only after all other funding possibilities have failed. The director indicated that only a few of the potential fellows identify this program/project as a top priority. One of the strategies used to rectify this problem has been an increased emphasis on its merits during visitation weeks when prospective minority graduate students visit the campus and meet with faculty representatives from departments in their fields of interests.

Concern 2: Limited Funding

Most of the fellowships offered to minority graduate students range between ten and fifteen thousand dollars per year. As mentioned, this stipend offers the student nine thousand dollars per year. Due to the expense of a graduate college education, this program does not provide the financial rewards/incentives offered by other minority scholarships such as the McKnight Foundation, the United Negro College Fund, doctoral grants or the Patricia Harris Fellowships. Thus, in order for this fellowship to be competitive and appealing to incoming minority graduate students, funding will have to increase. This is not likely given the budgetary restrictions/cutbacks facing the educational system in the state of Florida.

Concern 3: Limited Participants

The impact of this program on large numbers of minority students is minimal. Many of the black students at the University of Florida are not in the Ph.D. programs. On average, the maximum number of potential candidates for this program per year is fifteen. However, those numbers dwindle steadily if other fellowship offers are available. Since the program's inception, it has never had more than five students per year participating in the program.

Concern 4: Teaching Requirements

Another major drawback of this faculty development fellowship is the teaching requirements attached to the stipend. Many graduate students want to devote their full attention to their academic studies. However, if they receive this funding source, they are expected to teach a minimum of three courses per year. Classes at the community college can range upward to forty students per class— giving the graduate student less time to fully devote to his/her studies. Some of the potential candidates have indicated they do not want the added pressures of teaching while they are pursuing their Ph.Ds. Suggestions for a further reduction would increase the appeal of this fellowship. However, this reduction is not likely given the community college's dependency on adjunct professors. In many departments, adjuncts teach forty percent of the course offerings. All of the other major fellowship programs at the University of Florida allow the students to devote their full attention to their studies.

Concern 5: Minimal Teaching Experience

Some of the graduate students who teach at the community college have no previous teaching experience on the college level. If they are not properly monitored—their effectiveness in the classroom could be minimal. Efforts to rectify this concern include:

a. developing a mentoring program for those who have no teaching experience;

b. direct classroom observations by tenured full-time faculty; and

c. networking with others who can provide some insight into successful teaching strategies in the classroom.

If this support is not in place, future employment and the continuation of the fellowship are not likely.

Concern 6: Fellowship Restrictions

Those students agreeing to participate in the Santa Fe Community College and University of Florida Black Faculty Development Project cannot concurrently hold another University of Florida remunerative position or accept any other fellowship or assistantship without the approval of the dean. Unfortunately this limits the appeal of the project and students are likely to seek out other options. Efforts to alter this stipulation have been minimal.

Concern 7: National Hiring Freezes

Current national economic conditions have resulted in hiring freezes nationwide. In the state of Florida, many schools are currently limiting student enrollments and reducing course sections as cost-cutting measures. Consequently, they are not hiring new full-time faculty in many discipline areas. Further, Chatman and Jung (1992) suggest the increasing number of retirees will increase the need for new faculty only slightly and that higher education will find ways around hiring persons on a full-time basis. Such trends could prove "deadly" for those minority graduate students looking forward to employment in the community college system.

Concern 8: Negative Teaching Aspects

There is always the probability that some of the graduates may not want to work/teach in a community college setting. After investing a large number of years in completing a Ph.D. degree, the negative aspects of teaching in a community college setting may limit its appeal. The negative aspects of teaching in the two-year college setting include bureaucratic paperwork, lack of prestige within the higher education community, and perceived inadequate monetary compensation as compared to other career options (Sullivan, et. al, 1990).

Concern 9: Degree Completion

The most important goal for the graduate student is to complete his/her doctorate degree. Care needs to be taken to ensure they don't become too bogged down with teaching responsibilities and community based activities and lose sight of the their ultimate goal—the completion of the degree. Minority students should be given the option of deciding how many courses they want to teach per term as long as it equals three during the course of the year. Their options will depend on how much writing or research requirements are required during any given semester.

Shared Insights and Advice

If this program is to remain viable, several recommendations for improvement should be considered. According to the dean of the college, this partnership is not for everyone. Participants in the program must be well-prepared, focused, professional and be able to accept constructive criticism. Other specific recommendations/suggestions are based on the author's experience as a one of the first board fellows selected for this program in 1987. In retrospect, the author is convinced these strategies will enhance the overall quality of the program:

Recommendation 1

The development of a manual is needed, listing the specific kinds of professional experience, personal qualities and expertise that applicants for faculty positions should possess to be effective. This information should be reviewed in a special orientation session for all of the applicants to ensure they are capable of building positive cooperative relationships with full-time faculty, staff, and students at the community college. It might not be a bad idea for the minority graduates to submit teaching portfolios, or videos demonstrating classroom teaching and the successful strategies they use when working with students in different settings. If their roles are clearly defined at the outset, this can help minimize the ambiguity/discrepancies in the program.

Recommendation 2

The development of a structured mentoring program for the graduate students is needed. One way of encouraging minority faculty to remain on community college campuses is to ensure they have a "designated" mentor during the years they are working toward the completion of the degree. One can not assume faculty members on the community college campus will embrace the newcomer and provide valuable information that will ensure their success. If the graduate student has a "designated" mentor he/she has someone to interact with on a regular basis.

Under this arrangement senior faculty who enjoy working with new faculty, can help guide them through their first few years on campus. It is a fact that once recruited and on board, blacks are often overly patronized or patently ignored, and given little or no guidance on how to adjust to the new institution. A good mentor can assist the graduate student in teaching and feeling more "connected" to the community college setting. Having a mentor can provide a sense of familiarity and can contribute to the building of friendships. Such mentoring can be performed by several faculty representing diverse backgrounds. The most important point is a good mentor will assist the graduate student in gaining valuable experience needed to be a knowledgeable and effective college instructor (Sullivan 1990; Garcia, 1990). If ongoing personal contact is not possible, participants can continue to work with their mentor via telephone and mail during their period of employment. Since the fellowship is offered over a four-year period, it might be a good idea for the faculty mentors to rotate on a yearly basis. This would represent the ideal situation since it would allow the graduate students to network with varied faculty and would limit the need for any long term commitment from a select few.

Recommendation 3

Increase the minority graduate students visibility on Santa Fe Community College campus. Efforts should be made to encourage faculty at the community college level to involve the graduate students in as many-campus based activities as possible. While time constraints may limit their activities, increasing their visibility on campus allows them to serve as role models and communicate their talents to the college community. Their visibility can verify to the community college campus that these are potential faculty member "in the making." Their visibility on campus and in the community can be a testament to their professionalism, competence and maturity as fellows and "potential" full-time faculty members. Each fellow should have a broad set of experiences to initiate them into the world of academia.

Recommendation 4

Keep the lines of communication open. Efforts should be ongoing in improving the communication between the fellow and the prime decision makers on campus (student, faculty, mentor, administrator and board of trustee). Each key player should agree to meet formally at least twice a year to discuss the strengths and weaknesses of the program and what can be done to maintain the viability of the program. To date, the program does not have any procedure whereby the fellow formally interacts with the prime decision makers. Communication occurs, but it is, at best (as on many campuses), sporadic and inconsistent (Higgins, et. al.). Each player in this joint venture should be required to submit a brief narrative about their experiences at the end of each academic year.

Recommendation 5

Modify the teaching requirements. To address the possibility of increased academic responsibilities as the fellow nears the completion of the degree, it might not be a bad idea to offer them some flexibility with regard to when they want to teach their courses. The mandatory number of courses should not change. However, if the fellow chooses to teach all three in one semester or skip a semester—this flexibility should be allowed.

Recommendation 6

Since this fellowship can not compete financially with many of the other scholarships offered to graduate students, both institutions should continue to stress the non-tangible incentives of this program. Starting in the fall of 1995, arrangements for visit/tours of Santa Fe's campus coupled with audio visual presentations of the campus emphasizing its strengths and benefits could be instrumental in encouraging potential graduate students to matriculate at the University of Florida and participate in the program. Gaining teaching experience, establishing professional networks and professionally preparing for a career in academics are all "priceless" commodities of this program that might prove more valuable than monetary compensation.

Recommendation 7

Institute a faculty exchange program. Since the numbers of minority faculty are not likely to increase significantly in the next few years on Santa Fe's campus, it might be a good idea to expand the partnership to include those students who are master's level candidates (preferably in their last semester or two before graduation), since a Ph.D. degree is not a requirement for community college teaching. Serious consideration should be given to planning and implementing a supplemental program that would allow more minority adjunct faculty (on the master's level) to teach at the community college. The schools could offer term contracts for one semester or a maximum of one year. Such arrangements would provide the institution with a diverse, though frequently changing faculty population—while allowing the student to improve his teaching skills. These short-term arrangements would be quite appealing to many minority graduate students who are traditionally attracted to metropolitan areas and would be less willing/likely to seek a permanent position at the community college. This plan would also provide quality minority faculty to students without having to make long-term contractual arrangements/commitments. However, some permanent faculty may feel a degree of resentment toward those teaching who have not secured the master's (minimal) degree.

Better yet, according to the program's founder, it might be a good idea to expand the minority faculty development program to other community campuses that are in close proximity to the University of Florida. To date, four such colleges exist that are no more than one-and-one half hour from the University of Florida. These institutions include Central Florida Community College, Jacksonville Community College, Lake City Community College, and Gulf Coast Community College. If the dean of the graduate school at the University of Florida could secure a commitment from each of these community colleges, he could have as many as ten or more minority graduate students (per year) placed in schools throughout central Florida. This could result in as many as fifty potential candidates for employment over a five-year period. It is likely that most Ph.D. candidates would be very receptive to this arrangement, since they could still remain close to the university and work with their committee members without undue stress.

Conclusions

The value of this joint partnership is best expressed by those persons who have participated in the program. When asked how the program benefited them, these were their responses:

> *"The Faculty Development Program was the best thing that ever happened to me. I was able to gain valuable teaching experience and secure a job on campus without having to engage in an extensive national search. I was already familiar with my surroundings and my colleagues had a lot of respect for me because they knew what I was capable of producing in the classroom. I can't think of a better way to recruit quality minority faculty than through this program. Let's just hope the cutbacks in education won't destroy such a valuable program for students, faculty and institutions nationwide. Money is not everything. This program provided me with a lot of valuable insight that was priceless."*
> — Karen Cole Smith, Ph.D. 1989.

> *"Under this unique arrangement between the University of Florida and Santa Fe Community College, I am given the opportunity to survive as a full-time student as well as the privilege of keeping my teaching skills honed. Studying for a doctorate degree is an experience in itself. The students here are very much like the students I taught in Macon and I am grateful to continue teaching as I pursue my doctorate. It is something I never envisioned being able to do."* — Mary Mears, 1987.

> *"The University of Florida and Santa Fe Community College Faculty Fellowship has been very beneficial for me. It has provided financial assistance for me to pursue my Ph.D. Financial support is critical if I am to complete my degree. Most importantly, it has allowed me to apply my theoretical knowledge in the classroom. The mentor support I have received has been invaluable. The faculty on campus have provided encouragement, moral support, and greater insight into the teaching profession. I am constantly learning innovative teaching strategies and skills that will aid me in the future."* — Kim Battles, 1994-95.

These are just some personal testaments regarding the overall benefit of this program. One can only hope that a program of this magnitude is expanded and continuously funded for years to come. It is crucial to remain committed to increasing the ranks of qualified minority faculty in institutions of higher learning. Initiatives of this kind must continue to flourish locally, statewide, and nationally.

> *"We believe that the Black Faculty Development Project is one of the most innovative and imaginative programs yet conceived to recruit black Ph.D. students as well as faculty members."* — Dean Roderick McDavis, Program Developer.

—Dr. Karen Cole Smith is the Chairperson of the Social Sciences and History Department at Santa Fe Community College in Gainesville, Florida.

References

Baker, George A., Roveche, John E. and Gillett, Karorn Rosemary. Teaching as Leaders. A Theme for a New Decade. Community, Technical and Junior College Journal, 60 (5) 26-31, 1990.

Blackwell, J. E. Faculty Issues. The Impact on Minorities. Review of Higher Education, 11 (4) 417-434.

Chatman, S. and Jung, Loren. Concern About Forecasts of National Faculty Shortages and the Importance of Local Studies. Research in Higher Education 33 (1) 37.

Collins, M. Enrollment, Recruitment and Retention of Minority Faculty and Staff in Institutions of Higher Education Action in Teacher Education. 12 (3) 57-62, 1990.

Collins, Ronald, and Johnson, Judith. One Institution's Success in Increasing the Number of Minority Faculty: A Provost's Perspective, 1993.

Garcia, Jesus. A Commentary on Increasing Minority Faculty Representation in Schools of Education.

Gooden, John S., Leary, Paul and Childress, Ronald B. Initiating Minorities Into the Professorate: One School's Model. Innovator Higher Education. Vol 18, No. 4, pp. 243-253, Summer 1994.

Higgins, C. Steven, Elizabeth Hawthorne, Jane Cape and Laurie Bell. The Successful Community College Instructor. A profile for Recruitment. Community College Review, Vol. 21, No. 4, pp. 27-36, 1993.

Hischorn, M. W. Doctorates Earned by Blacks Decline by 26.5 Percent in Decade. The Chronicle of Higher Education. 34 (21) 1, February 1988.

Moore, W. Jr. Black Faculty in White Colleges. A Dream Deferred. Educational Record 68 (4) 69 (1): 116-121.

National Research Council. 1986 Summary Report. 1985 Doctorate Recipients from the United States Universities.

O'Brien, E. M. February 3, 1988. College Recruitment Strategies Varied and Innovative. Black Issues in Higher Education. 4 (22) 15-16.

Sullivan, G. M. and Nowlin, W. A. 1990. Recruiting and Hiring Minority Faculty: Old Story, Same Myths, New Opportunities. CUPA Journal 41 (2) 43-50.

Winbush, Donald. Trials and Triumphs: Compact for Faculty Diversity Institute Offers Ideas and Solutions. Black Issues in Higher Education, pp. 32-34, November 1994.

Appendix 1

African-American FACULTY
DEVELOPMENT PROJECT AGREEMENT

I hereby agree to participate in the SFCC/UF African-American Faculty
Development Project for the academic year and will abide by the
following stipulations:

1. I understand that I cannot concurrently hold another University of
    Florida remunerative position or accept any other fellowship or assistant-
    ship without the approval of the Associate Dean responsible for the
    SFCC/UF African-American Faculty Development project.

2. I understand that I must register and receive credit for at least 9
    Graduate School semester hours each semester (Fall and Spring).

3. I understand that I must maintain at least a 3.0 grade-point average.

4. I understand that my continued participation in the project is dependent
    upon satisfactory academic progress (3.0 GPA).

5. I understand that default on any of the above terms may terminate my
    participation in the project.

Signed _____ Date _____

I do not accept participation in the SFCC/UF African-American Faculty
Development Project.

Signed _____ Date _____

Please return a signed copy to: Associate Dean for Graduate Studies
                                  & Graduate Minority Programs
                                  241 Grinter Hall
                                  University of Florida
                                  Gainesville, FL 32611

Appendix 2

Program Summary:

Sante Fe Community College/University of Florida (SFCC/UF)
Black Faculty Development Project

Purpose: The SFCC/UF Black Faculty Development Project is designed to increase the number of African-American faculty at Santa Fe Community College while increasing the number of African-American students seeking doctoral degrees at the University of Florida.

Approved Areas: chemistry humanities physical sciences

English mathematics music (choral)

Eligibility: African-American U.S. citizens enrolled in or admitted into a doctoral program at the University of Florida are eligible for participation in the SFCC/UF Black Faculty Development Project. Applicants must have a master's degree in one of the approved areas.

Financial Support: Participants receive a $9,000 salary from SFCC for ten months, with payment of tuition and fees by the University of Florida. Non-Florida residents receive out-of-state tuition waivers.

Requirements: Participants must teach three courses (one fall, one spring, one summer) and assist SFCC in the recruitment and retention of minority students. Participants also must make satisfactory progress toward their doctoral degrees at UF.

Test Scores: The University of Florida requires GRE or GMAT scores before an application for admission is processed.

Application Deadline: Open

For further information, please contact:

Associate Dean of Graduate School
Human Resources & Planning
and Graduate Minority Programs or
241 Grinter Hall
University of Florida
Gainesville, FL 32611
(904) 392-6444

Sante Fe Community College
PO Box 1530
Gainesville, FL 32602
(904) 395-5843

The University of Florida and Santa Fe Community College are Affirmative Action/Equal Educational Opportunity Institutions.

The Effect of Institutional Change on Minority Student Retention: A National Model

by Pamela G. Arrington

Overview:

Thirty-six percent of all undergraduates (2,536,973) and thirty-six percent of all minority undergraduates (529,802) enroll at institutions which are members of the American Association of State Colleges and Universities-AASCU[1] (USDoE, 1991). To assist institutions in their retention and graduation goals, AASCU initiated a research project in 1991 and surveyed its members in the three succeeding years to document retention and graduation trends.

With support from Sallie Mae, AASCU began collecting data by survey and offering regional workshops. Using 1992 and 1993 survey data, pairs of institutions, selected for their similar characteristics (size, location, mission) and dissimilar outputs (student retention/graduation rates) were invited to work together. The project centered around the concept of teaming,—having campus teams at partner institutions working together on retention goals.

Partnering institutions have taken the following actions: cross-campus visits; exchange of information, particularly at the presidential level; functional analysis of academic support services (advising, tutoring, mentoring); and the appointment of task forces on admissions standards and retention. Evaluation reports show progress achieved in key areas such as establishment of baseline data; implementation of new admissions standards; development of a proposal for Freshman Year Experience; development of a retention plan, intrusive follow-up for stop-outs/drop-outs; and articulation agreements with community colleges.

Introduction

There are two components of the project: an annual survey administered to AASCU members and a national dissemination campaign. The goal of these research and dissemination efforts is to facilitate a national dialogue about effective teaching and learning practices, particularly practices with documented outcomes. Results from the annual survey are used to select institutions with significant experience in tracking and reporting student outcomes and providing campus conditions that facilitate undergraduate academic success. These institutions are invited to come together at regional conferences and provide insight into building institutional infrastructures that have been key in improving retention and graduation rates. One of the conditions for joining the project is an institution's willingness to designate senior administrators and faculty leaders to serve as resource persons in the area of academic student success for a state or regional network.

In addition to using the survey results to select project participants, survey data assist presidents who agree to host regional meetings in determining conference themes for three or four annual spring conferences. Program themes feature retention as a part of broader issues, such as the inclusive university, developing learning communities, and campus culture. The 1993 survey results indicated a need to promote ongoing meetings between staff at state colleges and community colleges on transfer issues. Because of this, the project's presidential leadership team agreed to invite all sectors of higher education, not just the invited project participants.

The annual retention survey, a research tool at the center of the data-gathering component of the project, permits AASCU to delineate the status of retention efforts among members; to identify student achievement issues needing further attention; and to classify respondents according to the three stages of retention program development — as defined by Richard Richardson's model: reactive, strategic, or adaptive.[2]

To date, the National Retention Project (NRP) has involved 284 institutions in data-gathering. They represent a cross-section of AASCU members and include twenty-six of the historically-black and minority-serving campuses. Using the 1992, 1993 and 1994 survey data, AASCU selected 132 campuses (see Appendix A) to join an effort to disseminate good retention practices and improve institutional effectiveness in bringing minority students to graduation. Each year, thirty-five to fifty presidents and campus teams participate in regional conferences hosted by leaders in student retention. A national advisory panel of retention scholars provides expertise in research and practice and consults with participants on activities, outcomes and dissemination of project results. AASCU has established regional networks and features a session on retention at its annual meeting to encourage continuing dialogue and learning on the topic.

Survey Research

AASCU has administered a survey for four years and modified the instrument each year. In 1992, they sought information on retention policies and practices, persistence and graduation rates. In 1993, they designed the survey to monitor institutions' progress through Richardson's model and standardized cohort definitions to conform with those in the first notice of proposed rule making under the student right-to-know legislation. Cohort data was collected so it could be analyzed at the aggregate level. Respondents were asked about the prevalence of fourteen desirable instruction and advising conditions on their campuses. The 1994 survey was comprised of two parts: a model programs profile sheet used to create an integrated database, and a section for reporting graduation and persistence rates. In addition, institutions were asked specific questions about student enrollment to assist AASCU in responding to the U.S. Department of Education regarding appropriate definitions for graduation rate reporting with the proposed Student Right-to-Know Act. The 1995 survey is planned to maintain the trend in data collection and establish the first cohort of longitudinal data using the fourteen administrative and campus climate conditions outlined in the 1993 survey.

Pertinent Survey Research Findings

Summary of 1992 Survey Results

After an analysis of the data collected from the presidents' questionnaire (N=165) and the data and characteristics questionnaire (N=140) in 1992, AASCU was able to delineate the status of retention efforts on member campuses and to identify issues that needed further attention. Survey respondents were classified by Richardson's paradigm. Several issues emerged as a result of the data analysis. All point to the need to enhance campus infrastructure in support of student retention.

Presidential leadership was the primary catalyst for campus retention efforts for 85 percent of the institutions who completed the Presidents' Questionnaire. After presidential leadership, respondents (60 percent) reported institutional research results as a primary catalyst for establishing offices and/or initiating programs to promote student retention and degree achievement. Sixty-three percent of survey respondents said they have stated goals for student retention and graduation. However, the majority (73 percent) do not have stated numerical retention and graduation goals. The primary modes of communication of stated goals include strategic planning documents (77 percent), presidential statements (60 percent), and freshman orientation (40 percent).

The majority (87 percent) of campuses routinely measure student retention. For each first-time freshmen cohort, 70 percent of the respondents annually collect retention data until graduation or withdrawal, versus by semester (29 percent) or upon completion of hours (.8 percent). Sixty-nine percent annually collect retention data for each transfer cohort. In addition, survey respondents stated they collect retention data by the following variables: native/transfer student (56 percent), other (43 percent), full- or part-time status (42 percent), academic major (41 percent), residential status (31 percent), and age (24 percent).

For all students, institutions reported first- to second-year persistence rates ranging from 27 to 93 percent. For African American students, respondents reported first- to second-year persistence rates ranging from 10 to 99 percent. For women, institutions reported first- to second-year persistence rates from 35 to 93 percent; and for men, from 23 to 93 percent.

However, only 70 institutions were able to report first- to second-year persistence rates for students by race/ethnic groups. Only 51 institutions were able to report graduation rates for students by race/ethnic groups. Only 20 institutions reported graduation rates for community college students transferring as juniors in 1987.

The literature addresses the importance of a student's sense of institutional fit (Tinto, 1993)[3] to student retention programs. The results of the study appear to support the premise that student retention programs improve students' comfort levels at state colleges and universities. A little more than half of the respondents (53 percent) stated they could document increased student satisfaction with campus and increased satisfaction with academic services (57 percent) as a result of campus programs to promote student retention and degree achievement.

Institutions noted the following as documented outcomes of programs to promote student retention and degree achievement: increased use of academic services (84 percent); increased retention rates (80 percent); and improved graduation rates (51 percent). In order to measure programs' outcomes, institutions reported using student tracking systems (91 percent), student surveys (84 percent), and individual student interviews (66 percent).

Orientation and tutoring were the most frequently cited administrative offices and student retention programs. Faculty referral (89 percent) was the primary way students were invited to participate in tutoring programs. While these efforts by colleges and universities improve retention rates, they do not have a similar impact on graduation rates unless a campus is willing to change its teaching and learning practices (Richardson, 1991).

For full-time, first-time freshmen admitted in fall 1985, the average SAT score reported was 844.3; the average ACT score reported was 16.8; and the average high school GPA was 2.98. For the same cohort, four-year graduation rates varied widely, ranging from 3 to 65 percent. For the same cohort, the range of six-year graduation rates was higher than the four-year graduation rate, ranging from 6 to 81 percent. Questions in the 1993 survey sought to clarify reasons for the low graduation rates.

With respect to graduation rates, AASCU was disappointed to learn that most institutions could not report four- and six-year graduation rates by ethnicity. Using NCAA data for Division I schools (1992), AASCU researchers examined the six-year graduation rates of different ethnic cohorts enrolled at AASCU institutions (N=127,732). This study showed high variance in graduation rates by race and gender, ranging from a low of 19.4 percent for Hispanic males to a high of 43.8 percent for Asian females.

From 1980 to 1992, 61 percent of the survey respondents reported an increase in six-year graduation rates for full-time, first-time freshmen; 27 percent stated their six-year graduation rates overall remained the same; and 13 percent reported an overall decrease in their six-year graduation rates.

As institutions change their environments to welcome diverse student groups, the relationship of faculty reward systems to faculty involvement in student assessment programs, learning assistance programs, and improved teaching should be considered. A majority (65 percent) of the survey respondents take into consideration activities such as teaching, academic advising, mentoring, and tutoring during the promotion and tenure process. Faculty/staff development programs on teaching/learning (73 percent) and cultural diversity (69 percent) were primary incentives provided to campus staff/faculty to increase their participation in student retention efforts.

A sizable majority (78 percent) of respondents' retention programs are funded by state appropriations. Almost all respondents (96 percent) noted budget cuts in state appropriations as a situation that would threaten the continuation of student retention programs. A sizable majority (77 percent) believed that if programs are funded by institutional base budgets and built into strategic planning efforts (74 percent), then the programs will become institutionalized. Top administrative support was noted by 86 percent of the respondents as an effort needed to ensure institutionalization of student retention efforts on campus. However, changes in top administrative personnel (board, 7 percent and president, 28 percent) or faculty (10 percent) were not seen by respondents as a threat to the continuation of student retention programs.

A majority of the survey respondents (64 percent) classified themselves as primarily commuter and 36 percent as primarily residential. The average percentage of undergraduate students who live on campus was 26.

When asked about programmatic retention efforts, institutions most commonly reported offering learning assistance such as orientation and tutoring. While such support does improve retention rates, it does not have a similar impact on graduation rates (Richardson, 1991). What works for graduation rates is a change in campus-wide teaching and learning practices (ibid., 1991) to accommodate diversely-prepared students.

Summary of 1993 Survey Results

In 1993, members were asked to report the actual number of students in various cohorts so data could be analyzed at the aggregate level.[4] The overall six-year graduation rate was 40.6 percent. The total range was 9.2 percent to 75.9 percent. For female students, the six-year graduation rate was higher than for male students, 44 versus 37 percent. The six-year graduation rates reported for white, non Hispanic students (43.8 percent) and Asian/Pacific Islander students (43.2 percent) were higher than those reported for African American (27.5 percent), Hispanic (29.9 percent) and American Indian/Alaskan Native students (25.1 percent). For all minority students, respondents reported a six-year graduation rate of 30.1 percent.

Using fourteen instruction and advising conditions cited in the national literature[5] as benefitting student retention and success, AASCU members were asked if these conditions were descriptive of their campuses. Responses to the 1993 AASCU Survey on Student Retention were occasionally contradictory. The first step in attacking retention problems on campus is to understand the consequences of key campus climate administrative conditions. Respondents acknowledged the benefit of having key administrative conditions (top administrative support, institution-sponsored funding, strategic planning and tracking) in place. Most reported progress toward these goals. While two-thirds of the respondents expressed campus goals for student retention and graduation in strategic planning documents, only forty-six schools reported that numerical goals existed or were being planned. No on-going meetings were reported for facilitating the dialogue between state colleges and community colleges around transfer issues. At the spring 1994 regional retention conferences, host campuses invited community college presidents to come to the conferences and bring campus teams in an attempt to begin a dialogue.

Respondents (sixty percent) reported they encourage and reward advising, mentoring and good teaching. Such factors are considered in the evaluation, promotion and tenure processes. This is consistent with the primary mission for most of the institutions that responded to the 1993 survey. More than half of the respondents (fifty-seven percent) wrote they provide merit pay/salary increases, grants, release time and opportunities for travel to workshops as incentives to encourage faculty participation in student retention efforts. On the other hand, less than one quarter (twenty-two percent) reported providing grants and release time to encourage faculty members to develop strategies for improving student achievement. However, further review of the descriptive comments revealed that many of the efforts to encourage faculty participation in student retention did indeed include strategies to improve student achievement.

Using the survey as an educational tool to shift the focus from access to student achievement, AASCU asked its members about the learning environments on their campuses. Generally, respondents were not engaged in student and faculty assessment. Over half of the respondents provide instruction in basic skills and tutoring to students who need these services. About a third offer students the opportunity to enroll in sections which provide extra hours of classroom instruction, tutoring or learning laboratories for diversely-prepared students; but almost half (49 percent) do not. Slightly more than a third of the respondents reported they use an early alert system to provide direct feedback to students, particularly those students in danger of failing, but almost two-thirds do not.

While respondents offer orientation programs for new students that emphasize sensitivity to cultural differences, most (fifty-five percent) do not require students to study at least one other culture, or require campus personnel to participate in cultural awareness sessions. The majority of responding institutions provide workshops to help faculty improve their teaching effectiveness with a diverse student population. Many provide monetary incentives to involve faculty in student retention practices on campus and, similarly, to encourage faculty to develop strategies for improving student achievement.

Research on student retention suggests that administrative commitment; strategic planning and assessment; early, direct and frequent feedback to students; commitment to student success, and a focus on teaching improvement are all effective campus strategies to improve retention and graduation rates at state colleges and universities. However, most AASCU respondents do not integrate key academic and social conditions in a systemic approach that would improve retention and graduation rates as well as the campus culture. Instead, an isolated programmatic approach continues to be used to change administrative, instructional and advising practices. Typically, there is no routine program evaluation.

Summary of 1994 Survey Results

The 1994 survey comprised two parts: a model programs profile sheet used to create an integrated program inventory database and a section for reporting graduation and persistence rates. Part I of the 1994 AASCU/Sallie May Survey on Student Retention asked respondents to report varied campus practices. Respondents reported on many different retention programs (n=324) to address key social and academic variables like assisting new students to acclimate to a new environment or helping students with undecided majors to identify academic strengths and career interests. The profiles received via the 1994 Survey were organized by program type: instruction and advising, administrative conditions, student and faculty assessment and partnership programs between state colleges and K-12 schools or community colleges. Part II of the survey solicited graduation rates for three cohorts (see Table 1).

Table 1: Results of the three Sallie Mae National Retention Project surveys

Year of Survey			
1992	1993	1994	
(1985 Freshman Cohort)	(1986 Freshman Cohort)	(1987 Freshman Cohort)	
170	188	213	institutions
6.5 to 80.6	9.5 to 75.9	3.3 to 75.3	Range
**	40.6	40.5	Average
15.4 to 51.0	36.6	35.8	Male
15.6 to 82.9	44.0	43.7	Female
**	27.5	28.0	Black, Non-Hispanic
**	25.1	24.5	American Indian/Alaskan Native
**	43.2	41.9	Asian/Pacific Islander
**	29.9	30.9	Hispanic
**	43.8	42.6	White, Non-Hispanic
All Minorities	**	30.1	**

** Data not available at this level of detail

As demonstrated in Table I, the number of survey participants has increased steadily. This growth is a result of extensive communication about the project, individualized feedback reports, and useful publications. However, despite increased participation, the graduation rate overall has not improved nor has the range moved upward, and marked differences in the average rates by ethnicity persist. Many institutions are still unable to track students by such critical factors as race and gender and have very low six-year graduation rates.

Institutional Mentoring Demonstration Project

When AASCU distributed its first feedback reports in the spring of 1994, it invited institutions with the lowest graduation rates to join a pilot project pairing them with an institution of comparable size, location and mission, which had achieved much better graduation rates and tracking capabilities. To date, sixteen institutions have volunteered to participate in the demonstration project and they have selected at least one partner each. The goal for this pilot project was change, and three results were envisioned:

1) to improve graduation rates at institutions reporting six-year rates below twenty percent;

2) to assist effective institutions in adapting the campus to support diversely-prepared students better, thereby increasing their rates of success; and

3) to increase the number of traditionally underrepresented students graduating from AASCU institutions.

Improving student retention rates is a priority in higher education. Colleges and universities have become skilled at recruiting students and now must find ways to keep them in school through graduation. A significant percentage (from 28.3 to 30 percent) of all institutional leaving occurs during the first year of college (Ibid, Tinto, 1993). Although institutions recognize this policy issue and have tried to address barriers to retention, it appears that permanent change can only take hold under certain conditions: locally based and managed implementation; evolutionary development; and sensitivity to institutional conditions. Institutional partnerships were created to improve graduation rates of all students, particularly underserved populations, and to adapt campus environments for diversely-prepared students. The results of the partnership efforts benefit other institutions, regardless of their status along Richard Richardson's (Ibid, Richardson, 1991) institutional adaptation continuum.

AASCU has taken steps to establish these links. First, with 1992 and 1993 survey data, seventy-six potential mentor institutions that had reached the strategic stage of Richardson's model and were ready to move to the adaptive stage were identified. With 1994 survey data, fifty-four more were identified. Most of these institutions report persistence/graduation rates by ethnicity and six-year graduation rates above 40 percent, for majority and minority students.[6]

Mentee institutions with low graduation rates have a different agenda: to improve data collection and tracking, as well as six-year graduation rates overall. The demographics of the original sixteen mentees differ from the mentors in minority student enrollment (ranging up to 95 percent), minority faculty (ranging up to 93 percent), and six-year graduation rates (from 11.4 to 40.9 percent). In 1994, another six institutions were identified with six-year graduation rates below 20 percent and 25 that did not report graduation rates by gender/ethnicity or transfer status.

Dissemination, Evaluation and Discussion

Nine regional conferences have served 173 campuses and over 830 faculty, administrators and presidents. Central to the conference design are program tracts for presidents and senior administrators, institutional research officers, and faculty. Institutions invited to join the project must agree to bring a campus team to a regional conference and presidents are encouraged to attend the regional conference and the national meeting where newly invited participants are recognized for their achievements in improved student persistence and six-year graduation rates. Papers presented at the regional conferences provide opportunities for campus personnel to showcase classroom research and model programs. A few of the papers presented at the regional meetings have been included in the national dissemination campaign. A cadre of retention scholars[7] advises project staff on goals and future initiatives. Also, they are the keynote presenters along with members of the presidential leadership team at the regional and national meetings.

In February 1995, a PBS video conference, Retention Strategies for Diversity, subscribed 328 schools including the fifty-nine North Carolina Community Colleges. The project was cited in testimony before the Senate Committee on Labor and Human Resources Subcommittee on Education, Arts and Humanities for increased attention to minority participation in higher education (May 17, 1994). Altogether, 410 institutions have benefited from National Retention Project (NRP) activities, leaving only seventy-seven AASCU institutions which have not participated.

As part of its responsibilities for technical assistance, data-gathering and dissemination, AASCU implemented a number of information clearinghouse activities, including: setting up a model programs database, and acquiring and organizing materials, models, practices, research and other information needed by institutions participating in this project. National Retention Project publications and resource materials[8] have been disseminated to 375 campus and twenty-nine system members.

The AASCU resources collected and made available to those interested in retention in higher education include relevant literature references, successful strategies and programs. The clearinghouse, located at AASCU, consists chiefly of printed material. Presidents participating in the NRP indicate they are willing to share this information, and report a long list of available resources: information on student retention data systems and initiatives in student tracking; descriptions of freshman-year experience programs; procedures for implementing faculty incentive grant programs, faculty advising programs and faculty reward systems affecting promotion and tenure; examples of computer databases to facilitate advising and placement for entering students; model mentor programs; information on general education curricula; examples of student surveys for diverse student groups, (i.e., entering students, current students, non-returning students); orientation programs and targeted programs for minority students.

Respondents to the surveys on materials and references needed reported the following would be most useful in assisting campuses in improving retention and graduation rates: expertise from documented successful programs; materials to disseminate to faculty that encourage their development and involvement in advising and curriculum reform; successful academic advisement programs/handbooks; expertise in improving tracking and reporting capabilities; and assistance with assessment techniques/data that will lead to improved retention.

To build upon the success of the 1993 Directory (circulation 2,000) and the 1994 Compendium (circulation 3,000) of model programs, AASCU established a national database of model programs to profile successful initiatives in retention and improvement of student achievement. The database will be used, much like ERIC, to extract programs and initiatives according to specific characteristics. Data elements include: institution name, contact name/title/ address/phone/fax/e-mail; name of program/initiative; description of goals; target population; cost of program/initiative; start/end dates; results of program evaluation; and program award status.

The database will assist AASCU staff when responding to inquiries about practices at other institutions (i.e. which AASCU institutions have developed initiatives targeting the first year experience? part-time students? African American male students? etc.). AASCU plans to make this feature available on-line for outside users. Database entries will be updated periodically.

Progress Report on the Demonstration Project.

At AASCU's Central Regional Retention Conference (Indiana, June 26-27, 1994) hosted by Ball State University, seven mentor/mentee teams met at a special program session. Each had prepared a retention project action plan addressing goals, indicators of progress, team members and proposed steps. During the late summer, AASCU surveyed these institutions via a campus team response form which focused on goals, resources, contacts, assistance needed from AASCU, and follow-up activities. Examples of services which AASCU could effectively provide to institutions include: identification of software packages for sophisticated tracking of retention and graduation rates for underrepresented groups; travel funding for team visits to campuses; information collection and dissemination on faculty development programs (to include an adviser's handbook) and institutional accomplishments (how successes were actually achieved).

The thirty institutions involved in the project to date were contacted again in February 1995 and asked to complete status reports listing actions taken, progress achieved, future plans, current team memberships and how AASCU could assist them. The institutional survey responses, gathered on a form called Status Request on Mentoring Project, are gratifying in that they reflect varied and committed efforts to improve retention and graduation rates. It is instructive to catalog representative responses and to sample some of the most interesting ones.

With respect to (a) actions taken, (b) progress achieved, and (c) future plans, the most common elements include: (a) campus visits; exchange of information, particularly at the presidential level; functional analysis of academic support services (advising, tutoring, mentoring); and the appointment of task forces on admissions standards and retention; (b) establishment of baseline data; implementation of new admissions standards; development of a proposal for freshman year experience; preparation of a Title III grant proposal to enhance technology infrastructure; completion of an action plan; development of a retention plan; intrusive follow-up for stop-outs/drop-outs; and articulation agreements with community colleges; and (c) recommendations for enhancing institutional efforts concerning new freshman and transfer students; reciprocal campus visits between mentor and mentee institutions; self-study of academic support services; and regular collection and reporting of retention rates by several cohorts. The following example is one university's succinct report of actions taken, progress achieved, and future plans: (a) The STARS (Student Advising and Retention Service) office has been in operation since September, 1994. (b) During the fall quarter STARS served 420 students with advising and retention services. Seventy students were retained that would have otherwise dropped out of the university and their educational program. A visit to XYZ was made by members of the team during the fall quarter of 1994. Helpful information was obtained to assist efforts at ABC. (c) In the future the STARS office will expand its services if funding is available. We need to serve approximately 800-900 incoming freshmen. University personnel will visit on the ABC campus during the fall of 1995 to interact with us on the services provided.

The second question on the AASCU Status Report on Mentoring Project form was developed to address two concerns: that the institutional team membership would include the highest level and most appropriate job functions; and that institutional team membership would be maintained at a full status. Therefore, the participating institutions were asked to list the names and job titles of their current team members. Two examples of institutional team memberships follow: One mentor lists its president, vice president for administration and fiscal affairs, dean of the school of library and information management, and the director of the student advising center; while its sister institution includes its vice president for academic affairs, executive assistant to the president, professor of education, dean of the school of science and technology, vice president for student affairs, director of admissions, instructor in journalism, associate dean of students, associate professor of English, and a professor of English and director of general studies. On the whole, the memberships of teams, while varying from institution to institution, demonstrated an ongoing effort to include administrators and faculty members deemed necessary to get the job done.

The third item on the AASCU Status Report on Mentoring Project form posed two questions: (a) what assistance or services from AASCU would help the institution to succeed in this project? and (b) if limited funds were made available, what would be the priorities? Typical responses cited the need for all or part of the expenses for reciprocal visits; availability of the latest research and literature in the field of retention; the sharing of innovations and success stories; statistical data for comparable institutions; and funding for research and service efforts. The response from one university nicely captures some sentiments common to most institutions:

"Everyone usually gets recharged while attending national and regional meetings. Unfortunately, the folks back home in the trenches are often not in attendance at these conferences. Perhaps by subsidizing the cost of visits to participating campuses by an assessment team of nationally-recognized experts, more staff and faculty members would be able to benefit from the ideas and, more importantly, be able to adapt concepts into workable solutions on the individual campuses. This leads to 'ownership' and improved outcomes."

The institutional responses to the items included on the Status Report on Mentoring Project convey important preliminary accomplishments, the need to continue, the teams of involved personnel, and the partnership roles for both the individual institutions and AASCU.

Discussion

Since the very first survey results, it was apparent that most colleges and universities have varied retention programs in place to address key social and academic variables, like assisting new students get acclimated to a new environment or helping undecided majors identify academic strengths and career interests. What has not been as apparent in the data is evidence of the integration of these efforts into the total campus culture. Typically, institutions invited to join the project have exhibited some evidence of initiatives that foster collaboration between student services and academic affairs. Data show this subtle systemic change increases the success of institutional programs like academic advisement, orientation, residence life, tutoring and supplemental instruction programs that are, of course, designed to improve students' retention and graduation. When staff from academic and co-curricular programs join together and collaborate on addressing key academic and social variables that effect student learning, student success is one outcome. Faculty and staff development is yet another outcome of such collaboration.

In reviewing the conference evaluations and notes from focus group discussions at the various regional meetings, one overwhelming trend is the perceived isolation most faculty and administrators still express when talking about efforts on their campuses to engage the total campus community in retention efforts. Often, administrators have stated they wish they could just get faculty involved. On the other hand, faculty have expressed dismay at being asked to do more with less, and that then, after doing more, not being appropriately recognized for their commitment by the same administrators who asked them to get more involved.

Even though many faculty participate in teaching orientation courses and academic advising, most express the need for additional institutional resources to help them adapt teaching and learning practices to accommodate a more diversely-prepared student body. The presentations at the regional conferences and the publications disseminated to faculty and administrators have fostered a continuing dialogue on student learning and achievement. One of the recurring conference themes for the past three years has been: the impact of learning communities on student learning and achievement.

Through a formalized national dissemination campaign, the project has heightened resource-sharing among members, while educating them about effective retention strategies. The project's dissemination efforts have advanced considerably with the establishment of the AASCU Clearinghouse: Resources on Practices and Software Supporting Retention. AASCU has compiled a collection of materials on student tracking, assessment, models of measuring student achievement, and mentoring.

In 1993, AASCU provided institutional reports to presidents showing how their six-year graduation rates compared to all other survey respondents. In 1994, they provided additional data that show how campuses compare with similar institutions according to mission (urban, rural) and size. Presidents were advised that institutional graduation rate data are confidential and only reported back to the responding institution

Conclusion

Through the AASCU/Sallie Mae National Retention Project, over 400 state colleges and universities and their affiliated systems of higher education have had the opportunity to look closely at their effectiveness and have begun to focus on these fundamental issues while preparing themselves to meet the emerging account-ability requirements. AASCU member institutions, by reason of their regional focus and special missions, have opened the doors to educational opportunity to many with varying degrees of success. They are now aware of the new challenges related to fostering student achievement and are examining the issue of how to convert access into success for a much larger proportion of their students.

In reviewing answers to the question, "How has participation in the NRP affected your campus practices?" the overwhelming consensus focuses on the project's education role. The project's tools (annual survey, publications, regional conferences, feedback reports, etc.) served to educate the campuses about the importance of institutional culture and learning environments to student success as well as provide normative data helpful in responding to state mandates. The following comment is representative.

> *"Participation in the National Retention Program has provided comparative and institutional data which I have shared annually with the University Administrative community. Thus, the University has stayed focused on improving student retention and graduation rates—issues demanding institutional changes in practices/culture. Further, participation in the regional conferences has provided an intensive learning experience for key University faculty and administrators who then share their learning with others on the campus thus affecting our learning community in a positive manner."*

To be successful, campuses will need to focus on strategies for effecting institutional change. Here, institutional change cannot be achieved by superficial means. It will require fundamental reform of campus cultures to support diversity and conversion of the learning environment from a teacher-centered one to a learner-centered one.

—Dr. Pamela G. Arrington is the Director of The National Retention Project at the American Association of State Colleges and Universities in Washington, D. C.

Footnotes

1. The American Association of State Colleges and Universities is a leading higher education association representing public colleges and universities and state higher education systems across the United States and Puerto Rico, Guam and the Virgin Islands. Ranging in size from 400 students to over 30,000, AASCU institutions enroll more than 3 million—one out of every five students in all U.S. colleges and universities.

2. "A Model of Institutional Adaptation to Student Diversity" in Achieving Quality and Diversity. New York: ACE/Macmillan, 1991. The reactive stage focuses on recruitment, financial aid, admissions, and scheduling activities. Institutions in the strategic stage focus resources on outreach, transition, mentoring, enrollment, and residence hall activities. During the adaptive stage (the more advanced and integrative stage) the institution focuses on student assessment, providing opportunities for students to acquire learning assistance, if necessary, and adapting curricular content to embrace the variety of learning styles inherent in diverse student bodies.

3. Vincent Tinto, Leaving College: Rethinking the Causes and Cures of Student Attrition, 2nd edition. Chicago: University of Chicago Press, 1993.

4. Survey results have limited generalizability: 188 respondents out of a total population of 361, with 114 reporting graduation rates on the fall 1986 freshman cohort overall and by ethnicity.

5. Likert-type items were modeled after Richard Richardson's (1989) Achieving Access with Quality: A Study of State and Institutional Practices for Increasing Enrollment and Graduation Rates for Black, Hispanic and American Indian Students: Survey for Institutions.

6. Among the current group of mentor institutions: two-thirds are urban and one-third rural; headcount enrollment ranges from 4,551 to 23,335; minority student enrollment is from 2.9 to 76.2 percent; minority faculty is from 3.8 to 70.5 percent; six-year graduation rates range from 22.8 to 48.4 percent; and six-year persistence rates range from 2.2 to 10.3 percent.

7. National Retention Project Advisory Panel: Drs. Clinita Ford, Coordinator, National Conference on Black Student Retention, Florida A&M University; Rosario Martinez, Dean and Founding Director, The Aldine Center, North Harris College (TX); Michael Nettles, University of Michigan, Researcher, undergraduate education, policy issues; Richard Richardson, Arizona State University, change theory, institutional adaptation to accommodate diverse student body, leading toward integration; Vincent Tinto, National Center for the Study of Teaching, Learning and Assessment in Higher Education, Syracuse University, Leader in teaching/learning reform since the 1970s; Julia Wells, Director of Higher Education Program Access and Equity, South Carolina Commission on Higher Education, Practitioner, state system and policy questions; and President Robert Glennen, Emporia State University (KS), AASCU president, extensive experience in advising systems and effective advising for retention.

8. These publications include: 1992 Survey Summary, Clinita Ford's Baker's Dozen of Retention Tips, 1993 Directory of Model Programs, 1993 Survey Results, Campus Practices for Student Success: A Compendium of Model Programs, Barbara Weaver Smith's Retention is the Outcome: Quality is the Goal, Roberta Matthew's Learning Communities: A Retention Strategy that Serves Students and Faculty, and Promoting Student Success: Improving Campus Climate for Under Represented Students.

References

Richardson, Jr., R. C. and Skinner, E. F. (1991). Achieving Quality and Diversity. New York: ACE/Macmillian.

Richardson, Jr., R. (1989). Achieving Access with Quality: A Study of State and Institutional Practices for Increasing Enrollment and Graduation Rates of Black, Hispanic and American Indian Students. Phoenix: National Center for Post-secondary Governance and Finance Research Center at Arizona State University.

Tinto, V. (1993). Leaving College: Rethinking the Causes and Cures of Student Attrition. Chicago: University of Chicago Press.

Appendix A
AASCU/Sallie May National Retention Project Participants

Adams State College	Longwood College (VA)
Alcorn State University (MS)	Louisiana Tech University
Appalachian State University (NC)	Louisiana State U.
Arkansas State University	Mansfield U. of Pennsylvania
Austin Peay State University (TN)	Marshall University (WV)
Ball State University (IN)	Mayville State U. (SD)
Bowie State University (MD)	McNeese State University
Bridgewater State College (MA)	Memphis University (TN)
California State University, Northridge	Metropolitan State College of Denver
California Polytechnic State Univ., San Luis Obispo	Michigan Tech U.
California Maritime Academy	Middle Tennessee State University
California State University, Sacramento	Millersville U. of Pennsylvania
California State U., Fresno	Mississippi University for Women
California Polytechnic State Univ., Pomona	Montclair State University (NJ)
California Maritime Academy	Morehead State University (KY)
Central Washington U.	Murray State University (KY)
Central Missouri State U.	Nicholls State University (LA)
Chicago State University (IL)	Northeast Louisiana U.
Clarion U. of Pennsylvania	Northeast Missouri State University
Cleveland State U.	Northern Kentucky U.
Clinch Valley College (VA)	Northern State U. (SD)
Coastal Carolina University (SC)	Northwestern State University of Louisiana
College of Charleston	Oakland U. (MI)
East Tennessee State University	Old Dominion University (VA)
East Texas State University	Prairie View A & M University (TX)
Eastern Connecticut State University	Pittsburg State U. (KS)
Eastern Illinois University	Plymouth State College (NH)
Edinboro U. of Pennsylvania	Portland State University (OR)
Emporia State University (KS)	Ramapo College of New Jersey
Fort Hays State U. (KS)	Rowan College of New Jersey
Georgia Southern University	Salisbury State U. (MD)
Governors State U. (IL)	Sam Houston State University (TX)
Grambling State University (LA)	San Jose State University (CA)
Indiana U. of Pennsylvania	San Diego State University (CA)
Jackson State U. (MS)	Shippensburg University of Pennsylvania
Kutztown U. of Pennsylvania	Sonoma State University (CA)
Lincoln University (MO)	South Dakota School of Mines and Technology
Livingston University (AL)	Southeast Missouri State University
Lock Haven University of Pennsylvania	Southern College of Technology (GA)

AASCU/Sallie May National Retention Project Participants

Southern Illinois University at Edwardsville
Southwest Missouri State
Southwest Texas State University
Southeastern Louisiana Univ.
St. Cloud State University (MN)
State University of New York-New Paltz
State University of New York-Potsdam
State University of New York-Old Westbury
State University of New York-Oswego
State University of New York-Geneseo
State University of New York-Cortland
Stephen F. Austin State U. (TX)
SUNY Institute of Tech. at Utica
SUNY College at Oneonta
SUNY College at Buffalo
Texas A & M U.- Corpus Cristi
The Richard Stockton College of New Jersey
The U. of the Virgin Islands
Towson State University (MD)
U. of Akron
U. of Alabama in Huntsville
U. of Wisconsin at Whitewater
U. of Tenn. at Chattanooga
U. of Wisconsin at Oshkosh
U. of Maryland, Baltimore Co.
U. of Houston-Victoria
U. of Southwestern Louisiana
U. of North Carolina at Asheville
U. of North Carolina at Charlotte
U. of Massachusetts, Boston
University of Southern Colorado
University of Maine at Fort Kent
University of North Florida
University of South Carolina at Aiken
University of Wisconsin - Green Bay
University of Wisconsin - Stout
University of Northern Colorado
University of Texas at Arlington
University of Nebraska at Kearney
University of Northern Iowa

University of Texas at San Antonio
University of Maine at Fort Kent
University of New Orleans
University of West Florida
University of Texas at El Paso
Wayne State College (NE)
Weber State U. (UT)
West Georgia College
West Liberty State College (WV)
Western Illinois U.
Western Washington U.
Western Carolina University
Westfield State College (MA)
William Paterson College
Winona State U. (MN)
Wright State University

The Minority Advising Program:
A System-Wide Approach to Retention of African-American Students in the University System of Georgia

by Joseph H. Silver, Sr.

Overview:

The purpose of this article is to share an example of a system-wide retention effort geared toward African-American students. The program is called the Minority Advising Program (MAP), and is a central component of the University System of Georgia's effort to retain African-American students. The program was developed as a response to the Adams litigation in which states were asked to dismantle their dual system of higher education and enhance minority participation.

In this article, the Minority Advising Program is examined with special efforts to describe the origin, nature, structure, and basic aspects of the program. Also included are basic characteristics of the program and funding information. This is a concerted effort to give and describe the components of a quality retention program.

Finally, several institutions within the University System of Georgia having successful programs are highlighted to give concrete examples of effective programs. While each institution is different, there exist several program characteristics that are the same and may be instructive to other institutions seeking to enhance the retention of minority students.

Introduction

The University System of Georgia, like many other state systems of higher education, was a part of the Adams litigation of the 1970s and 1980s. The gist of the litigation was to dismantle the dual system of higher education that existed in many states in the South and Southeast. Specifically, it was an attempt to enhance minority participation in higher education in the ranks of the student, faculty, and administrative population.

To respond to the issues and concerns raised as a part of the Adams litigation, the University System of Georgia adopted and implemented several programs, including the Administrative Development Program, Graduate Recruitment Seminar Program, Recruitment Missions, Regents Opportunity Scholarships, Summer Enrichment Programs, and the Minority Advising Program, among others. The purpose of this chapter is to provide a description of one of the above-mentioned programs, the Minority Advising Program. Specifically, information will be provided on the origin and development of the program, the organizational structure, and activities associated with the program. Also, the overall impact of the Minority Advising Program (MAP) at certain institutions within the University System of Georgia will be explored, with special attention to characteristics of successful programs.

Origin and Development of MAP

MAP was established in 1983 to address the specific problems faced by minority students within the University System of Georgia which impacted retention. There was also an intent to enhance the academic welfare of minority students.[1] The goals of the program include the promotion of academic success, the development of human potential, and the creation of an environment that fosters success and retention of minority students.

Originally, the Minority Advising Program was initiated as a part of the 1983 addendum to a 1978 desegregation plan of the University System of Georgia. After the University System of Georgia was relieved of reporting to the Office of Civil Rights in 1986, MAP continued as the system's effort to promote retention of minority students. In 1988, the program was reaffirmed and its continuation was recommended as a part of the University System of Georgia Steering Committee for Increased Minority Participation in Public Higher Education.[2] In 1994, the University System of Georgia appointed a new chancellor, and one of his first official acts was to again affirm the importance of the program. Support and intent to continue the program in the new administration were captured in a newsletter article to university system employees.[3] Each institution has a MAP on its campus, which is intended to supplement, not replace, normal advising activities. The overall program is coordinated at the central office level to provide leadership, direction, insight, and advocacy.

At the inception of the program, the Minority Advising Program on each campus was identical. The overall intent of this sameness was to assure a certain level of accountability and bases for measuring progress and success. It originally consisted of advising units of six to ten students, an advisor for each unit, and a coordinator for the overall program. Depending upon the size and the complexity of the institution, the coordinators may be full or part-time. In most cases, the MAP coordinators have other campus responsibilities, which is problematic in some instances. Initially, the program was coordinated through the Office of Academic Affairs on each campus.

The structure was reassessed in 1988 to address the special needs of institutions (example: residential, non-residential, universities, and two-year institutions). As a part of the recommendation of the University System of Georgia Steering Committee for Increased Minority Participation in Public Higher Education, each institution was given the authority to structure its program in a manner that best met its specific needs. Additionally, the institutions were given the flexibility of having the Minority Advising Program report either through the Office of Academic Affairs or the Office of Student Affairs. The original intent of having the programs report through the Office of Academic Affairs was more political than structural. It was felt that the program would be taken more seriously if housed in the Office of Academic Affairs. However, as the programs at given institutions gained in maturity and the overall support level increased, the institutions were given the flexibility of having the Minority Advising Program report either through the Office of Academic Affairs or the Office of Student Affairs. Even though the structural features of the program changed, each institution was expected to maintain the overall goals of MAP. When institutions were given the authorization for increased flexibility, only a few of the system's thirty-four institutions seized the opportunity to change various aspects of the program. Therefore, for the most part, MAP is uniform throughout the University System of Georgia.

The target population for the program is African-American freshmen and sophomores, even though any minority student can participate in the program. It should be noted that student participation is strictly voluntary. No student is mandated to participate in the program. However, students who have been identified as having problems navigating the specific institution in which they are enrolled are encouraged to participate. The programmatic concept was developed to address the cognitive and non-cognitive needs of students; therefore, factors impacting retention of minority students such as financial difficulty, cultural alienation, social isolation, academic difficulty, racial harassment, and family problems were factored into the program model.

In 1983, at the inception of the program, there were several basic guidelines for program. They were as follows:

1. Each institution within the University System of Georgia would establish

and maintain a Minority Advising Program. The MAP would supplement, not replace, regular academic advising activities.

2. Each MAP should establish advising units coordinated by faculty members with special training in the advisement of minority students.

3. The program should emphasize services to freshmen and sophomore students, but be open to any minority student seeking its services.

4. The MAP on each campus will be coordinated through the Office of Academic Affairs.

5. Each MAP will be structured to provide the following services:

   A. careful follow-up of drop-outs;

   B. special individualized counseling for at-risk students and students placed on academic probation;

   C. assistance to students in choosing a program of study and an academic major;

   D. help in examining the long-term implication of pursuing various courses of study and careful consideration of career opportunities presented by various academic programs;

   E. peer counseling to address a full spectrum of personal, social, and academic needs;

   F. access to appropriate and effective tutoring;

   G. help in identifying financial aid sources and review of procedures for obtaining financial aid;

   H. access to and facilitation of career counseling;

   I. reinforcement of the regular advisement system;

   J. access to study skills activities;

   K. articulation with high schools to help prepare minority students for college;

   L. provision of culturally appropriate programming and a forum to bring effective role models in contact with minority students to discuss their educational and other experiences; and

   M. periodic meetings with department chairs, academic officers, and presidents to maximize the interrelationship of the MAP with other aspects of the institution.

6. The president shall appoint a MAP coordinator who will oversee the program.

7. The president is responsible for the operation and success of the program, and provides institutional commitment and support to assure its success.

8. An annual conference for the purpose of staff development and improvement of strategies for making MAP more successful will be a part of the overall program.[4]

In 1988, several changes and/or additions to the guidelines were established. They were as follows:

A. The MAP will address students' academic and non-academic needs, addressing cognitive and non-cognitive dimensions of intellectual, personal, and social self actualization.

B. The MAP will be coordinated either through the Office of Academic Affairs or the Office of Student Affairs. In either case, there must be formal provision for close coordination with the other office in the governance of the MAP.

C. With the approval of the chancellor, institutions may modify the structure and functions of the MAP to render it more responsive to minority needs at that particular institution (example: size and nature of the institution, demographic profile, unique problems, etc.). Institutions seeking program modification should submit a detailed request specifying the unusual circumstances and modification sought.[5]

Other activities associated with the MAP include:

- improved articulation between high schools and the university system institutions to help recruit minority students;
- utilization of community groups and churches to assist in the recruitment of minority students; and
- utilization of alumni in the recruitment of minority students.

Until 1993, the guidelines for the Minority Advising Program were communicated to institutions via letter or Memorandum from the chancellor and vice chancellor for academic affairs of the University System of Georgia. This arrangement was problematic because when new leaders of institutions were appointed, they may or may not have been made aware of the memorandum of understanding pertaining to the Minority Advising Program. Also, in some cases, the institutional outlines of the reasons for the program could easily be compromised in the transition. However, this concern was addressed in July of 1993 when the guidelines for the MAP were made a part of the Academic Affairs Handbook, which is a system document containing the official actions and activities of the Office of Academic Affairs and other related system information. Each campus is expected to keep a copy of the Academic Affairs Handbook on file. Also, the entire document is available electronically.

Program Rationale and Structure

Across the United States, many minorities find the campus environment is often not hospitable and may even be hostile. Some minorities at University System of Georgia institutions face this same challenge. The MAP is designed to impact the campus environment in a positive way. Majority faculty, staff, and students are exposed to people, seminars and programs to help them understand the special challenges faced by minority students. Each of these groups is made aware of their obligation to assist in the retention of minority students. Each campus is asked to examine its programs, practices, and symbols to determine if they pose problems as far as climate is concerned. Minority students are afforded opportunities to meet with the president and other administrators to provide feedback on their perceptions and experiences on campus. The feedback becomes a valuable source of information to enhance program content and direction.

The purpose of the program is to assist in the retention of minority students. A fundamental premise in the development of the program was that minority students on majority campuses find themselves in unique situations requiring a great deal of adjusting and coping. Therefore, there was a systemic effort to identify those areas that created the greatest obstacles to retaining minority students. Once those areas were identified, the program was designed to address those concerns.

The essence of the MAP is to provide a supplementary support system to assure that minorities on majority campuses have every opportunity to succeed. As noted elsewhere, the program concerns itself with both the cognitive and non-cognitive aspects of the student's life on campus. Therefore, exposing the students to proper role models and appropriate cultural programming is as significant as monitoring academic progress; financial aid seminars are as significant as career counseling. Lack of proper attention to any of these areas could cause a minority student on a majority campus to leave.

Even though the MAP is a system-wide initiative, the actual content and name of the program may vary from campus to campus. There is a minimum level of program activities expected of each institution. However, the expected outcomes are the same for each campus. Some of these outcomes are as follows:

• Minority students' transition from high school to college should be made easy as a result of orientation programs.

• Minority students should have a clearer understanding of academic program offerings and career choices.

• Minority students' academic progress should be enhanced as a result of access to study skill seminars, tutoring, counseling, and personalized advising.

• Minority students should "see themselves" in campus activities as a result of culturally appropriate programs and the inclusion of proper role models in campus activities.

• Minority students should have access to information concerning financial aid through financial aid seminars.

• Minority students should be made to feel an integral part of the campus.

• Minority student retention should increase at system institutions.

To achieve these outcomes, each campus is expected to offer a minimum level of services and programs to assist minority students. A typical campus would offer the following components as a part of its Minority Advising Program: peer counseling; tutoring; study skills seminars; financial aid seminars; year-round culturally appropriate programming to bring in significant role models (local, regional, and national); special functions; field trips; special counseling for students on academic probation; and proper follow-up of dropouts to find out why they left the institution.

According to the university system guidelines, the president of each institution is ultimately responsible for the MAP, thus preventing confusion in the area of accountability. In most cases, a typical program would have a coordinator who reports to the chief academic officer of the campus. Majority and minority faculty and staff are identified as advisors for the program. Normally, a training program is in place and every advisor is expected to participate prior to actually being a part of the Minority Advising Program. Upon successful completion of the training, each identified advisor is assigned a certain number of students. It then becomes the responsibility of the advisor to be an advocate for each student and learn as much as possible about each student to assure every chance for success is realized. The actual advocacy may vary from campus to campus and from individual to individual, depending upon relationships that have been established.

The support provided as a part of the MAP is supplementary to the normal advising activities and support structures that exist on a college campus. While some might see this as a duplication of service, in its purest sense, it is seen as a safety net to assure that minority students will have every opportunity to be successful academically, socially, and emotionally, given the realities of life on a majority campus.

Also, in an attempt to assure accountability, the University System of Georgia requires each institution to submit an annual report detailing personnel involved; related activities, evaluation, and evidence of how the evaluation has been used; budget information; proposed budget for the upcoming year; and any expected changes. This report also allows for descriptions of the most successful and most challenging areas.

Funding for MAP

At the inception of the program, each institution was expected to provide funding for the administration and programmatic activities. Of course, there was (and continue to be) unequalled levels of funding earmarked for the program on respective campuses. As a result, program quality from institution to institution varied. In an attempt to address this, in 1990 the Central Office provided supplemental funds for the program to each campus (the institution is still the primary funding source). Each institution is given a base amount of supplemental funds with incremental funding based on minority enrollment. Even though the amount is nominal, it assures a minimum level of programming across the system and provides an avenue for increased accountability.

Also, the Central Office began to provide funds to supplement the Annual Minority Advising Program Conference in 1990. The supplementary funding for the annual conference assured that a blend of local, regional, and national presenters could be attracted to the conference. The pre-conference and post-conference newsletter is entitled "Just to Let You Know." The newsletter is a vehicle to keep the MAP Coordinators informed as to pre-conference planning as well as post-conference critiques and recommendations. The newsletter also serves as a vehicle to share information concerning programs at the various institutions and to provide commentary on popular topics impacting the program from a programmatic or implementation standpoint.

Characteristics of a Successful Program

Within the thirty-four University System of Georgia institutions, one can easily discern there is uneven implementation of the system-wide Minority Advising Program. What makes a program successful on one campus while other campuses are struggling or even failing? What can be done to bring sub par programs up to system expectations?

The very successful MAPs all have the following ten characteristics:

- *Their President is supportive of the program and its activities through both words and action.* The president is the CEO of the institution. If the president gives open support for the program, attends functions sponsored by the program when possible, and provides institutional funding for its activities, this sends a message to the entire campus that the program is an important part of the campus and serves a vital function for the college or the university. Empty words will not evoke the participation of the larger campus. The president must create the tone for an environment that is inclusive and encompassing, providing both rewards and sanctions to assure that every student is valued.

- *They receive support from high-ranking administrators (example: vice president of academic affairs, dean of students, chief financial officer, deans and department chairs).* The extent to which these senior level administrators support the program creates a cause-and-effect relationship with the rest of the campus. These significant administrators also have budgetary, personnel and facility control, all of which are necessary for a successful program. Employees who report to these senior administrators also take their cues from them.

- *They receive proper funding with a designated budget.* While many positive things can be done without funds, the fact of the matter is that any successful program needs adequate funding. In addition, those individuals responsible for the program should have budgetary oversight and control within stated guidelines of the institutional policy. Having access to funds which are a part of another person's or unit's operational budget becomes problematic. In most cases, the area or unit housing the budget will take care of its own operational needs first, and then secondarily look to support appendage activities. Therefore, it is important the program has its own budget to assure proper planning, programming, and accountability.

- *They take a holistic approach to programming that gives equal attention to the well-being of the student academically, socially, emotionally, and culturally.* The literature is replete with information suggesting there are many variables that impact a student's decision to leave or stay at a given institution. Therefore, a program designed to only look at one variable is doomed for failure from the outset. When the total needs of the students are known and attended to, more than likely the student will be retained. Therefore, the institution should be realistic not only about its academic offerings and academic support, but also equally as realistic about the social and cultural environment that exists and the impact that each has on the emotional, physical, and mental stability of its students, particularly its minority students.

- *Their program is marketed as an asset rather than a deficit.* The program must be given the most positive spin possible to be effective. If students see this as a "dumping ground" for minority students, they will shy away from the program. This is exasperated by the fact that some minority students do not want to be "singled out" for "special treatment." If the program is marketed and functions as a positive support service for minority students, both the students and the campus will benefit. That is why the holistic approach is very important. The program cannot be seen as only a program for students with academic deficiencies, even though addressing this need would be one component of the program. Bright minority students who are in good academic standing are also at risk of not being retained at majority campuses. Therefore, these students have to see the program as meaningful and also being able to address their special concerns. Every aspect of the program should be seen as an asset to the campus, the student, and the overall campus community. Anything less puts a significant drain on the image of the program and influences students' willingness to participate and faculty and administrators willingness to support the program. Having concerned and competent staff, who are able to interact on many fronts with the students and the campus community, also enables the program to be viewed as an asset.

• *Their minority and majority faculty support the program and its activities.* Very often on majority campuses, minority faculty members are stretched to the limit. Not only are they expected to conduct the routine activities of any faculty member, but they are expected to serve on many more committees, attend to minority students, and build bridges in the minority community, often without any reward or compensation. While the minority faculty are key components of the program, the majority faculty have a role also. Majority faculty not only serve as advisors, but in some cases they also serve as mentors. They sometimes "open doors" to which some minority faculty do not even have access.

• *They have a savvy coordinator who is dedicated to the program, linked to the campus community, and has the respect of his/her peers.* The administrator who heads the program must be able to articulate, in very clear terms, the essence of the program. He or she must be able to "cross campus lines" to gain support for the program and its activities. If the coordinator has the respect of his or her peers that translates into positive support for the program and its activities. This person not only should know and understand the politics of the campus, but also should be able, within that political environment, to project a positive image and increase support for the program.

• *They have students who are able to see the benefit and take advantage of the program.* The very successful programs are those in which the students themselves see the benefits of the program and take full advantage of the supplementary assistance. Often times, minority students use the program as an incubator and a springboard into mainstream campus activities. Students also have the ability to attract other students to the program.

• *They conduct evaluations that generate feedback used to enhance the program.* Successful programs have continuous evaluations. These evaluations include program activities, personnel, and overall impact on retention. Data gained from the evaluation process are used to enhance programmatic activities and program operation. Through the evaluative process, administrators are able to determine what is most or least effective in addressing the needs of the students. The students must know their input and suggestions are not only heard, but are included in the overall planning process associated with the program.

• *They have successfully institutionalized the program.* The MAP should be an integral part of the campus activities. It should have a life of its own.

Often, with programs of this type, the responsibility for its maintenance and existence rests in the hands of one person or group. If this one person or group leaves the campus for whatever reason, or ceases working with the program, continuation of the program becomes problematic. Therefore, it is important the program is not seen as an appendage, but rather as central to the operations of a given campus.

In determining the characteristics of those programs that are not successful, one only has to look for the converse of the characteristics previously listed. Once an institution is identified as not meeting system expectations, that institution must submit a detailed plan as to how the deficiencies will be remedied. The institution is provided technical support from the Central Office as well as other institutions identified as having successful programs. Depending upon the openness of the campus, this process is very useful and the majority of cases have resulted in programs being impacted in a positive way. Presently only about five of the thirty-four university system institutions are not up to full system expectations. Each of these five will be targeted for more specialized assistance and appropriate follow-up in the effort to have system-wide compliance.

Minority Advising Program Annual Conference

An integral part of the overall program is the annual conference. The conference is offered as a staff development conference and is mandated as a part of the program guidelines. It has grown over the years from an informational workshop to a professional conference that easily matches other state, regional, and national conferences in content and presenters.

At the outset, the annual Minority Advising Program Conference targeted program coordinators and advisors. In the early years, the conference lacked focus; however, this is not the situation today. Over the years, the conference has grown in scope and purpose, with the targeted audience now including faculty, staff, administrators, and students, as well. Since the retention of African-American students should be an institutional concern, representatives from all sectors of the campus should be present at the conference to learn and interact with colleagues. Sessions are developed that provide valuable information and insight to each of the groups. Pre-conference activities include: orientation sessions for new MAP coordinators and advisors, development and career workshops for students, and special training for system employees that will enhance their ability to interact with minority faculty and students.

The MAP Conference is also a forum to share program information, get new ideas, receive university system updates, and offer an opportunity to interact with regionally- and nationally-known speakers, authors, and presenters. The conference is coordinated by a statewide planning committee consisting of representatives from each institutional type (universities, four-year colleges, two-year colleges). In most recent years, the chair of the statewide planning committee has been the institutional representative from the campus hosting the annual conference. In the early years of the annual conference, it was difficult to get system institutions to host the conference. Primarily the annual conference was not seen as something that would "put a feather in their cap." However, as the conference grows in content and image, institutions routinely volunteer to host the conference, sometimes two years in advance.

The conference is managed in a very cost-effective manner, receiving its funding from the University System of Georgia's operating budget and additional support from a modest registration fee. Funding from the university system's operating budget assures a minimum level of programming at each conference. The assessment of a registration fee assures these programming efforts can be enhanced to assure high quality and the inclusion of regional and national presenters. However, it must be noted the majority of the presenters and professionals at the conference are university system employees. The chart presents a historical account of the annual conference:

Themes From Previous MAP Conferences

DATE	LOCATION	THEME
October 10, 1983	Athens, GA	Workshop on program concept
October 4, 1984	Macon, GA	Workshop on program structure
April 24-25, 1986	Atlanta, GA	"Reaffirming the Commitment"
April 30 - May 1, 1987	Atlanta, GA	"Total Institutional Involvement"
April 18-19, 1988	Savannah, GA	"Making a Difference: Early Intervention and the Successful Strategies in Recruitment and Retention of Minority Students"
March 2-3, 1989	Gainesville, GA	"Realistic Approaches to Recruitment and Retention: Linking the Community, Public Schools and the University System of Georgia"
March 1-2, 1990	Augusta, GA	"Achieving Diversity in the University System of Georgia: The Role of the Minority Advising Program and Minority Recruitment Officers"
February 28 - March 1, 1991	Albany, GA	"Minority Recruitment and Retention in the University System of Georgia: The Current State and Future Implications"
May 8, 1992	Milledgeville, GA	"Empowerment Through Pluralism: Strategies for Institutional Success"
May 6-7, 1993	Macon, GA	"Effective Recruitment and Retention: Restructuring the Dialogue"
April 14-15, 1994	Tifton, GA	"Empowerment Through Human Resource Coalition Building: From Dialogue to Implementation"
April 20-21, 1995	Valdosta, GA	"Creating a Positive Campus Climate: An Environment for Living and Learning"

326

There has been a methodical approach to the annual conference with each one building on the previous year's conference. The two initial conferences, after the workshops on the concept and structure of the program, were held in Atlanta, GA. This was by design, given the System's Central Office is located in Atlanta and the need to oversee the conferences to assure compliance with the expectations of the Central Office. The intent was to incubate and cultivate the conference until it had a wider acceptance within the University System of Georgia. When the acceptance was achieved, institutions were then identified to host the conference and to put their own signature on conference events.

Successful Models

No institution has a perfect retention rate of majority or minority students, so addressing retention issues is an enterprise in which all colleges and universities should be involved. Some institutions have spent a lot of time and resources trying to retain students. At some institutions, special efforts are made to retain minority students because of the realization of the special challenges they face. In fact, for the academic year 1995-96, it is reported the entire University System of Georgia will give renewed attention to the issue of retention. Yet, as plans are being made for this new system-wide initiative, there are several institutions that stand out among their peers as related to minority student retention.

Certainly one treads on dangerous territory when singling out a particular program among others as being a model, yet, neither space nor time will permit an indepth discussion on all of the worthy programs within the University System of Georgia. A few have been singled out because of the noticeable impact they have had on retention and quality of life for minority students on their respective campuses. Each of the campuses have a certain uniqueness in terms of its mission, location, and composition of its student body. Yet, the commonality among these institutions, for the most part, is that each has embodied in their approach to the Minority Advising Program, the ten characteristics identified as being essential to success.

The following institutions are highlighted in this section: Georgia Institute of Technology (Georgia Tech), Georgia Southern University, Valdosta State University, and Abraham Baldwin Agricultural College.

Georgia Tech—Georgia Tech has spent considerable time, energy, and resources in an effort to retain minority students. The Georgia Tech retention programs have been written about in national publications, such as the Wall Street Journal and Black Issues in Higher Education. Some might argue that Georgia Tech's high retention rates are due to the institution routinely recruiting bright students, including bright minority students. Yet, the fact of the matter is that even bright students are at risk of not being retained if special sensitivity and special efforts are not present.

At Georgia Tech, these efforts are a central mission of the institution and are seen as important by the president, other high ranking administrators, and faculty and staff. These efforts are coordinated out of the Office of Minority Education Development. The director of this unit is also special assistant to the president which also assures the program is given high visibility. Georgia Tech refers to its program as the Student Assistant Volunteer Program. The Office of Minority Education, referred on Georgia Tech's campus as OMED, has a comprehensive approach to its retention efforts, which include partnerships with local high schools, student organizations, community organizations, and educational consortiums to address the transition issues of high school students to Georgia Tech. Georgia Tech pays equal attention to the concerns of its dual degree students who transfer in from historically black institutions, as they, too, are dropout risks.

Georgia Tech has committed the financial support to the program and has identified a very competent staff to oversee and implement the various programs which are a part of OMED. Some of the outstanding programs Georgia Tech has as a part of its retention efforts are: Challenge program, Continuous Monitoring program, orientation, leadership retreats, Academic Enhancement program, team coaches and management letters.

It must be noted, as with other MAPs within the University System of Georgia, participation at Georgia Tech is voluntary. One of the ways in which Tech attracts its students is through information dissemination to parents and families of the students. Parents are provided information on all the services that OMED offers, assuring a cause-and-effect relationship to success at Georgia Tech. Parents, as a result, become recruiters of their own children. In addition, Georgia Tech directly contacts the students through letters, phone calls, and announcements at various events on campus.

Below is a brief description of programs offered through the Georgia Tech Office of Minority Education Development:[6]

Challenge: This is a six-week, non-credit summer program designed to help minority students adapt to the institution. Students take courses in math, English, and chemistry to prepare them for the rigors of the Georgia Tech curriculum. Students participate in counseling sessions to develop and enhance their leadership skills, interpersonal skills, study skills, and coping skills. Also, they participate in social and cultural programs and are given the opportunity to tour the city of Atlanta.

Team Coaches: All minority freshmen entering Georgia Tech are contacted by students who have been at Tech for one or two years. These students are referred to as Team Coaches. A letter is sent explaining the different activities and programs sponsored by OMED. Freshmen are actively pursued in an effort to get them to attend fall orientation and programs that will acclimate them to the Tech campus. Team coaches are also in correspondence with the students' parents to convince them to persuade their children to participate in OMED programs.

Orientation: Orientation is held at the beginning of every quarter. It is designed to meet the specific needs of minority students; within orientation, students may be grouped according to their special needs and a specialized program is offered to them. The orientation is publicized through a mass media campaign, and upper classmen and team coaches are used to entice the students to participate. A well-organized telemarketing plan is used to advertise and recruit student participation into the orientation program.

Leadership Retreat: This retreat targets freshmen and is held in the spring of each year. An off-campus site is used for the retreat. Students who have shown leadership potential are identified to participate. The retreat is staffed by personnel from OMED and minority alumni. The students participate in seminars on effective leadership strategies, how to become a campus leader, stress reduction, organizational skills, study skills, and time management. The retreat allows students an opportunity to meet and interact with alumni in both formal and informal settings.

Continuous Monitoring Program: Students are given a broad exposure to the various programs offered through OMED. They are also given information on the importance of evaluation. Students are given a grade-release form and asked to sign it so the Office of Minority Education can effectively track their progress. Through the grade-release form, the Office of Minority Education Development can interact directly with professors to determine the progress students are making in each class. Team coaches follow up on the grade-release forms throughout the quarter and are able to intervene before it is too late. The information generated as a result of the continuous monitoring program allows the Office of Minority Education to more specifically focus its intervention activities.

Academic Enhancement: Essentially, this program provides tutorial assistance to those students who have been either identified through the continuous monitoring process or who self-select this assistance. All minority students are informed that this service is available. Team coaches and mentors are also responsible for making students aware of this service. Advertisement through telephone and posters in dormitories are other examples of how the tutorial assistance program is advertised.

Management Letters: As with the student grade-release forms, the Office of Minority Education gets permission from students to communicate directly with their parents on academic issues. As a condition of participation in the Challenge program, students are required to sign a release form. Once the student signs the release form, he or she knows all of their academic progress information will be automatically sent to their family. The information is not only sent to families to give them an idea of how the students are doing, but also to solicit the assistance of the family in developing strategies that might make the next quarter more productive.

Georgia Tech has provided information which suggests those students who participate in the Challenge program are more than likely to have a higher grade-point average than minority students who have not participated in the program (Example: the data collected as a part of the 1993 Challenge Program suggest that participants for fall, winter, and spring quarters had grade-point averages of 3.0, 2.6, and 2.7, respectively, while the cohort of non-participants for the same period had grade-point averages of 2.7, 2.4, and 2.5, respectively). This information is widely published and helps students to understand participation in the Challenge program is a vital way to increase their academic success at Georgia Tech. Feedback is also used to continuously improve various aspects of the program. This comprehensive approach has yielded positive results. Georgia Tech's five-year retention rates for first-time, full-time minority students enrolled in 1989, admitted through developmental studies or as regularly admitted freshmen, are higher than the system rate and are also higher than the cohort of universities within the system.

Table 1
Multiple Retention Rates of Black Students—five years
First-Time Full-Time Entering Students
Enrolled Fall of 1989

	First Year	Second Year	Third Year	Fourth Year	Fifth Year
Georgia Tech	89.4	76.1	67.3	60.2	47.8
University Cohorts	78.5	62.8	54.0	49.4	43.0
System	63.5	44.5	36.8	33.6	29.8

DATA SOURCE: University System of Georgia Student Information Reporting System.

Georgia Southern University and Valdosta State University: Both Georgia Southern University and Valdosta State University have the distinction of being the only regional universities in the University System of Georgia at the time of this writing. Special designation was given to these institutions in 1990 and 1993, respectively, in an effort to address special education needs of the state of Georgia, and its southern region and southeastern region in particular. Prior to this designation, all of the system universities were located in the northern part of the state.

Having regional university distinction is not the only thing that Georgia Southern and Valdosta State have in common—both have fully implemented the MAP and both have retention rates of black students significantly higher than the system's average. Still another shared distinction is that both Georgia Southern and Valdosta State retain their black students at about the same rate that white students and other students are retained at their respective institutions. This is illustrated below, using 1989 cohort data:

Table 2
Multiple Retention Rates of Black Students—five years
First-Time Full-Time Entering Students
Enrolled Fall of 1989

	First Year	Second Year	Third Year	Fourth Year	Fifth Year
Georgia Southern University					
Black students	73.8	54.8	48.8	45.8	41.3
All others	71.1	55.1	48.7	45.9	42.8
Valdosta State University					
Black students	65.4	51.7	41.0	41.9	36.8
All others	60.0	48.7	43.3	41.5	37.6
System					
Black students	63.5	44.5	36.8	33.6	29.8
All others	69.0	52.0	44.4	41.5	39.0

DATA SOURCE: University System of Georgia Student Information Reporting System .

At Georgia Southern University,[7] the Minority Advising Program is part of the Division of Student Affairs, and recently found its home in the Office of Special Programs, which is a part of that unit. The Georgia Southern University program is also comprehensive, beginning at freshmen orientation (actually it begins with a letter to all incoming minority students who are new to the institution) and including interaction with faculty and staff; academic intervention programs; tutorial programs; study skills workshops; career-planning workshops;

financial aid workshops; Honors Day receptions; rap sessions with students; and seminars on racism and diversity.

While different, the thing that Georgia Southern does have in common with Georgia Tech is it has committed resources for staff and personnel to assure the needs of minority students are met in a systematic, comprehensive manner.

Valdosta State University has one of the more comprehensive approaches to minority student retention in the University System of Georgia.[8] Again, like Georgia Tech and Georgia Southern the institution has committed resources to assure the program is properly staffed and funded. The MAP at Valdosta State is housed in the Office of Minority Affairs and is called the Minority Achievement Program. The overall director of the program is also the assistant to the president for affirmative action and minority affairs. This gives the program high visibility and clout at all levels. One of the hallmark features of the Valdosta State program is the high degree of involvement and support by the institution's president. In addition to the director, a staff consisting of an assistant director, full-time coordinator, full-time counselors, and peer advisors are in place. Valdosta State University has over twenty-five faculty and staff who are serving as mentors to minority students and an equal number of students serving as peer counselors. In addition, there has been a cadre of other faculty and staff who routinely assist with the program.

The following are programs which are a part of the Minority Achievement Program at Valdosta State College: letter of welcome; summer orientation; fall orientation; general session with mentors/advisees/advisors; tutorial program; peer counseling program; Success Strategy Seminar; Financial Aid Seminar; lecture series bringing in significant African-American role models and professionals; personal contact between peer counselors and students; and peer mentoring.

According to data provided by Valdosta State, minority students participating in the Minority Achievement Program had a mean GPA of 2.49 for the academic year of 1993-94 compared to a mean GPA of 2.12 of minority students not participating in the program.

Abraham Baldwin Agricultural College: One thing that is consistent in the retention literature is the low- rate of retention of African-American students at two-year institutions. This is evident in the University System of Georgia, even though the rate of retention of minority students at the university system's two-year institutions is above the national average. One of the two-year colleges within the system, Abraham

Baldwin Agricultural College (ABAC), has given special attention to retention of minority students. For the last several years, a concerted comprehensive effort has been made and has yielded some dividends. While the retention rates for black students at ABAC are below the over-all system rates, they are above the system's two-year college cohort rate. The table below provides information supporting this contention:

Table 3
Multiple Retention Rates of Black Students—five years
First Time Full-Time Entering Students
Enrolled Fall of 1989

	First Year	Second Year	Third Year	Fourth Year	Fifth Year
Abraham Baldwin Agricultural College	54.0	33.3	19.0	15.9	14.3
Two-Year College Cohorts University System of Georgia	50.2	25.4	17.6	12.1	10.8

DATA SOURCE: University System of Georgia Student Information Reporting System.

While ABAC is above its system two-year college peers, the college has not been satisfied with the overall results. In this regard, a comprehensive approach has been developed to address the problem of retention of minority students. Part of this strategy has been to fully implement the MAP. The program is housed in the Office of Minority Student Programs, and interfaces with the entire campus through the Cultural Awareness Coordinating Council.[9] The hallmark of the MAP at Abraham Baldwin Agricultural College is similar to that of Valdosta State in that the president of the institution is highly involved and supportive of the program. As a result, the institution has committed considerable resources and personnel to assure the success of the program. Activities that are sponsored include: an orientation session for new students, session for peer advisors, receptions for new students, a newsletter, and a lecture series bringing in significant role models who bring a cultural perspective that is beneficial to minority students. Another hallmark is the significant involvement of the vice president for academic affairs. This high level administrative support sends a signal to the rest of the campus that this activity is important and is an integral part of the campus environment. Tutorial assistance, career planning and financial aid workshops, and peer counseling are all significant parts of the program.

Each of the programs mentioned above have fully implemented the Minority Advising Programs on their campus. Their respective retention rates suggest they are doing something right. The key to their success, however, is a dedicated staff whose director has campus-wide clout and access to higher levels of administration, including the president; adequate budget; and marketing their program from an asset model, rather than a deficit model.

Summary

The University System of Georgia developed a system-wide approach to retaining African-American students under the auspices of the Minority Advising Program. Even though at the institutional level there has been uneven implementation, for the most part the program has had a profound impact on the lives of minority students. Those institutions that have fully implemented the program have seen positive results. The system has attempted to identify those institutions not in compliance in an effort to help them develop viable programs. The problem has been, from the system's perspective, not enough staff to monitor the programs at the thirty-four institutions within the system.

One thing that is clearly evident, however, is that minority students on majority campuses are retained in greater numbers when special efforts and sensitivities are present in a comprehensive manner. Those programs that are successful develop a comprehensive program that is central to the institution's operation and mission, and receive adequate resources, both human and fiscal. Personnel associated with the programs constantly evaluate what is being done in an effort to enhance the programmatic activities and the approaches to delivering services.

In no way does the system-wide approach eliminate the need for institutions to develop their own initiatives. However, the MAP in the University System of Georgia assures each institution has a minimum level of programs and services geared toward the retention of minority students. As mentioned previously, the University System of Georgia will dedicate a significant portion of its resources and energies beginning in the 1995-96 academic year to the overall issue of retention. It is anticipated the MAP will continue to be a central component of the retention efforts; however, those institutions with consistently low retention rates of students, both majority and minority, will be given additional attention in an effort to assure the success of all students within the University System of Georgia.

—Dr. Joseph H. Silver, Sr., is the Assistant Vice Chancellor for Academic Affairs for the Georgia Board of Regents, in Atlanta, Georgia.

Notes

1. The Office of Civil Rights defined "minorities" as African-Americans for the purpose of desegregation in Georgia.

2. Upon being released from reporting to the Office of Civil Rights, the University System of Georgia conducted a study of its desegregation progress. The resulting recommendations were compiled in the document, University System of Georgia Steering Committee for Increased Minority Participation in Public Higher Education.

3. "Just To Let You Know." Fall, 1994 (an internal publication of the University System of Georgia which reports specifically on matters relating to the Minority Advising Program and its annual conference).

4. 1983 Addendum to the 1979 University System of Georgia Desegregation Plan.

5. University System of Georgia Steering Committee for Increased Minority Participation in Public Higher Education, 1988.

6. Georgia Institute of Technology Annual Minority Advising Program Reports 1990-1993.

7. Georgia Southern University Annual Minority Advising Program Reports 1990-1993.

8. Valdosta State University Annual Minority Advising Program Reports 1990-1993.

9. Abraham Baldwin Agricultural College Annual Minority Advising Program Reports 1990-1993.

Assessment and Evaluation for Student Retention Program Success

by Hazel Symonette

Overview:

Program development and evaluation processes are intimately intertwined. After implementation, effective program development requires monitoring and assessment to ensure goal attainment and program refinement. Effective program assessment and evaluation is an iterative, critically-reflective process that aims for continuous and cumulative improvement. Savvy program administrators and staff seize the initiative in crafting their vision and in "telling their story." They recognize and embrace the political as well as the technical dynamics of assessment and evaluation efforts. They transform the process into one with important a) *intrinsic benefits* for the program and the students it seeks to serve and b) *extrinsic benefits* when trying to deal with, satisfy and/or nullify external constituencies (whether in a defensive or offensive mode).

Savvy program administrators and staff integrate the assessment/ evaluation process into the natural rhythms of their program work so that it supports the *who, what, when, where, how and how much* issues associated with staff job duties in addition to the more macro-level program development and management issues. These program administrators and staff proactively prepare "their case" for program importance and effectiveness through critical reflection, collaborative brainstorming and the compilation of credible and meaningful evidence regarding program-relevant outcomes and improvement initiatives. Through it all, they keep students and their needs at the center of their agenda.

This article speaks in active "how-to" language. It strives to energize proactive claims on assessment and evaluation tools as crucial program resources. It presents six crucial skills that savvy program administrators and staff should develop. Although important at all times, such skills are an especially crucial program survival and development resource in times of political retrenchment and fiscal austerity.

Introduction

What qualifies a program to appear in a book on successful programs for recruiting and graduating students of color from postsecondary educational institutions? This volume, *Student Retention Success Models in Higher Education,* spotlights programs for increasing the postsecondary education presence and participation of students of color. How is it determined if a program is a success? What evidence convinces administrators and staff, as well as others, that the program intervention activities attained the intended results?

This article differs from others in this volume in that it focuses on a resource for program design and development efforts, rather than on a specific student retention program. That critical resource is program assessment and evaluation. Assessment refers to the systematic gathering and analysis of data from a variety of sources to guide instruction, advising, policy development and/or the allocation of resources for developing and improving individuals, groups, programs or processes. In its Latin origins, assessment refers to a constructively collaborative process: to sit down by or beside (as an assistant judge). Evaluation, although sometimes used interchangeably, focuses more directly on assessment in relation to stated or implied intentions like goals and objectives, in particular, the congruence between program design, implementation and outcome. Clearly, assessment and evaluation tools and techniques can provide answers to the program success questions cited earlier.

Program assessment and evaluation questions can be addressed at multiple levels of analysis. They may be framed for individual students, for various aggregates of students (e.g., by race/ethnicity and/or by gender) or for the program as a whole versus the total eligible population or the institution. Levels of success may vary across these different levels of analysis. To minimize confusion and errors of judgment, programs need to identify the specific focus and framework for their evaluative analyses, especially when and where there are shifts in levels.

All student retention programs need to set goals and objectives that are measurable, attainable, and yet ambitious, given the available resources and the retention-relevant characteristics of their target student populations. Effectively completing this task requires systematic review of past, present and future projected trends for relevant factors and characteristics, e.g., targeted student behaviors and activities. No other task is more pivotal. In delineating goals and objectives, programs are identifying the progress and performance benchmarks against which they will judge themselves and against which they implicitly ask others to judge them. In essence, programs are envisioning what success should look like as a result of their intervention activities. Without a doubt, the most crucial aspect of this envisioning involves specifying the appropriate student status baselines. They provide the frame of reference used to judge progress, especially in terms of "value added" contributions by the program. The fundamental importance of this task prevails whether the assessment model focuses on retention before versus intervention after the program, or on variations in retention associated with different patterns of program participation (levels and/or types).

Who Needs Assessment and Evaluation Skills?

Everyone needs them. In fact, everyone already uses at least a crude and informal variant of assessment skills when making decisions, especially those involving options or competing alternatives. The need for more systematic use of these skills is ever expanding. Assessment and evaluation mandates are everywhere. Rising throughout higher education, like other institutional sectors, is an increasing clamor for assessment, accountability and efficiency. All regional accreditation associations now require assessment.

Even if a program refuses to fully engage in the assessment process—it will occur anyway. It will be done by, at best, a partially informed outsider. For example, if inappropriate progress benchmarks or comparison baselines are used, questions may be raised and misjudgments made declaring the program is not working. At that point, it is often too late for a program to effectively intervene and challenge that conclusion. The program's mission is then reduced to basic damage control and disaster relief. Programs can do more. Programs can do better. Programs cannot afford to wait, somehow hoping assessment mandates will fade away. They will not.

Too often, usually by default, assessment/evaluation tools have been in the wrong hands and used against programs rather than for their improvement. Consequently, many a program has suffered an unnecessarily premature demise or cutback in resources. Student-centered diagnostic evaluation strategies provide a resource for empowered program improvement and strategic image management. Framing the evaluation initiative as a program resource that facilitates students' success makes it difficult to refuse participation and still maintain the persona of committed student development professional. These tools allow staff to identify practices that contribute to "revolving-door" attrition problems. In addition, these tools often help programs to push ahead in spite of external challenges and efforts to dismantle, or to at least, hold the line even when not able to fully advance their agenda.

A high profile case strongly affirms and reinforces these perspectives: the 1995 U.S. Congressional challenges versus the ultimate triumph of federal TRIO programs. TRIO programs and the National Council of Equal Opportunity Programs emerged from zeroed-out budgets to fully-restored budgets. Their exemplary models and strategies offer many important lessons. Politically savvy assessment and fast-mobilizing organization served them well in that battle for budget reinstatement.

Of course, there are no airtight guarantees. Making a solid case for program importance and effectiveness does not necessarily ensure that case will be fairly received, especially given the political context of many assessment/evaluation efforts. Regardless of the outcome, however, taking the initiative pays potent empowerment dividends that strengthen the program for the next "go-round." No comparable benefits accrue from just hoping and passively relying on others' social justice consciousness, benevolent indulgence or the "luck of the draw."

Developing these skills is worth the sacrifice of time and effort. That has been my experience in cultivating the will and the skills to engage in assessment and evaluation in the University of Wisconsin System. Accentuating intrinsic student benefits and program development and management benefits fuels the will to learn and engage in the assessment/evaluation process. Understandably, most program staff persons are necessarily hired for their "people skills" not their research and data analysis skills. The process is made less intimidating and more accessible by stressing an iterative, continuous improvement orientation. Given available resources, each program should map out its own developmental trajectory for assessment skill development and cumulative program improvement.

I developed this assessment/evaluation model for the University of Wisconsin System Office of Multicultural Affairs for our work with campus program administrators and staff who operate precollege, recruitment and retention programs that target African-American, American Indian, Asian American and Latino/Hispanic students and economically disadvantaged students. The model supports the systemwide Design for Diversity agenda for our 27 institutions: a comprehensive 10-year strategic plan for increasing the presence and participation of students, faculty and staff of color and economically disadvantaged students and for creating more multiculturally diverse and responsive educational environments.

The University of Wisconsin System now has a much more student-centered program evaluation process that is increasingly grounded in conditions supporting effective service delivery. Program evaluation is no longer strictly viewed as an externally-driven compliance activity with few intrinsic benefits for campus program administrators/staff and the students they serve. Using this model, we have made great progress in cultivating the belief that assessment and evaluation are worth the time and effort. Much work remains, however, to build the solid infrastructure of skills necessary for effective program evaluations. Program assessment/evaluation is becoming a self-diagnostic resource for continuous program improvement: a critically reflective, interactive and iterative process.

What Is Savvy Assessment and Evaluation?

Savvy program administrators and staff embrace the spirit of preparedness and proactively seize the initiative in crafting their vision and in "telling their story." To maximize accuracy, they ensure that persons at the point of service delivery and data collection have a vested interest in the value and validity of program data. More specifically, they integrate the assessment/evaluation process into the natural rhythms of their program work. Data collection and analysis efforts support the who, what, when, where, how and how much issues associated with staff job duties as well as the more macro-level program development and management issues.

Facility with assessment/evaluation tools and strategies is important at all times because program development and evaluation processes are intimately intertwined. After initial implementation, effective program development requires continuous monitoring and assessment to ensure goal attainment and continuous improvement. Savvy assessment skills are important in good times as well as bad times; they are especially crucial in times of political retrenchment and fiscal austerity.

Student recruitment, development and support program staff often articulate a desire to monitor, evaluate and improve the effectiveness of their programs. They seek to maximize the educational and career benefits for students. This article targets program administrators and staff who want to systematically use assessment and evaluation tools/strategies as a proactive student-centered diagnostic resource for critical reflection, empowered self-improvement and strategic image management.

Critical Reflection
Programs systematically examine the congruence between their missions/intentions and program intervention processes (implementation activities) and their congruence with desired program outcomes.

• Who was served by the program versus who was targeted for services (eligible)?

Types of students and their retention-relevant characteristics

• How were they served and for what purpose?

Program intervention components

Pattern and intensity of exposure to components

• What difference did the program intervention make with regard to desired educational outcomes?

Empowered Self-Improvement
Self-study evaluations give each program an opportunity to use the insights derived from critical reflection for continuous program improvement. Most importantly, this process offers the program an opportunity to speak for itself—articulating its vision and interpretation of the "appropriate" facts. To extract critically instructive insights, programs should contrast the model of program success that they initially envisioned and the level of success that they actually attained. They should honestly ask and

answer the question: "What lessons can be learned that will improve intervention efforts in the next program year cycle?"

Evaluative analyses may also reveal a lack of sufficient program resources to fully serve the needs of the eligible student population. For example, the numbers of tutors/counselors or tutorial/counseling sessions available may be inadequate to meet demand, or large numbers of applicants for a campus support or precollege program may have been refused. Both cases spotlight "unmet need," evidence that may substantively undergird proposals for additional resources. This is only one of a variety of situations where assessment data—properly collected, analyzed and packaged—are a valuable resource for program administrators and staff seeking to maximize the scope and effectiveness of student services delivery.

Strategic Image Management

Quality program evaluations are worth the sacrifice of time and effort for many reasons but especially because poorly crafted evaluations are typically presumed to represent poor/ineffective programs, just as poorly crafted personal work resumes are presumed to represent poor job candidates. Strategic image management is not a case for a public relations propaganda document. That would simply strain credibility. Rather, it is a case for critically reflective, evidence-based analyses of program strengths and weaknesses. It offers an opportunity for the program to communicate its data-grounded understandings of how and why desired educational outcomes do, or do not, occur for actual program participants. If attainment falls short of expectations, the program maps out an improvement initiatives agenda. Strategic image management involves packaging and sending the right message to primary stakeholders. These are the persons and organizations who are influenced by or who can influence a program's destiny. Crafting the right message involves juxtaposing both program participant needs versus available resources and relevant comparison baselines versus actual outcomes (vis-a-vis program interventions).

Student-centered assessment and evaluation strategies

The primary driving force should be student learning and progress toward degree attainment, life skills and career development. These tools and techniques should help maximize educational and career benefits for students. Maintaining this anchor-perspective is critical even though sociopolitical and fiscal realities dictate attention to other issues, such as external accountability and regulatory compliance. Without this perspective, programs may lose sight of the effectively-serving-students' priority. Such risks greatly increase when programs are bombarded by and try to accommodate multiple cross-cutting mandates and multiple stakeholders.

Seizing the initiative—baselines and benchmarks

Every program should claim the assessment mandate by "telling its story" while situating its programmatic agenda in the larger institutional agenda.

Through strategic image management—a political as well as a technical process, the program seizes the initiative by identifying and analyzing program intentions, intervention activities and program-relevant patterns of student outcomes. Program data are placed in the proper interpretive context.

Savvy program administrators and staff use assessment tools to proactively specify appropriate progress benchmarks for judging the program themselves and by which others should judge it. Taking off the conventional-indicators strait jacket, they periodically brainstorm regarding appropriate educational outcome indicators and then specify which measures are congruent with their actual intervention activities. They move beyond or at least complement the conventional easy-to-measure outcome indicators with measures that more fully and accurately capture desired changes in students' attitudes, awareness, knowledge, behavior, etc. Savvy program administrators and staff know that they need both quantitative and qualitative indicators to fully represent student transformations. Quantitative indicators provide the skeletal facts (broad scope but usually shallow depth) while the qualitative indicators flesh out that skeleton with often complex substantive content related to process, meaning and understanding (narrow scope with deep intensity).

Few tasks are more important than forthrightly addressing issues regarding appropriate progress benchmarks and comparison baselines. They provide the critical judgment and interpretive framework. Timing is most crucial. These efforts should long precede the questions raised by partially-informed "outsiders" who pass judgment—often incorrectly proclaiming a program ineffective. For example, a seemingly low student retention rate does not necessarily and automatically index program failure. That interpretation depends upon the comparison baseline, namely, the counterfactual: What would have occurred in the absence of the program? Apparent negative evidence simply begs for clarification and an explanation of why, for example, a large proportion of students dropped out despite the presence of support programs. With the appropriate frame of reference or comparison benchmark, one would be able to ascertain whether, in the absence of the program, retention rates would have been even lower.

Related to the above are issues of crude measurement indicators for student retention. In spite of the most diligent program support and retention efforts, some students will drop out or stop out. For some, there may be unresolved challenges and problems, either temporary or permanent, that are beyond the reach and resources of campus academic and nonacademic support programs. To the extent possible, program data and documentation (student baseline and monitoring information) should identify such cases as distinct from those cases where, for example, program services may not have been received by an eligible student in sufficient quantity or in a timely fashion.

For example, fall-to-fall cohort retention rates would represent only the crude beginning of a student retention program evaluation. Its complement, the cohort attrition rate, would ideally be disaggregated and "discounted" to take account of the above issues and other non-program related reasons for leaving. Only with that level of specificity can such rates serve as a useful diagnostic outcomes indicator that facilitates retention program improvement.

Self-diagnostic resource

Program staff and administrators need to be the first to know their assessment and program development blind spots and vulnerabilities, whatever the reasons. Again, those insights should long predate "outsider exposes" that may focus and capitalize on problems and weaknesses. They can, then, more self-consciously and strategically make decisions regarding improvement initiatives, future priorities and tradeoffs. Program staff, not outsiders, should be the first to use such critically reflective analyses to craft an explicit improvement initiatives agenda, especially if program outcomes fall short of program expectations/intentions.

Program administrators and staff should also constantly monitor the extent to which their services are perceived as important, if not indispensable, resources by their clients and other stakeholders. This involves not only effective service delivery but also effective public relations regarding the program's specific role and functions—notably, what it can and cannot deliver. The program's public relations agenda needs to speak to the fact that some program benefits may be transparent and taken for granted and thus potentially devalued. In general, the conceptual and operational bridge must reflect a solid articulation between the target population's needs and agenda and the program's agenda.

What Are Key Program Survival Skills?

Savvy program administrators and staff need to develop at least six crucial assessment-related skills. Although important at all times, such skills are an especially crucial to program survival and development in times of political retrenchment and fiscal austerity. Some of the research questions and the tasks associated with these skills may suggest a much more ambitious commitment than many programs may be willing and/or able to make starting out. Without a doubt, there are ongoing tensions associated with the often intense competing demands on limited resources for direct student services delivery versus conducting program evaluations (among other things). Moreover, program data often are unavailable to fully address these questions and, given budget constraints, may remain unavailable for a given program. However big or small the commitment, every program needs to start the process. As noted earlier, effective assessment/evaluation should be viewed as an iterative process that aims for a trajectory of continuous and cumulative program improvement.

Skill 1: Concretely Specify the Program Mission and Implementation Model.

Envisioning: program goals and objectives
What student needs are addressed and what are students expected to learn and to "look like" as a result of going through the program?

• Concretely specify what program success is expected to look like. Establish an iterative process for setting, reviewing and revising goals and objectives to ensure they are measurable and attainable, yet ambitious, given available resources vis-a-vis needs.

• Given the program expectations, and thus implicit (if not explicit) claims, what evidence would convince a reasonable person (among key stakeholders) those claims are accurate? (Choose program outcomes that primary stakeholders care about.)

• What are the appropriate outcome indicators that would best characterize the levels of progress toward program objectives, namely, those that best match the intervention activities?

Implementation Mechanism: Program Intervention Process
Through what organized actions and practices did the program seek to effect the expected changes?

• Program Logic. Are program activities, and the implicit causal model they represent, consistent with current realities and the actual causal model? More specifically, why are program activities expected to have the intended effects? More specifically, why should they result in desired individual or group changes in exposure, awareness, knowledge, interest, attitudes and /or behavior?

• Implementation Checks. What evidence is there to verify that your program has been fully implemented?

Target group effectiveness 1: To what extent has the program served the total population in need of its services (eligible population versus actual program participants)?

Target Group Effectiveness 2: How completely has the program served the students receiving its services (services requested/needed versus services received)?

The target group effectiveness criterion yields relative measures that spotlight "unmet need" in terms of eligible population participation and the intensity of participant exposure (amount and frequency) to a program's service components. They depend, of course, on how high program goals and objectives are set.

Clarifying the program's operational identity is crucial. Without some reasonably accurate and coherent definition of the implementation process, one does not know to what to attribute the observed outcomes or lack thereof. Such clarity is especially important when program outcomes differ across various types of participants. Ideally, program administrators/staff should compile measures that capture the type and quantity (frequency and amount) of program exposure as well as the qualitative dimension of exposure. More refined measures differentiate the programmatic features that do and do not work under various conditions. With the more refined measures, one can conduct more useful evaluations that move beyond "blanket endorsements" (it works) or "wholesale rejections" (it does not work).

Skill 2: Employ Appropriate Progress Benchmarks and Compile Compelling Evidence.

How is it determined if students have changed or are changing in the ways intended and expected? What tangible evidence exists that program goals and objectives—the desired state of affairs—have been attained?

Answering these questions focuses attention on the second key program effectiveness criterion, educational outcomes effectiveness. It complements the target group effectiveness criterion examined in the Skill 1 section. The Skill 2 effectiveness criterion spotlights the extent to which participation in the program's services resulted in the desired educational outcomes stated (or implied) as program goals and objectives. This could include, for example, improved academic performance, increased persistence to the completion of a course, a term and academic program and/or degree requirements (graduation). Effectively documenting program-relevant outcomes requires compelling evidence: the analysis and presentation of program data that are credible and meaningful given the expectations of the program's primary stakeholders. To be effective, program evidence should be accurate, representative, comprehensive, contextual, grounded and drawn from multiple sources and perspectives.

Mastering this most challenging skill (or more accurately, this cluster of skills) gets to the heart of core concepts undergirding effective program assessment/evaluation. Full mastery requires facility in addressing the questions and issues that follow:
- What evidence is there that the program model has been adequately tested?

- Are the progress benchmark indicators consistent with the program interventions—notably, the right things measured in the right ways?

- How well are student baseline characteristics, program activities, characteristics of exposure and program outcomes measured?

- What is missing? Are all relevant dimensions of the desired program outcomes represented in these measures? Can the student's voice be heard in assessment data? Is qualitative data used to flesh out and complement the skeleton of statistical facts?

What evidence is there that the program model works?

- Specify appropriate comparison baselines to identify what program-engineered changes occurred. This requires some variant of the following major program evaluation research designs:

   a) within-group design: before- versus after-the-intervention contrasts in knowledge, skills, attitudes or behaviors for program participants; or

   b) between-group design: cross-time contrasts among those exposed to program (or varied levels of exposure) versus those not exposed.

- Examine appropriateness of types/mix of services exposure.
- Examine adequacy of levels of exposure (minimum thresholds).

Use caution—the level of implementation for individual students (service delivery) and the quality of measurement of that implementation are crucial prerequisites for any meaningful program monitoring and outcomes assessment evaluation. One cannot occur without the other. In fact, one should not expect a program to have its intended effect if it has not been fully implemented for the population of students eligible for its services (target group). Furthermore, one should not expect to identify a program effect if program efforts have not been reliably and validly measured.

More specifically, misjudgment of program worth and value may result under any one of the following conditions:

The program is not implemented with adequate intensity (above threshold level) to effect the desired changes, e.g., may be the "right stuff" but the "wrong dose."

- The program inputs and/or outcomes are not measured well;
- wrong measures;
- crude and inadequately sensitive measures; or
- the model-testing and assessment window is too narrow, e.g., the desired changes involve time-sensitive latent manifestations.

Clarifying review.

The first two program survival skills are the most fundamental in terms of basic tools and techniques for student-centered, self-diagnostic program assessment and evaluation. With these skills, program administrators and staff develop facility with the key complementary program effectiveness criteria. Together, they determine the extent to which program exposure and performance are adequate given the total need for program services: target group effectiveness and educational outcomes effectiveness. With both criteria, the assessment addresses process as well as outcomes issues and concerns. Too often, program evaluations reflect a myopic focus on outcomes which, by default, treats the implementation process as a "black box." For the reasons cited earlier, this is a very unwise practice. It may result in serious errors of judgment. The following scenarios highlight the complementary importance and unique contribution of each program effectiveness criterion:

- Scenario 1:—a program has high impact yet still is ineffective: that is, it dramatically influences the thoughts and actions of actual program participants but program exposure is confined to a small fraction of the total targeted population (low target group effectiveness and high educational outcomes effectiveness).

- Scenario 2:—a program documents contacts with the entire target population yet registers minimal impact in terms of desired educational outcomes, e.g., increases in academic proficiency and performance (high target group effectiveness and low educational outcomes effectiveness).

Focusing on both effectiveness criteria encourages practices that are in the best interests of the population to be served. The target group effectiveness criterion encourages the broadest scope of coverage and service delivery among program participants and, thus, discourages "creaming," i.e., selectively involving as program participants only those who are most likely to be "successful." At the extreme, persons are selected who would be successful anyway—with or without the program intervention. On the other hand, the educational outcomes effectiveness criterion encourages monitoring of program participants to track the influence of program services, as well as the ongoing need for those services. This criterion encourages individualized plans (as resources allow) for maximizing students' prospects for academic success. Those plans should be based upon a documented assessment of "where the student is" at the time of initial program contact. With a complementary focus on outcomes as well as program inputs, there is no unintended incentive to, for example, pad and inflate student contact statistics. Most important, however, is the fact that these criteria jointly encourage a process- and outcomes-oriented focus on assessing "value added," given appropriate comparison baselines (e.g., student starting characteristics), rather than a strictly "black-box" outcomes-oriented approach. The latter approach often results in programs that simply screen and "cream" to identify (not cultivate) those who are already shining stars.

Skill 3: Cultivate a Continuous Quality Improvement Mindset.

Effective assessment is an iterative self-diagnostic process. It ideally involves continuous cycles of program improvement and refinement. More specifically, effective program development incorporates a feedback loop for ongoing program refinement. In total quality management terms, this process parallels Deming's plan-pilot-check-act model and the continuous quality improvement cycle. Reasoned analyses and plans are followed by "experimental" trials with continuous testing, learning and program refinement from those planned trials.

Improvement initiatives agenda.

To maximize educational benefits for students, this skill focuses on lessons learned and the resulting programmatic changes that are implemented and/or planned. Documenting these efforts are especially crucial when program outcomes fall short of program expectations. They verify that program administrators and staff are vigilant, critically reflective and responsive to needs for change.

Actual program improvement efforts—identify changes already made in the program to improve the quality and effectiveness of its operations, e.g., modes of service delivery, staffing practices, policies, procedures, etc.

Future improvement plans—recommend and explain what needs to be done to strengthen individual campus programs, as well as the overall array of, for example, precollege, recruitment and academic support programs. Identify any anticipated changes in program resources vis-a-vis the current or projected needs of the target population.

Insights regarding the improvement agenda should be informed by periodic needs assessments of the diverse and very likely changing needs of the program's target student populations. With this information, retention programs can continuously and critically review their inventory of intervention components for "goodness of fit." In ascertaining that fit, the student's voice needs to be heard.

Embracing the spirit of iteration and planned "experimentation" is essential because there are so many unknowns and uncertainties. There is no "one-size-fits-all" ideal academic support strategy that works on all campuses for all students of color or disadvantaged students. The particulars of what works varies over time, place and circumstances. Without an iterative spirit and an experimenting mindset, unknowns and uncertainties can be paralyzing.

Throughout the program development process, programs need to move beyond the more routine issues of efficiency—simply doing things right—to a more decisive focus on strategies for assessing whether one is actually doing the right thing—penetrating issues of effectiveness. To reduce the seductive web of procedural minutiae, constantly question yourself: Are we really doing the right thing, given students' needs and our expectations for their academic and career success? Or, are we just preoccupied with the right rhetoric and procedural routine? These are tough but crucial questions needed to clear the "busyness" smokescreen and keep programs honest.

Prospects for program effectiveness greatly increase if students' voices are fully represented in ongoing needs assessments and in outcomes assessments. In general, then, it is better to do the right thing poorly than to do the wrong thing well. If unavoidable, fail at trying to do the right thing rather than succeed at doing the wrong thing. At least the mistakes made yield lessons learned that are more likely to be instructive and suggestive of the next steps in the right direction. Each program/unit needs to map out the shape and pacing of its own developmental trajectory—given its changing configuration of resources, needs and short-/long-term priorities. Over time, that trajectory will probably change as resources and priorities change.

Skill 4: Establish the Program's Linkage to the General University Mission.

To ensure the viability of its place, each program/unit needs to link its mission and agenda to the fundamental values and principles of the university community: most notably, to excellence in teaching and learning outcomes, progress towards degree attainment, career development progress and mastery of competencies for ultimate success in the "real world," etcetera. In the absence of a program making a case for the centrality of its activities to the educational enterprise, program efforts may be viewed as peripheral or nonessential amenities that are easily dispensable.

Spotlighting program benefits.

Many of the benefits the university community accrues from student services programs and activities are transparent and taken for granted or misunderstood. This includes, for example, cocurricular and extracurricular support resources for academic and career readiness and progress, for leadership development, etc. These programs, especially those that promote multicultural diversity, support and "socialize" students. They help them to navigate and negotiate the sometimes bewildering, often frustrating challenges of the university culture and community.

Too often, myopic outsiders have a trivialized "food, fun and festivals" view of many student services programs and activities. From their shallow perspectives, the activities are simply and solely viewed as ends in themselves as opposed to means to connect, engage and facilitate students' transition and academic progress. Such activities create more conducive, supportive and responsive educational and sociocultural environments. Those environments can also become a broadly enriching resource that complements and humanizes the larger, sometimes alienating, campus community. They need not, as some contend, fuel or contribute to divisive balkanization.

Although some activities have strictly intrinsic social and/or aesthetic value, many often are used as "attention-getters." They create a forum that expands the scope and reach of direct student contacts beyond the more formal and more limited office contacts. They increase opportunities for "touching-base" connections and more informal monitoring-outreach status reports. They often "reel-in" the resistant and hard-to-reach in a neutral context that can set the stage for more directly working through academic issues and challenges. From these expanded points of access, program staff can more effectively help guide, energize and reinforce the student's learning path for academic growth, social and career development.

Program administrators and staff should forthrightly address the shallow misperceptions and misunderstandings of their work: notably, the fact that many view their services as making only a marginal contribution to the university mission. Such views are vocalized with ever greater frequency and intensity during "budget-crunch" times. Highest priority should be given to clarifying and making explicit the logic undergirding program activities and their connection to preparing students as future professionals and leaders.

Assessment data—properly collected, analyzed and packaged—can assist program administrators/staff in building a cogent case for their program's role and contribution. Student precollege, recruitment and retention/support programs cultivate the college pipeline and complement the university's basic "teaching and learning" mission. Without adequate numbers of students entering and being effectively prepared to live, work, develop and thrive in the 21st century, the educational enterprise would collapse.

Demographic imperatives—namely, the changing race/ethnic composition of the school-age population (kindergarten through twelfth grade) and ultimately the future labor force—are fueling major transformations in higher education. These imperatives, along with social justice and equity imperatives, increased the precollege, college recruitment and retention programming for students of color. In addition, these programs are also helping to increase campus multicultural diversity and thus to advance the university's educational excellence mandate: its agenda for preparing all students to effectively contribute to, negotiate and navigate the global society and economy of the 21st century. Students are being prepared to face and shape the dynamic and diverse challenges of an emerging new world. This educational goal is fundamental and broad-based, not a peripheral or nonessential amenity. Postsecondary educational institutions are challenged to cultivate the knowledge, skills, attitudes and commitments needed to effectively serve, empower and prepare all students for this new world.

Skill 5: Specify the Organizational Context Within Which the Program Operates.

In postsecondary institutions, few if any programs and units can fully accomplish their missions in isolation. Drawing upon the retention literature and the program's collective wisdom and experience, program administrators and staff need to formulate a campus retention model. The model would specify factors that influence student persistence to graduation and identify which campus units or programs, if any, address each of these factors. A useful next step in organizing this information would involve compiling a grid that classifies campus units and programs by the retention-relevant factors they address. This grid would be a valuable diagnostic resource in understanding how and why desired educational outcomes do or do not occur and for identifying where new interventions might be needed.

In general, this process will facilitate a more systematic mapping of the organizational context within which a student retention program operates. The map would include the network of "suppliers" and others that the program depends upon to effectively deliver its services and products. Programs need to identify, in a politically savvy way, those elements and forces that support/ reinforce versus those that undermine program efforts. Understanding that network and its dynamics is fundamental.

Within the university community, how are the teaching/learning enterprise and the student services network characterized?

• student-centered vs. not?

• coherent network of services to support student success vs. not?

• collaborative partnerships vs. not?

The probability of success for a student retention program greatly increases if it is part of a coherent student-centered support services network characterized by collaborative partnerships. With a partnership, the joint aim is to serve the whole student via comprehensive plans for maximizing students' prospects for academic success. This would require a documented assessment of "where students are" at the time of initial contact (academically-relevant baseline profiles of students' educational and social skills/resources) compared to projected needs for retention-relevant support services. Such planned interconnectedness is particularly crucial because student retention is a global educational outcome indicator. No one university unit working alone can really guarantee this outcome. One unit, however, could be responsible for effectively orchestrating a comprehensive retention agenda and plan.

Campus patterns of student retention reflect the net effect of a multiplicity of divergent factors. In varying degrees, most facets of the university community potentially influence retention. They influence the extent to which students develop a sense of academic and sociocultural connectedness and a congruent map between their educational/career goals and the university's resources.

352

Skill 6: Strategically Balance Commitments in Accommodating Shrinking Resources.

When absorbing budget and other resource cutbacks, programs should use great care in determining and packaging the tangible consequences—more specifically, the final configuration of services and modes of delivery. They should use special caution to avoid sending the wrong message: that cutbacks were easily absorbed. Skillfully document and highlight the special efforts and accommodations made, especially if services appear to remain intact. More specifically, seize every opportunity to highlight the consequences of inadequate resources in order to minimize programs getting "punished" for their commitment to students and their willingness to sacrifice much. Otherwise, difficult consequences and operating conditions may be discounted and ultimately ignored.

Selective self-serving amnesia and blindness may lead powers-that-be to, at best, continue the resource drought or, at worst, to further erode already inadequate resources. Expose even unintentional tendencies to institutionalize hard times and untenable working conditions: "You've done so much for so long with so little, you're now expected to do everything with nothing."

Strategically Balance

- Commitments to serve immediate student needs
- Commitments to send the right message—one that increases future resource prospects for initiatives whose institutional value waxes and wanes

Embrace the Spirit of Preparedness.

Effective program administrators and staff recognize the political and technical dynamics of assessment and evaluation efforts. They transform that process into one with important a) intrinsic benefits for the program and the students it seeks to serve and b) extrinsic benefits when trying to deal with, satisfy and/or nullify external constituencies (whether in a defensive or offensive mode). Too often, usually by default, assessment and evaluation tools have been in the wrong hands and used against programs rather than for their improvement. Proactive, student-centered diagnostic evaluation strategies offer a resource for empowered program self-improvement and strategic image management.

Even in the best of times, student services and support programs should stand in readiness to tell their own story and make their own case. In a retrogressive political and fiscal climate, all programs—especially those that target students of color and disadvantaged students—should expect probing challenges and quick turnaround time for response. That climate has been fueling fast and furious demands for programs to document and defend their value and contribution to the university community. Even if such attacks have not yet surfaced at your university, do not be lulled into complacency and self-satisfaction.

Programs must be able to defuse challenges and block those who are predisposed to discount, dismiss and dismantle cocurricular and extracurricular student services programs. For example, programs that increase the college presence, participation and success of students of color can resist marginalization by linking their efforts to macro-level issues, such as their universities' mission and values and 21st century demands. Educational excellence for universities requires the development of broad competencies in understanding and working with/in multiculturally diverse environments. Such competencies are high on the agenda for effectively preparing all students for the global society and economy of the 21st century. University of Wisconsin system President Katharine Lyall highlighted the pivotal importance of multicultural diversity initiatives in a March 1993 board of regents presentation:

> *"Design for Diversity articulated our commitment to significantly increase the number of minority students served by the UW System and to increase representation of qualified minorities among our faculty and staff. This commitment is based on the conviction that we must prepare our students through education and by experience to live and work effectively in a far more multicultural society and economy than any of us has experienced in our lifetimes. To do otherwise would be an educational malpractice equivalent to failing to teach foreign language or to provide exposure to computers."*

In conclusion, then, savvy program administrators and staff embrace the spirit of preparedness and proactively seize the initiative. They integrate the assessment/evaluation process into the natural rhythms of their program work. To maximize accuracy, they cultivate a vested interest through program data strategies that support the who, what, when, where, how and how much issues associated with staff job duties. These program administrators and staff have carefully crafted their vision and are already preparing their case through critical reflection, collaborative brainstorming and the compilation of credible and meaningful evidence regarding program-relevant outcomes and improvement initiatives. Through it all, they keep students and their needs at the center of their agenda. In the spirit of strategic image management, they have packaged that evidence in forms that are compelling for their primary stakeholders through successively "standing in the stakeholders' shoes."

—Dr. Hazel Symonette is a Policy and Planning Analyst in the Office of Multicultural Affairs, University of Wisconsin System Administration in Madison, Wisconsin.

About the Authors

Emma Amacker received the BS in Elementary Education from Grambling State University; the MA in Urban Education from Governors State University; the Ed.D. in Urban Education from Texas Southern University. Currently she serves as Assistant Professor in the Department of Curriculum & Instruction at Texas Southern University. She is responsible for the delivery of undergraduate teacher education courses. She has worked in public and private schools and continues as a special consultant. She is the founder and director of Awareness Institute, an educational consulting firm.

Pamela G. Arrington received the BA in Psychology from Spelman College; the MA in Guidance and Counseling from the University of Michigan; the Ph.D in Education from George Mason University. Currently she is Professor and Coordinator of the MA in Human Resource Development Program at Bowie State University and serves as Director of National Retention Project, American Association of State Colleges and Universities. Previous experience includes a faculty fellow, Office of the Secretary of Defense/Civilian Personnel Policy, Coordinator of Affirmative Action and Grants Development at Northern Virginia Community College and Counselor, Annadale Campus, Northern Virginia Community College.

Deborah F. Atwater received the BA in Secondary English Education and Speech and the MA in Speech Communication from Pennsylvania State University; the Ph.D in Intercultural Communication from State University of New York at Buffalo. She currently serves as Associate Professor of Speech Communication and African/African-American Studies at Pennsylvania State University. Her experience includes that of Senior Faculty Mentor in the Office for Minority Graduate Opportunities and Faculty Development, where she worked with junior minority faculty who were on the tenure track by providing different types of support.

Horace E. Belmear received the BA Degree in History from West Virginia State College in Institute, West Virginia and the MA in Physical Education from West Virginia University, Morgantown, West Virginia. He has been a high school teacher and coach and an education officer with the United States Defense Department. Presently, he is retired after having spent many years as a high school coach and teacher and as an Education Officer for the United States Defense Department in Oakland, Pennsylvania.

Donald Brown received the BA in Community Leadership and Development and the M.Ed in Rehabilitation Counseling from Springfield College in Springfield, Massachusetts; the Ed.D. in Educational Research, Policy, Planning and Administration from the University of Massachusetts, Amherst. For the past

355

seventeen years, he has served as the Director of the Office of African-American, Hispanic, Asian and Native Americans (AHANA) Student Programs at Boston College. His duties include the development and implementation of strategies that contribute to the retention and graduation of AHANA students.

John E. Bush received the BA from Delaware State College (University); the MS.Ed from Westminster College, Pennsylvania; the MA and Ph.D. from the University of Pittsburgh. He is Professor of Sociology and Special Assistant to the Chancellor for Multicultural Affairs at the University of Massachusetts, Dartmouth. Additionally, he directs the African and African-American Studies Program and established and advises the "Men of Color Discussion Group" and The Paul Cuffe Institute at the University. He has published numerous articles in popular journals and recently had his poem "Africa Revisited" accepted for publication in 100 Black Poets (Temple University). He serves as Editor of The National Journal of Black and White Men Together (Washington, D.C.).

Ann L. Carter-Obayuwana received her undergraduate degree in Business and English from Wright State University, Dayton, Ohio, and the MA and PH.D. in Counseling and Psychology from Purdue University, West Lafayette, Indiana. Presently she is an Associate Professor in the Department of Human Development and Psychoeducational Studies, School of Education at Howard University, Washington, D.C., where she teaches Counseling Psychology to graduate students. Her research has investigated the role of Hope and Coping ability in relationship to: (1) Retention rates of African-American students; (2) Women's health issues; and (3) The impact of various forms of communication media (e.g. film, music, print and broadcast) on the behavior of adolescents and young adults.

Constance A. Chapman received the BA in Education from Michigan State University and the MA in English and the Ed.D. in College-Level Writing from Columbia University. She is a 1995-96 Fulbright Scholar, who teaches English at the University College of Education of Winneba, Ghana, West Africa. Past teaching experience includes Georgia State University in Atlanta; John Jay College of Criminal Justice and Hunter College in New York; Rutgers University in New Jersey; the University of the West Indies in Jamaica; and 15 years of teaching "at-risk" students in New York and Detroit public schools. She has had numerous publications in regional and national journals.

Maurice C. Daniels received the BA in Psychology, the MSW and the Ed.D. in Higher Education Administration from Indiana University. Additionally, he did extensive master's level study at California State University, San Diego, and accepted the position of Assistant Director for Project Upward Bound at Indiana University. He was appointed Coordinator for Social Services for the Indianapolis Sickle Cell Center. In 1979, he joined the faculty at the University of Georgia, and was later appointed Director of the Patricia Roberts Harris Fellowship Program. Under his tenure more than $1,000,000 has been awarded to his program.

Barbara Evans received the BA in English Writing, the MA in Secondary Education and the Ed.D. in Policy, Planning and Evaluation from the University of Pittsburgh. Presently, she is an Assistant Dean at the University of Pittsburgh's Graduate School of Public Health (GSPH), where she is responsible for student academic services. She began in the Pittsburgh Public Schools as a teacher. This educator, evaluator, research assistant and former Lilly Fellow is a member of the Advisory and Steering Committees for GSPH's Center for Minority Health, where she conducts research assessing student perceptions of campus climate and retention issues.

John F. Gardenhire received the BS in Entomology and English from the University of Kansas at Lawrence; the MA in Educational Psychology from San Francisco State University; the Ph.D. in English from the University of Southern California. He has been successfully guiding "at-risk" black male students through Laney College's English composition and literature courses for nearly thirty years. He is a consultant and trains teachers to work with students in the areas of motivation and retention. Two of his books reflect this focus of his teaching: Reading Analytically and Sentence Analysis, English Grammar Made Accessible.

Lynda Law Harrison received a nursing degree from the University of North Carolina-Chapel Hill; the MSN in Maternal-Child Nursing from the University of Delaware; the Ph.D. in Child and Family Studies from the University of Tennessee. She is currently Professor and Director of Research at the University of Alabama Capstone College of Nursing. Previous experience includes hospital staff nurse, pediatrics nurse, child psychiatric nurse and public health nurse. Since 1978, she has been a nurse educator and served as Assistant Academic Vice President at the University of Alabama.

J. Blaine Hudson received the BS in Guidance and Counseling and History and the M.Ed. in College Student Personnel from the University of Louisville and the Ed.D. in Higher Education and Administration from the University of Kentucky. He has worked in higher education for more than twenty years. Experience includes Academic Counselor and Tutor Coordinator; Director of the West Louisville Educational Program; Associate Director of the Preparatory Division. In 1992, he joined the faculty of the Pan-African Studies Institute for Teachers. He is widely published and has received numerous awards, including appointments to the Kentucky Humanities Council and the Kentucky Institute for Educational Research.

Beatrice L. Logan received the BS in Health and Physical Education from Tennessee State University, Nashville, and the MA and PH.D. in Guidance and Counseling from Atlanta University. She is presently an Assistant Professor/Counselor in the Department of Learning Support Programs at Georgia State University, Atlanta. The last twenty years of her professional career have been spent working with "at-risk" college students. She is widely published in regional and national journals.

Catherine Geraldine Lyons received the BS in Home Economics from South Carolina State College; the MS in Educational Supervision and Administration from The Bank Street College in New York City; the Ph.D. in Agricultural and Extension Education from Pennsylvania State University. She completed additional studies in Curriculum Development at Teachers College in New York City. Presently she serves as Director of the Center for Minority Graduate Opportunities and Faculty Development at Pennsylvania State University. In her combined career, she has over twenty years of planning and implementing educational equity programs.

Reed Markham received the BA in Speech Communication from Brigham Young University; the BS in Political Science from Regents College; the MA in Organizational Communication from Brigham Young University; the MPA in Personal Management from the University of Southern California; the MA from the University of California, Los Angeles; the Ph.D. from Columbia Pacific University. He has served as a speechwriter for the United States Supreme Court. After several years of teaching in California state universities and community colleges, in 1993, he was appointed Director of the College of Arts Retention and Enhancement Services Program. He is the author of five books including Leadership 2000: Success Skills for University Students published by Simon and Schuster. He serves on the editorial board for several academic journals including the Journal of At-Risk Issues.

Kevin J. McCarthy received the BME from Notre Dame; the MM from Michigan State; the Ph.D. in Music Education from Case Western Reserve University; Post Graduate Studies at the University of Colorado, Boulder. Presently he serves as Associate Dean for Undergraduate Studies at the University of Colorado at Boulder. His performance career ranges from touring Europe with a Dixieland jazz group to singing under Robert Shaw in the Cleveland Orchestra Chorus. He has served as President of Colorado Music Educators Association and the Colorado Alliance for Arts Education. He is widely published. Among his many honors is the Bronze Medal from the Friends of the Kennedy Center. In 1992, he was inducted into the Colorado Music Educator Hall of Fame.

Katie M. McKnight received the BS and MS in Nursing from De Paul University; the Ph.D. in Education from Southern Illinois University at Carbondale. Currently she serves as Director of Minority Student Affairs and Assistant Professor at the University of Illinois at Chicago, where she is also Project Director for the I'M READY (Increasing Minority Representation through Educating and Developing Youth) Program, which is funded by the Robert Wood Johnson Foundation. Additionally, she has published several articles and book chapters relating to minority recruitment and retention in institutions of higher education.

Muriel A. Moore received the BA in Sociology from Richmond College, City University of New York; the ME in Elementary and Remedial Reading and the Ph.D. in Educational Organization, Administration and Policy from the University of Buffalo. Also she is a 1994 graduate of the Harvard Institute of Management. Presently she serves as Vice President for Public Service and Urban Affairs at the University of Buffalo. Her most recent professional and academic papers and presentations focus on the importance of professional service within the academy and the role of colleges and universities in the economic growth and development of urban areas. She has received many prestigious awards.

Quincy L. Moore received the BA in Business Administration, Sociology and Psychology from Culver-Stockton College in Canton, Missouri; the MS in Guidance and Counseling from the University of Nevada at Las Vegas; the Ph.D. in Counselor Education from the University of Iowa. Presently he serves as Director of the Office of Academic Support at Virginia Commonwealth University in Richmond, Virginia. Additionally, he co-authored a chapter on counseling African-Americans in Transcultural Counseling from An International Perspective in 1993 and published an article, "What if we Really Cared about Crime and the Future of Black Males?" He is currently completing a book, The Disappearing Educated Black Male!, a study of 120 black males and their journey through higher education.

Lillian B. Poats received the BA in Secondary Education from Purdue University; the M.Ed. in Guidance and Counseling and the Ed.D. in Higher Education Administration from Texas Southern University. Currently she serves as Associate Professor in the Department of Educational Leadership & Counseling at Texas Southern University. Previously she served as Director of Student Support at the University of Texas Health Science Center at Houston. She teaches graduate courses in the Higher Education program and conducts research on topics which relate to diversity in higher education. She is Chair of the American Association for Higher Education Black Caucus.

Roy Ann Sherrod received the BS in Nursing from the University of Alabama; the MS in Family Nursing from the Mississippi University for Women; the Doctor of Science in Nursing from the University of Alabama at Birmingham. Currently she is an Associate Professor of Nursing at the University of Alabama. She has served as a faculty member in the maternity area for over a decade. Scholarly activities have been in the area of infertility and disadvantaged students. She is widely published.

Joseph Howard Silver, Sr. received the BA in History and Government from St. Augustine College, Raleigh, North Carolina; the MA and Ph.D. in Political Science from Atlanta University. He was employed at Kennesaw College from 1977-1985 as an instructor, assistant and associate professor. Presently he serves as Assistant Vice-Chancellor for Academic Affairs for the University System of Georgia. His research interests are in the areas of urban politics and policy, civil rights issues in higher education and international relations. He is the author of several published works and is a frequent consultant on higher education and political issues and diversity in the workplace.

Forest Dent Smith received the BA in Government, the MA in Counseling and the Ph.D. in Higher Education Administration from Louisiana State University. Presently she serves as Minority Engineering Coordinator at Louisiana State University, where she has implemented a program to recruit, retain and graduate students. She has worked over 25 years in education and industry while maintaining a counseling practice. Her specialties are college retention, personal and professional development and multiculturalism.

Karen Cole Smith received the BA in Sociology from Bethune-Cookman College in Daytona Beach, Florida; the MA in Sociology from Ohio State University; the Ph.D. in Sociology from the University of Florida, Gainesville, Florida. She is presently the Chairperson of the Social Sciences and History Department at Santa Fe Community College in Gainesville. Previous experience includes seventeen years of classroom instruction in private, state and community colleges in the state of Florida. She is a frequent workshop presenter on multi-cultural and diversity issues in schools.

Hazel Symonette received the BA in Psychology from Central State University in Wilberforce, Ohio; the MS in Social Work, the MA in Sociology, and the Ph.D. in Educational Policy Studies/Sociology of Education from the University of Wisconsin-Madison. This researcher, educator and assessment specialist has cultivated assessment as a student-centered self-diagnostic resource for continuous improvement and provided technical assistance and training for the 27 University of Wisconsin institutions. Further she conducts statistical and policy analyses related to multicultural diversity initiatives.

Louise M. Tomlinson received the BA in English Literature from City College of New York; the MS in Behavioral Disabilities and the Ph.D. in Curriculum and Instruction from the University of Wisconsin-Madison. Presently, she is an Assistant Professor, Academic Assistant and Co-director of Patricia Roberts Harris Fellowships at the University of Georgia, and also national faculty for the Kettering Foundation's National Issues Forums. Publications include "Black Faculty Recruitment and Retention" in the NAFEO monograph, Desegregation in Higher Education, her own ASHE/ERIC monograph entitled, Postsecondary Developmental Programs: A Traditional Agenda with New Imperatives and in the National Reading Research Center Report No. 44, "The Effects of Instructional Interaction Guided by a Typology of Ethnic Identity Development: Phase One".

Order Form

If you would like additional copies of Student Retention Success Models in Higher Education, use this form.

To: CNJ Associates, Inc.
     P.O. Box 10042
     Tallahassee, FL 32302-2042

Please send _____copies of Student Retention Success Models in Higher Education at $49.50 plus $5 shipping. Florida residents, please add sales tax or a copy of your tax exempt number.

Print or Type

Ship to: _____   Bill to: _____
                Name & Title   Name & Title

_____   _____
                Address   Address

_____   _____
City   State   ZIP   City   State   ZIP

_____   _____
                Phone   Phone

All orders must be prepaid or have a Purchase Order Number. Make check payable to CNJ Associates, Inc. Please call 904-222-1087 or 385-1747 if you need additional information.

Amount Enclosed_____

Purchase Order #_____

Order Form

If you would like additional copies of Student Retention Success Models in Higher Education, use this form.

To: CNJ Associates, Inc.
     P.O. Box 10042
     Tallahassee, FL 32302-2042

Please send _____copies of Student Retention Success Models in Higher Education at $49.50 plus $5 shipping. Florida residents, please add sales tax or a copy of your tax exempt number.

Print or Type

Ship to: _____   Bill to: _____
              Name & Title   Name & Title
_____   _____
              Address   Address
_____   _____
City   State   ZIP   City   State   ZIP
_____   _____
              Phone   Phone

All orders must be prepaid or have a Purchase Order Number. Make check payable to CNJ Associates, Inc. Please call 904-222-1087 or 385-1747 if you need additional information.

Amount Enclosed_____

Purchase Order #_____

Order Form

If you would like additional copies of Student Retention Success Models in Higher Education, use this form.

To: CNJ Associates, Inc.
P.O. Box 10042
Tallahassee, FL 32302-2042

Please send _____ copies of Student Retention Success Models in Higher Education at $49.50 plus $5 shipping. Florida residents, please add sales tax or a copy of your tax exempt number.

Print or Type

Ship to: _____   Bill to: _____
           Name & Title   Name & Title

_____   _____
           Address   Address

City   State   ZIP   City   State   ZIP

_____   _____
           Phone   Phone

All orders must be prepaid or have a Purchase Order Number. Make check payable to CNJ Associates, Inc. Please call 904-222-1087 or 385-1747 if you need additional information.

Amount Enclosed_____

Purchase Order #_____

Order Form

If you would like additional copies of Student Retention Success Models in Higher Education, use this form.

To: CNJ Associates, Inc.
     P.O. Box 10042
     Tallahassee, FL 32302-2042

Please send _____copies of Student Retention Success Models in Higher Education at $49.50 plus $5 shipping. Florida residents, please add sales tax or a copy of your tax exempt number.

Print or Type

Ship to: _____   Bill to: _____
                  Name & Title   Name & Title

_____   _____
                  Address   Address

_____   _____
City   State   ZIP   City   State   ZIP

_____   _____
                  Phone   Phone

All orders must be prepaid or have a Purchase Order Number. Make check payable to CNJ Associates, Inc. Please call 904-222-1087 or 385-1747 if you need additional information.

Amount Enclosed_____

Purchase Order #_____

Order Form

If you would like additional copies of Student Retention Success Models in Higher Education, use this form.

To: CNJ Associates, Inc.
P.O. Box 10042
Tallahassee, FL 32302-2042

Please send _____copies of Student Retention Success Models in Higher Education at $49.50 plus $5 shipping. Florida residents, please add sales tax or a copy of your tax exempt number.

Print or Type

Ship to: _____   Bill to: _____
           Name & Title   Name & Title

_____   _____
           Address   Address

City _____ State ___ ZIP ___   City _____ State ___ ZIP ___

_____   _____
           Phone   Phone

All orders must be prepaid or have a Purchase Order Number. Make check payable to CNJ Associates, Inc. Please call 904-222-1087 or 385-1747 if you need additional information.

Amount Enclosed_____

Purchase Order #_____